ETHNIC

CHICAGO

PASSPORT'S GUIDE TO

ETHNIC

CHICAGO

A Complete Guide to the Many Faces & Cultures of Chicago

SECOND EDITION

RICHARD LINDBERG

Printed on recyclable paper

PASSPORT BOOKS
a division of *NTC Publishing Group*
Lincolnwood, Illinois USA

Cover Photos

American Egg Board (Front, upper left)
Government of India Tourist Office (Back, upper left)
Janice Gordon, Devon Northtown Business Association (Front, bottom right; Back, upper right)
Paula Martin (Front, lower left, upper and lower right)

For the family my father left behind in Sweden many years ago, and for the "new generation" of cousins I have met in my travels: Gunvor, Lars, Karl Ake, Ingrid, Eivor, Stig, Arne, Tommy, and Carolla.

Contents

List of Maps

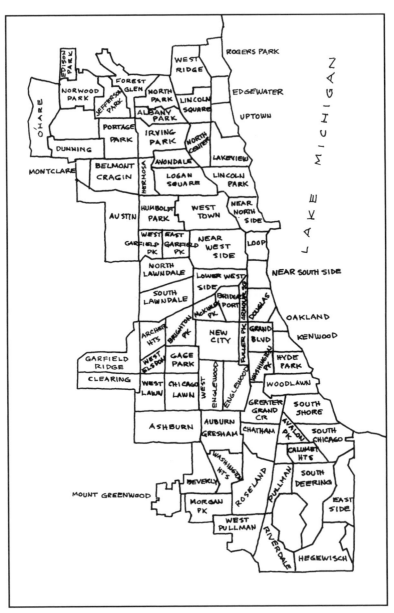

Chicago's Neighborhood Communities

Acknowledgments

For the first and second editions of this book, I am indebted to the following people who generously shared with me their rich insights about Chicago's ethnic treasures. Without their help, this book could not have reached its successful conclusion. Helen Alexander/UHAC; Elisabeth Angele/Goethe Institute; Laleh Baktian/KAZI Publications; Maria Bappart/Lincoln Square Chamber of Commerce; Robin Becker/Devon-Northtown Business Association; Roy J. Bellavia/WSBC-AM; Tony Burroughs/Afro-American Genealogical Society; Carol Carlson; George Cheung; Pauris Dadadahoi; Mrs. Raymond Dojinski; Jane Edwards/Mitchell Indian Museum; James Futris/ Hellenic Museum; Thor Fjell/Scandinavian American Cultural Society; Irene Gajeck; Dolly Galter; Marge Greenberg; John Griffin/Gaelic Park; Nazir Hasan; Teri Hays/Scottish Cultural Society; Stephen Hormann; Birute Jasaitis/Lithuanian Community Center; Gretchen Johnson/North Park College; the late Nathan Kaplan; Frank Kilker/Irish American Heritage Center; Gera-Lind Kolarik; Per-Hugo Kristensson/Swedish Cultural Society; Thelma Krupp; Kerstin Lane/Swedish American Museum Center; Denise Lindberg; Roy Lundberg; Anne Lunde; Paula Martin; Diane McKay/Museum of Science and Industry; Pawel Migacz/Polish *Zgoda*; Joan Murphy/British Club; Timothy O'Connell; Alice Palach/CSA Fraternal Life; Rodica Perciali/ Romanian Museum; Marie Piesko; Anilkumar Pillai/Federation of India Association; Val Ramonis/Balzekas Museum; Fred Randazzo/Joint Civic Community of Italian Americans; Roberto Roque/Filipino American Council of Chicago; Walter Roth/Jewish Historical Society; June Sawyers/Loyola Press; Norman Scaman/Cermak Road Business Association; Barbara Schaaf; Dana M. Sendziol; Dan Sharon/Asher Library; Charlie Soo/Asian American Small Business Association; Kathy Taylor/Irish Fellowship Club; Elaine Thomopoulos/Hellenic Museum; Adele Vacek; Faro Vitale; Anna Williams; Dee and Patrick Woodtar.

For the second edition I want to thank Patrick Flynn who helped canvass all of our previous entries and entered innumerable changes. And to my friend, agent, and fellow Chicago history buff Connie Goddard who helped revise the introductions. Thanks as well to editors Dan Spinella and Nick Panos who launched the revised edition and to NTC's Rosemary Dolinski who sheparded it through the production process.

Preface to
Revised Edition

My own experiences growing up in an ethnic household in the Chicagoland area weighed heavily on my decision to write *Passport's Guide to Ethnic Chicago,* a unique travel volume blending contemporary cultural attractions, parades, festivals, banquets and cotillions, tours, ethnic museums, and a comprehensive dining and shopping guide to accompany historical discussions.

The revised second edition of the enormously popular *Ethnic Chicago* continues our exploration into the heart of the city's immigrant settlements with an accent on the emerging Middle Eastern communities on the South and North Sides.

We have located exotic new restaurants, identified new museums and events, and tracked the progress of Chicago's diverse ethnic groups as they seek to preserve their heritage and culture in the Windy City melting pot.

Within the next several years Greektown USA, celebrating the Hellenic presence on the teeming Near West Side of Chicago, and Bronzeville, a snapshot of African-American community life in the South Side Douglas neighborhood during the years of the great Northern migration, will offer Chicagoans a privileged glimpse into a historic and sometimes overlooked past. The revitalization of Bronzeville is contingent upon legislative support and public funding. The initiative will provide a rare opportunity to preview a living museum patterned after the Beale Street re-development in Memphis, Tennessee, where the blues came of age as a musical art form.

Chicago remains in my estimation the most ethnic and culturally diverse of all American cities. Five years after the publication of the original *Ethnic Chicago,* my views have only been reaffirmed. We live in a spacious city (twenty-five miles long, ten miles wide) spread across the flat plain in an interlocking grid pattern of streets. Because of natural and manmade barriers—railroad embankments, expressways, and three branches of the

Chicago River, extending for fifty miles across the landscape—unintended "turf" boundaries have resulted. It is possible for one group of people to live in relative seclusion from the next, even though the distance of a few hundred feet may be all that separates them.

Hermetically sealed neighborhoods made it possible for immigrants to practice their social and religious customs, read the latest news from the old country in the foreign-language press, shop for imported foods and spices at independent grocers within a block or two of their homes, and virtually live out their entire adult lives unaffected by American culture.

If there is any lingering doubt that this culture exists in modern-day Chicago, immersed as we are in our home computers, fax modems, and journeys into cyberspace, a visit to the bustling Asian community centered around Argyle Street in Uptown or the Polish corridor on Milwaukee Avenue in the Avondale neighborhood takes you back to another time and place. The sights, sounds, and smells of Argyle Street remind one of the Maxwell Street open-air market during the formative years of this century, and it offers convincing proof that as much as things may seem to change, some fine old traditions will always remain with us.

There is an unshakable pride in who we are and from where we came, though most, if not all, would admit that there is no going back. Successive waves of European immigrants shaped the essential character of the city and contributed to its expansive growth and majestic splendor, reflected in spacious, baroque boulevards, towering skyscrapers, and the "green necklace" of parkways and forest preserves that dot Cook County.

Immigrant people encountered a city of shocking contradictions. Wealth and poverty; millionaires and slum landlords co-mingling in the chokehold of big city life. Those who lived in Chicago for a period of years before returning to their ancestral homes to visit or re-settle would very often voice complaints that the old country was not as they had remembered when they left, and that living conditions had changed. The frenzy to succeed within a new and highly competitive economic system, one that championed an entirely different set of values and mores, forced these European pilgrims to make a radical adjustment to the rigors of American life. By the time they returned to greet the friends and family who remained behind, very often their only shared experiences were nostalgia, the sentiments of the past, and the warm reassurances that can come only from kin.

In November 1924, my father, Oscar W. Lindberg, turned his back on a troubled past and set sail from Sweden aboard a lumbering transport ship called the *Drottningholm*. All he carried in his valise was a change of clothes, the collected works of playwright August Strindberg, and a handbill offering useful tips about negotiating a successful trans-Atlantic crossing.

Oscar was twenty-seven, a dark and rebellious young man who was instilled with the fiery convictions of the evolving Social Democratic Party led by Nobel Peace Prize winner Karl Hjalmar Branting. Branting was an advocate of universal suffrage, who had sought through his writings and speeches to circumvent the power of the monarchists and the privileged classes.

My father felt immense pride in having agitated for social reform and the cooperative movement in the taverns and trade union halls of Göteborg, the seaport city he had migrated to after running away from the family farm in Ronneby and the hardships of agrarian poverty. The trade unionists were squarely opposed to Sweden's temperance movement, religious piety as a matter of principle, and the stern mandates of the church governing social interaction between men and women. This also pleased Oscar, who had been known to take a drink in the company of a young woman on occasion.

He was one of eleven children, and in Sweden, the poor families were often separated through economic necessity, with the oldest and most capable youngsters sent away to earn their keep in factories or neighboring farms. An older brother heard a different calling and fled to Stockholm, where he rose to prominence in the Salvation Army. The eternal conflict between sobriety and abstinence against the temptations of the flesh split apart generations of Lindbergs and many other impoverished agrarian Swedish families for years to come.

Oscar toiled in a nearby brick factory but it was miserable, hard work and not to his liking. After his father angrily denied him the money to pay for a new suit to wear to church on Confirmation Day, Oscar ran away from the family home in order to see what was stirring in the city. He was restless and dissatisfied—proud, sardonic, and harsh in manner—traits well defined by his fourteenth birthday.

A socialist by conviction and a libertine by nature, my father balked at serving in the military when the time came for him to report for duty in 1924. Facing mandatory conscription into an army he detested, and the unhappy prospect of unexpected fatherhood (his girlfriend Elma Moller was about to give birth to a young son, whom she would name Osborne), my father chose to flee the country. However, the U.S. had recently imposed quota sanctions on European immigration—an isolationist backlash stemming from World War I—which made it impossible for Oscar to secure passage for Elma, now in her ninth month of pregnancy.

With the authorities probing his known haunts and making inquiries as to his whereabouts, my father purchased his ticket and hastily set sail for America under the assumed name of Waldemar Carlson, a hybrid of his own middle name and his father's first name—Carl (or Charles).

At some point in the voyage he jumped ship before the scheduled arrival in New York, entering the United States via Montreal, in order to avoid a legal wrangling with the American immigration authorities. From there he negotiated his way to Chicago, a city he would revile and cherish for the remainder of his life.

Oscar spent that first bewildering Chicago winter learning rudimentary English from an obliging librarian who worked with him late in the evenings after he had completed his daily chores as a carpenter and handyman.

Letters from home were sent to "Waldemar Carlson" in care of the Idrott Café on Wilton Avenue in the heart of the North Side "Swede Town" at Belmont Avenue and Clark Street. It was the general delivery address for many newly arrived Swedish immigrants who lived by their wit, imagination, and not much else. Idrott was a place to drink, to share stories, and to reminisce. And it still stands as a public house, to this very day.

In a messy two-flat near the city's rumbling elevated line, Oscar devoted much of his time to writing editorials in the foreign-language press catering to the free-thinkers in the neighborhood who happened to come from his province in Sweden. He spoke of the old injustices, the need to embrace a new social order to ease man's terrible suffering, but rarely did he divulge any details of his troubled private life, or those he had left behind who had depended on him the most.

It was in his cold-water North Side flat that Oscar received word from Elma less than a year later, on November 1, 1925, that the son he had never seen—little Osborne—had died of tuberculosis after a long and violent struggle against the ravages of the disease. I have often asked myself what thoughts ran through his mind as he read of the little boy's sufferings, told with simple but heart-rending poignancy by Elma.

There was no money left to pay for the funeral expenses, Elma explained. She pleaded with my father to send a portion of his earnings home to Sweden. When he was unable to respond in an appropriate manner within the allotted time, Elma was forced to rely on the charity of family and friends—Oscar's former socialist comrades—to help repay the funeral debt.

Elma still hoped to rejoin Oscar in Chicago, even after this great tragedy unraveled the meager threads of her own life. But her fears and apprehensions, coupled with the unyielding governmental policy toward renewed immigration from this corner of Europe, doomed any chance for my father to be reunited with his sweetheart. Elma never made it to America; her dream of securing an exit visa in order to begin anew in Chicago free of unpleasant memories was permanently shattered.

Her letters to Chicago, carefully preserved by my father in a weathered suitcase up until the moment of his death in July 1986, end mysteriously in 1930. A photo of Osborne, included with one of the earlier letters from Sweden, could not be found among his papers. We do not have a clue as to what the little boy even looked like. Whatever fate befell broken-hearted Elma Moller following the loss of her child is an imponderable riddle that lies buried in the records of one of the rural church parishes north of Göteborg.

During the years of the Great Depression my father launched the formative period of his career by constructing customized Sears & Roebuck bungalows. He put up houses up and down Belmont Avenue for those fortunate enough to be able to purchase the house-building materials from the catalog and live out the American dream of home ownership with a comfortable, well-stocked icebox and built-in ironing board.

According to an apocryphal family legend, Oscar approached General Robert Wood in the giant retailer's Chicago headquarters with a proposition to build the catalog homes for Sears customers. "Don't you know, young man, that there is a Depression on?" Wood thundered. My father, by his own account, looked the General square in the eye and scolded him for negative thinking. Ambition was his muse.

Following V-J Day in 1945, Oscar capitalized on the suburban land boom taking shape in Chicago's northern suburbs. Almost overnight, serene, picturesque farmlands and small suburban villages were transformed into sprawling subdivisions with schools, public parks, and interlocking expressways.

Returning GIs who had grown up in congested inner-city ethnic communities like Pilsen, Bridgeport, Lawndale, and West Town forsook their parents and immigrant grandparents in the old neighborhoods to begin the task of child rearing in suburbia, where the houses were cheap and durable and the backyards a lush green. Once again Chicago was on the move, and my father and fellow Scandinavian contractors like Ragnar Benson, a self-made millionaire whose imprimatur can still be found on various construction sites around town, were ready to supply the goods and services to pave over the vacant land linking the farms and fields to the central city.

My father incorporated his construction company on the theoretical principles of the Swedish cooperative movement he had feverishly embraced during his idealistic youth. When he wasn't cooking up deals with clients over V.O. Manhattans at the famed Morton House Restaurant in North Suburban Morton Grove, Oscar joined a bowling league, the Masonic order, and the Swedish choral societies. These cultural associations provided an important social outlet, status among his peers, and the means of preserving a rapidly vanishing culture which was just beginning to break apart in the old Andersonville neighborhood.

No longer fearing the wrath of the Swedish authorities concerning his fugitive status, my father made the first of three pilgrimages back to Ronneby in 1956. By now the famous "cradle to grave" socialism had taken deep root in the country, and the standards of living had evened out for the city dweller and peasant farmer alike. Life in rural southern Sweden had returned to its timeless ways.

The goals Karl Branting had outlined for his followers in the early 1920s had long since been achieved, but Oscar was sadly disillusioned by the profound political and social changes that had taken place while he was away. Why had the strong work ethic of former years been abandoned by the younger generations? My father groped for the answers to these riddles and returned to Chicago unwilling to accept the plain truth of the matter: He had become an American.

As a first-generation Swedish-American, it took me a long time to acquire a deeper appreciation for this distant foreign culture of which my father had spoken at a time in my childhood when life moved at its own leisurely pace. The desire to conform to a rigidly defined set of values and social customs defined by peer groups within one's neighborhood often runs counter to the wishes of immigrant parents, their love of homeland and desire to preserve at all costs old tribal customs in the American mélange.

The appreciation of our ethnic heritage is an acquired taste, and very often it comes much later in life when curiosity becomes a catalyst for independent investigation. That is why I set out to solve the seventy-year-old mystery surrounding the collection of brittle, yellowing letters I found in the suitcase at the time of my father's death. Elma's correspondence and dozens of family letters were translated with great care by surviving nieces and nephews in Sweden. Only then did this strange and evocative tale finally come to light. In his lifetime my father was a proud man possessed of the furies. He chose not to dwell on setbacks or misfortunes and governed his life accordingly.

Oscar's journey into the American heartland is but one of millions of anonymous untold stories forming a complex social history of the great immigration. He shared with his fellow travelers of a restless generation common fears, anxieties, and aspirations for the future, even as he was forced to come to grips with the certain knowledge that he would probably never again embrace Elma, nor the child in her womb. Nevertheless he rode the crest of the ocean's wave toward far-flung horizons and an unimagined destiny. Like so many others from foreign lands, he believed there was no percentage in looking back.

In this sense the immigrant shared a common historical thread with the earliest of the pioneering adventurers who followed the path of the swollen rivers and streams toward the land of the wild onion—which the Native Americans knew so well as *Checagou.*

Our journey into Chicago's ethnic past begins with the convergence of the French *voyageurs* and the native people on the shores of Lake Michigan, where the desolate, wind-swept frontier provided sanctuary for the Potawatomi, one of ten Great Lakes Indian tribes who inhabited the region. From a lonely frontier outpost skirting the edges of civilization to the thriving world-class city standing at the crossroads of the nation that we know today, Chicago history mirrors the remarkable accomplishments of *all* its people.

The commonly held view of Chicago as a corrupt, gin-soaked town reeking of slaughterhouses and steel mills, driven and ruled by Al Capone with help from a bevy of corrupt, unvarnished politicians on the make should only be taken at face value lest we lose sight of the human equation. This is a multi-faceted city whose essential character was shaped by the assimilation of its diverse tribes, who were absorbed into the mainstream of the melting pot. The immigrants coming from the four corners of the earth have vested in Chicago their fondest hopes for an unblemished future while cherishing their sacred remembrances of the past.

We hope you will enjoy reading about the epic of Chicago, and experiencing firsthand the city's unique international flavor by probing the soul of the *real* city beyond the Michigan Avenue boutiques and Wrigleyville coffee houses.

Discover for yourself the nation's most representative city that in every respect is a metaphor for the American experience.

The Wild Onion's Roots:
Native Americans,
French Traders,
and Settlers
from New England

History and Settlement

When the French voyageur Louis Joliet returned to Canada from his historic expedition of 1673 down the Mississippi River, he reported to the Comte de Frontenac, the governor of New France, on the many natural wonders he had observed. Joliet boldly declared that this land of the tall grass—described by an English cartographer as the "carriage of Chekakou"—was all that stood in the way of linking the Great Lakes to the drainage basin of the Mississippi River system. If there could be a way to successfully negotiate the "Chicago portage," French military power could encompass the western frontier from Canada to the Gulf of Mexico.

But as René-Robert Cavelier Sieur de La Salle was to find out later, any hope of turning the marshy swamp at the shore of Lake Michigan into a commercial trading port for France was marred by the natural barriers posed by the land and the water. The Des Plaines River could be navigated only by canoe, which thwarted any plan to bring goods into Chicago by barge. Spring flooding was another problem. This land had many possibilities as a strategic military outpost, but for purposes of trade and commerce, the obstacles seemed almost insurmountable.

In the winter of 1674, Father Jacques Marquette established a campsite at the present-day intersection of Damen Avenue and the south branch of the Chicago River, but it was La Salle who eventually succeeded in claiming the entire Mississippi Basin for the greater glory of France. On April 9, 1682, he named this land "Louisiana" in honor of the French king, and a year later established Fort Saint Louis at the Starved Rock site on the Illinois River, about sixty miles south of Chicago. But France was forced to relinquish all military and political claims to this territory by the terms of the February 1763 Treaty of Paris, ending what American colonists called the French and Indian War. For many years Chicago remained a desolate, marshy mudflat, inhabited exclusively by Indians.

There were ten indigenous Native American tribes inhabiting the Great Lakes region when the French voyageurs first set foot on Chicago soil: the Fox, Sauk, Menominee, Ojibwe, Winnebago, Ottawa, Huron, Chippewa, Illinois, and Potawatomi, a hunting-gathering people situated in their ancestral home at the foot of Lake Michigan. Their customs and way of life were profoundly altered by the rise of the fur trade in the west during the closing decades of the 18th century.

John Jacob Astor's Southwest Fur Company established a virtual trade monopoly in the lower Great Lakes region, and the demand for the prized pelts in the east encouraged adventurers and frontiersmen to seek their fortune in the Indian country. Fur-trading centers were opened in Green Bay, Detroit, Sandusky, St. Louis, and Fort Wayne. The wilderness quickly retreated before the steady advance of civilization. The native people were forced to abandon ancient customs and a way of life in favor of a new one that offered them a very small stake in the land they held dear.

One hundred years after Joliet completed his historic tour of the frontier for de Frontenac, Jean Baptiste Point du Sable, the son of a French merchant and a Haitian woman, became the first non-Indian resident of Chicago. His twenty-two-by-forty-foot cabin on the bank of Lake Michigan was the first permanent structure on the raw landscape. He conducted regular trade with other trappers, merchants, and adventurers who found the area desirable for commerce.

Du Sable was respected by the Potawatomi elders and was welcomed into their councils. He lived among them and took Catherine, the daughter of Chief Pokagon, as his common-law wife. The marriage was formalized at Cahokia on October 27, 1788, but the union had been sanctioned by tribal custom years earlier.

Intermarriage between Potawatomi women and the French and British traders was common during the formative years of the Great Lakes fur trade. Some of Chicago's most prominent early settlers who impacted the future direction of the community were of mixed blood. Billy Caldwell (called Sauganash by the Potawatomi) was the son of an Indian women and an Irish military officer stationed in Detroit. Torn between two irreconcilable foes locked in a bitter struggle for land, Caldwell chose to fight alongside the Shawnee Indian leader Tecumseh at the Battle of Fallen Timbers in 1794, where a coalition of Indian tribes were defeated by General "Mad" Anthony Wayne.

Caldwell later served as a messenger for the U.S. military garrison stationed at Fort Dearborn, on the shore of Lake Michigan. He carried dispatches to the increasingly hostile Potawatomi, who would later be aligned with the British during the War of 1812.

Before and during the hostilities, Fort Dearborn was home to a number of Chicago residents, including John Kinzie, one of Chicago's early citizens. Kinzie was the son of a Scottish army surgeon garrisoned in Quebec. He made his way to Chicago in 1804 and established a flourishing commercial business outside the walls of the stockade. For nearly eight years John Kinzie lived like a king.

When the war broke out in 1812, the Fort Dearborn regulars found themselves in imminent peril of Indian attack. Captain Nathan Heald, the commander of the strategically located outpost, was ordered to evacuate the area and retreat to a safe haven in Fort Wayne, Indiana. Kinzie had wisely sent his family away earlier aboard a Lake Michigan ship that conveyed them to safety, but now he held out, reasoning that at this point in the hostilities it was probably safer to remain at the fort than risk a dangerous expedition across open country. He later relented and agreed to accompany Captain William Wells, a company of soldiers, two women, and twelve children out of Chicago.

On August 15, 1812, Kinzie received a report from To-Pee-Nee-Be of the St. Joseph's tribe that the Potawatomi, commanded by Chief Leopold Pokogon, were preparing to mount an attack. When he advised Wells, Wells rode on ahead of the wagon party to scout the land and see if he could verify these reports. Suddenly, from the sand hills in the distance, he spotted a contingent of 400 to 500 warriors in full battle regalia. Frantic and desperate, Captain Wells raced back to his men and sounded the general alarm. "They are about to attack us!" he cried. "Form instantly and charge upon them!"

But it was already too late. Vastly outnumbered, the Wells party was overwhelmed and slaughtered on a marshy dune two miles due south of Fort

Dearborn near what is today the intersection of 21st Street and Indiana Avenue. The twelve children who had cowered in terror in back of the transport wagon were shown no quarter. They were tomahawked by a solitary Indian warrior and left to die. Fifty-four infantrymen, twelve militiamen, two women, and an escort of Miami Indians commanded by Captain Heald and Captain Wells were all massacred. The next day the Potawatomi completed their mission and burned Fort Dearborn to the ground.

Potawatomi chieftains would later deny responsibility and instead accused the Winnebago of instigating the attack. Regardless of where the responsibility for the deed rested, the Potawatomi left a trail of violence and murder in their wake. The attack upon the soldiers and settlers of Fort Dearborn exacted a terrible price and prompted the U.S. policy that sealed the final fate of the Native Americans in this region of the country.

Kinzie miraculously survived the attack and returned to Chicago four years later to survey the scene of devastation and try to reclaim what was left of his former holdings. He made a hideous discovery. The Indians had not bothered to bury the remains of the slaughtered men, women, and children. Bones were found lying scattered across the South Side lakefront. Fort Dearborn was rebuilt by American soldiers in June of 1816, the land reclaimed, and the dead interred in modest pine boxes. Life moved on.

John Kinzie moved into du Sable's house near the present site of the Chicago Tribune building, but he never regained the status in the community he enjoyed prior to the Fort Dearborn tragedy. His son John H. Kinzie returned to Chicago in 1834 and was instrumental in securing a charter for the city's first railroad line. He was later appointed the first president of the village.

Early chroniclers refer to the elder Kinzie as the "Father of Chicago." Latter-day historians are not nearly as flattering in their assessments. By some accounts the fur trader Kinzie engaged in ruthless, mercenary tactics in order to achieve his wealth and secure his reputation in Chicago. Caldwell, by some accounts, spared the life of a man who exploited the native people for personal gain and who had long been suspected of murdering his business rival, Jean Lalime, in a knife fight.

Lalime was an educated man. He was a French-Canadian fur trapper by trade who doubled as Fort Dearborn's language interpreter. It was his great miscalculation to try to compete with the volatile Kinzie by purchasing du Sable's trading post and real estate holdings for the sum of 6,000 livres in 1800.

The two men became bitter enemies in the next few years—settling their differences with a knife and a gun outside the gates of the Fort Dearborn stockade on a moonless night in 1812. According to Kinzie's account, Lalime accosted him in the dark and fired an errant shot that grazed his neck. In the ensuing struggle Kinzie wrested Lalime's knife away from him, and killed the Frenchman instantly.

"It was an act of self-defense. I was unarmed," Kinzie insisted. No one witnessed the altercation, but the villagers accepted at face value John Kinzie's version of events and exonerated him of any wrongdoing.

Kinzie paid Jean Lalime's funeral expenses and interred the remains in a burial plot less than 200 yards from his cabin. The Indian troubles weighed heavily on the minds of the settlers, and the Kinzie-Lalime scandal was quickly forgotten.

When questioned by historians years later concerning this unfortunate occurrence in frontier Chicago, the recollections of the old settlers concerning the death of Jean Lalime had dimmed. Efforts to plot the exact location of the Kinzie cabin and the grave of the French trapper based on eyewitness accounts failed to yield any tangible clues that would shed light on the mystery. However, on April 29, 1891, a crew of workers digging the foundation of a new building at the southwest corner of Cass Avenue (now Wabash Avenue) and Illinois Street unearthed a skeleton that did.

Medical examiners employing primitive methods of forensic science pegged the remains to be between 80 and 100 years old, consistent with the time of Lalime's death. Representatives of the Chicago Historical Society were reasonably certain, based on the existing historical record of where the Kinzie cottage was thought to have stood, that indeed the long-lost Jean Lalime had been located. Scraps of wood—all that remained from the modest pine casket John Kinzie laid in the ground in 1812—were found among the remains.

Kinzie, Lalime, and other French and British traders engaged in commerce with the Native American people to suit their purpose. Undoubtedly the growing hostility among the Potawatomi stemmed from the belief that they were being exploited for commercial gain, which only served to escalate the cycle of violence.

Others, like Alexander Robinson, the son of a Scottish trader and a Chippewa woman, and Antoine Ouillmette, hunter, farmer, and fur trader of mixed French and Potawatomi blood, cultivated friendly dealings with all and acted as mediators between white society and the Indian tribes.

Ouillmette and his Potawatomi bride Archange built their grocery store and trading post on the high bluffs overlooking Lake Michigan well north of Chicago in what is now the elegant North Shore suburb of Wilmette, named in his honor.

The Potawatomi, suffering from nearly 40 years of famine and starvation, made a swift transition from farming to commercial trading. Guns, hatchets, blankets, household items, and whiskey changed hands between the white settlers and the Indians in the normal course of business after Fort Dearborn was rebuilt from the ashes in 1816. But the days of the Potawatomi settlement along the banks of Lake Michigan were fast coming to an end.

The bitter memory of the Fort Dearborn massacre and the white man's persistent demands led to the removal of the Indians from the bustling settlement outside the old fort. A grand council was convened in Chicago on September 26, 1833, in an open shed on the north side of the river for the purpose of forging a binding treaty. Amid an atmosphere that alternated between gloom, drunken hilarity, despair, and triumphant jubilation, Alexander Robinson, representing the interests of the Potawatomi, the Chippewa, and the Ottawa, formalized the Treaty of Chicago.

In return for cash considerations, the remaining native people agreed to re-settle west of the Mississippi River no later than 1835. Robinson, however, chose to remain behind and was awarded 1,200 acres of land next to the Des Plaines River northwest of the city-to-be. This land, fronting Lawrence Avenue on the Northwest Side of the city, is now a forest preserve known as Robinson Woods.

The final exodus of the Indian tribes from Chicago on August 18, 1835, was marked by a simple but haunting refrain etched in the memories of all who formed along the parade route. Clad in loin cloth, ceremonial head gear, and war paint, the Potawatomi and their kin staged a grand farewell war dance down the boulevard before embarking on a westward journey to unfamiliar lands reserved for them in Clay County, Missouri. Historians tell us that the nomadic Potawatomi, unhappy with their new arrangements, drifted from Missouri to Council Bluffs, Iowa, then toward an inevitable and final rendezvous with oblivion.

Simon Pokogon, son of Leopold Pokogon, chief of the Potawatomi tribe that destroyed Fort Dearborn in 1812, related to his biographers that his father was forced to relinquish the land that became the City of Chicago for the equivalent of three cents an acre. Real estate property worth millions of dollars in the speculative frenzy yet to come was transferred to the white settlers for the sum of $14,000 in annual payments to be spread over the next twenty years.

"Almost every person I met regarded Chicago as the germ of an immense city, and speculators have already bought up, at high prices, all the building ground in the neighborhood," reported Patrick Shirreff, a local Scottish farmer in 1833. Soon, the settlers of solid New England stock, sensing the enormous investment potential, poured into Chicago by the thousands.

Transplanted Easterners—the Yankees of English, Welsh, and Scottish descent—came to dominate the cultural, mercantile, and social affairs of the primitive frontier village gradually being made over into a city. "It is a remarkable thing to meet such an assemblage of educated, refined, and wealthy persons as may be found there, living in small, inconvenient houses on the edge of the wild prairie," wrote Harriet Martineau around this time.

In 1837, the year Chicago received its city charter, William Butler Ogden, a New Englander embodying the Yankee values of ingenuity and thrift, was elected the city's first mayor. Ogden had held out few hopes for the future of Chicago after surveying the muddy quagmire in 1835. Dray wagons parked in a vacant field south of Fort Dearborn, the abandoned old relic from a bygone age, were axle-deep in the muck. Chicago was rough, uneven, and an altogether unpleasant place. "There is no such value in the land," he complained, "and won't be for a generation."

Two years later Ogden presided over a flourishing city of 4,000 hearty souls who had put little stock in his gloomy predictions. Apparently, even Ogden himself had not taken his words to heart fully. He accumulated a private fortune by taking control and directing the affairs of the city's first chartered rail line, the Galena & Chicago Union route, which soon linked the Mississippi River corridor to the Great Lakes.

The explosive economic growth of Chicago foretold by Joliet in the 17th century was hastened by events elsewhere. The opening of the Erie Canal in 1825 linked the Atlantic seaboard states to the Great Lakes region; for the first time, the westward movement of goods, services, and people shifted northward from the Ohio River.

Thus Chicago's strategic location on the Great Lakes made that city, rather than the older, entrenched river cities of Cincinnati or St. Louis, the major western terminus of the nation. The Illinois-Michigan Canal, linking the Great Lakes and the Mississippi systems (completed in 1845), and a pair of railroad lines that connected the city to the eastern markets beginning in 1852, permanently secured Chicago's place as the commercial heartland of the burgeoning West.

The canal's construction was the impetus for the arrival of the first great wave of European immigrants: the Irish, who came to the United States brimming with the expectation of good-paying jobs digging the costly new waterway. The unparalleled growth of Chicago during the second half of the 19th century was made possible by the hard work and industry of succeeding waves of immigrants. The Irish were followed by trainloads of Scandinavians, Germans, Poles, Bohemians, Greeks, Italians, Russian Jews, and other Eastern European groups. However, there were few Asians and Hispanics counted in the census during this earliest period of Chicago history; their numbers rapidly accelerated after World War II, particularly during the 1960s and 1970s. The city's African-American population was small before 1900, but changing social patterns in the South and improved communications with the urban corridors of the industrial North spurred the great migration beginning around 1907.

Population statistics tell us much about the demographic and ethnic makeup of the region. In 1970, for example, the major countries of origin represented in the city census included Poland, Germany, Italy, the Soviet Union, Sweden, and Ireland. Ten years later, African-Americans, Hispanics, and Asians were the fastest-growing ethnic groups in the city. These changing realities inevitably altered the city's political landscape. Blacks accounted for two-fifths of the city's population in 1980, and as a result they were able to wrest considerable power away from the white ethnics who had previously controlled the municipal departments and the appointment process. Racial fears predicated on real or imagined concerns about neighborhood safety, and a resulting decline in property values, compelled the children and grandchildren of many first-generation Europeans to abandon inner-city neighborhoods. The dilution of European culture is evident in such diverse neighborhoods as the West Side Pilsen community (formerly Czech-Bohemian, now almost entirely Mexican), and Lincoln Square on the North Side, where only the delicatessens, restaurants, and gift shops are left to suggest the heavy German concentration of former years.

Indeed, Chicago has changed in significant ways since Native Americans and the French, Scottish, and English traders roamed the prairie. There is no identifiable French-American colony in Chicago. The Scots are widely scattered throughout the suburbs, and the Potawatomi, all but forgotten, are a distant echo from the uncharted frontier. It is one of the supreme ironies of our history that as the Germans, Scandinavians, and Czechs decry the loss of community in their traditional neighborhood settings, Chicago's original settlers are today a tiny minority within the urban ethnic fabric of the city.

════ Native American History ════ and Attractions

Between 7,000–15,000 Native Americans, representing forty different tribes from across the country (but mostly drawn from the Chippewa, Winnebago, Sioux, Potawatomi, and Ottawa tribes), struggle to make ends meet in Uptown and other congested inner city neighborhoods of Chicago. Prior to 1950, there were only 775 American Indians living in Chicago, according to available census figures. As a result of a Congressional federal relocation program that began in the early 1950s, the figures increased steadily. The U.S. government encouraged American Indians to abandon tribal reservations in order to gain valuable work skills and begin a new and hopefully more productive life in the large urban corridors of Chicago and Los Angeles—the two main relocation centers selected by the Bureau of Indian Affairs. Today Chicago ranks third behind San Francisco and Los Angeles among the large cities in the reported number of Native American residents. The most recent census reveals that there are 7,000 American Indians living in the Chicago area, though community activists insist that this figure is much closer to 15,000. Native Americans own more than 100 local businesses.

The termination/relocation program, aimed at "getting the government out of the Indian business" and breaking up long-standing reservations, reached its heyday between 1951 and 1972. In 1972 the program officially ended. The general allotment policy had failed in its stated goals. Very often the jobs awaiting the American Indian in the designated city were nonexistent, and the prospects for enrolling in an accredited vocational school exceedingly slim. Receiving little more than a pat on the back, a wallet-sized I.D. card that categorized him as an "enrolled" member of a tribe, a one-way bus ticket, and $45 in spending money, the displaced Native American very often found himself suddenly abandoned and alone in Chicago. For Stephen Horman, an American Eskimo who came to Chicago in 1969, the only indoctrination he received was a Chicago Transit Authority route map of the city and fifteen minutes of agency time.

For the transplanted Native Americans, life in this rugged urban frontier has been an endless series of compromises between doing what is right and living from day to day. Unemployed parents stare out of their tenement windows unhappily as their children spend endless hours feeding quarters into the video arcade machines on Wilson Avenue, while groups of men huddle together underneath the Jackson Park elevated line in order to keep the swirling March winds that whip off the lake from searing their skin. Alcohol abuse. Poverty. Lines at the unemployment office. These all-too-familiar images of despair have acutely affected the Native American population of Chicago in many profound ways.

Amid the deprivation of Uptown there are hopeful signs that the Indian heritage has not been sacrificed. The American Indian Center, founded in 1953 at 411 N. La Salle, but eventually relocated to a converted Masonic Hall at 1630 W. Wilson, has sponsored many cultural events over the year to benefit its senior citizens, youth, and social services programs. The center continues the important mission of the Indian Council Fire, a general social services agency that existed from 1923 through World War II. It differs in one major respect: The American Indian Center was created specifically for the purpose of meeting the needs of the relocated Indians arriving in Chicago for the first time.

The presence of the American Indian Center is a major reason why the Native American population remains anchored to Uptown. In a similar vein, the All-Nations Assembly of God Church at 1126 W. Granville began its ministry in April 1981, and has served the Chicagoland Native American community as a part of approximately 160 worship centers across the United States. The ministry communicates the gospel to every tribe represented in the city and has sponsored training seminars, family-oriented social events, and counseling centers.

Incorporated on May 17, 1974, the Native American Educational Services (NAES) College at 2838 W. Peterson Avenue offers an academic program leading to a B.A. degree in community services for persons employed in American Indian programs and agencies. Affiliated with Antioch University, NAES College emphasizes the cultural and historic traditions of the tribal and Indian communities, and teaches the skills necessary for professional work. In this sense, Native Americans are made to feel an important part of the social milieu of Chicago, rather than strangers in their own land.

Cultural Institutions

Mitchell Indian Museum, *Kendall College, 2408 Orrington Ave., Evanston, (847) 866-1395. Closed Mondays and for the month of August. Donations accepted. Membership available.*

As a small boy, John Mitchell was fascinated by the history and culture of the Indian tribes of the Great Lakes and the Plains. His uncle served as an Indian agent in Oklahoma, and when John came to visit him one year, he was presented with several genuine Indian artifacts, which were to form the basis of a collection that was to grow to more than 2,000 pieces. John Mitchell was a successful businessman who was president of his own realty company and a trustee of Kendall College. When he retired in 1977, the extensive collection of Indian art and artifacts was turned over to the school, so that the whole community could benefit from his gift through ongoing exhibits, workshops, lectures, and an archive library. Betty Mitchell provided a generous endowment that enabled the college to turn her husband's vision into reality. The collection of items is maintained by curator Jane Edwards, and it illustrates Native American life through pottery, basketry, clothing, textiles, beadwork and quillwork. The artifacts are from four cultural areas: the Plains, Western Great Lakes, the Pueblo, and the Navajo. A children's table invites youngsters to experience history and folklore through touch, sight, and smell. Youngsters can build their own teepee, grind corn, or spin wool just as the Indians of the past did.

A permanent collection of items dating from 6000 B.C. to the twentieth century awaits the visitor to the Mitchell Indian Museum. *Recommended.*

Schingoethe Center for Native American Cultures,
Dunham Hall, Aurora University, Aurora, (630) 844-5402. Closed Mondays and Saturdays and for the month of August. Admission free.

Herbert Schingoethe shared John Mitchell's interest in Native American folklore. For much of his life he collected arrowheads and pottery, much of it unearthed from Kane and Du Page County farms. In 1960 Schingoethe began to manage ranches in Southwest Colorado, a job that afforded him the opportunity to roam through antique shops, Indian trading posts, and pawnshops. The collection grew until it numbered more than 3,000 objects. As a strong supporter of Aurora University, Schingoethe bequeathed much of his collection to the school. Dunham Hall, named in honor of the family of his wife, Martha, houses the collection of Southwest, Plains, Woodlands, Arctic, and Northwest Coast Indian artifacts in a 1,500-square-foot area within the main gallery. The gallery was inaugurated in the fall of 1990.

Webber Resource Center *at the Field Museum of Natural History, Main Floor, Roosevelt Rd. and Lake Shore Dr., Chicago, (312) 922-9410. Open daily. Standard museum admission fee charged. Free on Thursdays.*

A reading room and center for Native American lore since 1987. The resource center also stocks videos, which are available for viewing. All in all, the museum's permanent collection of Indian costumes, artwork, handtools and weaponry fills seven halls. The museum intends to combine the Webber Center with other cultural centers in 1996.

Native American Art Gallery, *810 Dempster St., Evanston, (847) 864-0400. Open daily.*

Owner Suzanne Ballew personally selects items for her collection during an annual buying expedition to the Southwest. She is able to pass on her appreciation of the Indian way to her customers as they shop for contemporary and antique Indian art, including pottery, baskets, rugs, drums, and lithographs (both original and limited editions).

Southwest Trading Company, *211 W. Main St., St. Charles, (708) 584-5107. Open daily. Credit cards accepted.*

A gallery of Native American art from the Plains states and the Southwest. Water color, acrylics, basketry, pottery, weavings, and a collection of sand art from the Navajo.

Southwest Expressions, *1459 W. Webster Pl.,*
Chicago, (773) 525-2626. Open daily. Credit cards
accepted.

A different kind of Chicago art gallery, specializing in contemporary Native American and Southwestern art. All media covered, including oils, basketry, lithographs, and pottery.

Annual Events and Celebrations

American Indian Center Annual Powwow,
alternating locations. Second or third weekend in
November. For dates and times, call (773) 275-5871.
Admission fee charged.

A three-day Native American festival. Since 1953 the American Indian Center has staged its annual powwow, which is regarded as a "unification ceremony," to promote the heritage and cultural diversity of the thirty to sixty tribes represented each year. Members of each tribe don the ceremonial headgear and costumes unique to their region before performing native dances. The corn dance, for example, salutes the fall harvest, while the snake dance is performed in long lines. The fest also includes an arts and crafts promenade, displays of tribal clothing, vendors selling Native American foods such as corn soup, fried bread jams, Sioux blueberry pudding, and tacos. All proceeds from the event go toward the American Indian Center to help meet their yearly operating expenses. A "Grand Entry" procession takes place each day. *Recommended.*

Native-American Powwow, *Governor's State*
University, Governor's Hwy. and Stunkel Road,
University Park, (708) 534-5000 (ask for the Office of
Student Life). Last weekend in March. Admission fee
charged. Free parking.

The Society for Native American Interests, a campus student organization, hosted its first day-long Powwow inside the university gymnasium in 1996. The day-long celebration features two dance troops appearing in the early afternoon and early evening. In between, one can sample a variety of Native American foods and purchase arts and crafts from vendors. Call in advance to confirm date and time.

Places to See

The Totem Pole (Kwanusila), *in Lincoln Park east of Lake Shore Dr. at Addison St., Chicago.*

During one of his forays to the Canadian Pacific Northwest in 1926, James L. Kraft, the founder of Kraft Foods, Inc., purchased a hand-carved totem pole with tribal symbols, family crests, and mythological depictions created by the Northwest Coast Indians. Kraft donated the artifact, which dated back to the turn of the century, to the Chicago Park District for the enjoyment of the city's school children. The pole remained in its familiar location until 1985, when concern arose over the physical deterioration caused by Chicago's changing climates and air pollution. The original pole was taken down and returned to Canada that year. A wooden replica was carved by Tony Hunt and paid for by J. L. Kraft. It has been chemically treated to withstand the elements and now stands in the same spot fronting Lake Shore Drive.

A Signal of Peace statue, *in Lincoln Park north of the Diversey Harbor entrance, Chicago.*

The statue depicts a mounted Sioux Indian giving the traditional gesture of peace. Sculpted by Cyrus Edwin Dallin (1861–1944), *A Signal of Peace* was on display at the 1893 World's Fair. It was rescued from oblivion and donated to Chicago by Judge Lambert Tree, who incidentally lent his name to the Police Department's medal of valor.

Bowman and *Spearman* statues, *adjoining the Grant Park entrance at Michigan Ave. and Congress Pkwy., Chicago*

The towering Indian warriors silhouetted against the Chicago sunset provide a poignant, historical image of a distant time and place. Sadly, few Chicagoans pay much attention to these statues. They are taken very much for granted, except by a handful of out-of-town tourists, who are struck by their simple yet majestic posture. They are the creation of renowned sculptor Ivan Mestovic (1883–1962) who was commissioned by the B. F. Ferguson Monument Fund to pay homage to the Native American. Erected in 1928, the Indians guard the entranceway to Grant Park, and were originally located on either side of a stairway that was replaced in the 1940s in order to permit automobile traffic to flow into the park.

***The Alarm* statue,** *Lincoln Park, east of Lake Shore Dr. (3000 North), Chicago.*

Dedicated on May 17, 1884, this was the first permanent monument to the Indians to be erected on Chicago Park District land. The bronze sculpture is the work of John J. Boyle (1851–1917), and it shows a man and a woman belonging to the Ottawa tribe. *The Alarm* was commissioned in 1880 by Martin Ryerson, a lumber magnate and commercial trader who worked with the Ottawa people early in his career. Ryerson was concerned that the artist present his figures only in the most favorable light, thus avoiding the usual prejudices against Indians common in those times.

NAES College, *2828 W. Peterson Ave., Chicago.*

The Native American Educational Services, Inc., is the only accredited institution of higher learning in the Chicago area specifically designed to provide a quality educational environment and job skills tailored to the needs of the Native American resident. NAES offers a selection of courses in tribal languages. At the Chicago campus, courses are taught in Menominee, Navajo, Lakota, and Ojibwe. Additional campuses are located on the Fort Peck Reservation, Poplar, Montana; Keshena, Wisconsin; and Minneapolis, Minnesota. The student body is comparatively small in relation to other liberal arts colleges in the area. Between 1975 and 1988, 108 students were enrolled in the degree program. Thirty-five graduated. But NAES is not a conventional college. Most of the students are older, with the average age in the mid-thirties. As a rule, the Native American student is usually the first member of his family to attend college, and therefore must balance the responsibilities to the family and earning a livelihood with the burdens of higher education.

Shops

American Indian Gift Store, *1756 W. Wilson Ave., Chicago, (773) 769-1170. Closed Sunday.*

An American-Indian-owned business specializing in authentic fine arts and crafts, including colorful and intricate beadwork from the Plains tribes; handwoven rugs from the Southwest; Indian stationery and note cards; paintings, prints, and sand paintings by Native American artists; Indian records and tapes; bone carvings by Stanley Hill; Kachina dolls; and hand-signed Indian pottery. The store also does some custom-made work and repairs Indian jewelry.

⎯⎯ Scottish History and Attractions ⎯⎯

Nobody knows for sure, and the figures are very approximate, but there are probably 100,000 Chicagoans with at least a trace of Scottish blood in them. The Scots, according to Wayne Rethford, director of the Scottish Home in North Riverside, dispersed rather quickly across Cook, Lake, and DuPage Counties, and never formed their own distinctive communities as did the Italians, Germans, or Poles, for example. The English-speaking immigrants were not encumbered by language barriers, and therefore were better able to assimilate into whatever neighborhoods they chose. But their Chicago roots run very deep, and up until the 1890s, the Scots were among the ten largest European ethnic groups in the city. The majority of Scots disdained the political arena, and chose instead to pursue careers in banking and commerce.

The Illinois St. Andrew's Society was organized the night of November 30, 1845, when a group of hearty Scotsmen gathered to celebrate in verse and song the Feast of St. Andrew, who was adopted as the patron saint of the Picts, a pre-Celtic people who assimilated with the Scots in the 9th century. In attendance that night was West Point cadet George McClellan, a fresh-faced nineteen-year old who happened to be passing through Chicago. McClellan, of course, went on to make a name for himself as one of the commanding generals of the Army of the Potomac during the Civil War.

An enduring city tradition was born, and for every year thereafter the oldest fraternal society in Illinois has donned the kilt every November to pay homage to the founding members, and to recall the exploits of one George Anderson. In every respect, George Anderson was the quintessential "common man." He served for a time as the postmaster at the substation located at 22nd and State streets. He was the driving force behind the St. Andrew's Society. He helped draft the first constitution and bylaws in 1853. He secured two plots of land for his fellow Scots who desired to be interred at the Rosehill Cemetery on the far North Side. At the time of his death in 1887, Anderson was the last surviving member of that historic 1845 banquet.

By reading aloud "Tam O'Shanter," a spirited narrative verse by Scotland's national poet Robert Burns (1759–96), George Anderson established a tradition for all future banquets. A restless and dissatisfied social rebel, Burns railed against religious orthodoxy, charming both the common folk and the literary social circles of Edinburgh. His enduring legacy extended all the way across the Atlantic, where in 1906, a Burns Monument Society was established in Chicago. Thousands of loyal Scots donated to a fund for the construction of a statue. Today, this Burns memorial fronts Washington Boulevard in Garfield Park, lovingly maintained by the Scottish Home.

Each year on the poet's birthday, residents of the home lay a wreath on the ground.

Cultural Institutions

The Scottish Home, *2800 Des Plaines Ave. (28th Ave. and Des Plaines St.), North Riverside, (708) 442-7268. Open daily. Admission free.*

The Scottish Home is the oldest non-profit corporation in Illinois, and has occupied this parcel of land since 1910, when the administrators moved from 43 Bryant Avenue (now 35th St.) on Chicago's South Side. A number of elderly Scottish people reside here under the auspices of the St. Andrews Society. A small, little-known museum and Hall of Fame honoring 200 prominent local Scots is located in the "undercroft" of the home. The museum is operated by the Scottish Cultural Society. The Robert Burns "corner" features original first editions and memorabilia from the poet's life. The Hall of Fame gallery, composed of 200 wall plaques, honors the notable men and women of Scottish descent in the city's history.

The Scottish Cultural Society, Ltd., *P.O. Box 486, Lombard, IL, 60148-0486, (708) 629-2227. Annual memberships available for individuals or families.*

The Cultural Society was formed by twelve Scottish enthusiasts in 1977 to bring the music, arts, history, and literature of the country into wide focus within the Chicagoland area. Meetings deal with a range of topics, including discussions on the life and times of famed poets and authors such as Robert Burns and Sir Walter Scott, proper highland dress, and musical entertainment. The society publishes the *Celtic Knot,* a monthly newsletter sent free to the more than 500 members.

Annual Events and Celebrations

Annual St. Andrews Society Anniversary Dinner, *Chicago Hilton and Towers, 720 S. Michigan Ave., Chicago. October or November. Call (708) 442-7268 for tickets. Membership in the St. Andrews Society is open to all persons of Scottish descent, and is available for individuals or families.*

What began in 1845 as a small, informal dinner affair continues more than

150 years later in one of Chicago's most fashionable downtown hotels. Scottish singers, accompanied by pipe bands, provide the entertainment, and a few of the more hearty members of the society will brave the brisk wind-chill factor to wear the traditional kilt.

Nicht Wi' Burns (A Night With Burns). *On or about January 26. Call the Scottish Home, (708) 442-7268. Admission fee charged.*

Dinner and celebration for the poet's birthday. Scottish folk songs. Readings from Burns's most famous works. Pipe bands. Native dancers.

St. Andrew Highland Games, *held at the Polo Grounds in Oak Brook. Mid-June. Call (708) 442-7268 for details and times. Admission fee charged.*

There is certainly more to Scottish culture than Robert Burns, bagpipes and folk dancing, evidenced by the Highland Games, an annual test of athletic stamina. Among the day's events is a rugby match, the 56-pound hammer throw, and sheaf and caber toss (lifting a 120-pound pole, and hurling it so that it rotates 360 degrees), by the representative Scottish clans in the United States. In addition to these grueling feats of strength, there are the customary pipe bands, genealogy booths, a Parade of Tartans—led by Scottish deerhounds—country dancers, vendors, continuous music, food concessions, stunt kite flying exhibitions, and a fiddle workshop. The proceeds benefit the Scottish Home. *Recommended.*

Annual Scottish Fair, *Odeum Sports and Expo Center, 1033 N. Villa Ave., Villa Park. Second weekend in October. For information, call the Illinois Scottish Cultural Society, (708) 383-0028. Admission fee charged.*

A two-day indoor festival sponsored by the Scottish Cultural Society, featuring famed local bagpipe bands including the Emerald Society and the Chicago Highlanders. During the solo bagpipe competition, over 100 local performers will compete for top prizes. A Scottish judge evaluates the contestants on technique, tuning, tempo, and musical performance. On Saturday night, the fair will host a "Ceilidh" (pronounced "kaylee"), which is a traditional Scottish sing-along led by the Canadian band Cromdale. The Scottish Fair has delighted Chicagoans since 1977. More than 10,000 people pass through the doors of the Expo Center each year.

Shops

Scottish Modern, *6115 S. Archer Ave., Summit, (708) 594-5773. Closed Sunday and Monday. MasterCard and Visa accepted.*

Seven thousand square feet of gift items, imported foods, jewelry, books, and Scottish clothing items, including a rich array of kilts. A tailor shop is on the premises.

Winston Sausage Co., *4701 W. 63rd St., Chicago, (773) 767-4353. Closed Sunday.*

Specializing in Scottish meat pies, but there is also a rich assortment of imported Irish and British foods.

Restaurants

Duke of Perth Restaurant, *2913 N. Clark St., Chicago (773) 477-1741. Open for lunch and dinner daily.*

Owned by a Scotsman from Aberdeen, who specializes in Scottish gourmet foods, including shepherd's pie, Hebridean leek pie, and smoked salmon. McEwan's Export and Newcastle Brown Ale on tap. The first Saturday of the month is "Open Pipe Night," when patrons are invited to bring along their own bagpipes and perform.

═══════ Anglo-Saxon Attractions ═══════

Cultural Institutions

British Club, *meets at the Latvian Community Center, 4146 N. Elston Ave., Chicago. Alternating Friday nights. Call Joan Murphy at (708) 673-6335 for additional information. Membership available for individuals or couples.*

Membership is open to persons of English extraction, or anyone with a passing interest in the history and culture of the British Isles. The club sponsors yearly travel excursions and sightseeing tours to the United Kingdom and Ireland; holds an Annual St. George's Day spring dance every May; offers discounts on merchandise at the various import shops around town; and publishes a newsletter for dues-paying members.

Annual Events and Celebrations

Bristol Renaissance Faire *(formerly King Richard's Faire), Bristol, WI. Saturdays and Sundays in August. Please contact the Bristol Renaissance Faire at 12420 128th St., Kenosha, WI, or call (708) 395-7773; (414) 396-4320; or Ticketmaster at (708) 395-7773. Admission fee charged.*

Journey back to the Renaissance and experience English Elizabethan village life in the Midwest. Each year 100 drama students are trained in Shakespearean dialogue, sword fighting, and country dance in order to authenticate the period. The Hammond-Lee Action Theatre performs three jousts a day, very often in the sweltering August humidity of Wisconsin. This is live, interactive outdoor theater at its best, combining history, culture, and medieval fun. Court jesters, panhandlers, and a delightful group calling itself the "Flaming Idiots" entertains at every turn in the road. The village merchants sell traditional foods from the Elizabethan period, and assorted souvenirs. One-quarter mile west of Interstate I-94 on State Line Road at the Illinois-Wisconsin border. Exit Russell Road, turn left, and follow the signs. *Recommended.*

Restaurants

The Red Lion Pub, *2446 N. Lincoln Ave., Chicago, (773) 348-2695. Open daily. Credit cards accepted.*

Chicago's kindred spirits who fancy kidney pie, Cornish pasties, and English beer meet and greet each other at the city's most famous English restaurant and pub; John Cordwell's Red Lion, across the street from the Biograph Theater, where John Dillinger was mowed down in 1934. There's no chance of that happening again. The Lincoln-Fullerton neighborhood is one of the most gentrified neighborhoods in the city, appealing to an urban mix of literary bohemians, artisans, and young professionals. But inside the Red Lion at least, the atmosphere is verrrrrry British. *Recommended.*

Outlying Areas

Medieval Times Dinner & Tournament, *2001*
Roselle Rd., Schaumburg, (847) 843-3900, or
1-800-544-2001. For groups of fifteen or more,
call (847) 882-0555. Closed Monday and Tuesday.
Admission fee charged.

The Count and Countess of Perelada welcome you to their home . . . an 11th-century English castle that looms over the Northwest Suburban landscape. The exterior of this imposing fortress is modeled after one built in Spain during the 11th century. Step back with them to the year 1093, when gallant jousters and knights defended the realm. Dine on roasted chicken, dragon ribs, and herb-basted potatoes served on pewter plates as you watch the Andalusian horses gallop about the 1,400-seat arena. Up above, a trained falcon swoops in a figure eight pattern as you digest the remainder of your four-course meal. The evening concludes with a fight-to-the-death jousting tournament and a battle for the sword of Charlemagne. Historical fact counts for little here. It's the skills of the horsemen, the wonderfully choreographed stage combat, and the food that matter. Medieval Times is one of Chicago's newest and most exciting attractions. The one-price admission includes dinner, show, beverages, and tax (cash bar service available).

Flatlanders Restaurant & Brewery, *Old Half Day*
Road and Milwaukee Ave., Lincolnshire, IL
(847) 821-9191.

A relaxed, pleasant experience in a comfortable brew pub and restaurant featuring a mix of beers of exceptional character from the Pacific Northwest and the British Isles utilizing ingredients from all over Europe and the United States. The adjoining brewery consists of a grain-milling room, the brewhouse, fermentation room, laboratory, and a two-story chilled serving room. The decor is very reminiscent of traditional mid-19th century European distilleries and malting works.

Irish Chicago

History and Settlement

Not so many years ago, virtually every policeman on the beat, street sanitation worker, and precinct captain was Irish. The sons of the Auld Sod dominated Chicago political and religious life for over 125 years, even though they were outnumbered by native-born Americans and German immigrants for much of that period.

The Irish brought with them a foreign culture that was often at odds with the Anglo-Saxon Nativists who branded them unworthy to share the new nation's bounty. In time, the Irish would overcome much of the ethnic prejudice and anti-Catholic phobia of the new world to take their place in the mainstream. It was a long, arduous journey, however.

From 1845 to 1847, Ireland suffered a disastrous famine that resulted from the failure of the potato crop. Nearly one-and-a-half million penniless, half-starved immigrants spilled in through the ports of Boston and New York. The overwhelming majority of them were tenant farmers who had suffered under a corrupt landlord system imposed upon them by the pro-British aristocracy. The Irish immigrants disdained the farmer's life in order to become manual laborers in America's burgeoning urban centers. Those who chose not to remain in Boston or New York made their way to the Pennsylvania coal fields or to the numerous canals then under construction along the East Coast.

The history of the Irish settlement in Chicago rightfully begins on July 4, 1836, when Dr. William B. Egan, a native of County Kerry, delivered the ground-breaking address to kick off the first phase of construction on the Illinois-Michigan Canal. The waterway was Chicago's first great civic undertaking, a link between Lake Michigan and the Illinois and Mississippi rivers. When completed in 1848, the canal quickly established Chicago as the most important transportation hub of the Midwest. Hundreds of Irishmen found their final resting place along the banks first on the Erie and then the Illinois-Michigan canals. The entry of the Irish into city politics coincided with the construction of the canal.

From just a few hundred canal workers in the 1830s, the Irish population of Chicago grew to 6,096 in 1850. As the city continued to grow, thousands more poured in to take advantage of job opportunities in packing houses, brickyards, construction, and municipal government. By 1870 there were 39,988 Irish in Chicago, accounting for 13.37% of the population.

The construction of the canal had spurred the growth of Bridgeport, a South Side community located on the South Branch of the Chicago River. The northeastern terminus of the Illinois-Michigan Canal (Canalport) was located there, in what was briefly a sleepy little village outside the main city limits. The original Irish settlement of Kilgubbin, just north of the Chicago River, was quickly dwarfed by Irish Bridgeport (so named because of a low-slung bridge erected across the Chicago River at Ashland Avenue in the 1840s). Thousands of workers' cottages sprang up almost overnight. Before 1848 the neighborhood was known as Hardscrabble, because disease, despair, and mortality ran high.

The first Catholic parish, St. Bridget's, was founded in 1850. The Irish, more than any other ethnic group, derived a sense of identity from their neighborhood parishes. The historic antagonisms between Catholic and Protestant that characterized much of Irish history since the 16th century were imported to U.S. shores. Irish nationalism is an important theme interwoven into the history of Chicago.

Following the completion of the canal, the Irish laborers were forced to seek alternative employment within Bridgeport. A steel mill opened at the southeast corner of Ashland and Archer in the 1860s, followed by breweries, brickyards, and meat packing firms. In 1865 the animal slaughtering and packaging was transferred to the Union Stock Yards immediately to the south. The industrial base of Bridgeport was cemented in 1905 when the Central Manufacturing District, an early industrial development, was founded on its western border.

Bridgeport is one of Chicago's oldest, most stratified neighborhoods. Its pleasant tree-lined streets are filled with modest wooden and brick two-flats, interspersed with ma-and-pa grocery stores and corner saloons. Symbolic of its ties to the Irish community, Bridgeport is the home of the Chicago White

Sox, a team founded in 1900 by Charles Comiskey, an Irishman whose immigrant father had served as alderman of the tenth ward. The son soon eclipsed his father's popularity and his ballpark, opened on July 1, 1910, was a monument to the Bridgeport Irish. On ground-breaking day—St. Patrick's Day of 1910—a "lucky" green Irish brick was laid in place by the architect Zachary Davis. Seventy years later Bill Veeck dug the brick out of the wall and certified to a disbelieving press that this was the genuine article. There was no trace of green on the brick, however. Comiskey Park, which stood at 35th and Shields (Bill Veeck Drive) was demolished during the 1991 season after a newer, more spacious ballpark opened across the street. It is called, appropriately enough, Comiskey Park II.

In the 1890s, political satirist Finley Peter Dunne captured better than most the spirit of Bridgeport. Writing for the *Chicago Evening Post,* Dunne introduced his readers to the fictional Martin Dooley, who provided a heart-felt glimpse at Irish social customs along "Archey" (Archer) Road. Dunne also lampooned a variety of less-than-circumspect politicians, men like Ald. Johnny Powers and the irrepressible "Bathhouse" John Coughlin. These men were representative of a generation of Irish politicians whose day has long since passed. But in their time, Coughlin, Powers, and their minions carved out an impressive power base by cultivating the "saloon vote," the liquor trade, and the denizens of the criminal underworld. Politics in the mid- to late-19th century was the lifeblood of the Irish community. The immigrants enjoyed an edge over the Germans, Italians, and Poles through their knowledge of the language and their inherent organizational skills.

The Irish had been quickly able to fill the political vacuum created by the Anglo blue bloods, who looked upon jobs in the government sector—be it police officer or city gas inspector—as less than honorable. Consequently, the Irish were there to weld a continuing "machine," from their precincts and wards. Their tolerance of public drinking and gambling flew in the face of traditional New England Protestant thinking, but was perfectly accept-able to other newly arrived Europeans who supported their elective bid.

The career of John Coughlin—Chicago's most colorful, notorious boss of the 1890s and 1900s—is illustrative of the path well traveled by Irish political figures of that era. Born in 1860, Coughlin helped his father tend the family grocery store on Polk Street, near the site where the Great Chicago Fire began. That conflagration swept away the store and much of the neighborhood, and young John was forced to strike out on his own. Recalling the event years later, Coughlin would say: "I'm glad that fire came along and burned the store. Say, if not for that bonfire I might have been a rich man's son and gone to Yale and never amounted to anything!"

As a young man Coughlin went to work as a "rubber" in a Turkish bath on Clark Street, hence his nickname Bathhouse John. There he laid the basis for his future career in the city council by rubbing elbows—quite literally—

with the city's leading political figures. With the help of a gambler, Coughlin was elected alderman of Chicago's bawdy, expansive First Ward, infested with bordellos, clip joints, and opium dens. Coughlin and his fellow First Ward alderman (at the time, each ward had two), Michael "Hinky Dink" Kenna, regulated vice on the principle that "Chicago ain't no Sunday school."

The Irish have a long history of dominating both the city council and the Chicago Archdiocese. The city has elected eight Irish mayors, while nine of the twelve men to head the Catholic church since 1844 were Irish born or of Irish parentage. Between 1844—when Bishop William J. Quarter was appointed to head the church—and the death of Archbishop James Quigley in 1915, only one non-Irishman presided over the diocese, and that was Bishop James Van de Velde, a Belgian who served from 1849 to 1854.

The Irish Democratic machine, however, did not extend much past Cook County. The Irish generally conceded state and national offices, concentrating their efforts on the local level. Since the early decades of this century, the days of "Boss" Roger Sullivan and his protégé Mayor Hopkins, a succession of ward bosses and Democratic Central Committee leaders have dispensed patronage jobs to the voting constituents. After Sullivan died in 1920, George F. Brennan took over the county Democratic party. He was followed by Pat Nash, and, in recent years, George F. Dunne, former president of the Cook County Board. The Irish machine developed over the years into an inclusive Democratic power base, with non-Irish leaders like Jake Arvey, Anton Cermak, and William Dawson taking turns leading the party.

The Irish have also made their contribution to Chicago literature, with James T. Farrell and the gloomy reality of his working-class hero Studs Lonigan the most widely known. An urban realist in the Theodore Dreiser tradition, Farrell created first- and second-generation Irish characters who struggled to make ends meet in a rough and unfriendly environment populated by street corner hustlers, Apple Annies, and inebriates. Against this backdrop is the family unit and the church, together buttressing residents from the chaos of the streets. Farrell's Irish lived in their three-story flats equipped with all the modern conveniences: steam heat, electricity, a folddown ironing board, and plumbing. Social life in the Washington Park area where he grew up centered around St. Anselm Parish, at 61st and Michigan Avenue, and the Corpus Christi Church, constructed at 49th St. and Grand Boulevard in 1915.

Washington Park, the larger neighborhood Farrell's characters lived in, extends from 51st Street south to 63rd, and from Cottage Grove on the east to Wentworth Avenue on the west. The South Side community was originally settled by stockyard workers during the Civil War. Washington Park underwent a period of expansion and accelerated growth after 1869—the year it was established. The crown jewel of the South Side, beautiful Washington Park was populated by succeeding waves of Germans, Irish, Poles,

Jews, and blacks. Farrell's people—the Irish who made the big move up from Hardscrabble/Bridgeport to Washington Park—began arriving in the 1880s. Still more of them came after 1906, when the famous Washington Park Race Track was razed to make way for more apartment buildings.

The blue-collar Irish who lived beside their beloved park were a secular, insulated people suspicious of the forces of social change swirling all around them. The racial dynamics of the city had everything to do with the great exodus out of the neighborhood beginning around the time of World War I. There were blacks counted in the 1880 Washington Park census, but they lived far west of the park for the most part. The boundary line set by the European ethnics held until 1915, when the first few blacks ventured into apartment buildings east of State Street, and still several blocks west of Washington Park. In the next few years the pace of racial change accelerated, so that by 1920, 15 percent of the neighborhood residents were black. Ten years after that only 10 percent were *white*.

Racial tensions on the South Side simmered for many years. In 1919 the collective hatred of both races spilled over into an ugly race riot that began at the 31st Street Beach when a young black lad violated the invisible dividing line between the races. He was stoned to death as he played in the cooling Lake Michigan waters with his friends. In the days that followed, much of the so-called "black belt" north of Washington Park and east of State became a veritable no-man's land.

In the years that followed, black immigrants from the South displaced large segments of the indigenous Irish, who fled farther east into Hyde Park, hoping that the University of Chicago campus would insulate them from the black population. The more upscale members of the community drifted into the fashionable South Shore neighborhood along the Lake Michigan shoreline between 67th and 79th Streets. Here the Irish encountered Swedes, English Protestants, and the wealthy, many of whom belonged to the South Shore Country Club, fifty-five acres of sprawling lakefront property at 71st Street.

South Shore's population doubled in the 1920s as the community absorbed the white flight from Washington Park and the communities to the north. New Irish parishes were established; one, St. Philip Neri, hosted an International Eucharistic congress in 1926. The splendor and opulence of this church on 72nd Street attests to the affluence of South Shore's Irish in the 1920s.

The pattern of racial integration finally caught up with South Shore in the 1960s, as it had in Washington Park forty years earlier. When the blacks broke down the color barriers, the Catholic Irish, the Protestants, and the Jews moved on.

The South Side today is a very different place today from when Finley Peter Dunne and James T. Farrell wrote of the customs and mores of their people. But the history and culture remain in the collective memories of the children and grandchildren who hear the stories handed down by their elders. The Irish traditions are interwoven into the fabric of the South Side, where the poorest of these immigrants raised their offspring in less than idyllic conditions in Bridgeport, Back of the Yards, Canaryville, and Brighton Park. Bound together by their faith and the cause of Irish nationalism, the immigrants soon came to grips with their environment and were able to rise above the wheel of poverty and the "No Irish Wanted" stigma in a short period of time.

Today Chicago is not nearly as Irish as it was once was. According to the 1990 census, the Irish account for only 8.89 percent of the metropolitan area's population, ranking third behind the Germans (16.1%) and the blacks (19.5%). Nationwide the Chicago Irish are low on the list of cities with 250,000 or more. (Boston is the center of Gaelic culture, with a fourth of its people claiming Irish descent.) Like so many other ethnic European groups, the Irish have abandoned inner-city neighborhoods. The South Side Irish tended to move farther south, to the Mount Greenwood community, where nearly half of the residents claim Irish descent, and nearby Ashburn and Beverly, communities that seem more suburban than city.

Politically, the times have changed, too. Irish politicians no longer dominate the city's political machinery, though a second-generation Daley now occupies the fifth floor of City Hall. The chief of police, the fire department chief, and the head of the Chicago Archdiocese, however, are all non-Irish. But on March 17 each year, *everyone* in Chicago, regardless of race, creed, or color, celebrates St. Patrick's Day. Even the Chicago River becomes green for the day.

St. Paddy's Day has been something special in Chicago ever since the early 1840s, when the Montgomery Guards, an Irish-American militia, decided to celebrate this most important of all holidays. For years various Irish organizations sponsored local neighborhood pageants on March 17. The Chicago St. Patrick's Day parade began on the West Side along Madison Street between Pulaski and Laramie in 1952. Four years later, newspaper reporter Dan Lydon suggested to Mayor Daley that he bring the parade downtown. So, beginning in 1956, the floats, the musicians, the politicians, and the clowns (though in some years, it's been hard to tell them apart) began marching through the Loop.

Dan Lydon, whose parents emigrated from County Galway years earlier, took charge of the St. Patrick's Day Parade in 1956 and supervised and choreographed the festive event every year thereafter until 1992, when at last he decided it was time to step down. For nearly three decades Lydon had fought a losing battle to have St. Patrick's Day declared a legal holiday and the celebration extended through the entire week of March 17th. He failed to interest local legislators in the proposition, but succeeded in turning a little-known event in 1952 into an internationally recognized *occasion,* symbolizing Chicago's Gaelic spirit.

Not to be outshined, the South Side Irish sponsored their own parade beginning in 1979 when forty children and their parents trekked up and down Washtenaw Avenue and Talman Street. Within a few years it became a full-blown extravaganza, featuring hundreds of different neighborhood organizations marching down Western Avenue from 103rd to 113th Streets.

Though the South Side has always attracted more Irish than the North Side, a spirited, good-natured rivalry has long existed between the fun-loving South Side Irish and their more staid North Side counterparts. Irish football, folk dancing, and choral singing dominate programs at Gaelic Park, just beyond the city limits on the southwest side. North Side Irish don't disdain frivolity, as a visit to the Abbey Pub on North Elston Avenue will testify. But the nearby Irish American Heritage Center is more likely to stage a Sean O'Casey play than mount a soccer team.

Attractions

Cultural Institutions

Irish-American Heritage Center, *4626 N. Knox, Chicago, (773) 282-7035. Closed Saturdays. Membership is open to anyone who is interested in Irish American culture.*

Located near the juncture of the Edens and Kennedy expressways on the city's Northwest Side, the Irish American Heritage Center occupies the former Mayfair College, an 86,000-square-foot Gothic-style structure that is slowly being transformed into a museum and showplace of Irish folk culture. The center is staffed by community volunteers whose "labor of love" is reflected in the work of the craftspeople who have donated many long hours. As you enter through the main doors on Knox Avenue, observe the lovely murals overhead in the foyer. They were painted by Ed Cox, and are based on the ninth-century Book of Kells. The slate floor installed in the spacious first-floor pub is done in a traditional architectural style common in Ireland.

Ditto for the flagstone fireplace replete with hobs and cranes. It was installed by volunteer worker Kevin Moran. The museum, which officially opened on October 6, 1991, with a visit from the president of Eire, Mary Robinson, houses an extraordinary collection of Belleek china. The museum spotlights the contributions of the Irish to American and Chicago history. It is not widely known, for example, that during one of the key battles of the Revolution, General George Washington used the secret password "St. Patrick."

During the year, the center sponsors myriad activities including concerts, fashion shows, beginning and advanced Gaelic classes, and step-dancing instruction. In October, and again in April, the Irish Heritage Players perform contemporary drama in the refurbished auditorium. The front row is reserved for the patrons and city dignitaries who have contributed substantial amounts of money or their time to make this project successful. The inscribed arm rests are a virtual "who's who" of Chicago. Mayor Richard M. Daley, for example, occupies his own reserved seat in the first row center.

Irish American Heritage Center Events

1. The Irish Heritage Players Theater Series. *For scheduled times and showings, call the center at (312) 282-7035. Free parking on the grounds. Handicap access. Admission fee charged.*

In April, and again in October and November, the 680-seat theater at the Heritage Center is usually filled to capacity when the community players stage the finest in Irish drama. In 1991, for example, the troupe performed Sean O'Casey's *Plough and the Stars,* directed by Pat Nugent.

2. Commemorative Easter Mass, *sponsored by the St. Patrick's Father's Group. Refreshments served afterward.*

As a result of the historic Easter Uprising on April 24, 1916, in which sixteen Irish nationalists lost their lives, Sinn Fein became the most powerful political movement in Ireland. Sinn Fein, sworn to securing a free Irish state, waged constant warfare against the British government until January 15, 1922. The anniversary of the pivotal 1916 uprising is marked in religious ceremony and a short program at the Heritage Center on Easter Sunday.

Regularly Scheduled Weekday Events

Mondays:	Music Workshops, call (312) 425-3564.
Wednesdays:	Bingo in the Social Center. Crafts and Needlework. Irish Step and Folk Dancing Classes. Gaelic Classes (Beginning).
Thursdays:	Irish Heritage Singers.

Fridays:	Francis O'Neill Céilí Practice. Production in November. (Francis O'Neill served as chief of the Chicago Police Department from 1901–1905. In addition to being one of the most honest, forthright lawmen in an age known for its rascality, O'Neill "collected" hundreds of long-forgotten Irish folk tunes and catalogued them on paper and published them. Many of these ancient folk tunes were overheard by O'Neill as he wandered the back alleys and boulevards of Chicago's Irish neighborhoods.)
Saturdays:	Scoil Baal-Tine, music lessons. Gaelic Classes (intermediate). Advanced Gaelic Classes.

3. Taste of Ireland Festival, *held on the grounds of the IAHC in mid-July every year since 1985. For times and prices call the center at (312) 282-7035.*

The event includes an abundance of Irish entertainment, children's games, Irish folk dancing and music, cultural exhibits, recent Irish films, and plenty of food for the entire family.

Gaelic Park, *6119 W. 147th St., Oak Forest, (708) 687-9323. Two miles west of Cicero Ave. on 147th St. Free parking on site. Membership available.*

Serving the needs of Chicago's large South Side Irish contingent, Gaelic Park was founded in 1984 as a cultural, athletic, and recreational facility. Local tradespeople donated their time, and building suppliers sold the materials at cost to ensure that the construction of the banquet hall, locker rooms, and playing fields could be built without delay. Today, the 18-acre Gaelic Park is the Chicagoland home of the Irish national pastime—hurling—and the most popular of all sports, Gaelic football. Four or five leagues from the junior and senior divisions compete here during the season. The park also provides satellite transmission of Irish football every Sunday morning during the season. The spacious meeting hall has hosted some of the biggest names in Irish entertainment over the years, including Foster and Allen, the Dubliners, Bagatelle, Mary Black, Brendan Grace, and many more. Vibrant and growing, the grand opening ceremonies marking the opening of the expanded facilities took place on March 10, 1991. In attendance were Rev. Robert L. Kealy, Chancellor for the Archdiocese of Chicago, and Gary Ansboro, Consul General of Ireland. "Gaelic Park is here to be a gathering place for the Irish and to allow Irish Americans to experience their heritage," explained President Tom Boyle. "The lounge, the games, our dances and concerts are all open to the public. We extend a warm Irish welcome to all."

Gaelic Park Events

1. Irish Mass and authentic Irish breakfast, *held the second Sunday of every month, between October and May. Admission fee charged. Breakfast includes sausage, eggs, bacon, black pudding, and soda bread.*

2. Chicago Gaelic Football League, *games played at Tinley Park (6119 W. 147th St.) on Sunday afternoons between April and October. Refreshments served. Admission fee charged.*

The sport has been played in America by Irish descendants since the 1920s. It is a fast-moving game utilizing a 15-ounce ball that can be advanced only if the player kicks it. Points are scored when the ball is kicked over the cross-bar and between the uprights. A goal, worth three points, is awarded when the ball goes under the crossbar and into the netting between the uprights. Other cities, notably New York, Los Angeles, San Francisco, Boston, Pittsburgh, Cleveland, and Detroit also host Gaelic football, but the sport enjoys a popularity here that is unique. The Irish football and hurling teams are always looking for new players. For further information, please contact the teams directly at the following numbers:

Men's Division, Gaelic Football

1. St. Brendans, (708) 614-8161.
2. Celtics, (708) 599-4733.
3. Wolftones, (708) 425-2024.
4. John McBrides, (312) 775-2826.
5. Rovers, (312) 239-4859.
6. Padraig Pearse, (708) 932-4518.
7. Parnell's, (708) 423-8794.

Women's Division, Gaelic Football

1. John McBrides, (312) 775-2826.
2. St. Brigid's, (708) 499-5311.

Hurling

1. Limericks, (708) 678-4465.
2. Harry Bolands, (708) 425-6622.

3. Erin's Own, (708) 422-0510.
4. Cu Chulainn's, (708) 633-0615.

Step dancing, céilí dancing, and bagpipe lessons are held every night in the main building at Gaelic Park. Céilí dancing consists of a number of dance routines from Ireland's principal counties, including the popular "Siege of Ennis," with eight dancers facing each other, moving across the floor in weaving, cross-over patterns. Céilí dancing classes are available to adults and children, and there is an annual competition. Step dancing, a regular feature at the various St. Patrick's Day ceremonies across the city, includes both jigs and reels in which the participants wear soft shoes. The hornpipe and treble jig, by contrast, are hard shoe dances whose sounds resonate on the hard wooden floors. During the year, folk dancing classes are generally held on Tuesdays.

Irish Fest, *Gaelic Park. Memorial Day weekend.*
Admission fee charged. Call the Gaelic Park Events
Club, (708) 687-9323.

Four-day festival. Four outdoor stages with continuous entertainment featuring national and international Irish and American musicians have attracted crowds in excess of 50,000, to make this one of the most successful Irish festivals in the United States. The merriment began in 1986, and each year virtually every inch of the 20-acre Gaelic Park has been filled to capacity. Food vendors sell an endless variety of ethnic foods and beer, with additional items from the Irish import stores in the city. Headlining the Irish Fest are such internationally known stars as the Barley Bree trio; the Clan, a Dublin rock band; and Tommie Makem and Liam Clancy. Count on seeing some down-home local talent, too. Joel Daly and the Sundowners, the Dancing Noodles, and 1960s rock singer Ronnie Rice have made appearances at the Irish Fest.

Rose of Tralee elimination contest and dance,
Gaelic Park. April. Call George Deady,
(708) 479-4978.

The Chicago Rose of Tralee competition determines who among the city's fairest colleens will represent the community in international competition in Ireland in August. The goal of the Rose of Tralee pageant is to locate the singularly unique Irish lass who is the "fairest maiden" of them all. It's quite a tall order, but the representative countries of the West send contestants every year. Young women between the ages of 18 and 25 who have never been married are eligible to join and compete.

Feis *(pronounced FESH)* **Competition,** *Gaelic Park.*
Saturday before Father's Day in June.

The Chicago Feis showcases some of the finest homegrown dance troops in Chicago at an annual competition held at Gaelic Park. The feis consists of traditional hard and soft shoe dances, including hornpipes, jigs, and reels.

Annual Events and Celebrations

St. Patrick's Day Parade (Downtown). *March 17.*
For additional information, call (312) 263-6612.

It is a grand, gala day for Chicago's Irish, who pay tribute to the patron saint of Ireland in the city's most lavish parade. But who was this celebrated figure from history, who is toasted in every pub from Bridgeport to Schaumburg on March 17? Historians believe that Patrick (389?–461? A.D.) was the son of a Roman-British government figure named Calpurnius. Tradition has it that he was born in the village of Bannavem (in what is now northern England) or possibly Kilpatrick, in Scotland. Educated in what is now France, Patrick was consecrated as bishop in 432 and assigned to Ireland by Pope Celestine to bring Christianity to the pagans. His mission was a difficult one, fraught with many perils, not the least of which was the local opposition of the Druids—pagan Celtic priests. Before he died in the Irish town of Downpatrick on March 17, the Apostle of Ireland reported the use of the shamrock as an illustration of the Trinity. Eventually the shamrock came to be regarded as the national symbol of Ireland.

Chicago's Irish have gone to great lengths to ensure that St. Patrick's achievements are not forgotten. The tradition of dyeing the Chicago River green began in the early 1960s when Stephen Bailey, parade chairman from 1958–66, seized on a novel idea. Bailey located 100 pounds of green-colored Air Force dye, and dumped it into the sluggish river. To Bailey's considerable delight the Chicago River retained its distinctive green hue for nearly a month. The outcry of the environmentalists eventually forced Bailey and his minions to change to a biodegradable dye. A peculiar local custom was born, one that was imitated in the large metropolitan areas of the United States.

The annual rite of St. Patrick begins with the traditional early morning Mass at old St. Patrick's Church at the corner of Adams and Des Plaines. An Irish brunch is served in the parish hall. Reservations for the brunch are strongly suggested, and can be made by calling the church at (312) 782-6171. Admission fee charged. An annual event since 1956.

The parade, replete with marching bands, lavish floats, the famous Shannon Rovers, labor groups, the mayor, governor, and a host of lesser lights from the Cook County Democratic and Republican parties lead an entourage that includes the parade queen and her court. The parade queen is chosen from among the most eligible young women of Irish descent between the ages of 17 and 26. The contest is held each year in February, when a reviewing committee selects the winner from the photographs submitted.

Parade festivities kick off at noon at Dearborn Street and Wacker Drive, then proceed south down Dearborn past thousands of spectators before winding up at Van Buren Street. On St. Patrick's Day, everyone is Irish. *Recommended.*

South Side Irish St. Patrick's Day Parade, *on Western Ave. between 103rd and 114th streets, Chicago. The Sunday before the holiday. Call (773) 238-1969 for additional information.*

Deep in the heart of the 19th Ward in the neighborhood of Beverly, the South Side Irish decided to begin their own St. Patrick's Day celebration for the benefit of the children who would otherwise be unable to attend the downtown parade which is always held on the traditional holiday. The South Side parade is billed as the "largest Irish neighborhood parade outside of Dublin." Recognizing the political hay from such a large turnout, numerous politicians have forsaken the big downtown parade in order to meet and greet the Irish-American residents of Morgan Park, Beverly, Mount Greenwood, and Oak Lawn. Massachusetts Governor Michael Dukakis joined the procession along with Senator Albert Gore of Tennessee as a tune-up for the 1988 presidential sweepstakes. Another presidential candidate, commentator Patrick Buchanan, marched in 1996.

The politicians are complemented by at least 70 floats, 199 marching units, and 44 bands. The Young Irish Club of Chicago, with more than 1,200 members in the Chicagoland area, usually has one of the most interesting floats in a parade that sometimes lasts three hours.

St. Patrick's Day Festival, *Irish-American Heritage Center, 4626 N. Knox, Chicago, (773) 282-7035. Admission fee charged.*

Continuous entertainment highlights the annual festival, which has been a Northwest Side tradition since 1986. Irish step-dancing, folk music, films, plus a special appearance by the Shannon Rovers (the favorite band of late mayor Richard J. Daley) are featured in the weekend activities. Only a limited number of tickets are sold in advance, so it is wise to call well before the big day.

Gaelic Park St. Patrick's Day Festival, *6119 W. 147th*
St., Oak Forest, (708) 687-9323. Admission fee charged.

Serving the South Suburban Irish community since 1979, the Gaelic Park
directors sponsor a morning Mass at the meeting hall, followed by a traditional Irish breakfast of bacon, black pudding, soda bread, and eggs. Following the South Side parade, the party returns to Gaelic Park with a dinner
dance held that Sunday night. Continuous entertainment provided by the
Gaelic Park Pipe Band, the Mullane Irish Dancers, and the Bannermen.

St. Patrick's Day Concert, *Friendship Concert Hall,*
Kolpin and Algonquin rds., Des Plaines, (708) 640-1000.
Admission fee charged.

Since 1980 the Mount Prospect Park District has sponsored an Irish folk
music concert featuring bagpipe players, folk dancers, and choral groups
direct from Ireland. The concert precedes a special Irish dinner that is open
to the public at the nearby Friendship Park Conservatory.

St. Patrick's Day Eve Concert, *Schaumburg Prairie*
Center for the Arts, 201 Schaumburg Ct., Schaumburg,
(847) 894-3600. Admission fee charged.

The northwest suburb of Schaumburg was originally settled by Germans,
but during the St. Patrick's Day celebration, everyone wears the green. An
annual event celebrating the holiday.

St. Patrick's Day Dinner, *Chicago Hilton and Towers,*
Grand Ballroom, 720 S. Michigan Ave., Chicago.
Sponsored by the Irish Fellowship Club,
626 S. Clark, Suite 400, Chicago, (312) 263-1200.

Membership in the club is open to any person of Irish birth or descent, or those
who have demonstrated a knowledge and sympathy for the ideals and aspirations of the club.

The Irish Fellowship Club, founded in 1902 to promote Irish culture and
the ideals of the great city, sponsors an annual dinner featuring the very best
entertainment and ballads in a convivial atmosphere. Dinner is preceded by a
cocktail hour. The price of the dinner is approximately $90.

Annual Fellowship Christmas Luncheon, *Chicago*
Hilton and Towers, Grand Ballroom, 720 S. Michigan
Ave., Chicago. On or about December 7. Call (312)
427-2926. Admission fee charged.

Semi-formal luncheon sponsored by the Irish Fellowship Club. Entertainment is provided by singer and balladeer Cathy O'Connell.

Chicago Irish Fest, *Gaelic Park, (708) 687-9323.*
Memorial Day weekend. Tickets available at the gate,
or in advance at most Irish import stores.

It's St. Patrick's Day one more time—only without the politicians and the blarney. Several stages of continuous entertainment light up the night. Count on seeing any number of Irish folk dancing groups, Barley Bree, the Shannon Rovers, Tommy Makem, and Carmel Quinn, who has appeared at Carnegie Hall for over thirty consecutive years. Irish culture area. Freckles contest. Free time-restricted phone calls to Ireland courtesy of AT&T.

Trinity Academy of Irish Stepdancing Fund Raiser,
Hyatt Regency O'Hare, 9300 W. Bryn Mawr,
Rosemont, (847) 246-2957. February or March.
Admission fee charged. For information, call Kathy
McDonnell, Trinity Co-President, (708) 771-2765.

Annual fund-raising event held to defray the costs of the dancers who tour the United States and various European festivals during the summer. The event includes a luncheon and dance performances by the troop.

Places to See

A Guide to City and Suburban Irish Pubs

Chicago pubs continue an old tradition that started when the Irish workers began digging the Illinois-Michigan Canal. Despite attempts by blue-blood reformers to close down the saloons in the 1850s, the custom has endured. Traditionally the pub was a place where a man could go to warm his bones in the winter and cool his palate in summer. Ward-level politics were practiced there, and sometimes the back room doubled as a gambling den, where faro, dice, and craps were played away from the watchful eye of the honest copper on the beat.

The Irish pubs are a slice of culture and blarney that is as much a part of Chicago as the green-colored river on St. Patty's Day. You won't find any slot machines or roulette wheels, but it's a fair bet that you'll find plenty of "crack"—the innocent variety, that is, in the Irish sense of a good time.

Kitty O'Shea's, *720 S. Michigan Ave., in the Chicago*
Hilton and Towers Hotel, Chicago, (312) 922-4400.

Authentic Irish pub named after the legendary pub in Dublin. Live music every night. Very popular with tourists and conventioneers.

Emerald Isle Pub, *6686 N. Northwest Hwy., Chicago,*
(773) 775-2848.

Northwest Side pub featuring folk and rock music, and an annual St. Patrick's Day celebration.

Schaller's Pump, *3714 S. Halsted St., Chicago,*
(773) 847-9378.

Chicago's best-known South Side bar and restaurant retains its Irish flavor by virtue of its location at 37th and Halsted in Bridgeport. Across the street the sachems of the tenth Ward Democratic party formulate strategy and dole out the patronage. But Schaller's is where they repair to afterward. The pump has been around for 100 years and is owned and operated by Jackie Schaller. The food is okay too, but the real attraction is the atmosphere. It's a real neighborhood kind of bar. Noisy, crowded, all Chicago.

O'Rourke's, *1625 N. Halsted St., Chicago,*
(773) 335-1806.

Chicago's literary left bank disappeared around 1930. The city of big shoulders has never been very kind to writers, choosing instead to bestow the laurel wreaths on captains of industry, hog butchers, and boodling aldermen. In the old days—that period of awakening before Al Capone and his minions re-defined culture in Chicago—the literary lions used to gather at the Whitechapel Club in the rear of the old *Daily News* building, and at Harriet Monroe's Little Room. At various times, Floyd Dell, John T. McCutcheon, Theodore Dreiser, Sherwood Anderson and others dropped by. But the writing renaissance they helped create ended abruptly when the siren sound of the New York publishing world beckoned them to the coast. The great flowering died, and in some ways it has never returned. O'Rourke's, the Old Town Ale House, Riccardo's, and to a lesser extent Billy Goat's Tavern, became the great writer hangouts of the post-renaissance period. There have been three O'Rourke's, beginning in 1964 at the original location on Wells St. In 1966, owner Jay Kovar reopened a few blocks away on North Avenue, and remained in business until October 21, 1989, when he moved to the present location. Photographs of William Butler Yeats, Oscar Wilde, James Joyce, and Brendan Behan adorn the walls, and if you're lucky you might run into Mike Royko and the rest of the *Tribune* and *Sun-Times* entourage. But the times have changed. Drinking to excess is no longer kosher, so it's unlikely you'll witness drunken barroom brawls between the journalists. For all the lurid details about the Friday night fights, ask the owner. *Recommended.*

Butch McGuire's Tavern, *20 W. Division St.,*
Chicago, (312) 337-9080.

The popular Rush Street bistro opened in 1961, and has long been known as one of the trendiest singles clubs in Chicago. The Hollywood film *About Last Night* (based on David Mamet's play *Sexual Perversity in Chicago*) was set at Butch McGuire's. Irish prints and photographs decorate the walls.

Harrigan's Pub, *2816 N. Halsted St., Chicago,*
(773) 248-5933.

A pub that is popular with both young professionals and newly arrived Irish immigrants, who enjoy the friendly neighborhood atmosphere. The bartender Tony Griffin was born in Dublin but came to the United States in 1988.

Harp and Shamrock Club, *1641 W. Fullerton Ave.,*
Chicago, (773) 248-0123.

The original Harp and Shamrock Club began in Canaryville, but now caters to a North Side clientele—mostly neighborhood people, Chicago police, and bagpipe players.

Coogan's Riverside Saloon, *180 N. Wacker Dr.,*
Chicago, (312) 444-1134.

Downtown resort that serves a traditional Irish meal of corned beef and cabbage on St. Patrick's Day.

Brehon Pub, *731 N. Wells St., Chicago,*
(312) 642-1071. Closed Sundays.

Neighborhood Irish pub just north of the Loop.

Cork and Kerry Pub, *10614 S. Western Ave.,*
Chicago, (773) 445-2675.

One of several pubs located in the Beverly neighborhood of Chicago.

Bucko's, *10910 S. Western Ave., Chicago,*
(773) 238-0784.

Another Irish pub on the "Western Avenue strip."

Keegan's Pub, *10618 S. Western Ave., Chicago,*
(773) 233-6829.

Fox's Pub, *9240 S. Cicero Ave., Oak Lawn,*
(708) 499-2233.

Entertainment.

Fitzgerald's, *6615 Roosevelt Rd., Berwyn,*
(708) 788-2118.

An Irish pub in Bohemian Berwyn.

Reilly's Daughter's Pub, *4010 W. 111th St., Oak*
Lawn, (708) 423-1188. Closed Sundays.

Popular rendezvous for South Side sports fans.

Shops

Abbey Productions, *3825 N. Elston Ave., Chicago,*
(773) 478-4408.

For a nominal price, Abbey Productions will convert Irish or British VCR tapes that are incompatible with U.S.-made players.

Gaelic Imports, *4736 N. Austin St., Chicago,*
(773) 545-6515. Closed Mondays. Personal checks
accepted but no credit cards.

Over ten years at this location (Austin and Lawrence). Irish gifts and deli items.

Donegal Imports, *5358 W. Devon Ave., Chicago,*
(773) 792-2377. Closed Sundays. All credit cards
accepted.

Located in the Edgebrook neighborhood on the far Northwest Side. Gift items, sweaters, fine crystal.

Shamrock Imports, *3150 N. Laramie, Chicago,*
(773) 286-6866. Closed Sunday and Monday. Cash
or check only.

Food, jewelry, fine china, baby items, hats, and sweaters directly from Ireland.

South Side Irish Imports, *3234 W. 111th St., Chicago, (773) 881-8585. Closed Sundays. Credit cards accepted.*

China, glassware, jewelry, and gift items. Located at 111th and Sawyer, one block west of Kedzie.

Joy of Ireland, *Level 3 of Chicago Place, 700 N. Michigan Ave., Chicago, (312) 664-7290 and (800) 235-8421. Open daily.*

Importer of a variety of Irish goods, including Waterford crystal, Belleek china, Celtic and Claddagh jewelry, handknit woolen sweaters, food, books, music, videos, and Irish newspapers. Offers a bridal registry and Irish wedding invitations. One of the few stores in the area to sell handmade linen and lace christening gowns.

Blarney Fine Irish Imports, *three locations: 4202J N. Harlem Ave., Harlem Irving Plaza, Chicago, (708) 453-1443; 999 N. Elmhurst Rd., Randhurst Shopping Center, Mt. Prospect, (847) 392-0044; and 1268 Springhill Mall, West Dundee, (847) 428-0303. Toll-free general number: (800) 788-7429. Open daily.*

According to the owner, Blarney's philosophy is to sell "everything Irish." This includes jewelry, Waterford crystal, Belleek china, clothing, books, music, videos, and food.

Outlying Areas

Fincara Irish Imports, *1700 Central St., Evanston, (847) 328-0665. Closed Sundays. Credit cards accepted.*

Clothing, gourmet foods, jewelry, tea, and jams from Ireland, Scotland, and the British Isles.

Touch of Ireland and Europe, *two locations: 4140 W. 95th St., Oak Lawn, (708) 422-3473; and 140 N. LaGrange Rd., LaGrange, (708) 579-3473. Closed Sundays. Credit cards accepted.*

Features Waterford crystal, Hummel figurines, handicraft items, records, tapes, sweaters, and shirts. The LaGrange location is the larger of the two stores.

Cleary's Irish Crystal, *815 E. Nerge Rd., Roselle,*
(630) 351-3722. Closed Sundays and Mondays. Credit
cards accepted.

Specializing in Tyrone crystal, which is comparable to Waterford but less expensive. No jewelry items sold here.

Irish Connoisseur, *1232 Waukegan Ave., Glenview,*
(847) 998-1988. Closed Sundays. All major credit
cards accepted.

Delicatessen and gift shop all in one. Irish sausage, bacon, black and white pudding, and soda bread direct from the "auld sod." The gift section features crystal items, jewelry, books, tapes, and sweaters.

Irish Treasure Trove, *17W424 W. 22nd St., Oakbrook*
Terrace, (630) 530-2522. Open daily. Credit cards
accepted.

Waterford crystal, elite china, records, jams, teas, and clothing items.

Irish Boutique, *434 Robert Parker Coffin Rd., Long*
Grove, (847) 634-3540. Open daily. Evening hours by
appointment. All credit cards accepted.

Books, gourmet foods, Waterford and Tipperary crystal, jewelry, china, and records. One of two affiliated stores in the historic village of Long Grove.

Paddy's on the Square, *428 McHenry Rd., Long*
Grove, (847) 634-0339. Open daily. Evening hours
by appointment. All credit cards accepted.

Sister store of the Irish Boutique. Two levels of merchandise, including heraldry items, woolens, hats, and records and tapes.

Shannon Imports, *5734 W. 95th St., Oak Lawn,*
(708) 424-7055. Closed Sunday. Visa, MasterCard
accepted.

Newspapers from Ireland delivered daily, gourmet foods, fine crystal, hats, caps, jewelry, and souvenirs.

All Things Irish, *P.O. Box 94, Glenview,*
(847) 998-4510.

Importers and distributors of Irish jewelry and quality Irish merchandise. Phone for a free catalog.

Irish Country Foods, *1555 Sherman Ave., Evanston,*
(847) 933-1212. Open daily.

Excellent source for Irish food. No other merchandise sold.

Restaurants

Irish Village, *6215 W. Diversey Ave., Chicago,*
(773) 237-7555.

Chicago's most famous Irish eatery, with entertainment six nights a week.
Free parking. Open Tuesday–Friday for lunch, Tuesday–Sunday for dinner.
Closed Monday. Credit cards accepted.

Abbey Pub and Restaurant, *3420 W. Grace St.,*
Chicago, (773) 478-4408.

Dining, sports telecasts, and a full card of entertainment acts including the
Dublin City Ramblers, the Dooley Brothers, the Drovers, and the Banshees.
Open nightly. Credit cards accepted.

Hidden Shamrock, *2723 N. Halsted St., Chicago,*
(773) 883-0304. Open for breakfast and lunch
Saturday and Sunday, and dinner daily.

Good food in a comfortable pub atmosphere.

Outlying Areas

Duke O'Brien's, *110 N. Main St., Crystal Lake,*
(815) 356-9980. Open for lunch and dinner daily.

Interesting combination of Irish and Southwestern food. Reservations
suggested.

Tommy Nevin's Pub, *1450 Sherman Ave., Evanston,*
(847) 869-0450.

Evanston used to be a dry town, but you would never know it on St. Pat's
Day. A new tradition was born on March 17, 1991, when the pub hosted its
first St. Patrick's Day celebration, with pan-fried liver and plenty of Guin-
ness to go around.

Robert's Roadhouse, *9090 Roberts Rd., Hickory Hills, (708) 598-8181.*

The South Suburbs of Chicago Ridge, Hickory Hills, and Oak Lawn are the newest ports-of-entry for young Irish immigrants seeking work in the lucrative construction industries. The building boom in the South Suburbs in the 1980s was a powerful lure, and Robert's is one of several pubs where the new arrivals can exchange information and swap stories about the homeland.

Houlihan's, *five locations: Chicago, 1207 N. Dearborn St., (312) 642-9647; Bloomingdale, Stratford Mall, (630) 351-2700; Oak Brook, 56 Oak Brook Center Mall, (630) 573-0220; Schaumburg, 1901 E. Golf Rd., (847) 605-0002; Skokie, Old Orchard Shopping Center, (847) 674-5490. Open at noon daily. Sunday brunch; happy hour. Credit cards accepted.*

Eclectic Irish-American pub and restaurant that caters to the Yuppie crowd.

Media

Irish Radio Programming

Mary Riordan and Harry Costelloe *play records, interview guests and comment on local Irish affairs on WCEV, 1450 AM, live from Gaelic Park every Sunday night from 7:05 P.M. to 9:00 P.M.*

Bud Sullivan, *Saturdays, 8 A.M. to 9 A.M., WPNA, 1490 AM.*

The Hagerty Family, *Saturdays, 9 A.M. to 11 A.M., WPNA, 1490 AM.*

Mike O'Connor, *Saturdays, 11 A.M. to 1 P.M., WPNA, 1490 AM.*

Martin Fahey, *Saturdays, 11 A.M. to noon, WJOB, 1230 AM.*

Mike Shevlin, *Saturdays, 6:30 P.M. to 8 P.M., WPNA,*
1490 AM.

Maureen Looney, *winner of the 1994 "Irish Person*
of the Year" by the Emerald Society of Illinois, a
police fraternal society, is a well-known Irish-
American merchant who hosts her own show,
Wednesdays, 9 P.M. to 10 P.M., WSBC, 1240 AM.

Irish TV

Cable Channel 25 *in Chicago offers viewers two Irish*
ethnic broadcasts each week. On Monday evenings,
the latest news, sports, and entertainment with a local
angle airs from 7 P.M. to 9 P.M. The Irish-American
Journal is a regular feature on Thursday evenings
from 6 P.M. to 6:30 P.M. For those without a cable
hookup, call channel 25 at (312) 477-4900 or write to
them at 1931 W. Diversey Ave., Chicago, IL.

Bridgeport:
Hardscrabble by Any Other Name

Bridgeport occupies a special place in Chicago history and is one of
Chicago's oldest, if not most colorful, neighborhoods. The neighborhood's
character was shaped by the Irish, who began arriving in 1836 to dig the Illinois-Michigan Canal. They lived in meager shanties along the banks of the
Chicago River, subsisting on a cabbage-rich diet—hence, the community's
derisive nickname, "Cabbagetown." With the coming of the canal, boatmen
dubbed the area "Bridgeport," because the Ashland Avenue bridge sat so
low over the river that barges had to be unloaded in order to pass safely
under it.

The organization of the Union Stock Yards in 1865 brought increased
employment opportunity for the area along with an awful nuisance. The
South Fork of the South Branch of the Chicago River became known as
"Bubbly Creek," an open sewer where the stock yard workers dumped rotting animal carcasses and offal at the day's end. Bubbly Creek is but an
unhappy memory today, though it is still possible to catch a glimpse of the
site at 35th St. and the Chicago River—Bridgeport's western boundary. The
stockyards closed permanently in 1971; all that remains is a stone entranceway designed by Burnham and Root at Exchange Avenue and Peoria, just

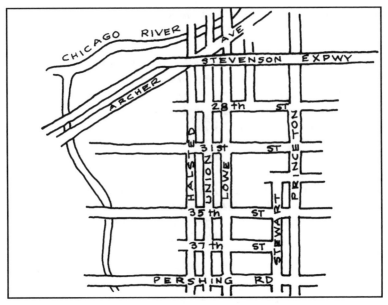

Bridgeport

west of Halsted Street. A limestone head, carved in the likeness of "Sherman," a prize bull belonging to Burnham's father-in-law, John B. Sherman, is carved over the central arch.

Bridgeport is still a densely populated residential and manufacturing neighborhood. Red brick worker cottages and two-flats, many of them with ground floors below the street level, can be found to the north and west of neighborhood landmark Comiskey Park. It is a secular, insulated community, where the neighbors look out for each other and tend to view outsiders with suspicion. On warm summer nights people will sit on the stoops of their buildings engaging in the kind of social interaction that has gone on in this neighborhood since the time of Finley Peter Dunne. The Maxwell Street Depot at 31st and Canal serves the best pork chop sandwiches and Polish sausages this side of Kansas City, and after a ball game it is the place to go for a late night repast. The Maxwell Street Depot never closes.

Politics and racial polarization have characterized much of the recent history of this community. For decades, blacks feared lingering in this neighborhood after dark. In a notorious incident that reflected the often brutal realities of modern urban life, two Chicago police officers picked up two black teenagers who were making their way home from Comiskey Park on August 14, 1989, and then drove them into the heart of Canaryville, where they were dropped curbside. The boys were assaulted by seven whites. Similarly, there are few white Bridgeporters who would venture into the Douglas neighborhood east of the Dan Ryan Expressway at nightfall.

Bridgeport served as the unofficial home of the Chicago Democratic Party long before "Hizzoner" Richard J. Daley became mayor. Early in life, Daley was a member of the Irish branch of the Hamburg Social Athletic Club (there was a Croatian and Lithuanian faction also), a gang of roughhouse "boyos" who were not afraid to knock a few heads on behalf of the local committeeman. You came up through the ranks and paid your dues like everyone else if you wanted to get ahead. That is how politics were conducted in the old days, and no one understood this better than Daley, the father of the "bootstrap theory" of American politics.

Richard J. lived in a modest bungalow on the 3500 block of South Lowe Avenue his entire adult life. On Sunday mornings, Daley, his wife "Sis" and their children would stroll by the homes of their friends and neighbors as they made their way to the Nativity of Our Lord Church at 37th and Union for Mass. The South Side Irish are deeply rooted in their local parishes. If, for example, you strike up a conversation with a stranger on the street, he will most often ask you the name of the parish you grew up in. That will tell him all he needs to know about your circumstances.

Though current Mayor Richard M. Daley moved into Central Station, a new and growing neighborhood south of Roosevelt Road, his mother "Sis" still lives in the family home on South Lowe, located conveniently down the block from the Deering District Police Station. The house is easily recognizable by the large American flag flapping in the breeze and by the unmarked squad car conspicuously parked in front. Within walking distance of the Daley home are the residences of former mayors Michael Bilandic (a Croatian), Martin Kennelly, and a host of lesser lights who comprised the fabled 11th Ward Democratic Machine headquartered across the street from Schaller's Pump at 37th and Halsted. "Da Mayor, Da Church, and Da White Sox"—so it goes in Bridgeport.

German Chicago

History and Settlement

"Discontent here is a German plant from Berlin and Leipzig!" snorted crusty old Michael Schaak, a police inspector assigned to the heavily German "Nord Seid" in mid-1880s Chicago. Himself a native of the Grand Duchy of Luxembourg, Schaak expressed the prejudicial attitudes of many Chicagoans who blamed the German immigrants for the 1886 Haymarket Riot.

Many Germans had come to America supporting socialism. Those who were politically active were called "anarchists" in the United States, and many became labor leaders. On May 3, 1886, police attacked a group of workers striking the McCormick Reaper Company. One worker was killed, and others called a protest for the next day in Haymarket Square. Police arrived in force and watched German anarchists speak passionately to the assembled protesters. A bomb exploded in the midst of the crowd. The workers blamed the police, and a riot erupted. The public turned against the anarchists. The belief that the Germans were here to foment revolution and unrest persisted through the labor troubles of the mid- to late-19th century, and through two world wars.

These factors contributed to many Chicagoans' decisions to deny their "German background, refusing to indicate that they were born in Germany, or born of German parents who had emigrated from Germany," contends historian Rudolf A. Hofmeister, author of the book *The Germans of*

Chicago. Only in recent years have historians looked past the "beer, bundist, and *Gemütlichkeit*" stereotypes to rediscover the cultural contributions Germans have made to Chicago.

Chicago's original German settler—Heinrich Rothenfeld—arrived in 1825, a dozen years before the city's charter was granted. Rothenfeld settled in Dunkley's Grove, now the village of Addison in the west suburbs. He was joined by Johann Wellmacher in 1830, and Matthias Meyer, who came here from Frankfurt am Main in 1831. Meyer opened one of the first bakery shops in the city.

When Chicago was incorporated in 1837, there were eighteen registered voters of German extraction. In the city election held that year, Clemens S. Stose, a German blacksmith, was elected alderman. On March 10, 1842, a German school was opened in the Dutch settlement between Chicago and North Avenues known as New Buffalo. It was the first Germanic settlement in the city, but it did not remain homogeneous for long. In the 1850s large numbers of Swedes and Irish began populating the area. The Germans pushed farther north to what is now known as Old Town, a neighborhood bounded by Division, LaSalle, Armitage, and Halsted streets. The area thrived, especially after the Great Chicago Fire of 1871, when improvements in public transportation provided the immigrants with easy, affordable access to the industrial corridor along the Chicago River and the famous breweries so closely associated with the German experience in Chicago.

William Haas and Konrad Sulzer—instrumental in Chicago's early development—opened the first brewery in 1836, churning out 600 barrels of foamy a year. Sulzer later went into partnership with future mayor William B. Ogden. Bavarian-born Mattias Best was the second brewmaster of note, founding his business on the South Side at 14th Street and Indiana. Eight years later, Adolph P. Mueller established a small brewery on the corner of State and Randolph—Chicago's famous *Bierstube*—where beer was manufactured and sold in the shadow of the original Court House across the street. By 1856, nine German breweries were churning out 16,270 barrels a year.

The Bavarians, Prussians, and the neighboring Irish who lived in close proximity on the North Side greatly alarmed the temperance advocates who feared that Chicago was about to become a beer-soaked den of iniquity. The Nativists, a loose coalition of teetotalers, Anglo-Saxons, anti-Irish, and anti-German Catholics, found a sympathetic ally in the person of Dr. Levi Boone, who was elected mayor in 1855. In his inaugural address, Boone outlined his promise to proscribe the liquor trade entirely, but the city council favored a compromise measure. So the saloon licensing fee rose to $300, and within days of the objectionable ordinance's passage, the city's small, untrained city police began to enforce the unpopular Sunday closing law. This affront to long-standing German traditions galvanized public opinion against the city administration. Some of the brewers, led by Valentin Blatz, attempted to thwart Boone and his minions by draping beer garden windows and constructing secret side-door entrances. Those less inclined to cloak-and-dagger tactics decided to take a stand against the unpopular constabulary.

On April 20, 1855, an angry mob of Germans and Irish tradesmen stormed the city's Court House at Dearborn and Randolph, crossing over the Chicago River on the Clark Street Bridge. They were met at gunpoint by the police and local militia, and the Lager Beer Riot was on. It was a short, bloody skirmish, over within minutes, then sixty rioters were herded into the lockup.

Though the mayor and his allies claimed a victory, their movement was thoroughly discredited and the prohibition law was rejected by a popular referendum two months later. The Germans earned the right to enjoy their Sunday afternoons in neighborhood beer gardens, but Nativist opposition to them did not end with the Lager Beer Riot. During some labor troubles in 1877, a detachment of police battered down the doors of the West Side Turner Hall at Roosevelt and Halsted in search of German agitators and "apostles of anarchy." A peaceable assembly of German workers were clubbed and fired upon in a flagrant abuse of police power that was typical of those paranoiac times, when foreign-speaking people often were perceived to be violent revolutionaries.

The Germans who gathered at the Turner Hall of Chicago for the most part were not anarchists or bomb throwers, but disciples of Friedrich L. Jahn (1778–1852), father of the *Turnverein* movement. A physical education teacher, Jahn believed that the moral fiber of his nation was intrinsically tied to healthy minds and robust bodies. The gymnastics and paramilitaristic regimens of his Turnvereins won many converts among the German youth, both at home and abroad. The first Chicago Turnverein was founded in 1852, and its impact was profound. When President Abraham Lincoln issued his call to arms in 1861, 105 members of the Chicago Turnvereine organized the Turner Cadets and volunteered for duty in the Union Army.

The 82nd and 24th Illinois Regiments, comprised of German-born Americans and commanded by Colonel Friedrich Hecker, served with distinction during the war. In 1866, a year after the Civil War ended, a proposal to integrate physical education classes into the public school curriculum was unanimously adopted by the city board. But it would take another twenty years before the schools finally implemented the plan. In that year—1886— the board hired eight "Turners" to teach gymnastics to Chicago's students. The German community paid tribute to the visionary Friedrich L. Jahn in 1907, when a grammar school bearing his name opened in the Lincoln Park and Belmont community on the North Side.

The generation known as the "48ers" left the greatest imprint on Chicago's history. Because of the political, social, and economic upheaval in several German provinces, Germans poured into Chicago in record numbers. Within a few years they were second only to the Irish as the most dominant ethnic group in the city. As the Irish had, many worked on the canal or in the packing houses; others found employment in the building trades, manufacturing, and public service. The Germans were prominent in the city police and fire departments. To reach a happy compromise between the Irish and German constituencies at election time, the mayor often found it necessary to guide the appointment process along these ethnic lines. By 1900, it was customary for the police chief to be Irish and his deputy superintendent German.

To the chagrin of their more conservative compatriots who had arrived several years earlier and had assimilated into the culture, the "48ers" were a revolutionary people. Among the political exiles arriving in Chicago during this period was Lorenz Brentano (1813–91), who had been condemned to death in Baden for his involvement in the Liberty Party. Brentano settled in Chicago in 1859. Taking an active interest in civic affairs, he served as president of the Chicago School Board from 1863 to 1868, then later as a member of the Illinois General Assembly and the Forty-fifth Congress. During this time he owned and managed the principal German language newspaper in the city, the *Staatszeitung.*

The Old Town neighborhood was once known as "German Broadway." Community life centered around St. Michael's Church, constructed in 1866 at Eugenie and Cleveland streets through money donated by Michael Diversey (1810–69), a prominent German brewer and Sixth Ward alderman. In his lifetime, Diversey founded three churches: St. Peter and St. Joseph in 1846 and, of course, St. Michael's, which became the largest German parish in the city by 1892.

To preserve the folk traditions of the distant homeland, the German settlers founded numerous fraternal societies, singing clubs, and social organizations. Among the earliest were the St. Peter Verein founded in 1847 by Catholic parishioners on the South Side, and the Männergesangverein (Male Singing Club) in 1850. The Freier Sänger Bund staged popular choral performances at the Deutsches Haus (German Hall) built at Grand and Wells Avenue in 1856. It was a focal point of the Old Town neighborhood until it was swept away in the Chicago Fire of 1871.

During that tragic conflagration, a German man single-handedly saved the city waterworks from destruction and thereby preserved an important Michigan Avenue landmark. Frank Trautman had arrived in New York in 1825, where he worked as an engineer on the first ocean-going steamboat. Soon afterward he settled in Chicago, and for thirty years he was the chief engineer for the city waterworks. When flames threatened to consume the pumping station on October 8, 1871, Trautman and his assistants covered it with woolen blankets and discarded sails from Lake Michigan vessels.

Keeping the covers soaked in lake water, they saved the station from certain destruction. Just two days later, Trautman was able to restore the water supply to the beleaguered city.

By the 1930s—the heyday of the European fraternal societies in Chicago—it was estimated that there were 452 such organizations. The Germania Club, founded in 1865, was the most influential in terms of its size and prestige. The founding members sang at the bier of the martyred President Abraham Lincoln when the funeral cortege passed through Chicago in 1865. The club later moved to its spacious headquarters at 1536 North Clark Street in 1889, near the present-day site of the Chicago Historical Society. Through these doors passed generations of Chicago Germans, many of them prominent in government, the arts, and finance. William DeVry, founder of the DeVry Institute of Technology, served as club president from 1961 to 1963.

Old Town remained a homogenous German community until the early 1900s, when a number of Hungarians and Eastern Europeans began to settle along North Avenue. To the north, the village of Lakeview, sparsely settled in the 1840s and 1850s, became the next major hub of German settlement. Konrad Sulzer was Lakeview's first resident, building his 100-acre farm on land that had recently been inhabited by Native Americans. One of the area's principal east-west arteries, Montrose Avenue, was originally known as Sulzer Road. The spacious Sulzer Regional Library at Lincoln and Sunnyside is named in honor of the early German pioneer and is considered to be one of the finest branch libraries in Chicago.

In 1881, 72 German families living in Lakeview petitioned the parish of St. Michael's for a church of their own. Feeling cut off and isolated from the city, these devout Bavarian settlers found it difficult to attend services at St. Michael's on a regular basis. In 1882 the Reverend Joseph Essing resolved the problem when he secured five acres of prime farmland at what would become Wellington and Southport street. In 1882, St. Alphonsus, a towering Gothic edifice, was constructed there. The church and a German school built on the same site solidified the Lakeview community.

Many other German churches were established in the city between 1881 and 1900, when the tide of immigration reached its crest. Of the forty-eight predominantly German houses of worship built between 1872 and 1892, twenty were Lutheran, fifteen Catholic, six Methodist, three Baptist, three Congregational, and one Presbyterian.

What made Lakeview particularly attractive to the ethnic Germans was the tolerant attitude toward social drinking by village officials. The beer gardens flourished in "Chicagoburg" thanks to the Saloon Keeper's Society, organized to "protect and demand their common interests by all lawful means and measures." The building boom in Lakeview between 1885 and 1894, along with improvements in public transportation, encouraged

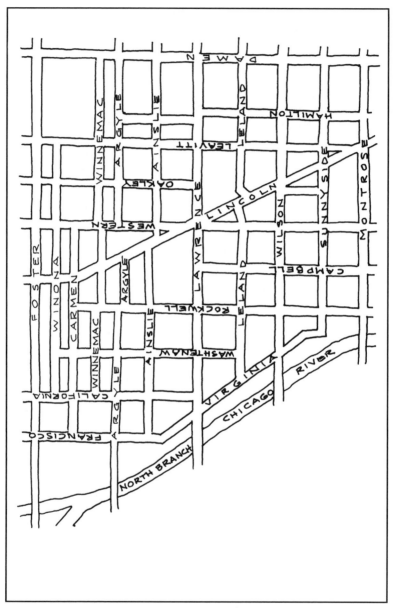

Lincoln Square

settlement of the north and west sections from the more crowded enclaves to the south and along the lake shore. Reflecting the growing importance of this up-and-coming neighborhood, the Lakeview Town Hall was built in 1872 at Halsted and Addison streets. Today, the 23rd Police District Station occupies the site.

The community reached residential maturity between 1910 and 1920, when the population swelled from 60,535 to 96,482. The Germans and Swedes dominated the cultural life of the community in the early years, but those of Hungarian, Polish, and Italian extraction pushed into the southern pockets of Lakeview near the industrial corridor to the southwest.

The coming of World War I presented new hardships for Chicago's German community. Torn between their loyalty to their adopted land and their nationalistic inclinations, the Germans came under sharp attack, especially after the fresh news of German atrocities galvanized public opinion against the Kaiser and his armies. The war, according to Professor Melvin Holli of the University of Illinois, "damaged German ethnic, linguistic, and cultural institutions beyond repair." Sizable amounts of money were expended by German propagandists in the U.S. to sway the neutrality of Americans— with little success. The Germania Club of Chicago attempted to raise ten million marks for the German chapter of the Red Cross, but did themselves a disservice by declaring that the conflict was a "war of the Teutonic race against the Slavic . . . whether the civilization of western Europe or the barbarism of Russia is to prevail."

On August 5, 1914, just a few days after the war broke out on the continent, 5,000 Germans, whipped into a nationalistic frenzy, marched through the Loop waving flags and banners and singing songs. A stirring torchlight rally was held in Grant Park, in which the speakers exhorted the crowd to support the cause with their hearts and purses. Never before had the city witnessed such a public showing for a foreign government. No other immigrant group was as well organized and financed as the Germans.

The United States entered the war on behalf of the Allies in April 1917, which effectively eliminated German *Kultur* in Chicago. Many fraternal societies dropped their Teutonic-sounding names. The Germania Männerchor, for example, became the Chicago Lincoln Club in 1918. When the war came, many Germans were arrested and held for seditious activities. German language instruction in the Chicago public schools was temporarily suspended, while many of the immigrants "Americanized" their names, partially out of embarrassment, more likely out of fear of reprisals from other groups. German Day, a cultural celebration and political rally held each year since 1893, was suspended in deference to the war effort. In the City Council, Alderman John Haderlein went so far as to propose a change of name for Goethe Street, to Nutwood Street. At the same time, the Theodore Thomas Orchestra became the Chicago Symphony.

The Second World War also undermined the German community. In the early 1940s, anti-German sentiment was such that hotheads in the community demanded that the beautiful statue of Johann Wolfgang von Goethe, in Lincoln Park since 1914, be melted down and made into a bomb. Despite these prevailing attitudes, the tide of German immigration into the city continued.

Completion of the Ravenswood elevated line directly west of Lakeview in 1907 opened up new communities to settlement. Three-flats, small apartment buildings, and beautiful brick homes constructed along the North Branch of the Chicago River sprang up almost overnight. Between 1920 and 1930, the Lincoln Square neighborhood northwest of Lakeview exploded in population, growing from 27,990 to 46,419. Lincoln Avenue, once a twisting Indian trail, became the principal business district and has retained a distinctive German flavor. According to 1980 census data, 22 percent of Lincoln Square's 45,954 residents were German.

During the next decade, sizable Greek, Asian, and Hispanic presences began changing the neighborhood's complexion. Like so many other ethnic European groups, the Germans have relinquished their city neighborhoods to the newcomers from Southeast Asia and Latin America.

German migration to the suburbs actually began in the 1840s, when a group of German immigrants settled the "Harlem" community, which was later named Forest Park. In 1885 the Altenheim (Senior Citizens Home) was founded in this western suburb, whose political history in many ways was defined by the Germans. Nineteen of the first twenty-one mayors of Forest Park were of German descent, which by comparison to Chicago's highly partisan political system tends to dwarf the accomplishments of the Irish in this regard. Chicagoans of German descent comprise 14.5 percent of Forest Park's ethnic composition, and 9.5 percent of the entire suburban population base in Cook and the surrounding collar counties. They are the largest ethnic group residing in the suburbs today, and have transplanted their Turner Halls, social clubs, and choral societies to River Grove, Elmhurst, Waukegan, Aurora, Bartlett, and Buffalo Grove.

Until recently, the German American National Congress (D.A.N.K.), with over sixty regional chapters in the United States., was headquartered in Mount Prospect, Illinois. However, the organization has returned to the Lincoln Square neighborhood to continue the task of bringing together Americans of German descent so that they may gain a full understanding of their ancestry and heritage. The decision on the part of the D.A.N.K. executive board to return to the old neighborhood suggests a reverse pattern of settlement, an urban phenomenon likely to continue into the next decade, as thousands of suburbanites rediscover the pleasures of the city.

From the city's earliest days the Germans have left their imprimatur upon Chicago's diverse ethnic culture. The sons and daughters of Deutschland have left behind a legacy of hard work and resourcefulness and a tenacious, unswerving pride in its institutions.

Getting There: The Lincoln (#11) bus begins at Congress and Wells in the Loop and runs north to Lincoln Square. By car from the Loop, take northbound Lake Shore Drive to the Lawrence Avenue exit and proceed west, until you reach Western Avenue.
For additional information, call the CTA at (312) 836-7000.

Attractions

Cultural Institutions

Goethe Institute of Chicago, *401 N. Michigan Ave., Chicago. Admission and rental of audio-visual equipment, including VCR tapes, are free with a library card. For further information, contact Elisabeth Angele, librarian, at (312) 329-0074. The lending library is closed Sunday and Monday.*

The recently renovated Goethe Institute in Pioneer Court sponsors a diverse program in the arts and humanities, while fostering cooperation between the German government and the people of Chicago. Founded in 1951, and sponsored in part by the Federal Republic of Germany, this nonprofit organization operates 149 branch libraries in sixty-eight nations. The Goethe Institute of Chicago has been at this location since 1978, and the collection includes a wide selection of magazines and newspapers imported from Germany, as well as video cassettes, slides, and music tapes that are available for rental. The institute offers beginning, intermediate, and advanced German language courses, and sponsors regularly scheduled musical concerts, contemporary German cinema, and lectures in the second-floor auditorium. Traveling art and ceramic exhibitions are held on the ground level.

German American National Congress (D.A.N.K.), *4740 N. Western Ave., Chicago, (773) 275-1100. Membership available for individuals or couples.*

Founded in 1959, D.A.N.K. brings together Americans of German ancestry interested in preserving the culture and language in the United States. With sixty active chapters, D.A.N.K. serves the needs of 52 million Germans, the single largest European ethnic group in the country today. Local chapters are free to sponsor whatever activities are of interest to the community, including parades, folk festivals, and German language classes. The society publishes a monthly newspaper printed in both English and German. Membership is open to individuals of German ancestry.

Outlying Areas

Dutch Heritage Center, *at Trinity Christian College, 6601 W. College, Palos Heights, (708) 597-3000. Open by appointment only.*

Dutch settlers began arriving in Chicago and the South Suburbs in the 1840s. By 1900—the peak year of the Dutch immigration into the city—there were some 20,000 of them who had arrived from the Netherlands. Many were poor truck farmers who tended their lands in close proximity to one another until they were forced to yield to the developers who planned towns, roads, and commercial businesses. A smaller enclave was located on the Near West side, in the vicinity of Ashland Ave. and 14th St. The history of the Dutch settlement in Englewood, Roseland, Lansing, South Holland, and Palos Heights is preserved in this little-known research center located on the second floor of the Jenny Huizinga Library at Trinity Christian College. Curator Henrick Sliekers has accumulated a fine collection of manuscripts, Dutch books, artwork, and historical artifacts donated by the descendants of the original settlers. Old church documents left behind are helpful tools in conducting genealogical research, and can be accessed at the library.

Annual Events and Celebrations

Annual Von Steuben Day Parade. *Saturday closest to September 17 (the birth date of Friedrich Wilhelm Freiherr von Steuben). Call Erich Himmell at (312) 561-8670 or (847) 647-9522 for details.*

In the darkest days of the War of Independence, the Continental Congress sought ways to reverse the ominous tide of British military advances. Through the intervention of Benjamin Franklin and Silas Deane, General George Washington was prevailed upon to enlist the support of Baron (Freiherr) von Steuben, who had previously been attached to the general staff of Frederick II. At the invitation of the beleaguered Washington, the Prussian aristocrat arrived in America in December, 1777, to train the Continental forces at their winter encampment at Valley Forge, Pennsylvania. Von Steuben whipped the troops into shape, and was rewarded with a field commission as major general, and later participated in the siege of Yorktown. Since 1966, the German societies in Chicago have sponsored an annual Von Steuben Parade, with over 200 groups represented by floats, bands, dancers, singers, and marchers garbed in traditional military regalia. It is, perhaps, Chicago's least publicized and most poorly attended ethnic parade. The newspapers and television stations give it little attention, and consequently the number of people who turn out each year is comparatively small. In 1990 the Mexican Independence Day parade was scheduled to follow close behind. The Hispanic community, which had lined up early on the sidewalks waving their colorful green and white flags, did not know what the city was up to when the German marching bands and choral societies passed in review. The parade is paid for every year through private subscription. Despite the city's apparent indifference, the colorful pageant continues, often under less-than-ideal circumstances. The German parade kicks off at Wacker Drive, and goes down Dearborn St., before winding up at Congress Parkway and Wacker Drive.

German-American Fest, *held in conjunction with the Von Steuben Day Parade, at Leland St., between Lincoln and Western avenues. Three days in mid-September. Call Erich Himmell at (312) 561-8670 or (847) 647-9522 for times and dates.*

Dancing, singing, and German foods, prepared by several of the area restaurants in two large tents. The talents of German organizations such as the Schwaebischer Singing Society and the Rheinischer Verein are on display in this annual celebration of German culture. Sponsored by the Lincoln Square Chamber of Commerce. *Recommended.*

German-American Day, *St. Benedict's Church, 2215 W. Irving Park Rd., Chicago, (773) 588-6484. Sunday on or about October 6.*

Since the arrival of the first German settler on U.S. shores, October 6, 1683, the number of immigrants and their offspring has grown to an estimated 52 million. In 1987 President Ronald Reagan proclaimed October 6 "German-American Day," to honor the accomplishments and contributions of this ethnic European immigrant group. St. Benedict's, one of the oldest German parishes in the city, sponsors an hour-long church service, with music supplied by the German choral groups, and guest speakers, which may include the mayor of Chicago, the vice consul of Germany, and other visiting dignitaries. No food or drink is served on the church grounds, but afterward it is customary to repair to one of the many excellent German restaurants in the area.

German-American Children's Concerts. *For information about the Children's Chorus and its performances, call Ruth Schuebel at (773) 477-7732 for dates and ticket prices.*

Three annual performances: (1) Mother's Day, at the Irish-American Cultural Center, 4626 N. Knox Ave., Chicago, (2) Christmas Concert, held the second week of December at the Irish-American Center, and (3) Christmas Around the World Festival, at the Museum of Science and Industry, throughout the month of December at 57th St. and Lake Shore Dr., Chicago. This choral group sings traditional and contemporary songs in German and English. The Children's Chorus is an adjunct of the German-American Singers of Chicago, and is one of eighteen singing societies under the auspices of the Combined German-American Choruses, an umbrella group organized several years ago and directed by Rudi Dick, who can be reached at (773) 763-1883. The adult choral societies come from all over the Midwest, and perform regularly at folk festivals, religious services, and the big downtown Von Steuben Parade. On the first Sunday of each month, one of the adult choral groups will sing religious hymns at the St. Alphonsus German-language Mass, held at 1429 W. Wellington Ave., Chicago. Call (312) 525-0709 for details.

Wicker Park Housewalk, *two-hour walking tour provided by the Chicago Architectural Foundation (CAF), 330 S. Dearborn St., Chicago. Generally held on a Saturday in May, June, and July. Commentary by CAF volunteers. Admission fee charged. CAF members admitted free. For dates and times, call (773) 922-3431.*

Listed in the National Register of Historic Places, the Wicker Park neighborhood is one of the city's few remaining nineteenth-century treasures. The community was given its name by philanthropists John and Charles Wicker, who donated the land to the city in 1870, and then capitalized on the real estate boom that followed. German immigrants poured into this area in the 1880s, and left their mark long after the Poles and Serbs became the dominant group in the community. The area made up of the 1300, 1400, and 1500 blocks of North Hoyne St. was once known as "Beer Row," for the many Queen Anne, and Second Empire style homes owned by prosperous German merchants. The Schlitz house, which stood on the corner of Hoyne and Pierce, was owned by the Milwaukee brewing family until it was torn down in the 1920s to make way for an apartment complex. Hoyne Street was the first paved artery in the district, and many fine Victorian mansions, including the Waixel-Borgmeir House (1521) still stand. Adolph Borgmeir was a

German craftsman who designed many of the fine furniture pieces sold by the A. P. Johnson Company. Wicker Park, once the home of Nelson Algren, who defined the essential character of the neighborhood in his gritty novel *Chicago: City On the Make,* is today a gentrified, rehabbed artist and Yuppie colony that is still worth a visit. The Architectural Foundation tour meets at Damen (2000 West) and LeMoyne (1500 North).

Wicker Park Greening Festival, *Damen and Schiller,*
Chicago. Usually the third weekend in August.
Sponsored by the Old Wicker Park Committee, at
1608 N. Milwaukee Ave., Chicago, (773) 342-1966.
Admission fee charged.

Two-day music, food, auto show, house tour, arts and crafts, and ethnic festival. A tour of historic homes, often including one of Nelson Algren's dwellings, and a garden walk are included in the admission price.

Christmas Open House at the Goethe Institute.
First or second Saturday in December.

Used book sale. Complimentary food and drink, and a prize drawing in the afternoon.

Outlying Areas

Fahrrad-Tour Von Schaumburg. *First or second*
Sunday in June. Register in advance by calling the
Schaumburg Park District at (847) 490-7015.
Admission is free.

A six-mile guided bike tour of Schaumburg's historic neighborhoods, with a special emphasis on the community's German heritage. The event kicks off from the Blackwell School, 345 N. Walnut Lane, Schaumburg.

Altenheim Home Annual Picnic, *7824 Madison,*
Forest Park, (708) 366-2206. First Sunday in August.
Admission fee charged.

Oompah bands, German bratwursts, beer, and a bake sale highlight the annual picnic and food fest in the Western Suburbs—a yearly tradition that dates back more than sixty years. Local dignitaries are always in attendance, and they might even partake in the dancing and bingo games, but don't count on it. There are pony rides for children, a dog show, and prize raffles. All proceeds benefit the Altenheim Home, a not-for-profit nursing home for the elderly.

Oktoberfest Celebrations

A festival with its origin in Munich, Oktoberfest dates back to October 12, 1812, when the Bavarian king Ludwig I celebrated his marriage to Therese Sachsen Hildburghausen by sponsoring a great horse race outside the city. A festive occasion with much pomp and revelry, the race was repeated each year. Nowadays the Munich Oktoberfest begins on the next-to-the-last Saturday in September and continues until the first Sunday in October, luring tourists from all over the world.

Basically, Oktoberfest is nothing more than singing, dancing, eating and drinking. Quantity is the operative word when you talk about beer drinking and food consumption, and several Chicago-area restaurants sponsor annual Oktoberfest celebrations to promote *Gemütlichkeit* within us all.

Berghoff Oktoberfest, *17 W. Adams St., Chicago,*
(312) 427-3170. Call for times and dates.

Three-day street festival held the second weekend in September, outside the restaurant between State and Dearborn streets. Chicken sandwiches, bratwurst, apple strudel, and the famous Berghoff beer are available for purchase. The scheduled entertainment is provided by any number of German bands, including Alpiners, the Red Castle Band direct from Heidelberg, and the Jan Wagner Bavarian Band, and is free. This festival began in 1985.

Outlying Areas

Schaumburg Oktoberfest, *at the Schaumburg Golf*
Club, 401 N. Roselle, Schaumburg. For further
information, contact Stacey at the Schaumburg Park
District at (847) 490-7015.

Bet you didn't know that Schaumburg, Illinois and Schaumburg, Germany, are sister cities. They are, and the special relationship between the two communities is celebrated each year in the parking lot of the hotel or the grounds of the golf course, where the Schaumburg Park District opens up a large beer tent, the first or second Sunday in October. A German band performs. Handicrafts are sold inside the tent, and the children can ride ponies or roller coasters.

Tinley Park Oktoberfest, *World Music Theater,*
191st St. and Ridgeland, Tinley Park, (708) 532-1733.
Late September or early October.

This annual event has become so big in recent years that the village has set up its own special hotline to call for information. Abundant food and traditional German music highlight the weekend festivities in this south suburb with its large German concentration.

Villa Park Oktoberfest, *Lions Field Park, 320 E. Wildwood, Villa Park, (630) 834-8525. Third or fourth weekend in September. Free parking and admission.*

Flea market, German food, children's games, and handicrafts. Entertainment provided by German bands.

Batavia Oktoberfest, *held along Wilson St. and N. Washington (Route 25), in downtown Batavia. Third weekend in October. For further information, contact Trudy MacLaren at (630) 879-6825.*

In addition to the usual sampling of German foods, the Batavia Chamber of Commerce sponsors an "herbal harvest," an antique panorama with fresh produce, fruits, and collectibles for sale by sidewalk vendors. The event runs for three days, Friday through Sunday. The Batavia VFW Post sponsors an Oktoberfest dinner dance the first week of October at the VFW Post on Highway 25. For ticket prices and times, call the VFW at (630) 879-6848.

Forest Grove Athletic Club Oktoberfest, *1760 N. Hicks, Palatine, (847) 991-4646. One-day event held in early October. Admission fee charged.*

A yearly fund-raising event for the athletic club, featuring Bavarian slap dancing, food, raffles, a German folk band, and arm wrestling contests.

Hans' Bavarian Lodge Oktoberfest, *931 N. Milwaukee Ave., Wheeling, (847) 537-4141. Every Friday and Saturday in October. Admission fee charged.*

The Oktoberfest celebration at Hans' Bavarian Lodge is a yearly tradition that has gone on since 1957. A large tent erected on the grounds can seat 2,500 people, who in any given year are entertained by such musical groups as Big Twist and the Mellow Fellows, and Epic, a traditional German band that plays waltzes and polkas.

Edelweiss Restaurant Oktoberfest, *7650 W. Irving Park Rd., Norridge, (708) 452-6040. Fridays through Sunday in September.*

A four-person band plays German folk songs while diners feast on pork shanks, bratwurst, and other belt-busting goodies.

Morgan Park Oktoberfest, *Morgan Park Academy,*
2153 W. 111th St., Chicago. First weekend in October.
Contact the Beverly Area Planning Association at
(773) 233-3100.

Three-day festival featuring German bands, bratwursts, and beer. Hours to
be determined.

Shops

Delicatessen Meyer, *4750 N. Lincoln Ave., Chicago,*
(773) 561-3377. Open daily. Checks accepted, but no
credit cards.

Imported German and Swiss chocolates, baked goods, beer, toiletries, colognes,
and ceramics. Sausages made on the premises in this old-fashioned German deli.

Inge's Delicatessen, *4724 N. Lincoln Ave., Chicago,*
(773) 561-8386. Open daily.

More than thirty years at this location. Imported French, German, Austrian,
Croatian, Danish, and Dutch gourmet foods and dry goods, including beer
steins, cosmetics, and homemade sausages.

Merz Apothecary, *4716 N. Lincoln Ave., Chicago,*
(773) 989-0900. Closed Sunday.

A delightfully quaint pharmacy that was formerly located in the 2900 block
of Lincoln Ave., from 1875 until 1982. The owners have recreated the look
and feel of an old fashioned ma-and-pa nineteenth-century retail store, with
dark wood paneling on the walls and glass display cases on either side.
Imported soaps, cosmetics, and medicines from Germany, England, Spain,
New Zealand, and Ireland. *Recommended.*

Finishing Touches of Europe, *4754 N. Lincoln Ave.,*
Chicago, (773) 784-0034. Open daily.

Women's clothing and jewelry imported from Germany and greater Europe.

Schmid Imports, *4606 N. Lincoln Ave., Chicago,*
(773) 561-2871. Closed Sunday and Monday. Accepts
all credit cards.

Gift items and souvenirs from Germany, including figurines, Nutcracker
and Smokeman dolls, pewter plates, music cassettes, decorated beer steins,
greeting cards, and magazines.

Small Fry, *4756 N. Lincoln Ave., Chicago,*
(773) 784-0506. Open daily.

The Graham family has owned this specialty clothing store continuously since 1949. Bavarian costumes, German and Austrian Lederhosen, Trachten, and knit goods for the "small fry."

Helga's Dolls, *4555 N. Western Ave., Chicago,*
(773) 769-0822. Closed Sundays. After-hours
appointments available.

Leading importer of modern collectible dolls (no antiques) from Germany, Italy, Spain, and France. The store in itself is a doll museum and well worth a visit.

Lincoln Market, *4661 N. Lincoln Ave., Chicago,*
(773) 561-4570. Closed Sunday.

The meat shop and delicatessen is well known all over Chicago, because the beerwurst and sausages are prepared in-house by master European butchers. German meats and food products from Poland, Hungary, and Yugoslavia.

European Pastry Shop and Café, *4701-03 N.*
Lincoln Ave., Chicago, (773) 271-7017. Open daily
for breakfast, lunch, and dinner.

Bakery in the front, with a dining area in the rear. The cakes, imported truffles, and tortes are sweet, gooey, and loaded with calories. Better stay away if you're on a diet.

Juergen's North Star Bakery, *4545 N. Lincoln Ave.,*
Chicago, (773) 561-9858. Closed Sunday and
Monday. No credit cards.

Homemade bread and cookies, but no fancy pastries.

European Import Corner, *4752 N. Lincoln Ave.,*
Chicago, (773) 561-8281. Open daily. No credit cards.

German beer steins, china, crystal, cuckoo clocks, magazines, and periodicals.

Alpine Meat Market, *4030 N. Cicero Ave., Chicago,*
(773) 725-2121. Closed Sunday.

Located one block north of "Six Corners" (where Irving Park Rd., Milwaukee Ave., and Cicero Ave. join), the delicatessen features Swiss, Austrian, and German foods. The marzipan candy may be cheaper here than anywhere else in Chicago.

Lutz Continental Cafe, *2458 W. Montrose Ave.,*
Chicago, (773) 478-7785. Closed Monday.

Bakery in the front, selling German and French pastries. Café in the rear.
Seasonal outdoor café.

Olga's Delikatessen, *3209 W. Irving Park Rd.,*
Chicago, (773) 539-8038. Open daily. No credit cards.

German imports, candy, and assorted foods.

Vienna Pastry Shop, *5411 W. Addison St., Chicago,*
(773) 685-4166. Closed Monday. No credit cards or
personal checks.

Specializing in fine German pastries. Owned by Gerhard and Hedwig Kaes.

Outlying Areas

Kuhn's Delicatessen and Liquors, *two locations:*
749 W. Golf Rd., Des Plaines, (847) 640-0222; 1165
S. Waukegan Rd., Northbrook, (847) 272-4197. Open
daily.

Established in 1929, Kuhn's is the largest and best-known of Chicago's delicatessens, specializing in imported European foods and beverages.

European Imports, *7900 N. Milwaukee Ave., Niles,*
(847) 967-5253. Open daily. Credit cards accepted.

Collectible dolls, crystal, and imported gift items from Germany, Italy, and
Spain.

Black Forest Delicatessen, *8840 Waukegan Rd.,*
Morton Grove, (847) 965-3113. Closed Monday.

Over thirty-five years at this location. Imported deli items, and chocolates
from Germany, Austria, and Switzerland. Fresh meats cut daily. Homemade
sausages.

Continental Delikatessen and Imports, *10 S.*
Evergreen, Plaza Shopping Center, Arlington Heights,
(847) 259-9544. Closed Sundays.

German, Swedish, and Norwegian food imports. Pastries, candies, tea, and
chocolates. Salads homemade on premises.

Restaurants

Chicago Brau Haus, *4732 N. Lincoln Ave., Chicago,*
(773) 784-4444. Open for lunch and dinner. Closed
Tuesdays.

Traditional German restaurant with entertainment and dancing nightly. The music is provided by a three-piece German band and accordion player. In August, the restaurant hosts a Summerfest with special low prices. On the weekend of the Von Steuben Parade, the Brau Haus sponsors its own German Fest celebration in the rear parking lot. April is "Bockbierfest" time, with entertainment and dancing nightly by the Brauhaus Band and Max Wagner on the accordion. Special lunch menu.

Huettenbar, *4721 N. Lincoln Ave., Chicago,*
(773) 561-2507. Open for dinner nightly.

A neighborhood tavern known for its *Gemütlichkeit.* The Huettenbar was formerly affiliated with the Brau Haus across the street, but the owner went off on his own a few years ago. Musical entertainment on Tuesday nights.

Heidelberger Fass, *4300 N. Lincoln Ave., Chicago,*
(773) 478-2486. Open for lunch and dinner. Closed
Tuesdays. Credit cards accepted.

Southern German cooking. Background music, but no regularly scheduled entertainment.

Great Beer Palace, *4128 N. Lincoln Ave., Chicago,*
(773) 525-4906. Open for lunch and dinner
Tuesdays–Saturdays and dinner Mondays. Free
parking. Credit cards accepted.

Bavarian beer garden in the rear seats forty people, and is a popular gathering spot during the Oktoberfest. It's also where the Beer Society of America meets each month. That ought to tell you something.

The Berghoff, *17 W. Adams St., Chicago, (312) 427-*
3170, and 436 W. Ontario, Chicago, (312) 266-7771.
Open for lunch and dinner. Closed Sundays.

Old Herman Berghoff left his home in Dortmund, Germany, in 1887, and began brewing his unique blend of beer in Ft. Wayne, Ind. In 1893, Herman introduced his special Pilsner to Chicagoans at the World's Columbian Exposition. Nowadays, the Huber Brewing Company of Monroe, Wisconsin, manufactures the beer that made the Berghoff Restaurant famous from the time it opened its doors on Adams St. in 1898. The sauerbraten, schnitzel, and seafood dishes are house specialties. The Berghoff is a real Chicago institution. *Recommended.*

Resi's Bierstube, *2034 W. Irving Park Rd., Chicago, (773) 472-1749. Bar open every day. Kitchen open during the winter months only, seven days a week. No credit cards.*

Austrian and German food you can enjoy in a quaint beer garden during the warm weather. Owners Herbert and Ingaborg Stover stock sixty bottled beers and eight on tap.

Zum Deutschen Eck, *2924 N. Southport, Chicago, (773) 525-8121. Open for lunch and dinner daily. Credit cards accepted.*

A classic German restaurant that evokes the nineteenth-century tradition of beer gardens, *Gemütlichkeit,* and "continental Sundays." Located across the street from St. Alphonsus Church in the heart of Lakeview, the restaurant is popular with the opera aficionados who regularly attend performances of the Chicago Opera Company at the Athenaeum Theatre inside one of the church buildings. A five-piece "oompah" band performs on Fridays, Saturdays, and Sundays. Be sure to join the sing-along.

German-American Restaurant & Lounge, *642 N. Clark St., Chicago, (312) 642-3244. Open for lunch and dinner. Closed Sunday.*

Over thirty-five years at this location. Modest little restaurant located just north of the Loop. Owned by the Hans Kief family. A variety of German foods are served. Catering.

Outlying Areas

Christi's German Inn, *45 W. Slade, Palatine, (847) 991-1040. Open for breakfast, lunch, and dinner. Closed Mondays. Credit cards accepted.*

Specializing in Bavarian dishes.

Bistro 1800, *1800 Sherman Ave., Evanston, (847) 492-3450. Open for lunch and dinner daily. Credit cards accepted.*

A quaint European restaurant and coffee house with a pleasing menu of German and continental foods.

Fritzel's Country Inn, *900 Ravinia Terrace, Lake*
Zurich, (847) 540-8844. Open for lunch and dinner.
Closed Mondays. Credit cards accepted.

Pleasing menu of German, Swiss, and Hungarian foods. Occasional entertainment, and Oktoberfest the last two weekends of September.

Hans's Bavarian Lodge, *931 Milwaukee Ave.,*
Wheeling, (847) 537-4141. Open for lunch and dinner.
Closed Mondays.

Owner Jane Berghoff's late husband owned the Adams Street eatery in downtown Chicago for many years. For over fifteen years, she has operated Hans's Bavarian Lodge, which is down the street from Wheeling's famous "Restaurant Row," which includes Bob Chinn's Crab House and Le Français, arguably one of the most expensive (but highly rated) dining establishments in the country. Imported bottled beers, delightful German rathskeller, and a bacon salad dressing that is out of this world. On Fridays, piano and zither players entertain patrons. Saturdays and Sundays feature live accordion music.

Heidelberg Restaurant, *122 S. York, Elmhurst,*
(630) 530-5115. Open for lunch and dinner. Closed
Sundays.

Food dishes from all over Germany. An accordion player performs on Fridays and Saturdays in the basement "Rathskeller." A special menu is offered during the Oktoberfest season. German Delicatessen on the first floor.

Edelweiss Restaurant, *7650 Irving Park Rd.,*
Norridge, (708) 452-6050. Open for lunch and dinner.
Closed Mondays. Credit cards accepted.

Edelweiss, an exceptional German-Austrian brasserie, has been a fixture in the Norridge community for more than twenty years. The restaurant offers pleasing German-Austrian cuisine in a casual old-world chalet setting. The menu has been upgraded and the interiors remodeled by Walter T. Kosch, the new owner who has served as chief designer for several award-winning hotels and restaurants in Austria, the West Indies, and the Caribbean over the years. Edelweiss sponsors a full calendar of special events throughout the year, including an Oktoberfest; a Valentine's Day celebration; a February pre-Lenten *Karneval* featuring much gaiety, good food, and drink; and the annual mid-winter serving of "Obstler," a smooth, invigorating liquor derived from apples and pears. German bands. Dancing and much more.

Golden Ox, *1578 N. Clybourn Ave., Chicago,*
(773) 664-0780. Open for lunch and dinner
Mondays–Saturdays, and for dinner Sundays.

Located near the intersection of Clybourn Avenue and North Avenue, which at the turn of the century was known as the "German Broadway," and was anchored by the Sieben Brewery at 1470 Larrabee and the Oscar Mayer Sausage Company on Sedgwick. Both firms provided jobs to the thousands of German immigrants who once lived in this neighborhood. Nowadays, the Golden Ox is one of the last vestiges of those times. The restaurant specializes in Bavarian food, including dumplings, Spätzle, and cherry and plum strudel. Delicious.

Schulien's, *2100 W. Irving Park Rd., Chicago,*
(773) 478-2100. Open for lunch and dinner.
Closed Mondays. Credit cards accepted.

An old-world restaurant and saloon in Lakeview. Professional magicians will sit down at your table and perform magic tricks in the evenings.

Mirabell, *3454 W. Addison St., Chicago,*
(773) 463-1962. Open for lunch and dinner.
Closed Sundays.

Small but charming Austrian-German restaurant with friendly waiters and a wide variety of dishes, which the owners proudly claim to be among the best in the city. Background German music.

Black Forest Chalet, *8840 Waukegan Rd., Morton*
Grove, (847) 965-6830. Open for dinner. Closed
Mondays.

Specializing in German and Austrian cuisine. Daily entertainment with live zither music Friday and Saturday nights. Special events every other month.

Media

International Historic Films, *3533 S. Archer Ave.,*
Chicago, IL 60609, (312) 927-2900.

This Chicago-based mail-order firm will send you a free catalog listing hundreds of classic movies and documentaries from Germany that are available for purchase. Included in their collection are a number of rare World War II era films from Germany including *Munchausen* and *Titanic,* both from 1943. Many of the documentaries and films in the inventory contain English subtitles.

The Lincoln Square Mall:
Chicago's Last Surviving Germantown

Lincoln Square dates back to three settlements founded in the second half of the nineteenth century: Bowmanville (1850), Summerdale (1855), and Ravenswood (1869). These three adjoining neighborhoods were annexed to Chicago in 1889. In 1925, small segments from each of these neighborhoods were partitioned off in order to form Lincoln Square, a bustling retail and residential community that was originally settled by German immigrants.

Through the efforts of the local Chamber of Commerce, the Lincoln Avenue business strip at the intersection of Lawrence and Western avenues was closed to two-way automobile traffic in 1978 and converted into a shopping mall. The outdoor plaza at its center became a popular meeting spot for many of the long-time German and Greek residents who have chosen to remain in the city.

Symbolic of the continuing Teutonic presence in this North Side enclave is the fifteen-foot Baroque-style lantern, which was donated to the Chamber of Commerce by the city of Hamburg in Germany. Made of heavy black cast iron with brass ornamentation, the lantern is located in back of the Abraham Lincoln statue in the plaza.

Scenes from the picturesque German countryside are depicted on a wall mural at 4662 N. Lincoln Avenue. This "concrete canvas" is the work of a native of Stuttgart who recruited talented high school students to help him complete the project. The mural, showing a medieval battle fortress and a quaint farming village, was dedicated during German Day festivities in 1991.

The mural is a good place to begin your shopping and dining tour of old Germantown on Lincoln Avenue—affectionately known to some as "Sauerkraut Boulevard."

Swedish and Norwegian Chicago

And because the young farmer couldn't continue creation where God had left off, he must be satisfied with his seven acres and all the stones wherever he looked; broken stones, stones in piles, stone fences, stone above ground, stone in the ground, stone, stone, stone. King Oskar had ascended the kingdom of Sweden and Norway. Karl Oskar had become king in a stone kingdom...

—Vilhelm Moberg, *The Emigrants*

══ Swedish History and Settlement ══

The land was cruel and uncompromising. Tall trees blocked the sun. The stones embedded in the lush soil broke the blade of many a good plow. Those peasant farmers of Småland, Sweden, tilled their land and paid the fealty to king and country believing that this was God's will. And then the first news of America reached them in the form of handbills and pamphlets. The circulars told of rich, fertile farmland and the great industrial city on the prairie—Chicago. The emigrants saved their *riksdalers* and dreamed of the day they would board the boat in the port of Göteborg to begin the perilous journey to America.

Olaf Gottfrid Lange, born in the port city of Göteborg in 1811, came to the United States as a sailor on board an American brig in 1824. Lange established permanent residence on September 18, 1838, and earned his keep by working as a druggist's assistant. As more Scandinavians began arriving in Chicago, Lange conducted English language classes inside the old blockhouse of Fort Dearborn.

Word of mouth played an important role in bringing rural Swedes to Chicago. Gustav Flack, a contemporary of Lange who operated a small store near the Clark Street ferry landing in 1843, sent home glowing reports about the city growing up around the fort. Flack encouraged many of his compatriots to emigrate, and within a few years they had founded a colony north of the Chicago River in the area bounded by Wells and LaSalle streets, from Division to Chicago Avenue. Community life centered around the St. Ansgarius Episcopal Church, built in 1851. It was known as the "Jenny Lind church," because the popular Swedish singer donated $1,000 to finance its construction.

The Larssons, Janssons, Karlstroms, and eighty other Swedes survived the deadly cholera epidemic of 1849 to prosper in the building trades as carpenters, welders, and skilled artisans. Polycarpus von Schneidau was probably the best known among the Swedes who populated frontier Chicago. In 1848 he was appointed superintendent of construction of the first railroad to run out of Chicago—the Chicago and Galena Railroad. In later years, such distinguished Swedish architects as Henry Ericsson and Andrew Lanquist helped to pioneer skyscraper construction in Chicago. Lanquist designed the People's Gas, Light and Coke Co. building on Michigan Avenue in Chicago, and the U.S. Steel headquarters in Gary, Indiana.

The Scandinavian Union (Skandinaviska Sallskadet) and the Svea Society were organized to foster cultural and ethnic unity, threatened by the melting pot called Chicago. Other organizations soon followed. The Swedish Club, organized in 1869, was the vortex of social and intellectual life in the city. Its restaurant and club room at 1258 North LaSalle Street was a favorite gathering spot for the city's most prominent citizens of Scandinavian descent. Carl Sandburg told many engaging stories about Abraham Lincoln and his own experiences as a crime reporter for the *Chicago Daily News* over drinks at the Swedish Club. Years later, Police Superintendent Orlando W. Wilson shared the camaraderie and fellowship with Chicago's Swedes—an irony, one would think, given the fact that the chief was of Norwegian descent.

During the heyday of Swedish immigration, there were numerous fraternal and choral societies scattered around Chicago, including the Svithiod Singing Club, organized in June 1882. It was natural for the European ethnic groups like the Swedes to find social identity and companionship in the churches where their native tongue was spoken and the hymns of the old country were sung. But the need for fellowship in a secular setting was strong, especially among the libertarians who preferred to adjourn to the local "sample room" after the lodge business was conducted.

The Svithiod Singing Club promoted social drinking in Chicago to be sure, but its members also participated in the 1981 unveiling in Lincoln Park of the monument to Carl von Linne (a Swedish botanist renowned for his classification of plants and flowers) and sponsored numerous charitable and philanthropic causes.

By 1871 the homogeneous community along LaSalle and Wells streets began to break up. Their improved economic position and the arrival of the Italians and other groups to the area hastened the departure of its inhabitants. A number of them relocated to the Belmont-Sheffield neighborhood, but this was only a temporary move. The new "Swede Town"—one that survives to the present day—sprang up near the corner of Clark and Foster avenues on the far north side, a sparsely populated neighborhood at the time. A tiny red-brick schoolhouse, an Evangelical Lutheran Church, and several itinerant farmers comprised what was then a distant suburb of Chicago.

This dramatic move outward from the city center was an attempt by the Swedes to preserve their native identity, yet forge a uniquely American community that was relatively isolated from the urban sprawl of Chicago. Swedish historians cannot agree which of the two Andersons residing in this area at the time lent their name to the community. Was it the Reverend Paul Anderson, who had arrived in Chicago in 1843? He served as pastor of the Lutheran church, which by 1854 had changed its name to the Swedish Immanuel Church of Chicago, but he was a Norwegian. The proud Swedes would argue that John Anderson, a highway commissioner and farmer who tilled an acre of land west of Clark Street, gave his name to the village.

Following the Civil War, Swedes began taking a more active role in city affairs. The original plan for Lincoln Park was submitted by a Swedish landscape gardener named Sven Nelson, who received his training in the old country on an estate that belonged to the royal family. Pehr Samuel Petersson (1830–1903) arrived in Chicago in 1854 to open a small nursery northwest of Swede Town. When the Chicago Fire reduced the city to cinders and ash, Petersson went to work planting trees and shrubbery along the ruined boulevards and side streets. It was estimated that he planted 60 percent of the city's foliage by 1901. Petersson founded Rosehill Cemetery and planted the trees at the 1893 World's Fair. Peterson Avenue, a major east-west street running just north of Andersonville, was named after him.

The Andersonville neighborhood experienced peak growth between 1890 and 1930, when 20 to 24 percent of the population was made up of foreign-born Swedes. Across the city in 1927 there were 125,000 people of Swedish birth or descent. It was the high tide of the Scandinavian immigration. The community experienced tremendous pride when the bronze bust of philosopher, scientist, and theologian Emanuel Swedenborg was unveiled before thousands of cheering Swedes in Lincoln Park on June 29, 1924, and when Crown Prince Gustavus Adolphus and Crown Prince William visited Chicago that same month.

The sixty-one Swedish churches that flourished in Chicago sponsored the traditional herring breakfast every Sunday. From the earliest times, the Swedes had fished the briny depths of the Baltic Sea in order to augment their food supply. The herring was carefully salted down in barrels before being served with boiled potatoes, sour cream, and cold beer. The Chicago herring breakfast, held in dozens of smoky church basements and fraternal meeting halls around the city, lasted only as long as there was a first-generation presence to sustain it. Like the polka traditions in the Polish community, the Swedish herring breakfast is a throwback to a vanished nineteenth- and early twentieth-century culture that is virtually nonexistent in modern-day Europe.

After 1930 the tide of Swedish immigration to Chicago slowed dramatically. New ethnic groups began moving into Andersonville, supplanting long-time residents who either passed away or abandoned the community altogether. As years passed, the neighborhood showed signs of benign neglect. Some thought was given to dropping the name of Andersonville entirely in favor of promoting cultural diversity among all the immigrant groups residing in the vicinity of Clark and Foster. However, the North Clark Street Business Men's Association and the long-time residents of the neighborhood favored preserving the status quo.

Andersonville was rededicated on October 17, 1964, a day of celebration for Chicago Swedes. Mayor Richard J. Daley and Governor Otto Kerner were on hand to cut the ribbon and extol the virtues of the Scandinavians who had called this neighborhood home for nearly eighty years. The bell-ringer tradition, now a quarter-century old, began that day. At 10:00 A.M. Dominick Lalumia marched up and down Clark Street, ringing a brass bell that symbolized a rebirth of the community. Shopkeepers emerged from their stores to sweep the sidewalk. The hue and cry had been sounded. Andersonville was back in business. Today the bellringer makes his weekly rounds on Saturday mornings at 10:30. He is often accompanied by Swedes in colorful folk costumes: Lucias, Vikings, Maypole dancers, and Lapplanders. Regardless of their ethnic identity, each store has its own special corn-broom, handpainted in blue and yellow. *Välkommen* to Andersonville.

Getting There: Take the Howard (North-South) line. Exit at Berwyn and walk west on Foster about four blocks. In January it is best to skip the walk and take the #92 Foster bus at the station. It is a short ride (about four blocks). By car from the Loop, drive north on Lake Shore Drive, exit at Foster Avenue and proceed west past Sheridan and

Broadway. When you reach Clark Street, you have arrived. Look for a parking spot (not always the easiest thing to do)—the side streets of Balmoral, Berwyn, Farragut, and Summerdale are your best bet.

For additional information, call the CTA at (312) 836-7000.

═══ Norwegian History and Settlement ═══

Mayor William Hale Thompson had no use for King George of England. During the 1927 mayoral campaign, the blustering demagogue of city politics made an issue of School Superintendent William McAndrew's alleged pro-English biases which, according to the unabashed Thompson, posed a threat to impressionable young minds. "This fellow McAndrew in the schools!" Big Bill thundered, "Teaching un-Americanism! If we don't look out our history books are going to have all kinds of things belittling George Washington, the great founder of our country!" The school text book issue struck a responsive chord with Chicago's 56,000-strong Norwegian community, who had felt the sting of history concerning the treatment of the legendary Viking explorer Leif Eriksson.

The history of the Norwegian immigration begins in 1836, a year before the incorporation of Chicago, when Johann Larsen and Halsten Torrisen settled in the city. Larsen was a sailor. Torrisen built the first two-story frame house within city limits, at Wells and Lake. He was employed as a gardener in the household of Walter L. Newberry, for whom the Newberry Library in "Bughouse Square" is named.

Ivar Lawson settled in Chicago in 1840 and made his fortune in real estate development. He was elected Chicago City Marshal in 1860. His son Victor embarked on a career in journalism with the *Skandinaven,* a Norwegian-language paper founded by John Anderson in 1866. Young Victor Lawson's apprenticeship ended when he struck out on his own in 1875 and founded the Chicago *Daily News,* the trail-blazing "writer's newspaper" published continuously until its demise in 1978.

The early-arriving Norwegians established community life at May and Erie Streets, near Chicago Avenue and the waterworks. Unlike the Swedes, who moved steadily northward, the Norwegians pushed farther west—into Logan Square in the aesthetically pleasing Humboldt Park neighborhood with its lovely gray-stone buildings and spacious boulevards. Wicker Park, home to poet and author Nelson Algren, was populated by a sizable Norwegian colony by the 1920s. The Norwegian Lutheran Church Memorial Church at 2614 N. Kedzie Boulevard anchored the community for a period of forty years or so until the Hispanics poured into the neighborhood in the

1960s. Today Norwegian-Americans are widely dispersed across the city and Northwest Suburbs.

In the 1920s, the heyday of the Norwegian singing clubs and fraternal societies, the sons and daughters of Thor and Odin seized upon Mayor Thompson's fiery campaign rhetoric to petition the city for an official correction of the historical record which snubbed Leif Eriksson. The "call to arms" was first sounded at the Norwegian Centennial Celebration of 1925. "It has been established as historical fact that Leif Eriksson set foot on the eastern shore of the American continent 500 years before the voyage of Columbus," declared Mrs. Berthe C. Peterson, vice-president and spokesperson for the Norwegian National League.

According to Professor R. B. Anderson, a foremost authority on the life and times of the Norseman, Eriksson lost his way and landed on the New England coast between Massachusetts and Rhode Island sometime around the year 1000. The exact location was never established. The Norwegians based their claim on purely circumstantial evidence. Eriksson called the land "Vinland," because of the abundance of wild grapes he found growing on the shore. These same grapes are indigenous to New England. President Calvin Coolidge, speaking at the 1925 Norwegian League convention in Minneapolis, accepted the findings without reservation. Mrs. Peterson went ahead and drafted a resolution calling on Thompson to support the Leif Eriksson movement. Her motives appear to have been something less than altruistic. "Our request is particularly timely because of the present controversy about un-American school books and because a $10,000 prize has just been offered for the best new American history written for the Chicago Public Schools!"

The outcome of this controversy was never resolved to Mrs. Peterson's satisfaction, nor to that of the combined Norwegian fraternal societies that abounded in Chicago at that time. But weep not for Leif Eriksson. The memory of the intrepid Viking, who established the first permanent European settlement in Greenland, was memorialized in Lincoln Park in the form of a curious nautical monument that arrived in the city in time for the 1893 World's Columbian Exposition. In honor of Leif Eriksson, Norway sent a replica Viking ship under the command of Captain Magnus Anderson to Chicago. The tiny vessel set sail from the port city of Bergen on April 30, 1893. Anderson and his men crossed the Atlantic, passed through the canals, the Great Lakes, and toward Chicago. Off the coast of Evanston, the latter-day Vikings were greeted by a small flotilla of Chicago boats, which escorted the craft to the foot of Van Buren Street, where the captain and crew were greeted by Mayor Carter Harrison I. The Viking long boat was placed on temporary display at the World's Fair, and was later donated to the Field Museum of Natural History.

Captain Anderson's boat was ignored and nearly forgotten when a group of ladies from the Norwegian Women's Federation started a campaign to relocate the boat to a more visible location in Lincoln Park. Money was raised to reinforce the rotting timbers, and when work was completed, the long boat was presented to the state as a historic monument. There it would remain for another generation: a Chicago oddity most people took for granted, or simply didn't understand.

The 25-ton Viking boat was maintained by the Cook County Commissioners and displayed in back of the Lincoln Park children's zoo for many years until the Chicago Park District reclaimed the land for expansion in 1993. The American Scandinavian Council agreed to purchase the boat for $1 contingent upon their ability to pay the relocation costs.

The Council planned to restore the boat to its former magnificence and display it permanently along the Chicago lakefront. The Council contracted with the Belding Corporation of West Chicago to remove the boat from its land-locked mooring in Lincoln Park. But instead of a long overdue restoration, the historic boat remains under a canvas tarp in the Belding yards in West Chicago, prisoner to a contract dispute between the Scandinavian Council and Belding.

The final fate of the Viking long boat remains in doubt as the warring parties attempt to thrash out an agreement suitable to all concerned. It is a sad plight for the boat, and for the Sons of Norway, a fraternal society whose Midwestern members representing Illinois, Indiana, Michigan, and Wisconsin celebrated their 100th anniversary on January 14, 1995—at a time when the Belding Corporation threatened to sell the boat to Vesterheim, a Norwegian-American museum located in (of all places) Decorah, Iowa.

Attractions

Cultural Institutions

Swedish American Museum, *5211 N. Clark St., Chicago, (773) 728-8111. Closed Mondays. Admission fee charged. Members free. Kerstin B. Lane, Executive Director.*

Begin your visit of Andersonville here, midway between Foster and Winona avenues, on the east side of Clark Street. From its modest beginnings in a tiny storefront on Clark Street in 1976, the Swedish American Museum today occupies a 24,000-square-foot gallery that is rich in history and folklore. The center provides space for permanent and traveling exhibitions, and various outreach programs for senior citizens, children, and the handicapped. Swedish language instruction, special concerts, "Svensk Gammaldans"

(Swedish dance lessons), and guest speakers are scheduled by Ms. Lane during the calendar year. Call for additional details. The new expanded center was dedicated on April 19, 1988, by his Majesty Carl XVI Gustaf, King of Sweden, who journeyed to the United States to celebrate the 350th anniversary of the founding of the first permanent Swedish settlement in America. *Recommended.*

Scandinavian-American Cultural Society, *2323 N. Wilkie Rd., Arlington Heights, (847) 870-1710. Membership available. Saga Restaurant is open for dinner Wednesday–Friday, and for Sunday brunch.*

In 1979, four old and venerable Scandinavian organizations faced the grim prospect of extinction.There was understandable concern for the future of the various Scandinavian fraternal societies in Chicago. The famous Swedish Club had already closed. The membership of the Dania Society, founded by Danish immigrants in 1862, was dwindling. Skjold Lodge #100, the local chapter of the Sons of Norway, and the Normennenes Singing Society, a 125-year-old Chicago institution, voiced the same concerns. So, in the spirit of cooperation, the fiercely independent groups joined with the Danish American Athletic Club and agreed to pool their resources and unite in the spirit of Scandinavia. The four organizations got together and purchased the former home of the Elks Lodge in Arlington Heights, just east of Highway 53. Today the flags of Sweden, Norway, Iceland, Denmark, Finland, and the United States fly proudly from the flagpoles on the grounds. The center features a wide variety of cultural activities. Saga Restaurant offers a smorgasbord of Scandinavian food. The Danish-American Athletic Club sponsors a soccer team—the Danish Dynamite—that plays matches around the city. The annual Christmas bazaar lures up to 2,000 visitors, and the folk dancing troops perform their routines at various times. Thor Fjell, a sales representative from Naperville whose father emigrated from Norway in 1927, is the President of the Society.

Annual Events and Celebrations

Midsommarfest (Midsummerfest). *Last weekend in June, traditionally June 25–26. For dates and times, call (312) 728-2995.*

This is one of the great neighborhood festivals in Chicago. The business district of Clark Street between Foster and Berwyn in closed off to automobile traffic to raise the Maypole for the Swedish ethnic dancers and folk groups. *Recommended.*

Leif Eriksson Day. *Saturday closest to Columbus Day, October.*

Any Swede worth his salt herring will tell you that the famous Viking explorer crossed the Atlantic around the year 1000 and stumbled across a country he named Vinland, four hundred years before Columbus. Well, at least the regulars at Simon's Tavern on Clark Street will tell you that. Call (312) 728-2995 for dates and information about the equally famous Viking performances in Andersonville.

St. Morten's Gos Dag (St. Martin's Goose Day). *Second or third week of November.*

An ancient festival celebrating St. Martin of Tours has gained new meaning in Andersonville's Swedish community. For centuries this holiday was important to farmers, marking the end of the autumn harvest and the beginning of the Christmas season. Roast goose was the traditional meal, served with "svartsoppa" (black soup). For the past 150 years St. Morten's Gos Day has been observed in Skåne, Sweden—the southernmost province.

Festival of Song, *Scandinavian-American Cultural Society, 2323 N. Wilkie Rd., Arlington Heights, (847) 870-1710. Friday evening before Palm Sunday. Free admission to the concert; charge for supper.*

Hosted by the Normennenes Singing Society, showcasing the talents of ten to twelve male choruses from around Illinois. The choruses represent Denmark, Estonia, Norway, Sweden, Finland, and Germany. Buffet supper.

Sons of Norway Heritage Night. *Scandinavian-American Cultural Society, 2323 N. Wilkie Rd., Arlington Heights, (847) 870-1710. Last weekend in April.*

Crafts show. Singing groups. Dance troops. Buffet dinner optional.

Easter Brunch at the SACS. *Scandinavian-American Cultural Society, 2323 N. Wilkie Rd., Arlington Heights, (847) 870-1710. Easter Sunday.*

All-you-can-eat smorgasbord includes roast pork, specially prepared herring, ham, and an out-of-this-world sweet table. Musical entertainment. Reservations required. Book early.

Norwegian Constitution Day Concert, *Norwegian*
Lutheran Memorial Church, 2614 N. Kedzie Blvd.,
Chicago, (773) 252-7335. On or around May 17.

Despite changing demographics in Humboldt Park, the Norwegian Church
has retained its uniquely Scandinavian flavor. During the year it sponsors
several musical performances from various traveling choral societies, such
as the K. C. singers of Kristelig Gymnasium, Oslo. The Constitution Day
concert is an annual event.

Christmas Events

Andersonville has recreated the traditional Christmas holiday with banners
hung from the street poles. Candles are placed in the storefronts, and roast
goose dinners are the featured entrees in the restaurants. Goose liver pate is
served in the shops along with the other Yuletide delight—Swedish glogg.
Prizes and giveaways at selected retail establishments. Call (773) 728-2995
for a schedule of events.

Lucia Day (The Festival of Lights). *Call*
(773) 728-2995 for additional information.

Andersonville commemorates this most important of all Swedish holidays
with a Lucia pageant sponsored by Ebenezer Lutheran Church. The Chicago
Lucia queen and her court will, weather permitting, lead a procession down
Clark Street from the Philadelphia Church, 5437 Clark at Rascher. At the
Swedish-American Museum the girls will lead the crowd in an hour of
Christmas carols and traditional holiday music. Santa Claus will drop by,
with hot apple cider and ginger-flavored cookies known as pepperkakor.

Outlying Areas

Swedish Days, *held at alternate sites in Geneva,*
located 36 miles west of Chicago (take I-29 west to
Ill. 88, to Kirk Road, exit north I-38, West). Held the
Tuesday through Sunday after Father's Day (June).
For additional information, call (630) 232-6060.

The festivities begin with a street carnival near the courthouse at 4th and
James Street. A craft show, a "Kid's Day," with such activities as a parade,
a Big Wheel derby, and jump-rope and free-throw competitions in the afternoon kick off the extravaganza. Nightly entertainment on a central stage
nearby. A "Swedish Days" parade closes out the festival on Sunday, beginning at 7th and State streets.

Scandinavian Day, *Vasa Park, Route 31, Elgin. Second weekend in September. Call (847) 774-SCAN for details.*

A multicultural outdoor picnic featuring the music, folk customs, gift items, and food delicacies of Sweden, Norway, Finland, Denmark, and Iceland. A huge event that lures Scandinavians from all over the Midwest.

Scandinavian Children's Day (Vasa Barnens Dag), *Vasa Park, Route 31, Elgin. Second Sunday in June. Call Marion Johnson at (847) 679-4774 for details. Admission fee charged.*

One-day ethnic festival. Music, folk dancing, games, booths, and entertainment provided by the children's auxiliary of the Swedish fraternal societies.

Annual Svithiod Day Outing at Vasa Park, *Route 31, Elgin. Third or fourth Sunday in June. Call Marion Johnson at (847) 679-4774 for details. Free admission. $1.00 parking.*

Varied entertainment and traditional refreshments served all day. In the old days, this was the one event on the Swedish social calendar that everyone circled. Salt herring. Cold beer. Mosquitoes. The combination was irresistible.

Swedish Day/Mid-Summer Festival, *Good Templar Park, 528 Eastside Drive, Geneva, IL. Weekend after Father's Day (June). For information, call Allan Peaslee at (630) 543-8909.*

This is the oldest continuing Swedish festival in Chicago, dating back to 1911 when it was held on the shore of Lake Michigan in Evanston. Good Templar Park was acquired by the International Order of Good Templars in 1925 for the sum of $32,000. Nowadays the Mid-Summer Fest coincides with Father's Day and Swedish Days in Geneva, and features a traditional herring breakfast, games, and performances by the children's dance troop Varblomman.

Places to See

Neighborhood Architecture

When initially settled, Andersonville and Edgewater were neighborhoods of single-dwelling homes. But by the 1920s, two-flats and high-rise apartment buildings were constructed to accommodate a growing population, and soon the communities became some of the most densely populated areas in all of Chicago.

If you leave the Clark Street business district and walk east down Berwyn to Wayne, you find yourself in the Lakewood-Balmoral neighborhood, where two-story walkups and courtyard apartment buildings coexist with the spacious single-family bungalows. Several fine examples of early 1900s architecture survive, including an example of the Prairie style at 5347 N. Lakewood Avenue near Balmoral, three blocks east of Clark Street.

A Queen Anne built by John Lewis Cochrane in 1893 survives at 5426 N. Lakewood. Cochrane was a real estate developer who purchased large tracts of land between Foster and Bryn Mawr and sold his Edgewater homes for prices ranging from $5,100 to $12,000. "No two alike," he promised. At 1430 W. Berwyn Avenue stands the Andersonville "Castle," a large, rambling, Gothic-Romanesque graystone home built for a prosperous Swedish family in 1904. An Italian garden complete with fountain is one of the charming features of this old landmark.

North of Andersonville at 1500 W. Elmdale stands the Immanuel Lutheran Church, whose congregation dates back to 1854, the time of the earliest Swedish settlement in this community. The modern facility was built in 1922; the three church bells in the center of the lawn are relics of the original building, destroyed in the Chicago Fire. The Immanuel Church is located at the northwest corner of Elmdale and Greenview, a block east of Clark. Phone (773) 743-1820.

North Park College

When the Swedish Evangelical Mission Covenant College and Seminary opened in Chicago on September 18, 1894, a published announcement cautioned students residing near the Loop not to attempt to make the long trip at night. The best way to reach the distant North Side, they said, was to take the Chicago and Northwestern railroad to the Summerdale Station on Foster Avenue. Standing forlornly out in the middle of what was then empty farmland, the tiny college and theological seminary founded by Swedish immigrant members of the Evangelical Covenant Church was a lonely sight.

Its one building, affectionately known as the Old Main, became the center of campus life for the modern North Park College and Theological Seminary, which occupies twenty acres of land four miles west of Andersonville on Foster Avenue. Today the school is a four-year liberal arts college. Cultural ties to Sweden, Denmark, and Norway are fostered through the Center for Scandinavian Studies, which began a student exchange program in 1977.

The Old Main, *3225 W. Foster Ave., Chicago,*
(773) 583-2700.

The focal point of the campus is the Old Main, constructed in 1892 and opened two years later. After the building was designated as a National

Historic Landmark, the Old Main Preservation Society raised nearly $1.2 million to finance an extensive renovation project. In November 1986, the building was reopened to the public. The Old Main houses the campus hospitality lounge, the reception lobby, and the public relations, admissions, and alumni affairs offices.

The Center for Scandinavian Studies. *For more information and a calendar of events, call (773) 583-2700.*

Located on the campus, the center serves the undergraduate student population and members of the community at large. Classes, lectures, special exhibits, and choral and dramatic performances are open to the public. Artisans, musicians, writers, and political figures from each of the five Nordic countries appear from time to time.

Shops

Andersonville is Chicago's very own Scandinavian community, with a variety of charming little shops, delicatessens, restaurants, and bakeries easily accessible by car or public transportation. Many of the retailers are second- and third-generation children of immigrants who have maintained the family business down through the years. The business district of Andersonville stretches from Foster to Bryn Mawr, with the greatest concentration of stores south of Catalpa. The small shops remain open until early evening, with extended holiday hours.

The Landmark of Andersonville, *5301 N. Clark St., Chicago, (773) 728-5301. Closed Mondays.*

Opened in 1987, the Landmark is a gallery of 21 different boutiques under the roof of a renovated turn-of-the-century building. Antiques, collectibles, toys, books, health food, and a sweet shop make the Landmark a place to see in Andersonville. Be sure to see Jan Baxter's blue-and-yellow broom, tucked in a corner behind the cash register.

O. M. Nordling Jewelers, *5249 N. Clark St., Chicago, (773) 561-9526. Closed Monday–Wednesday. Hours subject to change.*

Ossian Nordling was a jeweler's apprentice when he decided to open his Andersonville store in 1935. The family business is conducted in the same location today by his son Tom, whose customers come from as far away as Iowa and Minnesota, and with good reasons. Nordling's is perhaps the only jeweler in Chicago who can order custom-made items directly from Swedish craftspeople. There is a distinct Swedish style, reflected in the elegant gold chains and the bridal crowns that have been sold to many a proud parent whose daughter was about to walk down the aisle. Hand-made crystal from Orrefors, Kosta-Boda, and other leading Swedish glass manufacturers are on display and available for sale. *Recommended.*

Erickson's, *5304 N. Clark St., Chicago, (773) 275-2010. Closed Sundays.*

Silver, Waterford crystal, Lalique. Discounts on retail sales.

Wikstrom's Gourmet Shop and Catering Co., *5247 N. Clark St., (773) 878-0601. Open daily.*

Ingvar Wickstrom came to the United States in 1959 as an exchange student from Skåne. He's still here and serving up homemade limpa bread, imported smoked salmon, herring, vasa bread, and fine cheeses. Crawfish season is in August, and you can bet the old-timers who congregate in the front of his store will have their tables reserved. *Recommended.*

Erikson's Delicatessen, *5250 N. Clark St., (773) 561-5634. Open daily.*

Just an old-fashioned Swedish deli. No frills. Just lots of good food for sale. Fruk-soppa (fruit soup), potato sausage, herring, pea soup, crawfish (in season), and everything else needed for the perfect smorgasbord.

The Swedish Bakery, *5348 N. Clark St., (773) 561-8919. Closed Sundays.*

Fancy marzipan cakes, "vort limpa" bread, pepperkakor, coffee cakes, all freshly baked on the premises. *Recommended.*

Outlying Areas

The Sweden Shop, *3304 Foster Ave., Chicago, (773) 478-0327. Closed Sundays.*

Across the street from North Park College, between Kedzie and Kimball. A department store of Swedish merchandise, and it's not even in Andersonville. For nearly forty years the Sweden Shop has imported the finest Scandinavian glassware from the glass-blowing regions of Småland. Each piece is carefully hand-crafted, reflecting old-world detail and craftsmanship. Porcelain, hand-made wooden clogs, dolls, clothing, and pastries are available for sale. Gift items can be shipped directly anywhere in the country. *Recommended.*

Scandinavian Boutique, *18135 Harwood,*
Homewood, (708) 799-2150. Closed Sundays.

Billed as the southern suburbs' largest Scandinavian gift and needlework shop, Scandinavian Boutique celebrated its 25th anniversary in 1996. Features Orrefors, Bing & Grondahl, Royal Copenhagen, and Rörstrand china; clogs; Cairn gnomes; imported and domestic table linens; jewelry; dried food and candies; DMC Balger metallics; Danish flower thread; needlepoint and needlepoint kits; linen; and imported fabrics.

The Scandinavian Affair, *12246 S. Harlem Ave.,*
Palos Heights, (708) 448-4464. Closed Sundays.

Offers its shoppers complimentary Swedish coffee and pepperkakor. Specializing in Swedish imported goods, with a large number of Finnish and Norwegian goods as well. Woven rugs; lace curtains; table runners; crystal; Dale of Norway sweaters; dala horses; clogs; Christmas decorations; and gourmet food.

Restaurants

Ann Sather Restaurant, *two locations: 5207 N. Clark St., (773) 271-6677, and 929 W. Belmont. (773) 348-2378. Clark location: open for breakfast and lunch daily and dinner Saturday and Sunday. Belmont location: open for breakfast, lunch, and dinner daily.*

Ann Sather preserves all the warm memories of an old-fashioned Swedish country kitchen. Enjoy a traditional Scandinavian meal of herring, meatballs, potatoes, and rice pudding topped by lingonberries in pleasant surroundings. Roast goose dinner served on St. Morten's Day.

Svea Restaurant, *5236 N. Clark St., (773) 334-9619. Open for breakfast and lunch daily.*

"Simply the best Swedish pancakes in Andersonville," promises owner Kurt Mathiasson, cofounder of the Swedish American Museum directly across the street. Kurt is the resident Andersonville Viking. Costumed in traditional Viking clothing, he will, on occasion, lead the Saturday morning sweeping brigade.

Simon's Tavern, *5210 N. Clark St., (773) 878-0894. Open daily.*

Try Simon's for glogg (pronounced "glewg"). Simon Lundberg, the founder, has gone to his reward, but his son Roy still brews up the homemade glogg for the regulars on Clark Street every November. Glogg is a potent mix of hot port wine blended with raisins, aquavit (Swedish vodka) and other spices. They come by the busload to purchase this traditional Yuletide drink. Simon's is a real Chicago bar, dimly lit in deep earthy tones. Old Simon opened his bar in 1934, serving the rough-hewn Swede carpenters who sat for hours talking business, always business, and in the lilting tongue of Skåne, Småland, Dalarna, Dalsland, and the other regions of Sweden whence they came. Those were the days when a man could eat a meatball sandwich and potatoes for the price of a beer. It's no longer possible to feed an army of hungry working men in a tavern, but Simon's retains the look and feel of a real prohibition bar. This is the way a tavern used to be—no ferns, glass, or peppy waitresses. Escape the cold of winter or the heat of summer to trade gossip with someone you know.

The Bishop Hill Settlement

Though a few hours' drive outside Chicago, and about twenty miles northeast of Carl Sandburg's Galesburg, the Bishop Hill Settlement is worth the trip. It was established in 1846 by Erik Jansson, a self-styled prophet who ran into trouble with the leaders of the Swedish Lutheran Church. He told his followers that peace could be found in the American west and envisioned a village based on communal ownership of land with absolute devotion to the leader and the ideal.

After arriving in Chicago by way of the Great Lakes, the Janssonites walked the rest of the way, a distance of 160 miles. Western Illinois offered rich opportunities, and the colony flourished for fifteen years before dissolving in a sea of controversy, financial mismanagement, and a breakdown in its religious unity. When a spat with a stranger named John Root over Jansson's comely cousin Charlotte led the suitor to murder its founder, the community broke up.

Today Bishop Hill survives as a uniquely preserved museum listed as a National Historic Landmark in the Register of Historic Places. Swedish heritage is preserved year round, but Christmas at Bishop Hill is a special time for both the residents and tourists. Lucia nights are celebrated the second week of December, when Lucia queens serve pastries and coffee in museums and shops, all decorated for the holiday with brightly lit candles. Other good times to visit include Mid-summer Day at the end of June and Old Settler's Day in early September. For more information about Bishop Hill and nearby Galesberg, call the Heritage Association at (309) 927-3899.

A Publication for Scandinavians

The Sun, 637 S. Waukegan Road, Lake Forest IL (847) 295-5387, is an English language newspaper that keeps current with the latest doings in the Swedish, Norwegian, Danish, Finnish, and Icelandic communities of Chicago. A calendar of events is included in each issue. Subscriptions are $20 in the U.S. Call Karen Gagen for details.

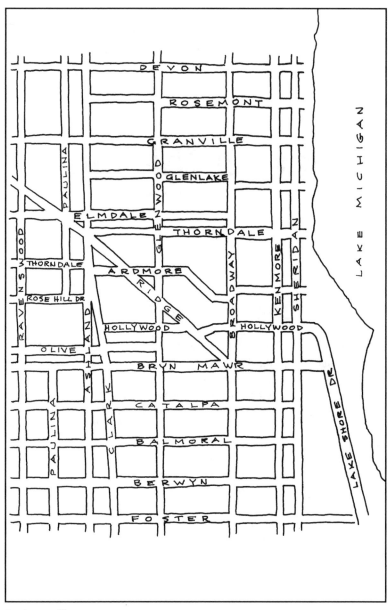

Andersonville

chapter five

Jewish Chicago

History and Settlement

Crowded, chaotic, noisy, and dirty—such were the images of the Maxwell Street open-air market that lingered in the shadow of the tall buildings on the West Side. This peculiar slice of ethnic culture came alive on Sunday mornings, in all its shabby glory. It was the world's largest flea market, where Gold Coast Yuppies rubbed elbows with the hustlers and con artists eager to make a few bucks selling hub caps, bootlegged video movies, and the kitchen sink. The bark of the carnival huckster and flimflam man filled the early morning air as the short order cooks grilled Polish sausage and the famous Maxwell Street pork chop for the Sabbath bargain hunters.

Maxwell Street, a symbol of Chicago's past vitality and Jewish immigrant culture, is no more. In the name of urban renewal the University of Illinois, Chicago campus laid claim to the last remaining vestige of turn-of-the-century immigrant life on the West Side. In the early 1960s urban planners flattened the Italian and Greek communities to make way for the new UIC campus. Now, the university has swallowed up the Maxwell environs for campus expansion. The impassioned pleas from community activists and neighborhood coalitions fell on deaf ears, and with the new construction came the demolition of eighty-year-old buildings and the final death knell to the essential *shtetl* character of old Maxwell Street. The city offered a pale compromise and said it would relocate the vendor booths from the marketplace east to Canal Street, but it was a token gesture that failed to stem the tide of lawsuits or soothe bruised feelings.

The old Maxwell Street ghetto, bounded by Canal, Halsted, Polk, and 15th streets, was densely populated by Eastern European Jews who lived in one- and two-story tenements in the back of kosher meat markets and second-hand furniture stores. Until 1923, when the city enacted stiff regulatory laws, real estate promoters would capitalize on the zoning loopholes by constructing two houses on one lot. Two, three, sometimes four families would be packed into these flimsy wooden lean-tos held together by baling wire and tar paper.

For the grandparents of the late Nathan Kaplan, their destiny was inter- twined with that of thousands of other Eastern European Jews who settled Maxwell Street from the 1880s until the outbreak of World War I. Their odyssey began in the tiny village of Bransk in Poland. "Myths of the new world stirred dreams," Kaplan wrote in his family genealogy. "My grand- parents, parents, aunts, and uncles were part of the historic European migration that poured into the U.S. between 1881 and 1923. The Jewish immigration differed from that of other Europeans in one major respect: Jews turned their backs on the land of their origin. Other Europeans came, but not all intended to stay. One of every three returned. Ninety-five out of a hundred Jewish arrivals stayed. The Orthodox Jews perceived America as a heathen country where Judaism would be endangered. Apparently my grandparents, though firm believers, did not have such fears."

Grandmother Shifrasrah Brinsky and Grandfather Nathan Brinsky, instilled with a sense of awakening and guided by their faith in the God of Abraham, settled on Maxwell Street. The Eastern European Jews faced the usual poverty, economic despair, and ethno-religious prejudices previously reserved for the Irish Catholics and Italians. The earliest arriving Jews came from the Germanic corridor: Prussia, Austria, Bohemia, and sections of modern-day Poland. The growth of the Jewish population in Chicago was in part due to historic oppression aimed against Jews in their native lands. By 1900 the Yiddish-speaking Jews outnumbered the earlier-arriving German Jews, whose presence in Chicago was noted as early as 1832—five years before Chicago's incorporation. In 1845, the first Yom Kippur services were conducted above a storefront at the southwest corner of Wells and Lake streets.

A year later the "Jewish Burial Society" was organized to provide for the dead. They purchased an acre of ground on the present site of the baseball field in Lincoln Park. This was Chicago's first Jewish cemetery. Within two years a deadly outbreak of Asiatic cholera filled the available plots. This, of course, only served to discourage future newcomers from settling along the banks of Lake Michigan. As the crisis worsened, community leaders welded together the Kehilath Anshe Mayriu (Congregation of the People of the West), or K.A.M.. In June, 1851, the congregation built the first Jewish synagogue, at Clark and Adams, a site now occupied by the Kluczynski Federal Building. By 1857 there were four congregations, but they were bitterly divided along ethnic lines. The Bavarian Jews, still the predominant group at the time, had little regard for their struggling counterparts from Eastern Europe.

Henry Greenebaum, an important figure in early Jewish Chicago, objected to the divisiveness of his own people, and wondered what steps might be taken to attain religious and cultural unity. Greenebaum was one of four brothers who arrived here in the midst of the cholera epidemic. He belonged to the Bavarian K.A.M. group, but vocalized his opposition to its exclusionary policies by joining the B'Nai Sholom Congregation. He served as the group's first secretary until the K.A.M. threatened him with expulsion. Young Greenebaum was vociferous in his criticisms. "And another thing, why so much concern about cemeteries? Why not provide for the living?" So, in 1857, he founded the first B'nai B'rith lodge—Number 33—and proclaimed a new era of cooperation between peoples as they united for common cause. "Here," Greenebaum exclaimed, "some of the best minds of German and Polish Jews joined hands to remove miserable provincial barriers existing in Chicago." In 1856 Greenebaum's organizational genius was rewarded with his election to the Chicago City Council. He became the first Jewish alderman, representing the old Sixth Ward.

A close friend of Stephen A. Douglas, Greenebaum was an ardent Unionist during the Civil War. He was one of the notable men in Illinois, not only in the political realm, but in the world of finance as well. When his bank smoldered in ruins during the Chicago Fire, he informed his depositors that they could come and receive their money once the vaults cooled down. It was an uncommon expression of charity and good will at a time of widespread looting and rapacity, when the civil authorities were hard put to safeguard the city.

The expansion of the Jewish community after the Great Fire of 1871 was steady if not spectacular. The flames swept away many German-Jewish residences near the downtown business district, forcing many of these people to move farther south along Michigan, Wabash, and Indiana avenues. By the 1920s, Washington Park, Kenwood, Hyde Park, and South Shore were heavily populated by prosperous German Jews. The University of Chicago, located in staid, austere Hyde Park, benefited from the warm financial support of such philanthropists from the retail business community as Julius Rosenwald and Leon Mandel.

Reflecting the outward movement from the central city, the K.A.M. Congregation relocated from downtown to Indiana and 26th streets, the first of seven moves in its long and storied history. The South Side German Jews were prosperous, upscale, and innovative. Despite claims to the contrary, they identified more closely with German culture than with the strict Orthodoxy practiced by the Eastern Europeans who lived in the Maxwell Street ghetto.

The assimilated German Jews published several newspapers, notably the *Jewish Advocate,* a weekly journal devoted to social issues and progressive Judaism. In 1880 the cornerstone for what was to become the future home of Michael Reese Hospital was laid at 29th and Ellis streets on the South Side.

The first Jewish hospital was erected at Schiller and Goethe streets on the North Side in 1868, through the efforts of the Hebrew Relief Association. When the facility was reduced to a pile of smoldering rubble in the 1871 fire, the relatives of Michael Reese set out to obtain a desirable site location on the South Side. Michael Reese, oddly enough, never set foot in Chicago. He made his fortune in the California Gold Rush, and willed his estate to his civic-minded kin back in Chicago for worthy causes.

The opening of the Michael Reese Hospital in 1882 on the site of the old Sherman Stockyards marked the beginning of an era of unbridled scientific accomplishment and service to the community. By the 1940s, the prestigious facility, with its 718 beds, had become the largest voluntary hospital in the Chicago area. However, much of the surrounding neighborhood became engulfed in urban blight in the 1960s. Hospital administrators were forced to make a hard decision about their future role in the community. The choice boiled down to denying the low-income residents essential medical services, or re-committing the available resources in their familiar urban setting. The planning board hired a professional staff to oversee a neighborhood expansion project, and today Michael Reese remains one of Chicago's major medical centers, even though the German Jewish "Golden Ghetto" is no more.

Before 1880 the Eastern European Jews represented a very small fraction of the city's Jewish population. The handful of Russian Jews who lived in Chicago before 1871 resided in an area near Federal and Harrison streets. The uprooting caused by the Chicago Fire and the period of civic rebuilding that followed pushed these people to the west of the central business district, and the Germans to the South Side. Events taking shape on the European continent spurred a tide of immigration that was to last a full fifty years (1880–1930).

Following the assassination of Czar Alexander II in 1881, the Russian government instituted a brutal crackdown against the Jews, who were falsely accused of subversive activity. The Jews were charged with the systematic murder of Christian children during the festival of Pesach or Passover. The "pogrom"—a Russian word meaning devastation—was an invention of the czarist government to divert political and social discontent from existing conditions toward a convenient scapegoat, the Jew. The suppression of Jewish culture and the murder of thousands of peasants occurred at a time of rising Jewish nationalism.

The movement to create a Jewish homeland of Zion was outlined by Leo Pinsker (1821–91) in Russia and by Theodor Herzl (1860–1904) in Austria. The Zionist movement ultimately led to the creation of the modern state of Israel in 1948, but not before decades of persecution at the hands of the host governments of Europe. Driven from their homelands with only the shirts on their backs and whatever could be carried in a torn and tattered valise, thousands of Russian and Polish Jews flooded into the near West Side of Chicago, displacing many Germans and Irish who once lived there.

The Jewish ghetto encompassed much of the area between Canal and Halsted streets—the Maxwell Street market—which was an embodiment of Russian Poland. Yiddish was spoken here, and the members of the community who subscribed to the Orthodox and Conservative movements of Judaism were free to worship as they pleased. Hebrew schools and Yiddish theaters were organized. Forty Orthodox synagogues were all within walking distance of the heart of the ghetto—the intersection of Halsted and Maxwell streets. By the early 1900s, it was estimated that 50,000 Eastern European Jews lived in close proximity to their houses of worship on the West Side.

Year	Chicago Population	Jewish Population	Percentage
1880	503,185	10,000	2.0
1900	1,698,575	75,000	4.5
1910	2,185,283	135,000	6.0
1920	2,701,705	225,000	8.0

The ghetto featured kosher food stores, matzo bakeries, and hundreds of peddler wagons and pushcarts, where down-and-out entrepreneurs tried to hustle a few cents selling fruit and vegetables in the muddy streets. Above the storefronts of the dilapidated wooden tenements, hundreds of Jews worked in the most squalid conditions manufacturing garments. The city's clothing industry quickly grew into a $50,000,000 business by 1900. Jews accounted for 68.6 percent of all Chicago tailors in 1910, but they earned less than $8 a week and were often required to put in twelve to eighteen hours a day. The famous clothing strike against Hart, Schaffner, and Marx and other large clothiers in September 1910 capped off an era of growing disenchantment among these laboring classes. The strike was spearheaded by Sidney Hillman, Jacob Potofsky, and Bessie Abramovitz, who organized Jewish workers against a powerful Jewish manufacturing concern—a phenomenon in those days when labor and capital represented different races, nationalities, and religions. Under the leadership of Hillman and

Abramovitz—who later wed—the newly organized Amalgamated Clothing Workers Union of America won important concessions from management, concessions which led to a better standard of living for the men and women who toiled into the night at the Maxwell Street sweatshops.

Maxwell Street exists only in the collective memories of the people who earned their livelihoods there. In its heyday, the street wore the trappings of free enterprise. The liveliest debate in town was not in "Bug House" Square, where orange crate orators espoused socialism, but between buyer and seller haggling over the price of a pair of knickers on Sunday morning at Maxwell and Halsted. It was a congested, overcrowded, reeking marketplace. Many of the residential dwellings lacked proper ventilation, plumbing, a bathtub, or a commode. By 1900 the Jewish population strained at the seams. In his 1952 survey of economic conditions in Chicago, Erich Rosenthal of Queens College in New York estimated that 50 percent of the Russian Jewish immigrants lived in ghetto conditions by 1915. The community was replete with gambling dens, houses of ill repute, and low cesspools of vice—which coexisted alongside synagogues and the beth hamedrash, or house of learning. Along Morgan and Green streets on the near West Side, Mike "de Pike" Heitler procured women of easy virtue, dice, liquor, and even cocaine, while paying a fealty to the Irish police captains who commanded the Des Plaines Street District.

The rise of the Jewish gangster after the turn of the century—Ike Bloom (née Gitelson), Jack Guzik, Davey Miller and Samuel "Nails" Morton—was an alarming, but not surprising, development. The ghetto was tough and mean, and fostered lawlessness in varying degrees when the teachings of the rabbi fell on deaf ears. Some, like Morton and Miller, were roguish Robin Hoods, interested to a certain extent in the welfare of their own people. Miller operated a restaurant and gym, and could always be counted on to come to the aid of elderly Jews who were attacked and beaten in Douglas Park by gangs of young hooligans.

Nails Morton was another product of Maxwell Street. During World War I he was awarded the Croix de Guerre after leading a raiding party "over-the-top" against a trench of German soldiers who had pinned down an entire company of American soldiers. Morton flushed them out, but met an untimely death several years later on the Lincoln Park bridle path, when his horse kicked him to death. Gangsters like Heitler, Bloom, and Guzik were vicious white slave traffickers who lacked the élan of Davey Miller. The *Jewish Courier,* founded in 1887 as a weekly (but later converted to a daily sheet), cautioned its readers to remain vigilant against this class of men and the "moral filth" of the ghetto.

After 1905 overcrowding and a changing economic picture resulted in an exodus from Maxwell Street for the safer, more pleasant residential neighborhoods of the South Side, and the Douglas Park-Lawndale communities farther west. Douglas Boulevard, fronting a fully landscaped park designed and laid out by architect William LeBaron Jenney in 1880, became the Jewish "Main Street" by the 1920s. At first the German and Irish landlords refused to rent apartment flats to the Jews, but through their sheer numbers and the availability of low-cost mortgages, Lawndale became a predominantly Jewish neighborhood by 1920. The Congregation Ansae Kneseth Israel was opened on Douglas Boulevard in 1913. It soon became known as the "Russian Shul" for the many Eastern European Jewish families that worshiped there. The rabbi of this temple was Ephraim Epstein (1877–1960), who rescued many Jewish exiles from Europe shortly before the outbreak of World War II. Epstein served his temple from 1911 until his death.

By 1927, there were more than 125 Jewish congregations scattered across the city. About 100 were Orthodox; the rest were Conservative or Reform. Yiddish newspapers were founded to emphasize the principles of Orthodox life in the United States, but increasingly the language underwent a subtle transformation, until a distinct Americanized Yiddish emerged. No doubt the change was a consequence of the desire among older Jewish residents of Chicago that the newer arrivals become more quickly assimilated. In a remarkably short time, the immigrants and their children absorbed American customs and participated directly in American institutions.

No longer excluded from the political process, the Jews of Lawndale exerted considerable influence at City Hall through their benefactors Mike and Moe Rosenberg, the 1920s patron saints of the 24th Ward Democratic machine. The brothers owned a junkyard and an iron metal company, but their rightful bailiwick was Chicago politics. The Rosenbergs pushed the selection of Governor Henry Horner in 1933, no small achievement during those highly partisan times. A decade earlier, the brothers had succeeded in placing 28-year-old Jacob Arvey in the alderman's chair.

Henry Horner, a distinguished probate judge who sat on the bench from 1914 to 1932, earned a reputation as Cook County's last "professional honest man." His compassion for widows, orphans, and the city's down-and-out was well known in legal circles. Horner was the grandson of one of Chicago's original Jewish settlers. In 1841, a young man, guided by ambition and instilled with the kind of forward-thinking outlook on life that turned dreams into reality, had arrived in frontier Chicago. Harry Horner laid the foundation for what was to become one of the city's largest wholesale grocery firms. He was also one of the founding members of the Chicago Board of Trade, and was well known among the old-timers until his illustrious grandson dwarfed his accomplishments a generation later in the political arena.

The generation of 1848 produced a number of business leaders less inclined to sully their reputations in the back alleys of Chicago politics. In the years that followed, German-Jewish parents encouraged their sons to pursue careers in law, finance, and the retail trade. Emanuel, Leon, and Simon Mandel founded a State Street department store that anchored the downtown shopping district for many years. Morris Selz and Sigmund Florsheim began their respective footwear businesses in Chicago.

Chicago's Jews were never a nationalistic people in the sense that the Germans were. The Russian, Polish, and Hungarian Jews who came later shared a common religious bond, and also a keen motivation to prosper within their chosen fields. Such was the case with the Rosenbergs, who succeeded in placing 28-year-old Jacob Arvey in the alderman's chair in the 1920s. Through the sheer force of his personality, Arvey, a Rosenberg protégé, became the floor leader of the city council and chairman of the finance committee. Arvey was a fixture in Chicago politics for many years, and might have become governor himself if not for the fact that the political sachems in the hall considered it politically expedient to avoid having one Jew in the mayor's office and another in the state house. To this day, there has not been a Jewish mayor of Chicago, though LaSalle Street businessman Bernard Epton waged an unsuccessful campaign against the late Mayor Harold Washington in 1987.

Mike Rosenberg served as 24th Ward committeeman and trustee of the Sanitary District until his death in 1928. Brother Moe succeeded him and went on to reshape the Democratic Party into the modern "machine" that endured in one form or another until the 1980s. Moe spent money like a drunken sailor in order to promote the election of friendly judges. He supported an ally from the Czech-Bohemian neighborhood, Anton J. Cermak, as the next mayor in 1931. Later, Moe Rosenberg outlined his strategy to a Congressional subcommittee that was investigating a powerful crony of his, utility magnate Samuel Insull: "We were not only looking to those judicial elections, to have Cermak become leader, but then we were looking to put Cermak in the mayor's chair, which we did."

Greater Lawndale remained a bustling Jewish community well into the 1940s, when it began to undergo profound racial changes. Erich Rosenthal estimated that 102,470 Jews resided here in 1940, but the numbers dropped by nearly half just six years later. The expansion of the black community, and the desire of many second- and third-generation Jews to leap-frog to the far North Side communities of Albany Park and Rogers Park, stripped the Lawndale community of its Jewish identity. The opening of the Ravenswood elevated line in 1907, and the Kedzie trolley seven years later, spurred the growth of Albany Park, annexed to the city when much of the property was farmland. Near the principal business district at Lawrence and Kedzie, thousands of transplanted Polish and Russian Jews from Lawndale and the greater West Side purchased two- and three-story flats and worshiped at the Orthodox, Reform, and Conservative synagogues that served the community's needs.

Jewish businesses from Lawndale were clustered along Lawrence Avenue between Pulaski and Kedzie for many years. By 1945, the Jewish population of Albany Park topped out at 35,000, but the area went into a slow decline, hastening the exodus to neighborhoods farther north. In the late 1960s and early 1970s, Asian Indians, Greeks, and Arabs began buying up commercial property. By 1979, there were only 13,000 Jews counted in Albany Park, most of them retired pensioners and senior citizens.

Today Chicago's Jewish community numbers some 240,000, but it is widely scattered across the metropolitan area and into the suburbs and collar counties. The largest concentration can be found in West Rogers Park between Kedzie, Western, Peterson and Howard streets, where a number of synagogues, bakeries, bookstores, restaurants, and fraternal associations keep alive the sense of community that seems to diminish each year.

West Rogers Park, like so many other diverse Chicago neighborhoods, is not restricted to just one group. Increasingly, the Jewish population is experiencing slow decline, while the Indian, Assyrian, and Asian presence is slowly transforming the composition of the area. Devon Avenue, from Ridge to California, resembles a miniature United Nations. Indicative of the rapidly changing patterns of settlement was the decision on the part of the Jewish community to sell Temple Mizpah (built at 1615 Morse in 1924) to the Koreans, who converted the facility into the Korean Presbyterian Church.

Where did they all go? To Skokie, Lincolnwood, and the North Shore suburbs, for the most part. By 1975, 40,000 of Skokie's 70,000 inhabitants were Jewish. The suburbanization of Chicago Jewry continues into the 1990s.

Many of Chicago's newer Jewish residents emigrated from Russia to escape Soviet discrimination and religious repression. The Soviet government listed their nationality as Jewish rather than Russian on their passports. With the doors of opportunity slamming shut in their face, the Soviet Jews who were fortunate enough to secure exist visas very often arrived in Chicago via the Joint Jewish Distribution Committee in Vienna. From there to Rome, and finally Chicago, where Rogers Park, adjacent Skokie, and parts of Des Plaines, Palatine, Wheeling, and Buffalo Grove have become "ports of entry."

Some 15,000 Soviet Jews have poured into Chicago in recent years. Many have found well-paying jobs in the industrial sector, and have saved up for the day when they can make their first down payment on a home in the quiet residential suburbs. Many older Jewish residents bemoan a corresponding loss of culture and tradition, perhaps forgetting that the younger generations often reassert their ancestral identities within the boundaries of the American value system.

Jewish Chicagoans are responsible for many of the city's most famous cultural institutions, including the Adler Planetarium, 1300 S. Lake Shore Dr. (planned and financed by Chicago businessman and philanthropist Max

Adler; dedicated in 1930); the Museum of Contemporary Art, 220 E. Chicago Ave. (founded in 1967 by Joseph Shapiro, a Russian Jew who started the museum with his own collection); and the Museum of Science and Industry, 57th St. and Lake Shore Dr., (rescued from neglect by the philanthropist and business tycoon Julius Rosenwald, who was also responsible for the construction of 5,357 schools, shops, libraries, and residential homes in 993 counties of the rural South).

In addition, the University of Chicago has produced several Jewish Nobel Prize winners, including Albert Michaelson (physics), Saul Bellow (literature), and Milton Friedman (economics). Professor Michaelson won the coveted Nobel Prize in 1907 for his studies of light, which contributed to Albert Einstein's theory of relativity. Bellow, who was actually born in Lachine, Quebec, a suburb of Montreal, captured the humorous and touching sides of Jewish life in Chicago in the *Adventures of Augie March* (1953). By the time he was eight years old, Bellow was fluent in French, English, Yiddish, and Hebrew. His Nobel Prize came in 1976, for *Humboldt's Gift*. Economist Friedman joined the University of Chicago faculty in 1946. He was awarded a Nobel Prize in 1976 for "achievements in the fields of consumption analysis, monetary history, and theory, and for his demonstration of the complexity of stabilization policy."

Getting There: The Howard Street elevated line links downtown with the Rogers Park community. The el makes six scheduled stops between Berwyn and Howard Street (at the city limit). The Devon (#155) bus begins at the Morse Avenue elevated stop and connects to West Rogers Park. By car from the Loop, take Lake Shore Drive north to the Foster Avenue exit. Follow Foster west to Western Avenue, and go north to Devon.

For additional information, call the CTA at (312) 836-7000.

Attractions

Cultural Institutions

Spertus Museum of Judaica, *618 S. Michigan Ave., Chicago, (312) 922-9012. Closed Saturdays. Admission fee charged. Membership available.*

Chicago's Spertus Museum teaches us the history of the Jewish people through traveling exhibitions, workshops, paintings, sculpture, costumes, and religious artifacts on permanent display. Founded in 1925 for the purpose of providing recent high school graduates with a basic program on Judaic studies, the museum was renamed in honor of Maurice and Herman Spertus in 1970. These gentlemen were the world's largest manufacturers of retail and wood frame pictures. Now in its seventh decade, the Spertus College of Judaica is an accredited graduate institution and a major learning resource center in the Midwest, offering classes in religious philosophy, Hebrew and Yiddish art, music, and culture. The Norman and Helen Asher Library on the fifth floor houses one of the greatest collection of Judaica in the nation, with over 70,000 volumes, back periodicals, musical collections, videos, and the Chicagoland Jewish Archives, which are available to serious researchers.

Bernard and Rochelle Zell Holocaust Memorial on the first floor of the Spertus museum relates the history of the Nazi persecution (1933–1945) through surviving artifacts, photographic documentation, and interesting sidelights into this darkest period of the human experience. The six pillars at the entrance record the names of Holocaust victims whose families reside in the Chicago area. The Paul and Gabriella Rosenbaum Artifact Center is considered to be a "hands-on" innovator in children's museum education, offering many classes and workshops for youngsters stressing the spiritual values of Jewish holidays. During the Hanukkah season, for example, children over the age of seven are taught how to construct menorahs. Through this kind of direct participation, they learn the significance of the holiday, which dates back to 165 BCE (Before Common Era), when a small army of Jews led by Maccabees reclaimed the second temple after it had been pillaged by the Syrian Greeks. With only a small jar of pure oil left behind, the Jews lit their menorah. According to legend, the lamps remained lit for a period of eight days. The miracle is celebrated by the Jewish people during the last week of December. *Recommended.*

Chicago Jewish Historical Society, *618 S. Michigan Ave., Chicago, (312) 663-5634. Membership available.*

Located on the second floor of the Spertus Museum, the Chicago Jewish Historical Society is interested in neighborhood settlement, the preservation of local archives, and issues of historical importance to the Jewish community. The Society sponsors a series of bus tours during the summer (see Annual Events), conducts monthly meetings, publishes a bimonthly periodical, and bestows a cash prize each year for the outstanding published monograph dealing with an aspect of Chicago Jewish history. Recently, the Jewish Historical Society reissued Hyman L. Meites' 1924 book, *History of the Jews in Chicago,* in a joint venture with Wellington Publishing.

National Jewish Theater, *5050 W. Church St., Skokie,*
(847) 675-2200. Admission fee charged. Credit cards
accepted.

A performing arts center featuring the works of Jewish playwrights, with themes of Jewish community. Four plays are given each year between October 2 and late June in a subscription series that has previously included such critically acclaimed presentations as *The Golem, Minnie's Boys* (a reverent look at the life of the Marx brothers), and *The Dybbuk.* Performances are given Wednesday, Thursday, Saturday, and Sunday afternoons at the 256-seat auditorium in the Mayer Kaplan Jewish Community Center. It is important to know that the plays are performed in English, not Yiddish.

Jewish Film Foundation, *6025 N. Christiana,*
Chicago, (773) 588-2763.

The JFF arranges special screenings of independent documentaries and dramatic films of special Jewish interest, at various commercial theaters throughout Chicago. These films would probably not reach a wider suburban audience if they were limited exclusively to the city's "art houses." While there is no membership or enrollment procedure, persons interested in being included on the mailing list are encouraged to contact the JFF.

Jewish Community Centers of Chicago

The neighborhood Jewish Community Centers of Chicago promote Jewish values in American life through a broad spectrum of educational, cultural, social, and athletic programs available to individuals, families, and groups. Each center is an independent Group Services Agency, with its own calendar of special events that may include dramatic presentations, lectures, classes, physical fitness, self-help sessions, counseling, child care, and various recreational programs. For more information, contact the appropriate center or the central offices of the Jewish Federation of Chicago, at 1 S. Franklin St., Chicago, IL 60606, (312) 346-6700.

Bernard Horwich JCC, *3003 W. Touhy Ave.,*
Chicago, (773) 761-9100.

Mayer Kaplan JCC, *5050 W. Church St., Skokie,*
(847) 675-2200.

Florence G. Heller JCC, *524 W. Melrose Ave.,*
Chicago, (773) 871-6780.

North Suburban JCC, *633 Skokie Hwy., Suite 407, Northbrook, (847) 205-9480.*

Northwest Suburban JCC, *1250 Radcliffe Rd., Buffalo Grove, (847) 392-7411.*

Anita M. Stone JCC, *18600 S. Governors Hwy., Flossmoor, (708) 799-7650.*

Hyde Park JCC, *1100 E. Hyde Park Blvd., Chicago, (773) 268-4600.*

Hamakor Gallery, *4150 W. Dempster St., Skokie, (847) 677-4150. Closed Saturdays.*

Full-service gift store and art gallery that sells ritual and ceremonial objects; limited edition prints and sculpture by American, Israeli, and other European artists; and Jewish books and audio and video cassettes. Periodic art exhibitions scheduled throughout the year.

Arthur M. Feldman Gallery, *1815 St. Johns Ave., Highland Park, (847) 432-8858. Closed Sundays, evening hours by appointment.*

Antique and contemporary Judaica; furniture, fine art, bridal registry, and appraisal service available.

Maya Polsky Gallery, *215 W. Superior St., Chicago, (312) 440-0055. Closed Saturday–Monday.*

Features the work of contemporary Soviet and Jewish artists, with a heavy emphasis on oil paintings and drawing. Maya Polsky, a Russian émigré, opened her gallery in February 1990 in River North. Since that time she has featured the first solo exhibition of Alexander Gazhur and Ukrainian painter Vladimir Bovkun.

Annual Events and Celebrations

Yom Ha'Atzmaut. *For location and additional information, call the Jewish Community Relations Council at (312) 357-4770. The event is free, but admission is by ticket only. Tickets available through major Jewish organizations.*

Annual celebration of the founding of Israel in 1948. The community-wide observance is sponsored by the Jewish Community Relations Council of the

United Fund, and the Chicago Zionist Foundation, and is held in mid-April. Special performances are given by the Combined Day Schools Choir, Israeli folk dancing troupes, and pop singers such as Aric Lavie. More than fifty organizations and synagogues participate in the traditional parade of organizations.

Annual Walk With Israel. *Call the closest Jewish Community Center (see list above) or the Jewish United Fund, (312) 444-2860.*

Fund-raising walkathon held at Jewish Community Centers and other locations in the Chicagoland area to provide financial support for essential humanitarian services in Israel, and for the care and feeding of Jewish refugees. This event has been held annually the first Sunday in May since 1971, and is a project of the Chicago Jewish Community Centers and the Young Leadership Division of the Jewish United Fund.

Annual Interfaith Dinner. *Westin O'Hare Hotel, 6100 River Rd., Rosemont. One Sunday in June or July. For ticket prices, advance reservations, and the date, call the Chicago Chapter of Magen David Adom, (773) 465-0664.*

Commemorating the anniversary of the State of Israel, and benefiting the Israeli Red Cross. Sponsored each year since 1966 by the Chicago Chapter of Magen David Adom. Banquet, oratory, and musical concert marking the founding of the Jewish state.

Jewish Community Center Hall of Fame Induction Banquet. *The Palmer House (or another downtown Chicago hotel). One Monday afternoon in June or July. For tickets and information, contact the Jewish Community Relations Council, (312) 357-4700.*

Banquet and ceremony honoring Jewish leaders who have demonstrated a commitment to worthy local causes and community service. Special guest speakers and presentations.

Raoul Wallenberg Humanitarian Awards Ceremony. *Sponsored by the Raoul Wallenberg Committee of Chicago, (312) 726-3555. Annually, usually in January; date and location vary.*

Swedish diplomat Raoul Wallenberg saved an estimated 100,000 Hungarian Jews from extermination at the hands of the Nazis in the closing months of World War II. This "righteous Gentile," as historians have tagged him, vanished without a trace in 1945, fueling speculation that the occupying Soviet armies arrested him and placed him in a gulag deep in the heart of Russia. Wallenberg's achievements are commemorated each year, with the presentation of a series of awards to community figures who best exemplify the spirit of the courageous Swede. A buffet reception follows the awards ceremony and speeches.

A Buffet of Jewish Thought. *Lunch program: North Conservatory (Lobby Level) of the Hyatt Regency Hotel West Tower, 151 E. Wacker Drive, Chicago. Dinner program: Gilson Park, Lakeview Center, Wilmette. Sponsored by the Chicago Community Kollel, 6506 N. California Avenue, Chicago, (773) 262-9400.*

A monthly lecture series on contemporary Jewish issues and concerns. The thought-provoking lectures are delivered by leading members of the religious and academic community of Chicago and abroad on the last Tuesday of the month. A brunch and buffet follow. Reservations are recommended, and a monetary donation is optional. The Chicago Community Kollel lending library contains both audiotapes and videotapes of each program.

Jewish Community Center Literary Series, *Mayer Kaplan JCC, 5050 W. Church St., Skokie, (847) 675-2200 x150. Tickets may be purchased at the door or by phone using Visa or MasterCard. Call for a schedule of events.*

Outstanding lecture series featuring contemporary Jewish-American authors discussing their careers and current projects. The lectures are scheduled throughout the year, and are supported in part by the Robert S. Fiffer Memorial Fund, established by his family and friends. Featured speakers have included Joyce Carol Oates, author of more than twenty novels and the winner of a National Book Award; Chaim Potok, whose most famous works include *The Chosen, The Book of Lights, My Name Is Asher Lev,* and *In the Beginning,* and Mordecai Richler, author of *The Apprenticeship of Duddy Kravitz.*

Yom Hashoah Commemoration (Holocaust Memorial Day). *Anshe Emet Synagogue, 3760 N. Pine Grove, Chicago, (773) 281-1423. On or about April 10. Admission free. Parking available.*

Dramatic readings, memorial service, candle-lighting ceremony, and community singing of Yiddish and Hebrew songs marking the events of the

Holocaust. Each synagogue in the city pays homage to those who perished in Nazi death camps, but the services at the Anshe Emet Congregation are among the most notable in Chicago. This annual event is open to the public regardless of religious affiliation.

Dr. K. Jeffrey Kranzler Memorial Concert, *Anshe Shalom B'nai Israel Congregation, 540 W. Melrose St., Chicago, (773) 258-9200. First Sunday in June. Admission fee charged.*

A different cantor each year presents a program of cantorial renditions, and traditional Yiddish and Israeli folk songs.

Prism Gallery and Performance Center, *620 Davis St., Evanston, (847) 475-7500. June exhibition, usually closed on Sundays. Admission to the Prism Gallery is free, but a cover charge applies to the live entertainment.*

A performing arts center and gallery that spotlights ethnic art, music, and culture at different times of the year. In June, Prism features an exhibition of fine arts and crafts holography, jewelry, and a mixed theme of artwork by Russian and Jewish artists. Live entertainment by Jewish musicians and performers is featured on the weekend. Paintings, sculpture, holography, textiles, pottery, jewelry, and furniture offered for sale.

Places to See

The First Synagogue in Illinois, *memorialized on a plaque affixed to the new Federal Building on Dearborn St., between Adams and Jackson Sts. and extending to Clark St., Chicago.*

On this site stood the first Jewish house of worship in the state. The plaque was originally dedicated on October 9, 1918, and moved to its present location when the old federal courthouse was razed.

Henry Horner Memorial Monument, *Horner Park, Montrose Ave. and California, Chicago.*

Dedicated on October 27, 1948, to the memory of the first Jewish governor of Illinois, this monument to Henry Horner was authorized by an act of the legislature in 1942; at its dedication ceremony, Illinois poet Carl Sandburg delivered the keynote address. Governor Horner was born in Chicago and died in office in 1940 after serving for eight years. He served as a judge on the Cook County Probate Court from 1914 to 1932 and was elected to the governorship on the strength of President Franklin Roosevelt's coattails. Horner was in many respects a visionary politician who attempted to shelve partisan causes to serve all of the people of Illinois fairly and without bias. For this, he was castigated by members of the Chicago Democratic machine.

Sidney Hillman Center of the Amalgamated Clothing Workers of America, *333 S. Ashland Blvd., Chicago.*

A Russian-born Jew, Sidney Hillman was one of the founders of the CIO. He served as the president of the union from 1914 until his death in 1946, and was actively involved when the CIO split with the AF of L. During World War II, Hillman was the number-two man in the War Production Board. The bust of this famous Chicagoan stands in the reception room of the Ashland Boulevard center.

Lessing Monument, *located in the Rose Garden of Washington Park, 57th St. and Cottage Grove Ave., Chicago.*

Gotthold Ephraim Lessing was not Jewish, but this German writer who lived during the Enlightenment did much to help the plight of 18th-century Jews through such published works as *Nathan the Wise*. His contributions were a factor in the emancipation of Jews in Western Europe. The Lessing monument was presented to the city in 1930 by Henry C. Frank.

Haym Solomon Monument, *Heald Square, East Wacker Dr. at Wabash St., Chicago.*

Known officially as the George Washington, Robert Morris, Haym Solomon Memorial, this imposing monument was dedicated on December 15, 1941, to commemorate the 150th anniversary of the ratification of the Bill of Rights. It shows Haym Solomon, a Polish Jew who helped finance the revolution, with General George Washington and Robert Morris, another financier of the Revolutionary War. The base of the statue contains the following inscription, taken from Washington's letter to the rabbis at the Newport, RI synagogue: "The government of the U.S., which gives to bigotry no sanction, to persecution no assistance, requires only that they who live under its protection should [conduct] themselves as good citizens in giving it on all occasions their effectual support." Solomon died penniless at age 45 after contracting a lung disease while incarcerated by the British for spying.

Jewish Waldheim Cemetery, *Harlem Ave. and Roosevelt Rd., Forest Park.*

Waldheim is one of the largest burial grounds in the world for people of the Jewish faith. There are roughly 175,000 graves located here, including those of the anarchist lecturer Emma Goldman (buried near the five condemned Haymarket men in the German section), her lover (the self-styled "King of the Hobos," Dr. Benjamin Reitman), former Illinois governor Sam Shapiro, theatrical mogul Michael Todd, and Clara Peller, best known for her comedy routine in the Wendy's TV commercials of the mid-1980s. The Waldheim cemetery has always served as a burial ground in one form or another, going back to the time when the Illini and Potawatomi Indians buried their dead here. The first Jewish interment took place in 1875, according to official records. Located due west of the old Maxwell Street ghetto, a trip to the cemetery was an arduous journey before the Metropolitan Elevated constructed a "funeral car" route out of the city in 1914. For twenty years, these customized train cars conveyed coffins and mourners to Waldheim, until they were put out of public service. These railroad cars were later used as examination rooms for motormen.

Shops

Rosenblum's World of Judaica, Inc., *2906 W. Devon Ave., Chicago, (773) 262-1700. Closed Saturdays. Credit cards accepted.*

Books on Israel and the Holocaust. Judaic video cassettes. Cantorial and Yiddish music. Games for youngsters. This is the Midwest's largest and oldest distributor of Judaica.

Chicago Hebrew Bookstore, *2942 W. Devon Ave., Chicago, (773) 973-6636. Closed Saturdays.*

Paperback and hardcover books. Tapes, gift items, religious goods.

Gitel's Kosher Bakery, *2745 W. Devon Ave., Chicago, (773) 262-3701. Closed Saturdays. Checks, but no credit cards.*

Breads, wedding cakes, pies, and pastries baked under the supervision of the Chicago Rabbinical Council (CRC).

Tel Aviv Kosher Bakery, *2944 W. Devon Ave., Chicago, (773) 764-8877. Closed Saturdays. No credit cards.*

Kosher cakes, pastries, and breads.

Levinson's Bakery, *2856 W. Devon Ave., Chicago,*
(773) 761-3174. Open daily. No credit cards.

Without doubt, the earliest-opening bakery in Chicago. Pastries and breads.

Kosher Karry, *2828 W. Devon, Chicago,*
(773) 973-4355. Closed Sundays. No credit cards.

A carry-out deli serving home-cooked gourmet kosher food, including meat blintzes, gefilte fish, and sandwiches. CRC-supervised.

New York Kosher, *2900 W. Devon Ave., Chicago,*
(773) 338-3354. Closed Saturdays. No credit cards.

Smoked fish, salmon, groceries, and kosher foods direct from the warehouse.

The Original North Shore Bakery & Deli
Restaurant, *2919-21 W. Touhy Ave., Chicago,*
(773) 262-0600. Closed Saturdays. No credit
cards.

A delicatessen in the front sells a full line of kosher foods, and a restaurant in the rear of the building serves hungry patrons. CRC-endorsed.

Outlying Areas

Selig's Kosher Delicatessen, Inc., *209 Skokie*
Valley Rd., Highland Park, (847) 831-5560.
Closed Saturdays. Checks, but no credit cards.

Located in the Crossroads Shopping Center, west of the Edens Expressway. Full line of kosher foods, including bakery products and imported items. The restaurant area serves up to forty people for a home-cooked lunch, dinner, or a quick snack. CRC-approved.

Door County Fish & Deli, *Dundee and Pfingsten,*
Northbrook, (847) 559-9229, and Grove Point Plaza,
Route 83 and Lake Cook Rd., Buffalo Grove,
(847) 459-7040. Closed Saturdays. Credit cards
accepted.

Famous for their smoked fish, which is prepared on the premises. A small counter serves the lunch crowd. This Jewish delicatessen is better known for catering Bar/Bat Mitzvahs, Bris, Shiva, graduations, and Mother's Day celebrations.

Hungarian Kosher Foods, Inc., *4020 W. Oakton St., Skokie, (847) 674-8008. Closed Saturdays. No credit cards.*

Full-line delicatessen and grocery selling kosher foods.

Kaufman's Bagel & Delicatessen, *4905 Dempster St., Skokie, (847) 677-6190. Open daily.*

Imported foods from Israel. Kosher foods available for carryout.

Restaurants

Belden Restaurant and Deli, *two locations: 7572 N. Western Ave., Chicago, (773) 743-4800; Arlington Heights, 902 W. Dundee Rd., (847) 398-7750. Open for breakfast, lunch, and dinner daily. Credit cards accepted.*

A Jewish deli reminiscent of the old days, even though they have been in existence less than two decades. Noisy and very crowded during the noon hour, Belden sells sandwiches to go, fancy bakery items, and kosher foods in the fronts of the restaurants. Catering available.

The Chocolate Bar, *2957 W. Devon (773) 381-1770.*

Owner Menachem Emanuel has opened Chicago's first kosher espresso café serving Cholov Ysroel cappuccino along with kosher gourmet pastries. The café is nestled inside his elegant kosher chocolate shop which features a full line of homemade, parve Belgian chocolates. Gift baskets and shipping are available. Credit cards accepted. Open 7 A.M.–10 P.M. Closed on the Sabbath.

Tel Aviv Kosher Pizza, *6349 N. California, Chicago, (773) 764-3776.*

Pizza and dairy restaurant that is CRC-supervised. Open for lunch and dinner. Closed Fridays. No credit cards.

HaShalom, *2905 W. Devon Ave., Chicago, (773) 465-5675. Open for lunch and dinner. Closed Saturdays and Sundays.*

Storefront featuring inexpensive Israeli and Moroccan cuisine in a casual atmosphere. Specialties include hummus, baba ghannouj, bourekas, kebabs, and tahini.

Whistler's Restaurant, *3420 W. Devon Ave.,*
Lincolnwood, (847) 673-9270. Open for breakfast,
lunch, and dinner daily.

Extensive menu specializing in Jewish-American cuisine.

Outlying Areas

Ken's Diner/Bugsy's, *3353 W. Dempster St., Skokie,*
(847) 679-2850. Open for lunch and dinner
Sunday–Thursday; open for lunch Friday; closed
Saturday. Free parking. No credit cards.

Owner Ken Hechtman promotes his deli as a kind of "Kosher Ed Debe-
vic's"—patterned after the kitschy 1950s motif that made the River North
diner famous. People come from all over the Midwest to partake of the food
(certified by the CRC) and festivities. Music. Pinball games. "Comedy
Night" every Tuesday. This is the home of the "Burger Buddy."

What's Cooking?, *6107 N. Lincoln Ave., Chicago,*
(773) 583-3050. Open for breakfast, lunch, and dinner
Sunday–Friday; open for breakfast and lunch
Saturday. Credit cards accepted.

Jewish-American cuisine located in the Lincoln Village Shopping plaza.

The Bagel Restaurant and Deli, *two locations: 3107*
N. Broadway, Chicago, (773) 477-0300, and 50 Old
Orchard Shopping Center, Skokie, (847) 677-0100. Open
for breakfast, lunch, and dinner daily. No credit cards.

Non-kosher Jewish-oriented restaurant formerly located in Rogers Park.
Specializes in blintzes and stuffed whitefish.

Falafel King Israeli Restaurant, *4507 W. Oakton St.,*
Skokie, (847) 677-6020. Open for lunch and dinner,
Sunday–Thursday; open for lunch Friday. Closed
Saturday. No credit cards.

Kosher meat and vegetarian dishes.

Manny's Coffee Shop, *1141 S. Jefferson St.,*
Chicago, (312) 939-2855. Open for breakfast and
lunch. Closed Sunday. Credit cards accepted for
catered orders only.

Years ago, when there used to be a "real" Maxwell Street and it spilled over
onto Roosevelt Road, with its hundreds of tenement buildings, discount

clothiers, and butcher shops, afternoon shoppers would satisfy their appetite at either Lyon's Deli (now known as Nate's, 807 W. Maxwell Street) or Manny Raskin's, where you could feast on lamb shanks, matzo soup, baked chicken and fish, and other kosher-style foods that made the strip famous. Manny went on to his reward, but his son Ken continues to run the business at 1141 S. Jefferson. He moved to this location in 1965, a few years after the Dan Ryan Expressway tore through the neighborhood and sapped Maxwell Street and Roosevelt Road of much of its local color. No matter; the food is still good, and the new-old Manny's remains one of the favorite lunch spots west of the Loop. *Recommended.*

Russian Tea Time, *77 E. Adams St., Chicago, (312) 360-0000. Open for lunch and dinner daily.*

Traditional Russian Jewish cuisine. The extensive menu includes a number of excellent vegetarian dishes.

Russian Palace, 24 E. Adams St., *Chicago, (312) 629-5353. Open for lunch and dinner daily.*

Traditional Russian Jewish cuisine. Live ethnic music for Sunday brunch.

West Rogers Park:
A Community in Transition

The West Rogers Park neighborhood on the city's Far North Side has been home to thousands of Jewish families since the end of World War II, when they began moving out of Lawndale on the South Side. Settled in the mid-nineteenth century by the Swedish and Irish, West Rogers Park was a part of the village of Rogers Park until it was annexed to Chicago in 1893. The growth of the community was accentuated by the addition of a Northwestern el line that was constructed in the 1900s, linking downtown Chicago to Wilson Avenue. Bounded by Howard Street and Western Avenue on the north and east, and Kedzie and Peterson on the south and west, it is a quiet residential community revolving around devotion to the family and religious traditions.

Orthodox Jewish families began settling West Rogers Park as early as the 1920s, but the numbers increased significantly during the 1950s. By 1963 there were more than 48,000 Jewish residents living in the 50th Ward, which has been represented in the city council by two of the more flamboyant aldermen of their day: Jack Sperling (1955–73), and Bernard Stone (1973 to the present). Both men championed the neighborhood's best interests with only a passing regard for partisan issues.

The growing Jewish community that moved into West Rogers Park purchased Georgian, ranch, and bungalow-style homes and two-flats closest to the nearly two dozen synagogues serving the area, many of them originally located along Maxwell Street and in North Lawndale. On the Sabbath, Orthodox Jews are prohibited from driving and therefore must walk to the congregation nearest their home. The Jewish businesses centered near Devon and California avenues are closed on Saturdays, which is the traditional day of prayer and meditation.

West Rogers Park has undergone significant changes in recent years. In addition to many Russian Jews who arrived during the 1980s, the area has also seen an influx of East Indians and Pakistanis.

Congested Devon Avenue is a wildly exotic shopping street between California and Western avenues near the city's northern border. The western part of this commercial strip is called Golda Meir Way in honor of the late Israeli prime minister; Russian and Ukrainian Jews (Meir was born in Kiev and grew up in Milwaukee) have made the area less Orthodox but more distinctly ethnic. Residents queue up in stores not only to purchase goods but to engage in neighborly conversation, as though they were still in the U.S.S.R.

A few blocks to the east, Devon becomes Gandhi Marg in honor of the great pacifist and Indian leader. Indian grocery stores, video rental shops, restaurants, and sari stores crowd this part of the street. More recently, the Assyrian-American Association, representing Chicago's small but growing Iraqi-Christian community, established headquarters at 1618 W. Devon. And further west, the Croatian Cultural Center of Chicago occupies a large building at 2845 Devon Avenue, suggesting that this most cosmopolitan of Chicago's North Side streets may undergo yet another ethnic transformation.

Czech and Slovak Chicago

History and Settlement

In October 1918, a nation called Czechoslovakia was carved out of the remnants of the old Austro-Hungarian empire. It was a Slavic nation composed of the former imperial provinces of Moravia, Bohemia, Slovakia, and Sub-Carpathian Ruthenia. Though not all Czechs are Bohemians, that is what many of these immigrants have been called since they first set foot on these shores in the eighteenth century. Bohemia is a lush region, with vast mountain ranges, fertile valleys, and rich deposits of coal, graphite, silver, iron ore, and uranium, but the history of the area is pockmarked by the violent struggles.

In 1848 a nationalistic uprising against the Hapsburg monarchy to combat a rising tide of "Germanization" within the provinces spurred the first wave of immigration into the United States. The "48ers" and all those who were to follow in the next 140 years were among the most literate and highly skilled Europeans to immigrate here. Their love of freedom echoed through the provinces in the long-suppressed work of Jan Hus, the immortal fifteenth-century author who championed the Czech language. A new generation of thinkers awakened the national conscience and fueled the growing movement toward independence during the Victorian era. Journalist Jan Neruda (1834–91) encouraged the Czech people to improve their economic lot through public education. Tomas Garrique Masaryk, Czechoslovakia's greatest political figure, who became the first president of the new republic in 1918, bridged the widening gulf between two schools of thought: the Parnassians, who wove foreign themes into Czech literature, and the Nationalists, whose most eloquent spokesman was the poet Suatopluk Cech (1846–1908).

Though Czech William Paca was one of the signers of the Declaration of Independence, the greater number of freedom-loving Czechs didn't begin arriving in the United States until shortly before the Civil War. They fanned out across the Midwest and the Plains states of Nebraska, Kansas, Wisconsin, and Texas; the terrain was reminiscent of the land they had recently left behind. Those who settled in Chicago in the 1870s established the first Czech community along De Koven Street—*Mala Jinzni Strana,* or "Little Prague."

After the Chicago Fire, the Czechs began to build on the open prairies near Eighteenth Street and Racine Avenue. One of the first buildings to be erected in the neighborhood was a Czech restaurant and saloon owned by an immigrant from the West Czechoslovakian city of Plzen. He named his establishment the Pilsen Cafe, and gradually the name was adopted by the immigrants who inhabited Blue Island Avenue from Sixteenth to Twenty-Second Streets.

The Pilsen neighborhood was for many years an important manufacturing center. The McCormick Reaper Works, at Blue Island and Western avenues, and the Chicago, Burlington, and Quincy railroads provided jobs and meager wages for the workers who crowded into modest two-story cottages with high basements, tiny grass plots in front, and a garden in the back yard. Describing the assimilation of his people into the Chicago culture, an anonymous Czech WPA writer penned these thoughts during the height of the Depression:

> The economic adjustment of the Czech community to American conditions seems almost to be perfect, due to a strong tendency for economic cooperation. Here and there only minor conflicts arise with other nationalities, as for example with the Irish, whom the Czech hate on account of their Catholic religion, favoritism and rough dealing with their subordinates. They (the Czechs) are very anxious to get prestige in the group, knowing that there is much community spirit, patriotism, and solidarity among the people, which will be to their advantage. It is among the working men and among the intellectuals, where the Czech culture finds its place.

Pilsen was a highly secular, insulated neighborhood, hemmed in by railroad tracks, heavy industry, and a flourishing retail trade centered along

18th Street. For nearly eighty years, English was a second language here. The old-timers organized mutual aid benefit societies to promote the culture, and the financial welfare of the immigrants who worked at the Peter Schoenhofen Brewery on 18th Street or the Chicago Stove Works Foundry. According to WPA writer Theodore Przydryga, "the great mass of Czech people are skilled workmen and craftsmen. The second generation tends to prefer office employment, business and professional careers such as the law, dentistry, medicine, teaching and banking."

The immigrants received the latest news through four daily newspapers representing the political extremes of the day. The mainstream *Svornost Daily* (Harmony) was the first Bohemian newspaper published in the United States. The "Free Thinkers," who were violently opposed to Roman Catholic clericalism, published the *Spravedlnost,* which advocated a liberal school system and socialism—unpopular views that contributed to the hard feelings existing between the Irish-run city administration and the fledgling trade unionist movement of the 1870s and 1880s.

The Czechs organized their "Sokols," or free-thought schools, to fill an educational gap in the immigrant community. The Sokol movement began in Czechoslovakia in 1862 in order to promote the physical, spiritual, and mental well-being of the people. Dissident poet and journalist Karl Havlicek (1821–56) was the prime mover of the Sokol ideal. Havlicek, whose statue was placed in Douglas Park on the West Side, was the editor of a Prague newspaper until he was imprisoned by the Hapsburg government for his views. In his memory the Chicago Czechs dedicated the Sokol Havlicek-Tyrs at 2619 S. Lawndale.

The largest Sokol unit in the United States met there, in the heart of "Ceska California," the second most influential Czech neighborhood in Chicago. Bounded by California Avenue on the east, the city limits on the west, and from 14th St. on the north and 33rd on the south, Ceska California was inhabited by Czechs from the 1880s until the Mexican immigrants changed the ethnic composition of the neighborhood.

Today, throngs of Mexican bakeries, restaurants, thrift stores, and community centers line the main business thoroughfares of Pilsen. For many newly arrived Mexicans, Pilsen is their first real encounter with American culture. The Czech residents abandoned these West Side neighborhoods by the 1950s, leaving behind only a few solitary reminders of their heritage, like the St. Procopius Catholic church at 18th and Allport, built in 1883, and the "mother parish" of Pilsen.

Ceska California (or Lawndale) was the political power base of Anton Cermak, Chicago's only Czech mayor, who was tragically shot down while in the company of President-elect Franklin D. Roosevelt at Miami's Bayside Park on February 13, 1933. Cermak was the architect of the legendary Democratic machine. Born in Prague, Cermak came up the hard way—

working for a few cents a day at the Braidwood mines. But he was resourceful and ambitious. This favorite son of Lawndale attracted the attention of George "Boss" Brennan, future Democratic kingmaker who came up through the coal mines, taught school for a time, and then drifted into state politics.

In 1931, the industrious Cermak, whose personal wealth was estimated to be $7,000,000, was elected mayor by Chicagoans fed up with the antics of William Hale Thompson and his gangster coalition. Cermak came down hard on the gangsters who turned the city streets into a shooting gallery. He was loved and respected by his Czech-Slavic constituency, the majority of whom supported his anti-Prohibition platform.

Through his brief mayoral term, Cermak continued to reside in Lawndale at a modest residence located at 2338 W. Millard Avenue. The real estate office of Cermak and Serhant was located on the main thoroughfare of Ceska California at 3346 W. 26th Street. Farther down the street stands the fortress-like Criminal Court Building and lockup, constructed for the sum of $7.5 million and opened on April 1, 1929. Thanks to Cermak, these city institutions were permanently located in the future mayor's home ward.

Appropriately, 22nd Street was renamed Cermak Road in honor of the martyred mayor, who in his earlier years took an active role in community affairs as the director of the Czechoslovak-American Chamber of Commerce. The steady westward drift into Cicero, Berwyn, Riverside, Brookfield, and other suburbs along the path of the old Burlington Railroad line, which had begun after World War I, continued into the 1950s and 1960s. But during the time of Cermak's political ascendancy, 22nd Street between Cicero and Harlem avenues became known as the "Bohemian Wall Street."

"The neighborhood," according to author Norbert Blei, who grew up in Cicero during its halcyon days, "was a current, a circular field of motion. Much coming and going. Everything stood still, yet everything revolved (by the hour, the day, the season, the year) and came back to you. You departed and returned. And you were the same but different." For Miles Pancner, who arrived from Lisov, Czechoslovakia, in the 1920s to open an import business on 22nd Street, Cicero and Berwyn was the "Tailor City," reflecting the many skilled garment workers who plied their trade on Bohemian Wall Street.

Evidence of the legendary Czech penchant for thriftiness abounds. Up and down the street can be found the savings and loan institutions that do not bother to place withdrawal slips on the counter. It was customary for the Czech families who lived in the red and brown brick bungalows off 22nd Street to visit the savings and loan every Saturday morning to deposit their paychecks, fulfilling their dream of home ownership. In good times and bad, the Czechs of 22nd Street are wary of the permutations of the stock market, putting their faith in the old adage that a penny saved is a penny earned.

Cermak Road has been an extension of Czech folk life for nearly 80 years. The Western Electric Hawthorne Works in Cicero provided steady employment for many of the 40,000 Czechs living nearby from 1903 until the doors of the old factory closed for the last time in the 1980s. Norbert Blei described the significance of Western Electric in his nostalgic memoir, appropriately titled *Neighborhood:* "Though the boundaries of the town were fixed streets, addresses [and] directions were of less significance to a kid than the fact that Western Electric (the tower, the huge green and red sign that glowed from the roof at night) marked the spot where Chicago began; the Sanitary District (which you could smell when the wind blew from that direction) and the race tracks (Sportsman's Park and Hawthorne) and the Burlington Railway (home of the Silver Zephyr) and the Red Arrow (famous jazz joint) were south; the factories, the Dutch settlement, the Town and Ritz shows, [and] Columbus Park were north and also Chicago; and Cicero turned into Berwyn just after the Olympic show and Sokol around Lombard Avenue across the street from the Hole in the Wall Tavern. . . ."

The neighborhood. It wasn't prettified or sissy. Al Capone sweated out four years of Mayor Dever's reform administration at the Hawthorne Smoke Shop during the 1920s. And the all-night saloons of Cicero have raised the hackles of many a church-going reformer. But there have been greater threats in recent years. With the departure of Western Electric, Cicero and Berwyn faced the economic drag that accompanies the defection of heavy industry from an area. How well the Czechs maintain their identity in Cicero and Berwyn remains to be seen, though the loosening of border restrictions and the retreat of communism in Eastern Europe fostered a new wave of immigration into the United States.

During the "Prague Spring" uprising of 1968, some twenty to thirty refugees a week stepped off the bus in Chicago with little more than the clothes on their back and a few dollars in their pockets. Those new arrivals could count on the warm assistance of their American relatives, or the Czechoslovakian National Council of America (CNCA) to help them find affordable housing, a job at Western Electric, and neighbors of Bohemian descent to converse with in their native tongue. But this is a changing time, and the old rules no longer apply.

The stirrings of freedom in Czechoslovakia have given rise to ethnic nationalism, and this is a grave concern to all Chicagoans who celebrated the peaceful overthrow of the old communist regime on December 11, 1989 when the hard-line President Gustav Husak relinquished power to a coalition government of Czechs and Slovaks. The "Velvet Revolution" offered great hope for the future and inspiration to freedom loving people everywhere.

The former Czechoslovakia split into two republics, where two similar but distinct languages were spoken. Slovakia, more closely aligned to Hungary in language and culture, fell under the spell of Prime Minister Vladimir Meciar, a nationalistic strong-man who distanced himself from the more industrialized Czech Republic led by President Vaclav Havel, the former playwright. Debate over Slovak separatism dominated the political life of the post-Soviet era.

In the face of rising ethnic hostilities Czechs and Slovaks prepared for the eventualities of a "Velvet Divorce" which finally transpired on January 1, 1993 when two new states were carved out of the ever changing map of Central Europe. The challenge that lies ahead for both Slovakia and the Czech Republic is to foster economic growth through peace and unity.

A proud people who embraced the American way of life in all aspects, the Czechs and the Slovaks of Chicago will endure despite future developments in the troubled regions. George Halas of the Bears, sportscaster Chet Coppock, former Chicago Blackhawk center Stan Mikita, actress Kim Novak, former assistant public defender Mary Jane Placek (a.k.a. "Empress of the Bohemians"), crime writer Gera-Lind Kolarik, and Cicero's former poet-in-residence, Nobert Blei, are Czech-Americans who have left their imprint on the community. There will certainly be more.

Getting There: Board a Douglas train going west (originating in the Loop). Take this train to 54th and Cermak, where you should board a West Cermak (#25) bus, which will take you to Austin and Cermak. By car from the Loop, use the Eisenhower Expressway (I-90), either by driving west on Congress Street which becomes the freeway just west of the Loop, or by exiting the Kennedy Expressway (from the north), or the Dan Ryan (from the south) at the clearly marked ramps. Head west on the Eisenhower until you reach Austin Avenue. Exit at Austin, turn left (going south) until you hit 22nd Street. Turn left and you are entering Cicero; right, and you are in Berwyn.

For additional information, call the CTA at (312) 836-7000.

══════════ Attractions ══════════

Cultural Institutions

Czechoslovak Heritage Museum and Archives
Library, *122 W. 22nd St., Oak Brook, (630) 795-5800.*
Open Monday–Friday.

The CSA Fraternal Life (formerly the Czechoslovak Society of America) is a fraternal benefit organization founded in 1854 in St. Louis to provide its members with a full line of insurance products and annuities, and for the broader purpose of preserving the history and customs of the native land.

The museum was started in 1974, when the CSA moved into its spacious new offices in Berwyn. The museum houses a colorful collection of authentic folk costumes from the many different towns and regions of Czechoslovakia. A fine collection of blown glass, and lead crystal in many colors and styles, are proudly displayed by the CSA side by side with decorative Easter eggs, embroidery, farm implements, musical instruments, and paintings and sculptures. The library houses a collection of papers and archives pertaining to rural village life in Czechoslovakia, and to the Euro-American immigration, which commenced in the late 19th century. The museum is located only a few minutes from the Harlem Avenue exits of I-55 and I-290.

The Anne and Jacques Baruch Collection, *P.O. Box 11078, Chicago 60611, (312) 944-3377. Hours by appointment only.*

Jacques and Anne Baruch opened their Chicago gallery in 1967 just before the events surrounding the Soviet crackdown, which became known as the "Prague Spring." Anne Baruch now operates the gallery as a private dealership, and continues the work by featuring the work of previously "forbidden" Czech artists and other Central and Eastern European artists.

Annual Events and Celebrations

International Houby Festival. *Second or third week in October. For more information, write the Cermak Road Business Association, 2134 S. 61st Ct., Cicero 60650, or call (708) 863-8979.*

A "houby" (or *hribky*) is a mushroom. To the Czech people, this wild fungus, which we take for granted, is sacred. The houby is akin to the Irish shamrock, and every year around Columbus Day, the Cermak Road Business Association sponsors a week-long celebration of the houby. A Houby Queen is crowned; the ball and dinner-dance follow; the merchants sponsor a sidewalk sale during the week, which is followed by the centerpiece of the festivities: the Sunday parade, featuring food booths, floats, arts and crafts, horseshoe-throwing contests, and races. The Houby Festival has been going strong since 1969 from Central Avenue to Oak Park Avenue. According to local legend, and the wit and wisdom of Norbert Blei, the seasoned houby hunters will leave their homes in Cicero, Berwyn, or Riverside one morning in the early fall, armed with a bushel basket, knife, and the fabled "houby stick." Then, with the quarry in hand, the hunter returns home to have his wife prepare mushroom soup, pickled mushrooms, sacred mushrooms. . . .

Moravian Day (Moravsky Den). *Fourth weekend in September. For more information, please call Jospeh Borysek, President of the United Moravian Societies, at (708) 562-2307. Admission fee charged.*

The ethnic traditions of Moravia, the central province of Czechoslovakia, are celebrated in song, dance, and colorful costumes during the annual Moravian Day at the Operating Engineers Hall, 6200 Joliet Road, in Countryside. The festival is one of the longest-running ethnic events in Chicago. It dates back to 1939, when the newly formed United Moravian Societies sponsored their festive outing at Pilsen Park (26th and Albany), and then later at the Sokol-Havlicek Tyrs at 26th and Lawndale. In the early years a stately procession of horsemen decked out in Moravian folk costumes paraded to the fairgrounds. The pageantry and dash of those earlier times have been transplanted to the western suburbs under the auspices of the United Moravian Societies and the Moravian Folklore Circle. The finest Czech dance troops from Indiana, Wisconsin, and Canada assemble to perform a singing and dancing program depicting a different theme each year. A Welcome Dance at the Sokol Berwyn Hall, 6445 W. 27th Place in Berwyn, precedes Moravian Day, to welcome the out-of-town performers. The following morning a Holy Mass conducted in the Moravian dialect at the Engineers Hall begins the day-long events. General dancing, and a rich harvest of Moravian food including tripe soup, dumplings and sauerkraut, dill pickles, and pastries, await the public.

Czechoslovak Day Festival, *at the National Grove No. 4, 27th St. and Des Plaines, North Riverside, the last Sunday in July. Sponsored by the Czechoslovak American Congress, (847) 795-5800.*

The day-long festival rekindles happy memories of Pilsen Park at 26th and Albany, where for years the Czech community of the West Side gathered every weekend to eat, drink, and dance. Pilsen Park had an outside stage and a dance pavilion with a wooden floor. On warm summer nights when the crocuses were in bloom, and the music soft and gentle, young people gathered under the stars to dream . . . and to romance. Pilsen Park was razed in the mid-1970s to make way for the Little Village Mall, which serves the Mexican community. The Czech Festival began in 1985 as a kind of Pilsen Park "revival." The event was an immediate success, attracting people from all over Chicago, Indiana, and even one person from Australia. The picnic is held on the last Sunday in July. There is music, dancing, entertainment and plenty of Czech food including potato pancakes, sausages, kolacky, and more.

American Sokol Organization Anniversary Celebration. *For location, ticket prices, and dates, call the American Sokol Organization, 6426 Cermak Rd., Berwyn, (708) 795-6671.*

The word *Sokol* means "falcon"—a symbol of strength and independence to the Czech people. In the United States, roughly 10,000 adults and 50,000 children participate in American Sokol Organization activities. The movement was founded by Dr. Miroslav Tyrs, who was inspired by the customs of ancient Greece. The Sokol ideal—"Physical Fitness Through Gymnastics"—has been kept alive in the United States since the post-Civil War period. The anniversary celebration is held each year, featuring dinner, cocktails, and a cultural program.

Czechoslovak National Council of America (CNCA) Debutante Ball (downtown). *Admission fee charged. For further information, or to join the CNCA, please contact Olga Kovar, at 2137 S. Lombard Ave., Cicero, (708) 656-1117. Annual membership available.*

The Czechoslovak National Council of America was founded during World War I. It grew out of an urgent need for a united national war effort of Americans of Czech and Slovak descent. In recent years the CNCA has sponsored many worthwhile activities, including classes in English for newly arrived immigrants, the creation of a permanent chair of Czech and Slovak studies at the University of Chicago, and numerous publications, including a 1976 bibliography, *Czechs and Slovaks in America,* and a monthly newsletter, *Vestnik.*

The CNCA is divided into six main districts: Washington, DC; Cleveland; Chicago; Michigan; New York City; and the Pacific (San Francisco, Los Angeles, San Diego). Greater Chicago is the largest district, with six local chapters. Each year since 1951, the CNCA sponsors a black-tie debutante ball, honoring local girls of Czech descent. The 1991 event was held in the Grand Ballroom of the Ritz-Carlton Hotel in Chicago. In attendance were the Honorable Shirley Temple Black, U.S. Ambassador to Czechoslovakia; Illinois Governor Jim Edgar; and Mayor Richard Daley of Chicago.

Czechoslovak Allied Organizations in Chicago (Suburban Ball). *Drury Lane Oakbrook, 100 Drury Lane, Oakbrook Terrace. First or second weekend of February. Contact Jerry Rabas, Sr. at (708) 788-9770 for additional information. Admission fee charged.*

The Czechoslovak Allied Organizations began holding formal dinner dances a few years after the CNCA, but this group was the first to have debutante balls. The tradition began in 1965, but unlike the CNCA, which limits participation to girls of Czech extraction, the Allied Organizations will accept young women between 16 and 21 of any ethnic background. The main purpose of the ball is to formally introduce the debs to society, but is also aimed at bringing together recent arrivals from Czechoslovakia with the older and younger generations of Chicagoans whose links to the old country may not be quite so strong. Tickets for this gala event include prime rib dinner, musical entertainment, and debutante presentation.

Czechoslovak Independence Day. *Observed on or about October 28 in Chicago and Cicero. Call (773) 656-1117 for details, or call the village of Cicero at (708) 656-3600.*

The Chicago celebration occurs at the Daley Civic Center Plaza in a noontime ceremony sponsored by the Czechoslovak American Congress and the Department of Cultural Affairs for the City of Chicago. The national anthems of both countries are sung, and various folk dance troops perform native dances. A second ceremony is held on the grounds of the Cicero Town Hall in conjunction with the Czech Congress. Colors are presented by the Cicero Police Auxiliary, and the national anthems are sung by the CSA Fraternal Life Singers.

Shops

Minarik's, *5832 W. Cermak Rd., Cicero, (708) 652-2854. Closed Sundays.*

"Chleb nas vezdejsi." The sign over the cash register reads "bread from us is best," and there are few people in Cicero and Berwyn who will argue the point with Stanley and Maria Zolnierczyk, who specialize in Czech pastries, cookies, and imported foods from Europe.

Vesecky's Bakery, *6634 W. Cermak Rd., Berwyn, (708) 788-4144. Closed Sundays.*

A fixture on 22nd Street since 1929. To understand the Czech culture, visit Vesecky's on a busy Saturday morning when the neighborhood people show up for their specially made Bohemian Rye. Kolacky made from three kinds of dough, each filled with cheese, jam, or poppy seed, is recommended for those with a sweet tooth.

Prague Delicatessen, *6312 W. Cermak Rd., Berwyn, (708) 863-1106. Closed Sundays.*

As you step into this old world deli, notice the copies of *Denni Hlasatel* (the *Daily Herald*) and other Czech language publications on the counter. The

Prague Delicatessen caters to the needs of the Bohemians who live in the neighborhood. This is no tourist trap to be sure, just the finest *sledzie, pierogi, kana, jaternice,* and *sery* available in the neighborhood.

Crawford Sausage Company, *2310 S. Pulaski Rd., Chicago, (773) 277-3095.*

It goes without saying that the wonderful Bohemian prazsky (favored by the Czechs of Berwyn, Cicero, and Riverside) must come from the old neighborhood in Chicago. Since 1925 Crawford has distributed their Daisy-brand sausage to many Chicago area stores, notably the grocers in the Czech neighborhoods. Prazsky is a derivative of "Prague." It is a stick-to-the-ribs kind of meat that goes best with rye bread and beer, and is not recommended for calorie counters or vegetarians.

Joseph A. Starosta Meat Market, *2617 S. Ridgeland, Berwyn, (708) 788-2934.*

Joe Starosta is one of the few butchers in the area who still makes his own sausages and meats.

Jim's Meat Market, *1538 S. 61st. St., Cicero, (708) 863-6308.*

Jim Ruda is another who does it the old fashioned way—he grinds the meat for the sausages himself.

Pancner's, *6131 W. Cermak Rd., Cicero, (708) 652-3512.*

Miles Pancner opened his greeting card and stationery store at this location in October 1929—the same month the stock market crashed and plunged the nation into the worst depression in its history. Miles Pancner hung on gamely, and within a few years his small import business began to thrive. When he passed away on February 5, 1989, Pancner was hailed as the "last great pioneer merchant of 22nd Street," by the *Berwyn Life.* Pancner's is a gift shop specializing in fine imported glassware, crystal, Czech greeting cards, and an impressive collection of ornate dolls and marionettes. The costumed dolls, imported from Czechoslovakia, are a delight to behold for children of all ages. Books by Vaclav Havel, and by Cicero's native son, Norbert Blei, are available for sale. The store is owned by Jean Pancner-Lundberg, the daughter of the founder, who maintains the family business with loving care. The creaking wooden floors and ancient display cases hearken back to a time in American history when private entrepreneurship was the attainable dream for the poorest immigrant—when people did their shopping in the neighborhood and not at a distant suburban mall. *Recommended.*

Restaurants

Klas Restaurant, *5734 W. Cermak Rd., Cicero,*
(708) 652-0795.

In 1922 Adolph Klas opened his castle-like restaurant on 22nd Street, and it was an immediate hit . . . with Al Capone, who swapped stories, drank beer, and played gin rummy with the proprietor in the back room during the wild and woolly Prohibition days. The playing cards are on display in a glass cabinet near the front door, reminding patrons that Cicero was a lusty town in its heyday. The current owners of Klas advertise themselves as the "pork specialists" of Chicago, which is hard to refute. Hand-painted murals in an Eastern European motif decorate the walls. Wood carvings and stained glass windows are featured in the "Dr. Zhivago" banquet room—upstairs. Is this where Al Capone hid from the police? Come and find out. Catering. Special luncheon prices. *Recommended.*

Chateau Rose, *5830 W. Cermak Rd., Cicero,*
(708) 656-5690. Open for lunch and dinner daily.
Credit cards accepted.

Pilsner, *6725 W. Cermak Rd., Cicero, (708) 484-2294.*
Open for lunch and dinner. Closed Mondays.
Visa/MasterCard accepted.

Czech Plaza, *7016 W. Cermak Rd., Berwyn,*
(708) 795-6555. Open for lunch and dinner daily.
No credit cards accepted.

Home Restaurant, *6831 W. Ogden Ave., Berwyn,*
(708) 788-4104. Open for breakfast, lunch, and
dinner. Closed Mondays. No credit cards accepted.

Outlying Areas

Westchester Inn Restaurant, *3069 S. Wolf Rd.*
(near 31st St.), Westchester, (708) 409-1313 or
(708) 409-1391. Open for lunch and dinner daily.
No credit cards accepted.

Bohemian-American cooking brought to you by Mary and John Bosela.

The Dumpling House, *4109 S. Harlem Ave., Stickney,
(708) 484-6733. Open for lunch and dinner daily.
MasterCard and Visa accepted.*

Pleasant chalet exterior. Home cooking.

Bohemian Garden Restaurant, *980 W. 75th St.,
Downers Grove, (630) 960-0078. Open for lunch
and dinner. Closed Mondays.*

Moldau Restaurant, *9310 W. Ogden Ave., Brookfield,
(708) 485-8717. Open for lunch and dinner. Closed
Wednesdays. No credit cards accepted.*

Bohemian-American cooking.

Little Bohemia Restaurant, *25 E. Burlington,
Riverside, (708) 442-1251. Open for lunch and dinner.
Closed Mondays. No credit cards accepted.*

Same menu the entire day with specials.

Czech Kitchens, *6731 Pershing, Stickney,
(708) 749-7868. Open for lunch and dinner.
Closed Sundays. No credit cards accepted.*

Daily specials and fresh carry-outs.

Little Europe, *9208 Ogden Ave., Brookfield,
(708) 485-1112. Open for lunch and dinner.
Closed Mondays. American Express accepted.*

European Village Restaurant, *11141 W. Roosevelt Rd.,
Westchester, (708) 531-1115. Open for lunch and dinner.
Closed Mondays. Visa and MasterCard accepted.*

Corner Restaurant, *9201 Broadway, Brookfield,
(708) 485-5660. Open for lunch and dinner. Closed
Tuesdays. Visa/MasterCard accepted.*

Riverside Family Restaurant, *3422 Harlem Ave.,
Riverside, (708) 442-0434. Open for lunch and dinner.
Closed Mondays.*

Large, bustling restaurant owned by a Czech immigrant, Peter Stanga. Moderately priced.

Zenona Restaurant, *3218 Harlem Ave., Riverside,*
(708) 442-1002. Open for lunch and dinner. Closed
Mondays.

A tiny storefront restaurant. Very charming.

Bohemian Crown Restaurant, *7249 Lake, River*
Forest, (708) 366-8140. Open for lunch and dinner.
Closed Mondays.

Located west of the Oak Park Mall, with convenient parking in the rear.
Unpretentious decor, with good food at reasonable prices.

Bohemian Crystal, *639 N. Blackhawk, Westmont,*
(708) 789-1981. Open for lunch and dinner. Closed
Mondays. American Express, MasterCard, and Visa
accepted.

Hearty portions of traditional Czech foods—duckling; pork with lots of dill
gravy for the asking.

Media

Czech-Language Radio Programming

Sunday's Czechoslovak Radio Hour, *Sundays, 9:00*
to 10:00 A.M. Louis Kolarik has hosted this show for
more than 25 years. He doubles as the executive
secretary of the CSA Fraternal Life, and is treasurer of
the Czechoslovak American Congress.

Czechoslovak-American Radio Show, *Wednesdays,*
8:00 to 8:30 P.M. and Thursdays, 8:30 to 9:00 P.M.
Host: Jerry Jirak, who is the director of the Bohemian
American Concertina Association.

Both programs are aired on the voice of ethnic Chicago, WCEV Radio, AM-
1450, located at 5356 W. Belmont Ave., Chicago, IL 60641, (312) 282-
6700. The program director is Lucyna Migala.

Baltic Chicago

History and Settlement

Not much is known about Antanas Kaztauskis, except that he worked in the stockyards side by side with hundreds of other disillusioned Lithuanian émigrés who had abandoned the fertile valleys and lush woods of their Baltic state in search of political freedom and economic opportunity. But Kaztauskis recorded the despair felt by his compatriots in a 1904 article titled: "From Lithuania to the Chicago Stockyards—an Autobiography," and because of his shocking account of the grimy, disease-ridden Packingtown, a 26-year-old journalist named Upton Sinclair decided to investigate the situation firsthand.

The hitherto-unknown writer donned a set of shabby working clothes and joined the immigrant work force to observe the true conditions inside the empires of Cudahy, Swift, Armour, and Libby, McNeill. The result of his year-long investigation was *The Jungle,* the muckraking novel published in 1906. The real-life inspiration for the fictional Jurgis Rudkis in *The Jungle* may in fact have been Antanas Kaztauskis. At the very least, elements of the 1904 exposé formed the premise of the landmark novel, which not only tugged at the heartstrings of America but also led to the passage of the Pure Food and Drug Act.

Lithuania was a province of Imperial Russia before World War I, a free nation in the 1920s and 1930s, and an incorporated state of the Soviet Union after 1940. In 1991, it regained its independence. With 100,000 immigrants living in Chicago and adjacent suburbs, the city became the center of Lithuanian culture in the United States. It has remained that way since the 1920s, when the population topped the 100,000 mark. Most of the early arrivals came to Chicago around the time of the 1893 World's Fair.

The immigrants were, by and large, born on farms in Lithuania, where livestock breeding and dairy farming were the dominant agricultural activities. They came to Chicago equipped with healthy, strong bodies, keen minds, and a will to work hard—ideal qualifications for employment in the Union Stock Yard and Transit Company. The Lithuanians poured into the neighborhoods south and west of the stockyards in the 1890s, following succeeding waves of Irish, German, and Polish workers.

Packingtown was a vigorous, thriving community, seemingly created overnight. The stockyards had opened on Christmas Day 1865, on what was once a parcel of swampland formerly owned by Mayor John Wentworth. Within a few short decades, Chicago became the center of the meatpacking industry in the United States. But the honor was not without a price, because poverty, high crime, polluted air, and vermin-infested streets characterized the Back of the Yards community.

Like other European ethnic groups, the Lithuanians did not settle in just one neighborhood. There were scattered pockets of settlement in Bridgeport and Brighton Park—an Irish-German enclave west of the Yards along 43rd and 47th streets. In 1892 the Lithuanians built their first church in Chicago—St. George's on Lithuanica Street. This roadway, which cuts through the heart of old Bridgeport, was named in honor of two Chicago aviators of Lithuanian descent, who took off from New York City in 1933 in a celebrated race across the ocean with Wiley Post. Their plane was named the Lithuanica and had been purchased by subscription from the Chicago *Daily News.* The two flyers, who had been headed for Lithuania, never completed their mission. They crashed in a forest deep in the heart of Germany on July 13, 1933. A monument honoring the pilots was erected in 1934 at California Avenue and Marquette Road.

The building boom witnessed in Brighton Park in the 1920s lured many of the Back of the Yards Lithuanians into this solid, working-class neighborhood. In 1906 work began on the Immaculate Conception Church at 44th and California. Ten years later a parochial school was opened. Describing the notable achievements of his people, Joseph Elias, president of the Lithuanian-American Chamber of Commerce, wrote in 1927:

They began their careers here very humbly. Yet it was a relatively short time before they were recognized as a valuable part of Chicago's melting pot of varied racial groups. Today the Lithuanian people have their own churches and parochial schools, newspapers, societies, and clubs, all of which foster the spirit of American ideals.

By the 1920s there were more than 200 Lithuanian societies and clubs with an aggregate membership of between 2,500 and 2,800. The oldest and most successful choral and dramatic society in the city was the Birute. Founded in 1907 and headquartered at the Lithuanian Association at 31st and Halsted streets, the Birute has sponsored a number of concerts and stage plays. Indeed, the world of music and art embraced a number of Lithuanians who gained considerable prominence. Joseph Bobrovich, the noted opera tenor, for example, was born in Lithuania, where he grew up as a peasant fisherman. Bobrovich went on to become a member of the Russian Imperial Opera. After the 1917 Revolution he escaped to America, where his resonant voice echoed through the concert halls of Chicago and other cities. A highlight of one of his many tours was his celebrated appearance with Chaliapin at the Chicago Civic Opera Company. The Lithuanians are great lovers of the opera. Since 1956 the Lithuanian Company at Maria High School, 6727 S. California, has produced lyric opera on a grand scale. Such rarities as Amilcare Ponchielli's *I Lituani* premiered in Chicago.

Through hard work and thrift came the realization of the American dream: home ownership. By being able to earn more than the bare essentials for food, clothing, and shelter, the thrifty Lithuanians were able to pool their savings and climb the socio-economic ladder. By the 1920s there sprang up two Lithuanian state banks with deposits of more than $5,000,000. Building and loan associations were organized in the neighborhoods—grassroots banking for the community. Through these institutions, the immigrants were able to purchase homes in the expanding "bungalow belt" of Marquette Park on the city's Southwest Side.

Bungalow construction—inexpensive but durable housing—reached its peak in Chicago during the boom years of 1926–27. Prospective buyers who had accumulated money during the war years and early 1920s took advantage of easy credit terms and the availability of land. Improvements in public transportation, especially the electrified trolleys, linked the once-isolated townships on the far Northwest Side and Southwest Side to the Loop.

Much of the land that formed the nucleus of the Chicago Lawn community (Marquette Park) was owned by a real-estate millionaire, Hetty Green, who kept the area undeveloped and decidedly rural until 1911, when she finally disposed of the property. Then almost overnight, new subdivisions were carved out of abandoned cabbage patches. The Lithuanians who settled west of Western Avenue beginning in the mid-1920s typically paid $5,500 for the distinctive "Chicago school" contribution to the architectural landscape—the much-maligned but durable bungalow. It featured deep overhangs, an unfinished basement, dormer attics, central heating, and a tiny one-car garage in the back yard.

By 1930 the combined population of Marquette Park and the adjacent community of Gage Park stood at 78,997. The numbers started to decline in

Gage Park during the 1930s, but Marquette Park showed continuous growth up to 1960. By virtue of their numbers, the Lithuanians became the dominant ethnic group in the community by 1927. That year the Nativity of the Blessed Virgin Mary parish opened at 69th and Washtenaw. Today it is the largest Lithuanian parish outside Europe, with 2,500 families.

Marquette Park was the last of the pre-World War II neighborhoods to evolve out of the Union Stockyards, when the meat packing industry was still a vital concern to Chicago's economic well being. This Southwest Side community is now home to 150,000 ethnic Lithuanians—more than any place outside Europe. Yet many members of the younger generation have abandoned the "bungalow belt" for suburban Downers Grove, Clarendon Hills, and Lemont, where one can visit the Lithuanian World Center—which has been the nerve center for Lithuanian-Americans monitoring the political turmoil and fight for independence in the homeland.

Today the heart of Chicago's Lithuanian community is centered near Western Avenue and Marquette Road. Lithuanian Plaza Court, a small commercial strip between Washtenaw and Western avenues, features many charming ethnic restaurants and stores. For many summers the Homeowners' Association of Marquette Park sponsored a folk fare along West 69th Street, featuring the work of native craftspeople and merchants.

The Lithuanian community is one of the better organized, most cohesive immigrant cultures in Chicago today. The past is kept alive at the Balzekas Museum of Lithuanian Culture at 6500 S. Pulaski Road. Founded by Stanley Balzekas, owner of a car dealership on Archer Avenue, this is one of Chicago's lesser known but more interesting folk museums, highlighting the history, customs, artwork, handicrafts, and armaments of Lithuania.

When *glasnost* opened a crack in the door to Soviet Russia, worshipers at St. George's Church in Marquette Park gathered to celebrate Mass and pray for a free Lithuania. Some wore native costumes, while others carried the yellow, green, and red flag of the homeland. At the back of Tolius Slutas's bookstore in Marquette Park, an impressive array of equipment stood primed to receive telefaxed messages from Vilnius, Lithuania's capital city. Since 1988 Slutas and his wife, Helen, have broadcast the Lithuanian-American Hour, a news and information service for the Southwest Side. Tolius fled Lithuania as a boy during the Nazi terror. Since that time he has maintained his ties to his homeland by communicating with the *Sajudis,* the underground movement that championed independence in the Baltic region.

Lithuania has finally won its long battle to gain freedom and the right to self-determination. Chicago, with the largest concentration of Lithuanians outside the capital of Vilnius, tolled the bell of freedom on March 11, 1990, when Vytautas Landsbergis, the President of the Supreme Council of Lithuania, proclaimed the restoration of the independent republic in a special session of parliament. In May 1991, Mr. Landsbergis (who did not run for president in the first democratically held election, February 14, 1993) was warmly greeted by the City of Chicago and the South Side Lithuanian-American community at a special luncheon in his honor at the Balzekas Museum.

Freedom is an eternal vigil for these Lithuanians. As a dissident writer has summed it up: "On the road to independence it's raining."

Attractions

Cultural Institutions

Balzekas Museum of Lithuanian Culture, *6500 S. Pulaski Rd., Chicago, (773) 582-6500. Open daily. Free parking. Admission fee charged. Members free.*

It's really three museums in one. Upstairs, across the hall from the 13th Ward Democratic Organization, the Lithuanian Folk Art Institute offers instruction in weaving sashes and national costumes from the seven ethnographic regions of Lithuania. The Folk Art Institute was founded in 1980 as a not-for-profit educational and cultural organization whose main goal is to preserve, research, and create Lithuanian folk art. Seventy to 100 members attend classes, where they learn the skill of using the inkle loom under the direction of Vida Rimas and her artisans.

Downstairs, the main exhibit "Lithuania Through the Ages" transports the visitor through the history of the Baltic state, with special emphasis on folk costumes, amber jewelry (the stone is worn by Lithuanians for health), military items, numismatics, and philately. The Balzekas Museum was formally opened on June 22, 1966, next to Stanley Balzekas's Chrysler showroom on Archer Avenue. The family moved into larger quarters at 6500 S. Pulaski in 1986. The Children's Museum of Immigrant History teaches school-age youngsters about the importance of their heritage through a tour of the Medieval World in the castle "Armory," and a journey back to the 19th century in the "Passport to Lithuania" exhibit. Children are permitted to dress up in authentic folk costumes and play the traditional musical instruments such as the *kankles.*

For serious researchers, the museum is the largest Lithuanian resource depository outside of Europe, housing 20,000 books, periodicals, monographs, and photo archives. *Recommended.*

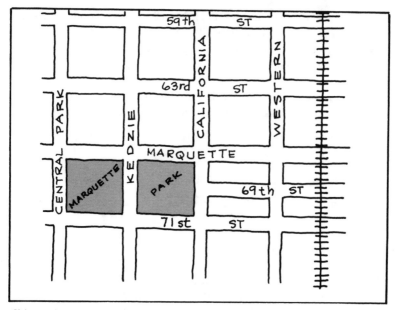

Chicago Lawn

Lithuanian American Community and Human Services Council, *2715 W. 71st St., Chicago, (773) 476-2655.*

Adjacent to the Seklycia Restaurant, the L.A.C. provides English-language instruction, a senior citizens' aerobics class, medical lectures, and folk dancing to Lithuanian immigrants. Some 100,000 members belong to this fraternal society, which is dedicated to helping newly arrived immigrants achieve self-determination. For the friends and relatives in need, the L.A.C. sends books and food supplies back to Lithuania. During the non-binding referendum conducted by Lithuanian voters over the question of separation from the Soviet Union (held over the weekend of Feb. 8–9, 1991) a telex number was set up to connect Chicagoans directly with the parliament in Vilnius. (Because all mail was routed through Moscow, local officials were concerned that printed telegrams would be confiscated by the officials.)

Latvian Community Center, *4146 N. Elston Ave., Chicago, (773) 588-2085.*

Chicago's Latvian population numbers less than 8,000, but this small-but-determined immigrant group shares a common cause with the Lithuanians:

liberating the Baltic states from Soviet rule. On August 5, 1940, the Soviet Union annexed the Latvian territories, effectively ending the republic's brief encounter with democracy. Thousands of Latvian citizens became refugees. Many of them settled on Chicago's Northwest Side between 1945 and 1950. Today their needs are served by the Latvian Community Center. The meeting hall is upstairs from the Latvian Folk Art Museum (see the following entry), and it is where members of the Latvian Welfare Association, their senior citizens' group, and various community organizations meet in a congenial atmosphere. At various times during the year, the center sponsors concerts, art shows, and plays that are produced locally, and performed by visiting troupes from midwestern cities and from Canada.

Latvian Folk Art Museum, *4146 N. Elston Ave.,*
Chicago, (773) 588-2085. Open Monday–Friday.
Other hours by appointment. Donation requested.

The museum as it exists today is the outgrowth of an earlier effort by the Chicago Latvian Association and several artisan groups in Illinois and Wisconsin to establish a permanent home for a collection of archival artifacts (Senmantu Kratuve). Beginning in the mid-1960s, and continuing for the next decade, Osvalds Grins and his daughter Astra Revelins scoured the United States in search of historic items brought from Latvia. Grins painstakingly assembled an impressive collection of folk art, which made its way into the permanent exhibit, established at this location in 1978. As the years passed, Chicagoans of Latvian descent donated family heirlooms and artifacts. Today the museum features a collection that is particularly rich in textiles. Also noteworthy are some of the less-familiar items, such as the musical instruments: *kokle* (a string piece) and the *giga* (a monochord). Visitors can listen to an unusual collection of Latvian folk music, preserved through the decades on audio tapes. Supported in part by the Illinois Arts Council.

Lithuanian Youth Center *(adjacent to the chapel of*
the Lithuanian Jesuit Fathers), 5620 S. Claremont,
Chicago, (773) 778-7500. Open Monday–Friday.

The Youth Center serves Chicago's Lithuanian community as a cultural, educational, and social center, housing the Lithuanian World Archives and the Ciurlionis Art Gallery (named for M. K. Ciurlionis, whose emblem of the knight Vytis—the Lithuanian national emblem—stands on the lawn outside the building). Special events, concerts, and dance troupes scheduled periodically.

Sisters of St. Casimir Lithuanian Library,
2601 W. Marquette, Chicago, (773) 776-1324.
Open by appointment only.

Since it was built in 1911, the Sisters of St. Casimir have maintained this museum and archive of Lithuanian history. The sisters also staff Holy Cross Hospital, opened at Lithuanian Plaza Court and Western Avenue in 1925.

Outlying Areas

Lithuanian World Center, *511 E. 127th St.,*
Lemont, 60439 (630) 257-6777.

Formerly St. Andreas Church. Lithuanian Mass is still conducted in this church and cultural center in south suburban Lemont, but in recent years the center has served the dual purpose of museum and folk art institute. The basement houses a collection of folk art, costumes, and works of fine art. Saturday school classes are conducted between 9:00 A.M. and 1:00 P.M. for schoolchildren, and private parties are scheduled throughout the year.

Annual Events and Celebrations

St. Casimir's Day (Kaziuko Muge). *Lithuania Youth Center, 5620 S. Claremont, Chicago, (773) 778-7500.*
First weekend in March.

In Lithuania, the coming of spring and the warm weather is marked by the annual St. Casimir celebration, honoring the memory of a canonized saint born in 1458 in Krakow, Poland. St. Casimir was the grand prince of Lithuania, whose progressive social programs greatly benefited both Poles and Lithuanians. The annual event is something akin to the New Orleans Mardi Gras, according to Birute Jasaitis, community leader. The weekend festival is sponsored by a Lithuanian "scouting" movement similar to, yet different from, the American Boy Scouts in that the members are active for life. Three floors of the Lithuania Youth Center are transformed into a replica of a market center from old Vilnius, featuring handicrafts, woodwork, decorated eggs, amber jewelry, and entertainment. The weekend celebration continues at the Balzekas Museum with a Sunday afternoon Lithuanian film festival, and a folk art show with a depiction of key events from St. Casimir's life. *Recommended.*

Draugas **Community Festival,** *4545 W. 63rd St.,*
Chicago, (773) 585-9500.

Run by the Marion Fathers, the *Draugas* Lithuanian-language newspaper is the only daily sheet to be published outside of Europe. The community fest is held either the last Sunday in July or the first Sunday in August, at the Marion Fathers seminary at 63rd and Pulaski, and is a special fund-raising event to sustain the publishing venture. Food booths, book sale, raffle, and special exhibits.

Easter Brunch at the Balzekas Museum of
Lithuanian Culture, *6500 S. Pulaski Rd., Chicago,*
(773) 582-6500. Easter Sunday.

Throughout the year, the Balzekas Museum sponsors many fine programs that promote Lithuanian culture. The Easter Brunch and egg-decorating classes are community favorites.

Brighton Park Lithuanian Homeowner's Festival.
Mid-July, or the Friday and Saturday immediately
following the Taste of Chicago Festival in Grant Park.
Call Bob Zebrauskas at (773) 778-5237 for
information. Free admission.

A city-sponsored ethnic folk fair with a variety of musical styles to suit all tastes. Country, rock, Polish, and Lithuanian folk music. In the past, the Brighton Park residents have brought in Lithuanian entertainers—eleven in 1991—to authenticate the European flavor of this event. The Homeowner's Festival takes place on S. Western Boulevard between the 4300 and 4700 blocks.

Balzekas Museum Anniversary Dinner, *Amber*
Ballroom, 6500 S. Pulaski Rd., Chicago, (773) 582-
6500. Second weekend in December. Admission fee
charged.

Buffet dinner of Lithuanian cuisine. Dancing. Cash bar.

Places to See

Nativity of the Blessed Virgin Mary, *Lithuanian*
Plaza Court and Washtenaw, Chicago, (773) 776-4600.

The late Mayor Richard J. Daley proclaimed 69th Street "Lithuanian Plaza Court" in 1966, to honor the ethnic Europeans who settled in this community.

Many of them worshiped at Nativity B.V.M., founded in 1927. Begin your tour of the neighborhood here, and pay close attention to the colorful exterior mosaic murals, painted by Lithuanian artist Adomas Varnas. The modern church was dedicated in 1957. It was designed by John Mulokas, who drew from elements of the baroque, Lithuanian folk themes, and Christian designs. Inside, the church maintains an impressive collection of artifacts and curios pertaining to Lithuanian history.

St. George's Parish, *33rd St. and Lithuanica,*
Chicago.

Here stands the mother church of Lithuanian immigration to the United States, though the facility is closed now and imperiled by the wrecker's ball. The handsome Gothic structure was built piecemeal between 1892 and 1908, as money became available. The Rev. George Kolesinskas was appointed by Archbishop Patrick Feehan on Mar. 2, 1892, when it was determined by the archdiocese that there were enough Lithuanians in Chicago to support their own parish. Nearly a hundred years later, the final Eucharist was celebrated by a handful of remaining parishioners. Ironically, the archdiocese had decided that there were no longer enough people in the community to keep the historic church open.

Shops

Baltic Bakery, *2616 Lithuanian Plaza Court,*
Chicago, (773) 737-6784, and 4627 S. Hermitage,
Chicago, (773) 523-1510. Open daily.

Nothing fancy about either store, but the Lithuanian and Polish residents of the South Side have patronized the Baltic Bakeries for years. A variety of fresh breads, imported cheeses, kolacky, stollen cakes, beer sausage, and a few German imports thrown in for good measure make this one of Chicago's best bakeries.

Restaurants

Nida Delicatessen and Restaurant, *2617 W. 71st St.,*
Chicago, (773) 476-7675. Closed Sundays and
Mondays. No credit cards accepted.

The small restaurant sells bacon buns, *kugilis,* hazelnut cakes, Lithuanian "Andriulis" cheese, and some Polish delicacies. Open for lunch and dinner. Seats only five to six people at a time.

Neringa Restaurant, *2632 W. 71st St., Chicago, (773) 476-9026. Open for breakfast, lunch, and dinner daily. No credit cards.*

Joseph and Janina Galica are your hosts, and if you want alcohol, they suggest you bring your own. No matter. The food and the soup—their specialty—are top drawer. The house specialties—*kugilis,* dumplings, and duck—are highly recommended in this, one of the largest Lithuanian-cuisine restaurants in Chicago.

Seklycia Lithuanian Manor Inn, *2715 W. 71st St., Chicago, (773) 476-1680 or 476-2655. Open for breakfast, lunch, and dinner daily. No credit cards accepted.*

A favored gathering spot for Americans of Lithuanian descent—particularly for older people who have remained unassimilated into the community. The restaurant and its adjacent banquet hall have been serving the local residents for over a decade as a dining establishment and meeting place. Specials every day. No liquor served.

Outlying Areas

Healthy Food, *3236 S. Halsted St., Chicago (773) 326-2724. Open for breakfast, lunch, and dinner daily.*

Far removed from the Lithuanian community, Healthy Food is located in Irish-Hispanic Bridgeport. The latest news of the community can be found at the front counter in the form of handbills and notices. The standard Lithuanian dishes, *koldunai, kugelis,* and *blynai* (pancakes with sour cream) are served, along with American entrées.

Media

Lithuanian-Language Radio Programming

Voice of Lithuania, *hosted by Balys Brazdzionis. Airs on WCEV-1450 AM, Monday through Friday, 8:30 to 9:00 P.M.*

Margutis II, *hosted by Petra Petrutis. Airs on WCEV-1450 AM, Monday through Friday, 9:05 to 9:30 P.M. Long-running program, first heard in the Chicago area in 1966.*

Lithuanian American Radio, *hosted by Anatolijus Slutas. Airs on WCEV-1450 AM, Sundays, 7:00 to 8:00 A.M.*

Latvian-Language Radio Programming

Latvian Music, *broadcast on WNIB-FM (97.1 on the dial) and WNIZ-FM (96.9, aired in Zion) every Monday evening at 11:00 P.M. The Folk Art Museum has produced this program since 1985.*

71st Street, Between California and Western

The commercial district and unofficial center of Lithuanian culture in Chicago is 71st Street and Lithuanian Plaza Court (formerly 69th St.) between California (2600 West) and Western Avenue (2400 West). The small commercial/residential strip that comprises Lithuanian Plaza Court still features several ethnic-European restaurants and businesses, but increasingly these merchants are leaving the neighborhood in light of a changing ethnic composition.

The remaining little stores and the restaurants continue to serve the neighborhood people and Lithuanian visitors who return each day to sample the culture, regardless of the racial and ethnic differences that have cast Marquette and Gage parks in an unfavorable light over the last twenty-five years.

In some ways, Lithuanian Plaza Court has been eclipsed by the 71st Street merchants, who have become recommitted to the neighborhood, now composed mostly of Lithuanians. According to Birute Jasaitis, Vice President of the Lithuanian Community Organization in Chicago, few of these old-timers have ventured outside of the neighborhood even though they have raised their children to adulthood. Many of them can only speak a few words of broken English, but they count on the Lithuanian-American Community Organization to provide important social services, job referrals, and a conduit to their relatives back home.

Estonian Chicago

Estonian House, *Estonian Lane, Lincolnshire, (847) 537-8016. One-half mile north of Deerfield Rd. on Milwaukee Ave. Open Sundays only. Admission to the grounds is free. Membership available.*

The tiny Baltic nation Estonia, bordered on the north by the Gulf of Finland, on the west by the former Soviet Union, and on the south by Latvia, was ruled by Sweden until 1721, when it was ceded to Russia. Estonia would remain under Russian rule for all but twenty years of its history—until the fall of communism in 1989. The tiny colony of Estonians who settled in Chicago—less than a thousand, according to an unofficial census conducted in the 1970s—celebrates its heritage at Estonian House, a private mansion turned into a cultural center celebrating the performing arts. The Estonian House is off the beaten path—a tiny blue road sign hanging from a pole on northbound Milwaukee Avenue provides the only clue to the passing motorist—but inside the building on any given Sunday there may be folk dancing, musical concerts by the Finnish/Estonian Chorus, or a light lunch served by the ladies of the club. The Mid-Summer Festival (Saturday closest to June 24th) draws large crowds who partake in dancing, dining, and the joys of being Estonian . . . and Scandinavian. Enno Toomasalu is the Director of Estonian House, and he invites one and all to stop by, say hello, visit the library, tour the center, and sample Estonian culture

Hungarian, Serbo-Croatian, and Romanian Chicago

═ Hungarian History and Settlement ═

The struggle to establish a free and independent Hungary during a period of revolution and upheaval in European history drove many of its citizens into a self-imposed exile. The history of Chicago's Hungarian community rightfully dates back to the closing months of 1849.

The brutal crackdown against nationalistic insurgents by Austria's Franz Joseph I, ruler of the Hapsburg Empire, encouraged freedom lovers from the flat plains of the central European monarchy to begin anew in the United States.

Only a handful of Hungarian families made it to Chicago prior to the Civil War, but they established the city's first private foreign-language school. During the period of peak immigration from Eastern and Southern Europe (1890–1920), Chicago's Hungarian population swelled from a paltry 3,600 to more than 70,000. However, the census data from this period is imprecise due to the confusion and ignorance of Chicago's head-counters who often confused the Hungarians with Czechs, Germans, Austrians, and other former residents of the old empire.

There is no mistaking some of Chicago's more prominent citizens of Hungarian descent, however. Sir Georg Solti and Fritz Reiner, the great maestros of the Symphony Orchestra, were Hungarian-born. The makers of Vienna Sausage, Chicago's preferred fast-food culinary delicacy, are also of solid Hungarian stock.

The second-wave immigrants of the late 19th century established community life on the edges of the original German settlement on the North Side from Wells Street to North, and across Lincoln Avenue.

Immigrant Magyars who had departed the agricultural provinces of Hungary settled near the heart of Chicago's South Side industrial core at 95th Street and Cottage Grove Avenue. Plentiful jobs in the steel mills and railroad yards awaited them. Hungarian Jews found acceptance and a new identity near the Maxwell Street ghetto on Roosevelt Road.

On the West Side, the immigrants erected a parish at 2015 W. Augusta Boulevard—St. Stephen, King of Hungary Church, named for Stephen I, patron saint of Hungary and in 1083 the first king to be canonized. The South Side faithful were served by Our Lady of Hungary Roman Catholic Church, built at 92nd and Avalon, now a Haitian church. The Hungarians are long gone.

The Calvin Reform Church, originally serving a predominantly Hungarian congregation, has pushed steadily southward from 92nd and Langley in Chicago to 2895 Glenwood-Lansing in suburban Lynwood. The faithful observe Hungarian Independence Day every year on March 15, marking the 1848 revolt which ushered in a brief period of peace and harmony in a troubled land. Throughout the year the church publishes a cookbook and hosts numerous festivals, bazaars, and community events, including Hungarian sausage-making. Each year hundreds of pounds of tasty *kobacz* are prepared with loving hands in the basement of the church and sold to the community. Alcoholic spirits are strictly prohibited on the premises of this church, according to author Barbara Schaaf, a second-generation Hungarian-American. However: "It's almost impossible *not* to find a Hungarian church without a bar in the basement."

The third wave of immigration occurred in the late 1950s. Popular discontent against the post-World War II Soviet-controlled regime fostered dissent and rebellion that claimed the lives of many of its citizens. After four weeks of resistance and demonstrations, Russian tanks and manpower crushed the revolt in Budapest on November 4, 1956. Nearly 200,000 refugees fled the country for the safety of the Western democracies. A loophole in the immigration laws permitted 30,000 displaced Hungarians to resettle in the United States.

From the make-shift "Freedom Camp" established in Camp Kilmer, New Jersey, thousands soon made their way into Chicago where they were welcomed in the spirit of friendship by many other ethnic Europeans who had experienced similar political repression over the years.

The Hungarians who fled to America as a consequence of the 1956 uprising tended to gravitate to the South Side in search of steady-paying jobs in the steel mills and railroad yards. They purchased affordable homes in neighboring West Pullman, along Commercial Avenue (the main thoroughfare of South Chicago), and near Burnside (89th Street and the Illinois Central Tracks), during the prosperous post-World War II era.

The erosion of the manufacturing district and the loss of jobs in the 1960s forced many second-generation Hungarians to re-evaluate their economic prospects. Many abandoned the old neighborhoods in favor of the outlying suburbs of Lansing, Calumet City, and Burnham, and the North Shore suburbs of Skokie, Niles, and Northbrook.

Fragments of the old North Side Hungarian neighborhoods could still be found along Clark Street, Belmont Avenue, and Lincoln Avenue in the 1970s and 1980s, but with urban gentrification many of the original European settlements have been swept away.

Croatian & Serb History and Settlement

Amid the steam and smoke of the nearby steel mills, and the odiferous stench emanating from the Union Stockyards several miles to the west, Chicago's Croatian community stands tall and nurtures a proud ethnic heritage on the Southeast Side. They occupy a necklace of working class neighborhoods stretching along the Calumet River from Lake Michigan to Lake Calumet, roughly fifteen miles from downtown Chicago.

Here, amid swampland, waste disposal sites, decaying rustbelt factories, and corner saloons in the bungalow neighborhoods of the 10th Ward, live the Croatians and Serbs. The 10th Ward was once ruled by the colorful and flamboyant Alderman Edward Vrdolyak, whose Croatian parents owned one such neighborhood tavern years ago.

A troubled past and an uncertain future characterize the history of Croatia, a rectangular Southern Slavic parcel of land across the Adriatic Sea from Italy. Today Croatia is torn by ethnic strife, instability, and war as the various ethnic minorities (Serbs, Slovenes, Bosnian Muslims, and Hercegovinians), seek to establish autonomous rule following the disintegration of the former republic of Yugoslavia and the collapse of communist rule.

For much of its history, Croatia has endured the rule of occupying foreign powers. At the time of the 1893 World's Fair in Chicago, Croatian music, folk customs, and national identity were on display at the gala celebration along the lakefront, even though the region was still a province of the old Austro-Hungarian empire and subject to the will of the foreign crown.

A tanburitza orchestra from Croatia entertained and delighted World's Fair visitors with its unique arrangements using this string instrument, a cross between a mandolin and the familiar Greek bouzouki. The musicians were garbed in traditional ethnic costumes and their appearance marked the first public presentation of Croatian music in the United States.

By the onset of the Depression in 1929, there were four recognizable Croatian neighborhoods in Chicago: 18th and Racine, established in the heart of Czech Pilsen in the mid-1920s; 28th Street and Princeton to the south; 28th and Central Park further west; and 50th and Throop. It was estimated that there were 38,000 Croats living in Chicago at that time. Today that number has grown considerably, to more than 100,000 in Chicago and its neighboring suburbs, primarily to the south of the city.

As Chicago continued to expand and newer immigrant groups staked their claim on the Near South Side, the Croat settlement moved farther away, first to Bridgeport, then ultimately Hegewisch and the Lake Calumet region brushing up against Northwest Indiana.

It is one of the great ironies of Chicago's ethnic history that the Serbs should settle in close proximity to the Croats, their ancient enemies from the old world. Long-simmering ethnic and sectarian tensions between these two Balkan republics erupted after the creation of Yugoslavia in 1918—one of the consequences of World War I, which destroyed the last vestiges of monarchical rule in Central Europe. The Roman Catholic Croats, whom the Serbs accused of pro-Nazi activity during World War II, will argue that they were denied an independent nation in 1945 because the Serbs were communist sympathizers.

Serbs, Croats, and Slovenes imported their hostilities to South Chicago and the surrounding communities. Through sheer economic necessity they were compelled to work side by side in the steel mills and residential communities of Slag Town and Memorial Park, the mill neighborhood that took shape at the turn of the century.

Chicago's Serbs probably outnumber the Croats in the city. There are 60,000–300,000 Serbs compared to 75,000–200,000 Croats, according to one estimate. Serb immigration began before World War I, and in each South Side neighborhood where they established a presence, construction of a Serbian church followed. The newest Serbian Orthodox Church is Holy Resurrection, near Cumberland Avenue and the Kennedy Expressway on the far Northwest Side of the city.

As these two warring groups continue to struggle in the remnants of the former Yugoslavia, Serbs and Croats manage to co-exist—albeit uneasily—in the Windy City. Cultural, political, and religious differences remain and are almost unsolvable, particularly among the younger people who have immigrated to the United States in the last 35 years. Serbians and Croats speak a dialect of the same language, but the Serbs use the Cyrillic alphabet and are Eastern Orthodox. Croatians use the Western alphabet and are Roman Catholic.

A unifying force between the Croatian and Serbian communities following World War II was the familiar call for freedom from communist tyranny. The stirrings of a "Free Croatia" movement took shape in the 1960s and 1970s, when a new wave of immigration from the Slavic states occurred. At the same time, members of the Serbian National Defense Council engaged in anti-communist activity marked by random terrorist attacks here in Chicago.

In 1963 a bomb exploded outside the Yugoslav consul at 38 E. Bellevue, not far from the lakefront. Fifteen years later the home of the Yugoslav consul was again bombed. This time the Freedom for the Serbian Fatherland (SOPO) claimed responsibility. Then, one of the editors of the weekly anti-communist newspaper *Liberty* was tragically slain in the editorial offices, 3909 W. North Avenue, in apparent retaliation. With the fall of communism, the various ethnic groups comprising the troubled Balkans redirected their hostilities toward each other.

Today, the hated communists are an echo of the past, but in their place ethnic and religious nationalists prolong a conflict that seems almost unfathomable in the United States. In Chicago, the Serbs and Croats will undoubtedly continue to debate the correctness of their causes within the traditional framework of fraternal societies and private clubs. The Croation Fraternal Union, one such club, is an amalgam of twenty separate lodges. It promotes close ties to the motherland and sponsors numerous activities and social events.

Chicago's Croatian-American community is widely dispersed across the city. Many of the second- and third-generation Croats moved to the North Shore, congregating near the foot of the Devon Avenue melting pot where a parish was opened at Ridge Avenue. Then they later moved to suburban Morton Grove, Skokie, and Northbrook.

In the 1970s, the non-profit Croatian Culture Center of Chicago purchased a converted supermarket at 2845 W. Devon Avenue in the middle of the Jewish and Indian communities. A social hall, classrooms, conference area, a library, and a small museum under the auspices of the Reverend Francis Eterovich enthusiastically promotes the long history of Croatian culture. The imposing building adds to the diverse multiethnic flavor of Devon Avenue—truly a boulevard of the United Nations.

Hungarian

Hungarian Books and Records, *561 W. Diversey Ave., Chicago, (773) 477-1484. Closed Sundays.*

Located on the second floor of a Hungarian travel agency, the shop sells Hungarian-language books, videos, and English texts pertaining to the history of Hungary.

Kenessey's Cypress, *500 E. Ogden Ave., Hinsdale, (708) 323-2727. Open daily for breakfast, lunch, and dinner. Accepts all credit cards.*

American restaurant that serves certain Hungarian delicacies including beef *guylas* (stew).

Serbo-Croatian

Feast of the Assumption, *St. Jerome's Church, 2805 S. Princeton. Mid-August.*

This long-running festival lures up to 10,000 celebrants, who sample roasted lamb, pig, and sauerkraut in a festive picnic setting. St. Jerome's is where Chicago's first and only Croatian-American Mayor, Michael A. Bilandic, attended Croatian-language classes as a youngster.

Holy Trinity Croatian Church, *1850 S. Throop, between 18th and 19th Streets, Chicago, (773) 226-2736.*

Built in 1914, this small church and school in Pilsen served Chicago's Croatian community for many years. Mass is still conducted in Croatian, and it still serves as a cultural center for many Chicago residents of Croatian descent.

Miromar's Serbian Club, *2255 W. Lawrence Ave., Chicago, (773) 784-2111. Visa and MasterCard accepted.*

Czech and Yugoslavian fare served daily for dinner. Entertainment and floor show, Friday and Saturday evenings.

Rada's Inn, *2824 N. Ashland Ave., (773) 472-1900. Open for dinner. Closed Mondays.*

Traditional cusine, including shish kebab and stuffed peppers.

The Cafe Continental, *5515 N. Lincoln Ave.,*
Chicago, (773) 878-7077. Open for dinner Thursday
through Sunday.

Croatian specialties served, including sausages (*kobasice*), apple strudel and crepes (*palacinke*), and standard American fare. Entertainment nightly.

Skadarlija Restaurant, *4024 N. Kedzie Ave.,*
Chicago, (773) 463-5600. Open for dinner
Wednesday–Sunday. Closed Mondays and Tuesdays.
All credit cards accepted.

Full Serbian menu, with entertainment nightly.

Romanian

Little Bucharest, *3001 N. Ashland Ave., Chicago,*
(773) 929-8640. Open for dinner daily.

Authentic Romanian cuisine in a lively, casual atmosphere. Specialties include ciorba soup, Romanian sweetbreads, smoked homemade sausage, and Romanian apple strudel. Live continental music Friday and Saturday nights. Delivery available. Reservations recommended on the weekends.

Romanian Kosher Sausage Company, *7200 N.*
Clark St., Chicago, (773) 761-4141. Open daily.

A popular North Side deli and butcher shop since 1966, when the Loeb family first opened their doors for business. Old world ambience. Kosher meats manufactured on the premises.

Media

Croatian American Radio—*Saturdays, 1:00–2:00*
P.M. *on WCEV, 1450 AM.*

Free Croatia—*Sundays, 2:05–4:00* P.M.*, on Sundays,*
followed by the Voice of Croatia *at 3:05 until 4:00* P.M.
on WCEV, 1450 AM.

Ukrainian Chicago

═══════ History and Settlement ═══════

Ukraine, a republic of the Commonwealth of Independent States, has ethnic traditions and a culture that dates back to the ninth century, when the
lands southwest of Russia proper were known as the Kievan-Rus. The
name Rus came to signify the lands around Kiev, an important trade center
in Eastern Europe. Various other states existed in the region, and it wasn't
until the late nineteenth century that the inhabitants began to think of themselves as a Ukrainian people with a similar culture and shared values.
Those who lived under Austrian rule in Galicia fostered the nationalist
movement—one that began as a literary revival and ended in a great awakening in 1917. The Russian Ukrainians established an independent republic in the aftermath of the Bolshevik Revolution, and on November 1, 1918,
Austrian Ukrainia proclaimed itself a republic and was federated into the
U.S.S.R. as the ZUNR.

Then, in January 1919, warfare erupted in the Russian Ukrainian Republic. Under the leadership of Symon Petlyura, ZUNR was united with the
Ukrainian National Republic. Between 1917 and 1921, several governments
struggled for control of the Ukraine. The situation remained chaotic until
1924, when the Ukrainian Soviet Socialist Republic became one of the con-
stituent republics of the Soviet Union.

There was widespread famine in the 1930s, which the Ukrainians blamed on Josef Stalin and his collectivization of agriculture. Some 5,000,000 persons perished. Many of them were victims of Stalin's dreaded secret police, which enforced a policy of "Russification"—the suppression of non-Marxist cultural and scholarly activities.

The common thread of ethno-Ukrainian history through World War II was the growing awareness among these people that there was more to preserve from Bolshevism than just a religious tradition. The immigrants who escaped the Stalinist terror—and who found a better life in America—continued the struggle to win freedom for their families back home. As they will tell you, the former Soviet Union was not Russia (though essentially dominated by Russians), nor are Ukrainians Russians.

The immigration to U.S. shores began in the early 1870s with the arrival of the sub-Carpathian Rus (or Rusins, the ancient name of the Ukraine). Many of them were fleeing from the horrors of the Czarist regime; others were in search of a fortune in the mythical cities of gold. For the most part, the political exiles settled in the cities. Others, who were seeking work in the industrial sector, founded colonies in the iron manufacturing regions of Pennsylvania. In 1884 they organized the first Ukrainian church in the United States—St. Michael the Archangel in Shenandoah, Pennsylvania.

The first large settlement of Ukrainians arrived in Chicago around 1873. Dr. Volodymer Simenovych, a law student in his native land, was the Ukraine's foremost poet and a scholar in his own right. After emigrating to the United States in 1887, Simenovych edited *Ameryka,* one of the first Ukrainian newspapers to be published in this country. In Shenandoah, the early cultural center for these people, he organized a Ukrainian cooperative store, a children's theater troupe, and a reading circle. He left his mark on the community before moving on to Chicago, where he was a vibrant force in ethnic-Ukrainian life until his death in 1932.

A small pocket of Ukrainian immigrants had colonized Packingtown on the South Side. They erected a church in 1903 that stood in the shadows of the large slaughterhouses. The First Greek Catholic Church of St. Mary's of Chicago featured a three-barred cross in the steeple. Beneath the cross was a crescent, symbolic of the "victory" of Christianity over Islam. St. Mary's soon became an integral part of the Rusin-Ruthenian culture that was predominant in Chicago's Ukrainian community. An important part of the service in those days was the plain chant of the congregation. No instrumental music was permitted. The Ukrainian church followed the forms of the Catholic Church of the Greek Rite.

By the 1930s there were five Ukrainian parishes dotting Chicago's neighborhoods, including the lovely Byzantine-Slavonic style of St. Nicholas's Roman Catholic Cathedral at Rice and Oakley streets on the near Northwest Side. The Cathedral of St. Nicholas stood in the heart of an emerging Ukrainian neighborhood south of Wicker Park and along Chicago Avenue.

Built between November 1913 and January 1915, this fine old church emulated the style of the Basilica of St. Sophia in Kiev.

St. Nick's anchors Chicago's famous "Ukrainian Village," whose boundaries extend from Chicago Avenue to Division and from Damen to Western. The neighborhood north and west of downtown Chicago was first settled at the turn of the century by Polish and Slavic immigrants who purchased plain, unassuming red brick "worker cottages" dating back to the early 1870s when the city was rebuilt from scratch following the Great Fire. Some of the oldest housing stock in Chicago is remarkably well preserved and on view along Cortez and Thomas, quiet, tree-lined side streets in West Town. Along Hoyne Avenue, wealthy German merchants built elegant Victorian homes, including the mansion at 1036 N. Hoyne, where the famed Polish pianist Ignace Paderewski once performed a private recital for its owner, Edward Bankes, a coffee seller. But with the rise of Ukrainian nationalism, and the influx of political refugees during World War I, the Village assumed a Ukrainian cultural identity that lingers to this day.

Among the folk traditions imported into the United States by the Ukrainian immigrants were the melodic native songs that date back to prehistoric pagan times. There are the *koliadky* (Christmas songs), *kupalo* (mid-summer night songs), and the harvest songs, most notably the *Kolo-miika,* which is accompanied by native dancing. The *Kolo-miika* portrays the sound of the waving wheat fields so familiar to the immigrant farmers. The dance steps

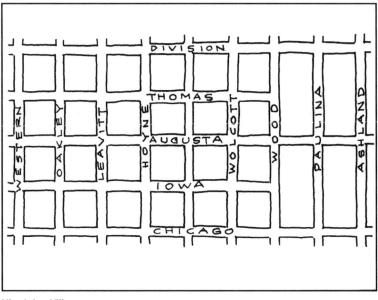

Ukrainian Village

of the *Kolo-miika* are intended to create a visual image of crossing swamplands or stretches of arid deserts. In some of the more thrilling moments of the dance, the movements portray the life of the Tartar as he was chased through the woods by wolves and bears. It is said that when five or more Ukrainians get together it is inevitable they should form a choral or dance group. The famous Ukrainian National Chorus, under the direction of Alexander Koshetz, introduced the translated version of the classic "Carol of the Bells," a Christmas melody.

Also important to Ukrainians is the plight of their compatriots who have suffered under the yoke of oppression since the time of the czars. On Jan. 4, 1917, Dr. Simenovych led a delegation to the White House, where he prevailed upon President Woodrow Wilson to proclaim a national Ukrainian Day. Wilson, with support from both branches of Congress, designated April 21, 1917, as Ukrainian Relief Day. A month later, on May 19, 1917, Simenovych and his colleague Dr. Stephen Hrynevetsky founded the first Ukrainian newspaper in Chicago—*Ukrayina*—in an attempt to unify the various ethnic coalitions that were often at odds over religious and social matters into a common cause. Indeed, Dr. Simenovych was a driving force in Ukrainian Village during the early years. On May 30, 1918, he sponsored a massive rally at Pulaski Park (Noble and Blackhawk streets) that drew a crowd of 10,000 supporters of the democratic movement. At the time there were fewer than 40,000 Ukrainians residing in the city.

The Ukrainians settled in Chicago in three successive waves, the first occurring before World War I, the second in the 1920s, and the third between 1945 and 1950, when thousands of political refugees from Eastern Europe found their way to America. Included in this group were many people from the professional classes—physicians, lawyers, writers, and intellectuals who stood in opposition to the Stalinist regime. The population surge energized Ukrainian Village and spurred construction of new churches.

The new arrivals were a thrifty, self-reliant people who created a new life for their children in the United States, while retaining much of their European heritage. The story of the First Security Federal Savings and Loan Association is a living reminder of Chicago's "I Will" spirit, and the faith of the Ukrainian immigrants in their public institutions. During the 1950s and early 1960s, the Savings and Loan pumped millions of dollars back into the Ukrainian Village, providing mortgages on easy terms to immigrants who otherwise had no chance of establishing credit in their new homeland.

Then in 1964, state regulators informed First Security that it was nearly insolvent when $360,000 in assets were reported missing. Julian Kulas, the embattled president of First Security, appealed to the community for help. The residents answered the appeal. Borrowing a page from the classic movie *It's a Wonderful Life,* they streamed into Kulas' office with cash gifts, some as high as $1,000. Kulas recalled that he had to "physically restrain" some of them so that he could write out receipts.

Flush with $300,000 in new investments, the Savings and Loan reopened its doors days later. In 1966 board members and depositors granted First Security three-year interest-free loans totaling $70,000 to replace the decrepit frame building that had served as office headquarters for years. First Security became a bank in 1985, and today controls assets of more than $136 million. On the occasion of the firm's twenty-fifth anniversary in March 1989, board members conducted their meeting entirely in Ukrainian at a neighborhood youth hall.

The resurrection of First Security stabilized Ukrainian Village at a time when many second- and third-generation residents were moving out to the suburbs. The neighborhood realtors were discouraging investment, a practice known as red-lining, because of it's racial and ethnic overtones, and banks refused to invest much-needed dollars into the community. Many old-timers—the bedrock of the village—began to wonder whether the time had come to move their cherished cultural institutions.

In 1969 St. Nick's switched from the traditional Julian calendar to the Gregorian, which sparked an angry outcry of protest among the traditionalists in the congregation. A dissenting group of parishioners broke away and started their own church—Saints Volodymyr and Olha—a few blocks away, at Oakley and Superior streets. The church was dedicated in 1974 by the head of the Ukrainian Catholic Church, Patriarch Joseph Slidyi. Its parishioners take credit for the resurgence of Ukrainian Village. With urban gentrification, many of the suburban Ukrainians began to return to the old neighborhood in the late 1970s to purchase homes and raise their children.

Ethnic pride is reflected in the various Ukrainian cultural centers that have opened in recent years. The Ukrainian Museum of Modern Art, at 2453 W. Chicago, celebrates the work of Ukraine's contemporary artists, many of whom had seen their works banned by the Soviet government. In 1988, after nearly ten years of hot debate with some of the other European groups that permeated the Northwest Side community west of the Kennedy Expressway, the $2.5-million Ukrainian Culture Center opened at Chicago and Oakley.

Each year on January 22, Ukrainian Independence Day is celebrated in Chicago. It is a symbolic event that commemorates that all-too-brief period following the Bolshevik Revolution, when the republic was established.

Ukrainians today take pride in their Americanism. At the same time they are mindful of the diminution of their national identity under the Soviets. In the 1930s, a Ukrainian writer who wrote a brief history of his people for the Works Project Administration (WPA) summed up the hopes and dreams of his people by saying: "This new generation, with its modernistic tendencies for progress, will no doubt in time be the making of Ukrainia as one of the world nations."

The long-desired goal of a Ukraine free of communist repression was an idea born of hope, courage, and faith; a faith at long last rewarded on August 24, 1991, when the nation's parliament declared its independence from Russia following a failed coup by communist hardliners. Ukrainians by the millions voted in a national referendum five months later to sever all ties to Russia and the faltering government of Mikhail S. Gorbachev.

In Chicago, where an estimated 40,000–60,000 Ukrainian Americans had kept close watch on the historic developments in their ancestral homeland, it was a time for celebration and revelry. On the day of the landmark vote, many gathered inside old St. Nicholas church on Rice Street to give thanks and pray. But most of all, these Ukrainians looked to the future with a sense of renewed hope.

It was time to build a new nation and to assist the republic in its effort to forge a strong democracy. Some, like Evanston Police Officer Michael Shep, would journey to Ukraine in the coming year to work with the local authorities. Shep, who grew up in Chicago, would make several more pilgrimages to Ukraine in order to train the civilian police force in the latest Western law enforcement techniques. Others would simply savor the moment. "I thank God for letting me live long enough to see this day," wept 60-year-old Anthony Kit, summing up the attitudes of the people of Chicago's Ukrainian community.

Getting There: Take the CTA O'Hare elevated line northwest to the Chicago and Division stop. There you can transfer to the Chicago (#66) bus. From Michigan Avenue, take the Chicago bus (#66), originating on Fairbanks, to either Damen or Ashland. Connecting buses run on Milwaukee Avenue (#56), beginning at Michigan and Washington; Damen (#50), beginning on the West Side at 35th Street and Archer; or Division (#70), running from Clark to Austin. By car or taxi from the Loop, drive north on Michigan Avenue to Chicago Avenue, where you turn left. Continue west to Ashland or Damen, which places you in the middle of Ukrainian Village.

For additional information, call the CTA at (312) 836-7000.

Attractions

Cultural Institutions

Ukrainian National Museum, *721 N. Oakley Blvd., Chicago, (773) 421-8020. Open Thursday–Sunday.*

*Monday–Wednesday by appointment. Donations
requested.*

Olha Kalymom (who will remind you that Olha is Ukrainian, Olga is Russian) is your host and guide during the tour of the customs, history, and folk art of Ukraine. Olha will show you a wonderful collection of wood carvings, costume dolls, sculptures, and bas-reliefs by modern Ukrainian artists. Pay particular attention to the intricate and highly detailed Easter eggs (*pysanka*)—a staple of Ukrainian folk art. The oldest designs are called ideograms, but the painted eggs share a common theme: the sun (represented by a tripod); a rose; and stars in various patterns. Ukrainian embroidery, a highly developed folk art, is included in this collection. Many of the articles were made by village women to satisfy their innate sense of decorative beauty. The art can be found in common household items such as tablecloths, scarves, and smocks. Also displayed are 17,000 Ukrainian-language books received in donation from immigrants and visitors coming from Europe. A military room and a room dealing with the history of Chicago's Ukrainian community are included in the tour. *Recommended.*

Ukrainian Institute of Modern Art, *2320 W.
Chicago Ave., (773) 227-5522. Closed Mondays.
Donations accepted. Annual memberships available.*

UIMA, as it is called, was opened in 1971 in a rehabbed storefront. Since that time, the museum has presented an average of five major art exhibitions each year, and has featured the work of independent artists whose avant-garde style has come to the attention of the curator and a panel of professional artists.

Annual Events and Celebrations

Ukrainian Heritage Festival, *Smith Park, 2526 W.
Grand Ave., Chicago, (312) 227-0020. Second
weekend of September. For additional information and
a listing of times and scheduled events, contact the
Ukrainian Congress, 742 Oakley Ave., Chicago, (773)
252-1228.*

Food booths, dance troupes outfitted in colorful Ukrainian costumes (the women all wear knee-high boots), folk art, wood carvings, and *pysanka* eggs are featured in this celebration sponsored by the Ukrainian Congress of Chicago. The highlight of the festival is the main stage event held on Saturday night, where a variety of performers ranging from traditional to popular entertain.

Ukrainian Independence Day Celebration,
Ukrainian Village Cultural Center, 2247 W. Chicago Ave., (773) 252-1228. On or about January 22.

A short-lived Ukrainian independence was achieved on Jan. 22, 1918, and to mark this day, the Chicago Ukrainians hold a banquet and a symbolic flag-raising ceremony at St. Volodymyr and Olha Ukrainian Church at Oakley and Superior streets. The dinner and ceremony are sponsored by the Ukrainian Congress.

Taras Shevchenko Festival, *various locations, including the Ukrainian National Museum; the American-Ukrainian Youth Association, Inc., 2455-59 W. Chicago Ave., (773) 486-4204; St. Andrew's Church, 300 E. Army Trail Rd., Bloomingdale, (630) 893-2827; and St. Joseph's, 500 N. Cumberland Ave., Chicago, (312) 625-4805. Throughout March.*

Taras Shevchenko, Ukraine's greatest poet, championed the independence movement at the expense of his own personal freedom. Shevchenko was exiled to Siberia for his beliefs, but his memory is preserved in the Ukrainian schools across the United States. Shevchenko was born on March 9, 1814, and died on March 10, 1861. The museum features month-long exhibitions of Shevchenko's artwork, his writings, and depictions of his life. The churches feature tributes during March.

Christmas Celebration, *St. Nicholas Ukrainian Cathedral School, (773) 276-4537. First week of January.*

The 20-member children's choir from St. Nicholas Ukrainian Cathedral School, dressed in traditional costumes, sing Christmas carols in English and Ukrainian on the Ukrainian Christmas holiday. The choir performs at local business establishments on Chicago Avenue, including the National Security Bank at 1030 W. Chicago Ave.

East European Arts and Crafts Exposition,
Ukrainian Village Cultural Center, 2247 W. Chicago Ave., (773) 252-1228. Mid-December. Admission prices vary with the days of operation.

Icons, paintings, hand-carved wooden boxes, ceramics, glass, and some great food are offered for sale.

Places to See

Ukrainian American Publishing Co., *2315 W. Chicago Ave., (773) 276-6373. Open daily.*

What began as a printing house disseminating newspapers and political pamphlets to newly arrived Ukrainian immigrants is now a gift shop, selling Easter egg coloring kits, greeting cards, embroidery, and school books for children attending St. Nicholas. The spirit of those former times is not lost, however, because the store also sells copies of the *Independent Ukraine,* a political journal published quarterly out of Toronto, Canada, where there is a sizable Ukrainian population. The UAP has been at this location for more than 30 years.

Delta Import Company, *2242 W. Chicago Ave., (773) 235-7788. Open daily.*

Since 1963, the Delta Importing Company has sold folk jewelry, figurines, fabrics, crystal, greeting cards, decorative eggs, and other items from Ukraine. The trident is the national symbol of Ukraine, and the nautical image abounds at Delta, in rings, posters, T-shirts, and pennants. Irene Bodnar, the third of three owners, will ship parcels to the old country. *Recommended.*

Ukrainian American Youth Association, Inc., *2455-59 W. Chicago Ave., (773) 486-4204. Open daily.*

Busloads of school-age children come here every week and practice their folk dancing—the Hutzuk and Hopak are the traditional steps. The building is home to the famed dance ensemble "Ukrainia," which has performed at Epcot in Orlando, Florida; the Trump Castle; and Las Vegas. The troupe performs here in July. For times and dates, call the UAYA. Lesson fee charged.

St. Nicholas Ukrainian Catholic Cathedral, *Oakley Blvd. and Rice St., (773) 276-4537.*

This beautiful Byzantine-style cathedral was modeled after the Basilica of St. Sophia in Kiev, but only thirteen of the original 32 copper-clad domes were built into the Chicago version. When a serious rift in 1968 over the proposed adaptation of the Gregorian calendar split the followers of the Eastern Rite (called Uniate Catholics) from the immigrants of the Western Ukraine, the decision was made to construct a second parish. Those who observe the Gregorian calendar chose to remain at St. Nicholas.

**Saints Volodymyr and Olha Church and Cultural
Center,** *Superior St. and Oakley Blvd.,
(773) 276-3990.*

Built between 1973 and 1975, St. Volodymyr features gilded Byzantine
domes set off by a two-story mural on the façade. The mosaic commemorates the conversion to Christianity in 988 A.D. by St. Volodymyr. The saints
of the church were painted on a lovely mural in back of the nave by an 82-
year-old neighborhood resident. Church and community planners envisioned a time when a united Ukrainian community could take advantage of
the spacious Cultural Center and auditorium constructed adjacent to the
church on Chicago Avenue.

Shops

Ann's Bakery, *2158 Chicago Ave., (773) 384-5562.
Open daily.*

A neighborhood institution specializing in wedding cakes, fine pastries, and
Ukrainian twist bread.

Self Reliance Co-op Grocers, *2204 Chicago Ave.,
(773) 342-9560. Closed Sundays.*

The co-op is a European concept that is practiced here in Ukrainian Village.
This independent grocer offers a wide array of items, including beets,
borsch, dried mushrooms, *kutiya* for the Christmas celebration, Ukrainian-
language publications, and the usual staples of American food.

Restaurants

Sak's Ukrainian Village Restaurant, *2301 W.
Chicago Ave., (773) 278-4445. Open for lunch and
dinner. Closed Mondays.*

Nothing fancy, no pretension, just lots of good food. Sak's is for people on
a budget, or, as one person told me, where the real Ukrainians eat. Try the
borsch soup and the *holubtsy* (cabbage rolls). You won't leave hungry.

Galan's Restaurant and Lounge, *2212 W. Chicago
Ave., (773) 292-1000. Open for lunch and dinner daily.*

For a slightly more upscale atmosphere, try Galan's, and be sure to order the
Kozak Feast, which is a random sampling of borsch, *holubtsy, varenyky*

(filled dough dumplings), *kovbassa* and *kapustka* (Ukrainian sausage and mild sauerkraut), *kozak spys* (tenderloin of beef and pork on a skewer), and *kartpolyanyk* (potato pancakes). In the "Land of the Trident," Galan's lovingly adheres to the old world customs and features Ukrainian music Friday and Saturday evenings. Cool jazz is featured afterward. *Recommended.*

(A popular anecdote tells of a Zaporozhian Cossack who died several centuries ago and found himself in hell. Though not perturbed by his new surroundings, he considered his plight a sorry one because there was no borsch in hell!)

Outlying Areas

A Taste of Ukraine Café, *127 S. Rand Rd., Lake Zurich, (847) 550-8506. Open for lunch and dinner. Closed Sundays.*

Authentic, inexpensive Ukrainian cuisine in a casual setting. Specialties include cabbage rolls, pierogi, and homemade desserts.

Media

Ukrainian-Language Radio Programming

Ukrainian Variety Hour, *hosted by Maria Chychula. Airs on WCEV-1450 AM, Mondays, Wednesdays, and Thursdays, 7:05–8:00 P.M.*

Voice of Hope, *religious programming. Airs on WCEV-1450 AM, Mondays, 8:00–8:30 P.M.*

Religious programming from Saints Volodymyr and Olha Ukrainian parish. *Airs on WPNA-1490 AM, Tuesdays, 8:00–9:00 P.M.*

Ukrainian Evening Tribune. *Airs on WPNA-1490 AM, Fridays, 8:00–9:00 P.M.*

Religious programming from St. Nicholas and St. Volodymyr. *Airs on WPNA-1490 AM, Saturdays, 3:00–5:00 P.M.*

Ukrainian Voice of the Gospel, *religious programming. Airs on WSBC-1240 AM, Tuesdays at 9:00 P.M.*

Polish Chicago

History and Settlement

As Chicago was once the center of Irish-Gaelic culture in the Midwest, it is today the most important port of entry for thousands of Polish immigrants who share the same hopes and aspirations as earlier arrivals. Indeed, more than one million Poles and descendants of people of Polish heritage call Chicago home. They are the largest of the city's non-Hispanic white ethnic groups, followed by the Irish and Germans. They come from all backgrounds and socio-economic classes. A cousin of Lech Walesa—the democratic conscience of Poland during the days of political and economic discord following the declaration of martial law in December 1981—lives in suburban Park Ridge, just across the city boundary line; a cousin of his successor Aleksander Kwasniewski lives here as well.

Since 1980, the year that Walesa and his band of patriots launched the Solidarity Movement, courageous Poles possessing the wherewithal to buck the system have come to Chicago to live under less-than-ideal circumstances, if only to breathe the fresh air of freedom. Back home, many of these immigrants were pillars of the local community—lawyers, teachers, and skilled craftspeople. But they suffered under a stagnant economy and high unemployment.

During the height of the Solidarity crackdowns in 1982–83, thousands of Poles arrived at O'Hare Airport as political refugees. Members of the professional classes, including lawyers and accountants, were forced to accept menial employment, cleaning other people's houses or scrubbing the floors of Loop office towers. They do it happily—for now. Freedom and economic opportunity exact a heavy price, but one that must be paid.

The crossroads of Chicago's "old Polonia" was once located at Milwaukee and Division streets, directly northwest of the Loop. Today Milwaukee Avenue is still very much the "Polish Main Street," but new arrivals now settle farther north in Avondale; the neighborhood around St. Hyacinth's Roman Catholic Church between Central Park and Pulaski is called Jackowo, a nickname for the church. The Milwaukee Avenue corridor is a rich tapestry of sights and sounds that heads through some of Chicago's most colorful, ethnically diverse neighborhoods—from West Town at the foot of the Loop, up through Wicker Park, Logan Square, Avondale, Portage Park, and Jefferson Park—where many second- and third-generation Poles live—all the way to the Illinois-Wisconsin state line.

The residents of Jackowo speak Polish and attend St. Hyacinth's. The average weekly attendance at mass numbers 8,000, which is double the turnout at any other parish in the Chicago Archdiocese. These immigrant Poles may on the surface have little in common with their American-born compatriots whose parents arrived before World War II, but they are united in thought and spirit. Together they funnel an estimated $1 billion in cash and material goods back to Poland every year—private foreign-aid packages sent through the United States postal system.

Chicago's Polonia—the name is derived from an ancient Slavic tribe known as the *Polanie* (field or plain we live in)—first took shape in 1851, when Anton Smarzewski escaped the Prussian regime that had enslaved his homeland. He became the first settler from that region to establish residence in Chicago. A carpenter by trade, Smarzewski decided to add the German-sounding "Schermann" to his last name. He opened up a small grocery store near Division and Noble streets. Thus, the first Polish colony was born on the near Northwest Side.

In 1864, Peter Kiolbassa, a Pole from Texas who had fought in the Civil War, came to Chicago, where he hoped to make his mark in public life. Widely known for personal integrity and charisma, "Honest Pete" was elected city treasurer in 1891. He established a precedent, later incorporated into law, that made it obligatory for state, county, and city officials to pay into the public treasury all interest on public money. Kiolbassa believed that he was ethically bound to teach the lessons of citizenship not only in word, but in deed. His political advisers reminded him that he was not legally required to do so, but Kiolbassa made good on his promises at a time when politicians were less circumspect in their dealings.

Kiolbassa and Smarzewski-Schermann organized the St. Stanislaus Kostka Society in 1864; five years later it evolved into Chicago's first Roman Catholic parish. The St. Stanislaus Kostka Church, standing at the corner of Noble and Evergreen streets on the Northwest Side, is the oldest and grandest Polish Catholic parish in the archdiocese. Forty of the first fifty-six houses of worship erected for Chicago's Poles were replicas of the great churches of Europe, with paintings, statuary, stained glass, and wood carvings hand-crafted by artisans. St. Stanislaus in Chicago houses a masterpiece painting created by the famous Polish artist Stanislaus Zukctynski during one of his visits to the city. To a generation of Poles who attended services at this parish, the church will always be equated with the memory of Father Vincent Barzynski, who helped found the Polish Roman Catholic Union in 1874.

The arriving immigrants fanned across the greater Northwest Side in record numbers, especially after 1871 when Otto von Bismarck enforced a policy of Germanization in the Polish provinces. During that time of repression, many ecumenical figures were exiled or jailed, and the German language was required learning for all Polish schoolchildren. The tide of immigration between 1871 and 1918 was fostered by the desire to escape political subjugation and by the quest for greater economic opportunity.

Poles found jobs in the industrial basin along the North Branch of the Chicago River—Goose Island, the Lower West Side near the Burlington Railroad, and the Bridgeport and Back-of-the-Yards neighborhoods on the South Side. The Polish ghettos that sprang up in the waning years of the nineteenth century circled the factories and slaughterhouses. The unskilled Poles were happy to accept jobs in heavy industry, which paid an average of $8 per week. With these meager earnings they clothed and fed their families while paying for the upkeep of the neighborhood parish, even though it involved tremendous self-sacrifice. St. Hedwig's, founded in 1888 at Webster and Hoyne, was built and paid for by the immigrant parishioners, who absorbed 90 percent of the construction costs.

In 1904, the generosity of the Poles was again called upon, this time to finance the construction of a monument to the Revolutionary War hero Thaddeus Kosciuszko. In that year, the statue, sculpted by Casimir Chodainski, was unveiled amid much fanfare in Humboldt Park. (It has since been moved to Achsah Bond Street and Lake Shore Drive, west of the Adler Planetarium.) To participate in such a worthy cause was seen as a great honor and was encouraged by the political and religious societies, which fostered closer ties to the mainstream American establishment.

There were two major Polish settlements in Chicago at the turn of the century, Polonia on the North Side and smaller pockets on the South Side at 47th and Ashland; 32nd and Morgan; and 88th and Commercial in South Chicago. The "Polonia Triangle" at the intersection of Division, Milwaukee, and Ashland formed the nucleus of the original "Polish Downtown." It was a cohesive neighborhood about three-quarters of a mile long and a half-mile wide. Eighty-six percent of the population was composed of foreign-born Polish immigrants, according to 1898 census figures.

At 1520 W. Division Street stands a modest gray building that once housed the Polish National Alliance (PNA), an ethnic-political fraternity organized in 1880 by a group of exiles committed to the liberation of the homeland from the various occupying powers. By 1927, PNA membership in the United States stood at 250,000, with assets totaling $17,000,000, and a publishing house at 106 W. Division. The PNA first published *Zgoda* (Harmony) in 1880, and was less concerned about religious and moral issues than a rival organization that sprang up six years earlier—the Polish Roman Catholic Union (PRCU), which sought to promote religious ties between the immigrant community and the church.

For years these two powerful fraternal organizations were at cross-purposes with each other. The PNA was assailed by the PRCU as a godless collection of anarchists, unbelievers, and troublemakers. Then, following the collapse of the Central Powers in 1918, the Poles moved rapidly toward statehood. In November of that year, the short-lived republic was established on democratic principles, and a government was installed the following January. With the goal of unity achieved, the religious PRCU and the nationalistic PNA closed ranks. The cultural gap that previously separated them dissipated.

By 1920, Chicago's Polish community had moved ahead of every foreign-born immigrant group in the strength of their numbers. Catherine Sardo Weidner of Butler University estimates that 31 percent of all European Poles over the age of 21 became American citizens in the 1920s. The attainable dream of home ownership in the expanding "Bungalow Belt" on the Southwest and Northwest Sides during this period was a powerful lure, and it convinced many of the new arrivals to invest in property instead of saving their money for a trip back home.

To preserve the links in the face of "Chicagoization," community leaders officially dedicated the Polish Museum at 984 Milwaukee Avenue on January 12, 1937. Under the direction of its first curator, Mieczyshaw Haiman, the museum became an important repository for items of historical significance pertaining to the Polish settlement of Chicago. The museum has expanded from two to three floors in the PRCU building, and it features a wide assortment of ethnic folk costumes, religious art, and murals depicting the scientific accomplishments of the Polish-American people.

One of the most popular exhibits over the years has been the Ignacy Paderewski collection, honoring the famed classical pianist who made three celebrated visits to Chicago during his illustrious career. Paderewski performed for the first time on New Year's Eve, 1891, at Adler and Sullivan's

Auditorium Theater. Though he collected only $300 for the performance, he left the city with some vivid impressions. He would recall the metropolis on the lake as a city of colossal dimensions, rivaled in the United States only by the majestic Niagara Falls.

Paderewski returned in 1893 to play at the World's Colombian Exposition. This time he struck up a lifelong friendship with Theodore Thomas, Chicago's famed symphony director. Then in 1916, Paderewski played Chicago for the last time before embarking on a political career. The Polish pianist performed before 4,000 people. The proceeds went to the Polish relief fund. In 1960, to honor the 100th anniversary of Paderewski's birth, the Chicago Polish Museum completely restored the New York hotel room where he had passed away.

The significance of Chicago as a Polish-American cultural center is illustrated by the visits of Pope John Paul in October 1979 and Lech Walesa, the Solidarity leader, who visited the city in 1989 to appeal for financial aid for Polonia. But even as the last vestiges of communism in Poland were swept away, the exodus continued unabated. In 1989, 150,000 people traveled to Chicago, where 25 U.S. dollars was the equivalent of two months' pay in Warsaw.

Today there are two Polonias in Chicago. Jackowo is representative of the earlier, 19th-century immigrant settlement. Polish is spoken there, and the parents of school-age children see to it that their youngsters receive instruction in the Polish language and customs. Small grocery stores, travel agencies, and other shops carry Polish newspapers and conduct business in the Polish language. There is a sense of togetherness in Avondale—pride amid despair. Triumph over adversity. But there is still a long way to go.

This is inner-city living; a noisy, congested urban kaleidoscope of sights, sounds, and smells. A few miles to the north, the landscape changes ever so slightly. In Jefferson Park, Norwood Park, and Edison Park, the more affluent Poles who arrived before and after World War II manicure their lawns, keep a watchful eye on the property values, and drive to the suburban malls to shop. Few, if any, go back to Milwaukee Avenue and Central Park unless it is by necessity. There is a friendly rivalry between the newcomers and the old-timers.

Younger Poles profited from an improved postwar educational system, but have chosen to emigrate to the suburbs in recent years for purely economic reasons. They do not dance the polka (some have never heard of it), and they look upon the quaint folk traditions of the far Northwest Siders as relics of a vanished era of Polish history. The older residents, for their part, may view the new immigrants as communists or free thinkers.

For years the Poles were represented in the City Council by 41st Ward Alderman Roman Pucinski, whose office on North Milwaukee Avenue was a favored gathering spot for Polish Americans eager to share in the latest news of the old country. Pucinski, a former Chicago *Sun-Times* news reporter and wheel horse in the two Daley mayoral administrations, is a personal friend of Lech Walesa and has visited him in Poland. Roman is retired now, but his daughter carries on the family tradition. Now in her third term as clerk of the circuit court of Cook County, Aurie Pucinski is the foremost Polish-American office holder in the county.

The far Northwest Side still retains its Polish identity. Przyblo's White Eagle banquet hall skirts the city boundary line on Milwaukee Avenue in Niles. Przyblo's is built on the site of an old ethnic picnic ground. It stands across the street from St. Adalbert's Cemetery, arguably the largest Polish burial ground in the city. It can be said of restaurateur Ted Pryzblo that he gets them coming and going. Hundreds of young couples have celebrated their nuptials in the banquet hall by donning aprons featuring baby toys. It is an old Polish custom that foretells many children and a long, prosperous life. The White Eagle also hosts the numerous funeral processions that file in and out of St. Adalbert's every day. Ted Pryzblo, a second-generation Pole, is quick to point out, however, that two presidents and Pope John Paul have also been fêted in his eating establishment.

The White Eagle is not only a great ethnic restaurant, it also celebrates Poland's national symbol in its name. According to popular legend, Lech, Czech, and Rus—three brothers who were said to have lived in Central Europe 1,500 years ago—were at one time betrayed to a common enemy by their sister. They fled the ancestral home to escape their persecutor and to find fortune wherever it might lie. After crossing the Danube River they parted, each continuing in a separate direction. Lech and his followers came upon the Wartha River, where one of the Slavic tribes dwelt. Lech, who was an ancestor of Poland's first ruler, Miecrzslaw I, came upon a nesting white eagle. Startled by the presence of Lech, the eagle fluttered its wings and flew off toward the sun. Observing the graceful beauty of the soaring eagle in flight at sunrise, Lech settled near the spot and founded a city which he called Gniezo (the Nest). A popular and benevolent ruler, Lech's people honored him by identifying themselves as *Polaki* (derived from *po Lochu* or followers of Lech). For a national symbol they selected the white eagle on a red background, which down through the centuries has become Poland's national symbol.

Getting There: Take the CTA O'Hare elevated line to Belmont, where you can connect with the Belmont (#77) or Addison (#152) bus, which conveniently serve this Northwest Side neighborhood. Take either bus to Milwaukee Avenue, which places you in the heart of Avondale. For a real slice of ethnic culture, you may wish to consider a leisurely bus ride on the CTA Milwaukee Avenue line (#56), which begins at Michigan and Washington in the Loop, and ends at the

Jefferson Park station on the far Northwest Side. The ninety-minute ride will take you through some of the oldest immigrant settlements in the city, including West Town, Logan Square, Avondale, Portage Park, and Jefferson Park. By car from the Loop, take Lake Shore Drive north to Belmont, and follow Belmont west to Milwaukee Avenue.

For additional information, call the CTA at (312) 836-7000.

════ Attractions ════

Cultural Institutions

The Polish Museum of America, *984 N. Milwaukee Ave., Chicago, (773) 384-3352. Lending library closed Thursdays and Sundays. Museum open daily. Admission is free, but donations are encouraged.*

With 60,000 volumes housed in the lending library, a collection of rare and unusual historical artifacts, and a gallery of paintings and sculptures, the Polish Museum is one of the oldest and largest ethnic museums of its kind in the United States. Located in West Town, the hub of the original Polish Downtown, the museum is a tribute to the many struggles of this immigrant group in adjusting to the hardships of American life. It has on display the sword presented to Poland's King Bolesaw the Brave by Holy Roman Emperor Otto III in the year 1000 A.D.; books that were printed in the 1500s and 1600s; and some personal effects of Ignacy Paderewski, pianist, statesman, and composer.

The Main Hall features a Casimir Pulaski exhibit and a Maritime Room contains scale ship models. There are ethnic and military costumes, and a gift shop selling souvenirs and Polish folk art. The art gallery on the fourth floor features the works of some noted Polish painters, including Jozef Czapski, Leon Polzycki, Wojciech Kossak, Konstanty Mackiewicz, and Eugeniusz Geppert.

The museum is sponsored by the Polish Roman Catholic Union of America (PRCUA), which shares offices in the building. Special exhibits throughout the year. *Recommended.*

Copernicus Foundation Cultural and Civic Center,
5216 W. Lawrence Ave., Chicago, (773) 777-8898. Membership available.

Founded in July 1972 by the Illinois Division of the Polish American Congress, the Copernicus Foundation is a nonprofit corporation that sponsors a wide variety of programs and activities aimed at preserving and celebrating a rich ethnic heritage. In 1973, the Foundation presented the City of Chicago with the Nicolaus Copernicus Monument, honoring the 15th-century Polish astronomer who advanced the theory that the earth and the other planets revolved around the sun. The monument commemorates the 500th anniversary of the astronomer's birth, and is situated on the grounds of the Adler Planetarium.

The Foundation's most ambitious project to date has been the conversion of the old Gateway Theatre at 5216 W. Lawrence Avenue into a community arts and cultural center. The Foundation completed its purchase of the former movie palace on June 17, 1979. Six months later the first major renovation took place when the original theater lobby was converted into a three-story area that now houses offices, conference rooms, and a small ballroom. The theater itself seats 2,000 people. Funding for the project was obtained from private individuals, organizations, and corporations who wanted to invest in the future of the Northwest Side Jefferson Park community, while at the same time preserving Polish culture for future generations.

The Center sponsors an annual Taste of Polonia, a Polish film festival, the spring Copernican Award ceremony, a Christmas holiday festival, art exhibits, lectures, musical events, and senior citizen seminars. Members receive the *Copernican Observer* (a quarterly newsletter), special reduced rates at the yearly events, and voting privileges (with a donation of $500 or more).

Polish Highlander Alliance, *4808 S. Archer Ave., Chicago, (773) 523-7632.*

Founded in October 1929 by Zigmund Lokanski, the Highlander Alliance is a South Side not-for-profit cultural society representing 5,000 members (4,500 reside in Chicago alone) who were born in the extreme southern regions of Poland, or who descend from families who resided in the Carpathian Mountains and its foothills. The Highlander Home on Archer Avenue is an educational and cultural center that offers English language classes three times a week to immigrant Poles, sponsors a Sunday afternoon radio program on WPNA, provides studio space for the dozen or so folk dance troupes that regularly practice there. A reference library of Polish literature and nonfiction books, several banquet halls, and a restaurant are also on the premises. During the year, the alliance sponsors a number of cultural activities, including a fall festival, a February Christmas pageant, a Queen of the Highlanders contest in August, and regularly scheduled performances given by the Hyrni and Szkolka dance troupes, plus other worthwhile events to help pay for a scholarship fund established in 1984.

Annual Events and Celebrations

Polish Constitution Day Parade, *Dearborn St. from Wacker Dr. to Van Buren St. On or about May 3.*

Commemorating the signing of the short-lived constitution in 1791, which established a democratic monarchical government with a senate, a house of deputies, and a judiciary. The document included the concepts of people's sovereignty; majority rule; religious freedom; and most importantly, universal liberty. The Poles modeled their democratic constitution after that of the United States, which had been ratified into law two years earlier. However, Poland was invaded by Catherine II of Russia in 1792, and by 1795, the fledgling democracy was partitioned into three spheres of influence, controlled by the Russians, Austrians, and Prussians. Poland did not become an independent state until after World War I, and then came the long period of Nazi occupation followed by forty-four years of Soviet repression. The first glimmer of hope came in 1980, when the Solidarity movement was founded. In 1989 the archaic, repressive communist government fell, and now the Polish people are working to restore the 1791 constitution.

In 1891, the Polish National Alliance (PNA) decided to mark the anniversary of the signing of the constitution with a gala parade and celebration. The PNA's observance has continued more than twenty-five times as long as the constitution was in effect. The big downtown parade features 12,000 marchers in traditional Polish costumes, drum and bugle corps, and 100 floats. The day begins with a wreath-laying ceremony at the Thaddeus Kosciuszko monument at Lake Shore Drive and Solidarity Drive, near the Adler Planetarium. The parade kicks off in the late morning.

Taste of Polonia, *Copernicus Center, 5216 W. Lawrence Ave., Chicago, (773) 777-8898. Thursday–Monday over Labor Day weekend.*

Continuous entertainment on two stages (a variety stage and a polka stage), featuring such musical acts as the Average Polka Band, Grazyna Auguscik (Polish jazz), and an array of 1950s–60s nostalgia groups. Special performances by the Lechici Folk Dancers of the Polish Youth Association are held at various times during the festival. The food vendors are representative of the restaurants and delicatessens that proliferate on the Northwest Side and have participated in this event since its inception in 1979. They sell traditional menu items such as potato and meat *pierogi, nalesniki* (blintzes), cabbage rolls, mushroom soup, *bigos, zurek,* and *flaczki.* Local merchants will allow patrons to use their parking lots at specified times to attend this festival.

Annual Copernican Award Ceremony, *Gateway Theater at the Copernicus Center, 5216 W. Lawrence Ave., Chicago, (773) 777-8898. First or second Friday in May. Call the Center for tickets.*

The foundation has paid tribute to an outstanding member of the Polish-American community each year since 1979. The 1991 recipient was Robert F. Martwick, former assistant state's attorney and noted trial lawyer in Chicago. Roman Pucinski was honored in 1994. The Polish National Alliance was fêted in 1996. The award is presented during a concert given by the Lake Shore Symphony Orchestra in the 2,000-seat Gateway Theater. A lavish buffet supper is served in honor of the recipient. Tickets are sold for the buffet supper and the concert, or for the concert alone. All tickets may be purchased at the Center during normal office hours, or concert tickets (only) will be available at the door one hour before the concert.

Copernicus Center Holiday Festival, *Copernicus Center, 5216 W. Lawrence Ave., Chicago, (773) 777-8898. First Saturday in December. Admission free.*

Arts and crafts booths, featuring the works of Polish artisans from the Chicago area. The handmade items (which do not always pertain to Christmas themes) are offered for sale to the public.

Pulaski Day Reception, *Polish Museum of America, 984 N. Milwaukee Ave., Chicago, (773) 384-3352. March 4. Admission free.*

Pulaski Day is a city and county holiday. In 1929, on the 150th anniversary of the Polish martyr's death, President Herbert Hoover proclaimed March 4 Pulaski Day. But few people who are given the day off work have the slightest idea what they are supposed to celebrate. The answer may be found at the Polish Museum, where a special exhibit chronicles the life and times of this freedom fighter who helped save George Washington's army from disastrous defeat at Brandywine and West Tavern in 1777. Casimir Pulaski was living in exile in Paris when he was recruited by Benjamin Franklin to join the War of Independence in America. Pulaski, known as the father of the U.S. Cavalry, met a hero's death while leading French and American troops in the attack against Savannah, Georgia.

An overflow crowd usually attends the reception, concert, and museum tour. In the past, public notables, including Governor James Edgar, have scored points with Polish-American voters on the Northwest Side by appearing at the museum to spread the good word about this forgotten hero.

Holy Trinity Polish Church Parish Bazaar, *1118 N.*
Noble, Chicago, (773) 489-4140. Weekend in
September or October. Admission free.

Arts and crafts booths, Polish foods and merchandise for sale, and musical entertainment in the parish hall.

Christmas in Poland, *Museum of Science and*
Industry, 5700 S. Lake Shore Dr., Chicago,
(773) 684-1414. Sunday before Christmas.

The holiday traditions of Poland are celebrated in song and dance during the museum's annual Christmas Around the World festival held throughout the month of December. A special one-hour appearance by the Lechici Folk Dancers of the Polish Youth Association of Chicago is featured. This famous dance troupe, founded by Czeslaw Orzel-Orlicz, marks its thirtieth anniversary in 1996. The troupe consists of forty-five teenagers and young adults who perform the regional dances of ten Polish provinces under the direction of choreographer Ted Wiecek.

Bal Amarantowy (White and Red Ball), *Chicago*
Hilton and Towers, 720 S. Michigan Ave., Chicago.
Last Saturday in February. For information, contact
the Legion of Young Polish Women, c/o the Copernicus
Foundation, at (773) 777-8898. Tickets may be
purchased from the Foundation.

Sponsored by the Legion of Young Polish Women, the White and Red Ball (white symbolizes the debutante before her formal introduction into society, the red represents the post-deb) is regarded by many as the crown jewel of the Polish-American social season in Chicago. The annual fund-raising event, which benefits various Polish charitable causes, dates back to 1941, when the Legion of Young Polish Women donated the proceeds of the Ball to the exiled Polish armies and resistance movement battling Nazi aggression. The league was founded in Chicago by Helen (Lenard) Pieklo on Sept. 2, 1939—the day after the Nazi armies invaded Poland. In 1945, the first formal debutante cotillion was held for young women of Polish extraction between the ages of 16 and 20. The tradition continues into the 1990s. Even though the league does not have an office or phone listing, interested parties are encouraged to contact the Copernicus Foundation, where many of their meetings are held. Formal attire requested.

Cinderella-Prince Charming Ball, *sponsored by*
the Polish Roman Catholic Union of America,

(773) 278-3210 (1-800-772-8632 outside Illinois).
Call for date and location.

The Presentation Ball is given for both the young men and young women of high school age who belong to the PRCUA. The teenagers are taught the social graces and formal ballroom dancing prior to their presentation at the dinner dance, held around Thanksgiving. Tickets may be purchased from the PRCUA. In addition to the Prince Charming-Cinderella Ball, the PRCUA offers other social activities during the year, including athletic tournaments, bus tours to Polish cultural events outside Chicago, the traditional Easter *Swiecone* and a Christmas *Oplatek*.

Traditional Easter Celebration, *sponsored by the Polish Women's Alliance of America, 205 S. Northwest Hwy., Park Ridge, (847) 384-1200. Admission fee charged. Held at alternating restaurants on the North Side and South Side on a Sunday afternoon at Easter time.*

The Polish Women's Alliance (which is not affiliated with the PNA) has been in existence for nearly a century, and has 63,000 members in a seventeen-state area. It is a fraternal benefit society offering life insurance to its members and a calendar of social events. The Easter celebration includes the traditional blessing of the food, singing of Polish Easter carols, folk dancing in colorful ethnic costumes, and children's events. Every other year the Easter party is held on the South Side at various banquet halls and restaurants including the Landmark, the Mayfield, and the Polonia. The sponsoring North Side halls include Przyblo's White Eagle, and Aqua Bella.

Traditional Christmas Celebration, *sponsored by the Polish Women's Alliance of America, 205 S. Northwest Hwy., Park Ridge, (847) 384-1200, held at alternating restaurants on the South and North Sides. First Sunday afternoon in December. Admission fee charged.*

Includes dinner, a Santa Claus for the youngsters, ethnic dancers in folk costumes, and the blessing of the food. To find out where the event will be held in a given year, please call the Polish Women's Alliance of America. The cost of the dinner varies with the location.

Swietojankie **(St. John's Day Festival),** *Allison Woods Forest Preserve, Des Plaines. (The grove is located on Milwaukee Ave. between Sanders and River*

roads.) June 24. Sponsored by the Legion of Young
Polish Women, c/o the Copernicus Foundation,
(773) 777-8898. Admission is free.

The League of Young Polish Women hosts this charming ethnic event, which recreates the folklore and customs of St. John's Day. The eligible young women of the Polish community are given plastic wreaths to float down the Des Plaines River. According to ancient European customs, the young man who rescues the wreath from the churning river is sure to become the fair maiden's betrothed. The Des Plaines River is a tepid, polluted artery nowadays, but the quaint custom is interesting to observe anyway. A Polish kitchen serves food on the grounds. Prize drawing. Music.

Easter Basket Festival at the Polish Highlanders
Home, *4808 S. Archer Ave., Chicago, (773) 523-7632.*
Admission is free.

A one-day festival held the Saturday after Good Friday in the Highlander Hall. A panel will judge children's Easter baskets and award prizes.

Fall Festival at the Polish Highlanders Home,
4808 S. Archer Ave., Chicago, (773) 523-7632.
Second weekend of November. Admission fee
charged.

A two-day ethnic festival held in the Highlander Hall, featuring an assortment of ethnic foods from twelve different nationalities. Folk dancing contests and sales of Polish ethnic costumes are included in the festivities.

Places to See

Baby Doll Polka Club, *6102 S. Central Ave.,*
Chicago, (773) 582-9706. Open nightly.

Owner Irene Korosa bubbles over with enthusiasm when she describes her off-the-beaten-path nightclub and cocktail lounge, with its panoramic view of Midway Airport's majestic runways. We don't know of any other club in the city that caters to the polka set, which makes this place so unusual. Irene has been at this location for over ten years, and seems to be doing well despite the fact that she does not charge an admission fee to the seventy-five or so patrons that can be squeezed onto the dance floor. The house polka band starts playing at around 9:30 P.M. *Recommended.*

Shops

Joe and Frank's, *5620 N. Pulaski, Chicago,*
(773) 581-0639. Closed Sundays.

Located on the northern tip of Avondale. Old-fashioned bakery and delicatessen that manufactures its own sausages. Brought to you by Joe Ligas and Frank Ratulowski.

Teresa Deli, *3184 N. Milwaukee Ave., Chicago,*
(773) 282-5515. Closed Sundays.

Freshly cut meats, imported gourmet items, homemade sausages, and baked goods.

Iry's, Inc., Deli and Liquors, *2922 N. Milwaukee*
Ave., Chicago, (773) 227-5424. Open daily.

Iry's is the kind of place you remember from the old neighborhood. They always used to be on the corner. This place isn't, however. It's tiny, and cluttered, and the owners will probably give you the big eye if you happen to be 9 or 10 years old and just want to hang around. It is helpful if you speak Polish. Gift baskets, liquors, baked goods, and meats.

Bristol Liquors, Deli, & Lounge, *two locations:*
3084-86 N. Milwaukee Ave., Chicago,
(773) 545-7072, and 5205 W. Belmont Ave.,
Chicago, (773) 545-6097. Open daily.

The delicatessen is in the front, the restaurant area in the back, just like the old-fashioned neighborhood places used to be. Polish foods and newspapers.

Mulica's Deli & Liquors, Inc., *3118 N. Milwaukee*
Ave., Chicago, (773) 777-7945. Open daily.

Wally Mulica's place is one of the busiest gathering spots on the street. The deli is located in the rear. Frozen foods, liquor, pastries, produce, and Polish magazines and newspapers are sold in the front.

Andy's Deli, *two locations: 3055 N. Milwaukee Ave.,*
Chicago, (773) 486-8160, and 1737 W. Division St.,
(773) 486-8870, and 5438 N. Milwaukee Ave.,
(773) 631-7304. Open daily.

The place is nearly always busy. The overextended clerks sell imported food items, greeting cards, and Polish newspapers.

Pasieka Home Quality Bakery, *3056 N. Milwaukee Ave., Chicago, (773) 278-5190. Open daily.*

A real old-fashioned Chicago bakery, with wooden cupboards and sales clerks who smile at you. Pastries. Bread. Cakes for all occasions.

Ann's Bakery, *2923 N. Milwaukee Ave., Chicago, (773) 489-6562. Closed Sundays.*

Sister store to the one in Ukrainian Village. Baked goods, delicatessen items, Polish newspapers, and candy.

Toys and Gifts Store (*Paczki do Polski*), *two locations: 3114 N. Milwaukee Ave., Chicago, (773) 685-1517, and 4406 N. Milwaukee Ave., Chicago, (773) 545-4300. Open daily. No credit cards.*

A fine little toy shop, with a large inventory of Lego kits, Polish greeting cards, and ethnic dolls.

J. D. Jewelers, *3022 N. Milwaukee Ave., Chicago, (773) 252-6140. Closed Sundays.*

Jewelry items. Gold bought and sold; Polish music on cassettes. Repairs while you wait.

Calisia Imports, *3026 N. Milwaukee Ave., Chicago, (773) 222-3268. Open daily.*

Dimly lit, cluttered gift store with the look and feel of an old-fashioned neighborhood rummage and resale shop. The gift items are imported from Poland, India, and China, among other places. Some of the merchandise is expensive, some not. Cards, jewelry, Czech and German crystal pieces, religious icons, woodcarvings, and dolls.

Syrena Department Store, *3004 N. Milwaukee Ave., Chicago, (773) 489-4435. Open daily.*

Before there were suburban shopping malls, interstate highways to whisk you there, and coldly impersonal retail chains that swallowed their competition like a Pac-Man character gone berserk, there were cozy, intimate neighborhood department stores with creaking wooden floors and merchandise displays that did not titillate the visceral senses. They were not supposed to. Your parents took you there on Thursday nights (never on Tuesday—that was when *I Love Lucy* was on, and the slowest night of the week for retailers) to buy school clothes, a Sunday-go-to-meeting outfit, and sensible oxfords. Syrena's evokes powerful childhood memories. The customers and sales clerks are all Polish, so it might help if you speak the language.

Anna's, *2992 N. Milwaukee Ave., Chicago,*
(773) 227-5221. Open daily.

Children's and adult's clothing in the same kind of neighborhood setting that makes Syrena's so interesting.

Polonia Bookstore and Publisher's Co., *2886 N.*
Milwaukee Ave., Chicago, (773) 489-2554. Closed
Sundays. Accepts credit cards.

The largest Polish bookstore in America offers a wide selection of books in Polish, fiction and poetry, historical and religious books, books for children and students, dictionaries, travel guidebooks, and books in English on Polish subjects. Sells both paperbacks and hardcover. Albums and cassettes also available.

Outlying Areas

Bacik's Super Meat Market, *4249 S. Archer*
Ave., Chicago, (773) 247-2253. Open daily.

Pierogi, lunch meats, liquors, dairy products, Polish imports, newspapers, and magazines.

Forest View Bakery, Inc., *6454 N. Milwaukee*
Ave., Chicago, (773) 775-7740. Open daily.

Fancy tarts, cakes, and homemade breads.

John & Ray's Market, *5760 N. Milwaukee*
Ave., Chicago, (773) 774-1924. Closed
Sundays.

Specializing in choice meats and Harczak sausages. Located a few doors down from the busier Kalinowski market.

Kalinowski European Style, *5746 N. Milwaukee*
Ave., Chicago, (773) 631-4640. Open daily.

All foods made on the premises. Serving the Gladstone neighborhood of the 41st Ward, this deli is busiest on Saturday mornings. Fresh meats, party trays, and catering.

Kasia's Polish Deli, *2101 W. Chicago Ave., Chicago, (773) 486-6163. Open daily. Cash only.*

Imported foods from Poland and Greece.

Gilmart Quality Food and Liquors, *5050 S. Archer, Chicago, (773) 585-5514. Open daily. No credit cards.*

The South Side's choice for imported Polish, Yugoslav, Czech, and German delicatessen foods. The proprietors also serve smorgasbord-style foods in a small dining area in the store.

Petrov Enterprises, *6203 W. Montrose Ave., Chicago, (773) 545-2277. Closed Sundays.*

Offering the finest Polish, Yugoslav, German, and Austrian crystal and imported Italian figurines to the public for wholesale prices.

Dunajec Bakery and Delicatessen, *5060 S. Archer, Chicago, (773) 585-9611. Closed Sundays.*

Homemade bakery and Polish deli foods; sausages, *pierogi,* etc.

Gorski Bakery and Deli, *5222 W. Diversey, Chicago, (773) 736-0805. Open daily. No credit cards.*

Fine selection of sausages and baked goods.

Kolatek's Bakery, *5405 S. Kedzie, Chicago, (773) 737-2113. Open daily. No credit cards.*

Old-fashioned South Side Polish bakery where the layer cakes, fruit slices, cookies, and breads are all homemade.

Sobczak's Avondale Sausage, *8705 N. Milwaukee Ave., Niles, (847) 470-8780. Closed Mondays, but phone orders accepted.*

A slice of the Avondale neighborhood transported to serene, tranquil Niles, a world removed. European-style homemade sausage, salads, and party trays. Extensive catering menu for house parties, graduations, banquets, showers, and anniversaries. A real favorite of the suburban Poles.

Sophie's Polish Deli, *418 W. Northwest Hwy., Mount Prospect, (847) 590-5489. Open for lunch and dinner Monday–Saturday and for Sunday brunch.*

Popular off-the-beaten-path destination point for homemade breads, sausages, and Easter delicacies including imported Polish candies, sweet braided bread, and Easter *babkas*. Located opposite the Metra railroad line on Route 14.

Restaurants

Wigry Restaurant, *3027 N. Milwaukee Ave., Chicago, (773) 342-5636 or (773) 278-1311. Open for breakfast, lunch, and dinner daily. No credit cards.*

The truly amazing thing about the restaurants in Avondale is the prices. A full meal can be ordered at the Wigry for less than $10. Cocktail lounge on premises.

Home Bakery Inc., *2931 N. Milwaukee Ave., Chicago, (773) 252-3708. Open for breakfast, lunch, and dinner daily.*

Eat and shop at the same time. The delicatessen sells baked goods, sausage, candy, AND imported foods and newspapers. The restaurant features herring blanketed by onion-and-cucumber sour cream, potato pancakes, and *bigos* (hunter's stew).

Czerwone Jabluszko Restaurant, *two locations: 3121-23 N. Milwaukee Ave., Chicago, (773) 588-5781, and 6474 N. Milwaukee Ave., Chicago, (773) 763-3407. Open for lunch and dinner daily.*

Two locations, one in Avondale, the other a stone's throw away from Roman Pucinski's old office in the 41st Ward. The owners promise that you will never leave hungry if you dip into their big smorgasbord, with a variety of *pierogis* and crepes, pork chops, roast beef and pork, goulashes, sauerkraut, potato pancakes, and fritters. If you get tired of the smorgasbord, you can choose something else from our small menu, they say, and I believe them. The prices are a real bargain.

Congress Restaurant and Nightclub, *3200 N.*
Milwaukee Ave., Chicago, (773) 286-5105. The
restaurant is open for breakfast, lunch, and dinner
daily. Open at noon on Sundays.

The Congress is one of the hot spots of Avondale. The Polish music and dancing are featured every Friday, Saturday, and Sunday evening.

Outlying Areas

Alex's Deli, *6247 N. Milwaukee Ave., Chicago,*
(773) 792-1492. Open for lunch and dinner daily.
No credit cards.

A tiny, family-owned restaurant where mom, dad, and the kids strive to make your visit a pleasant one. The food is served buffet-style, and is always warm and fresh thanks to the extra attention shown by the owners. Not to be missed is the Polish-style cabbage casserole, the thin-sliced roast pork, or the sweet-tasting blintzes. You'll also enjoy the prices.

Teresa and Magnolia Polish Restaurants, *4751 N.*
Milwaukee Ave., Chicago, (773) 283-0184. Teresa is
open daily for lunch and dinner; Magnolia serves only
dinner and is closed Mondays.

Two adjacent restaurants. Teresa is a very inexpensive little Polish kitchen. The *gollabki* (stuffed cabbage) and *naiesniki serery* (cheese blintzes) are house specialties.

Pierogi Inn, *5318 W. Lawrence Ave., Chicago,*
(773) 725-2818. Open for lunch and dinner daily.
Cash only.

Owner Richard Zawadzki has a cable TV cooking show, and he once served as Hugh Hefner's personal gourmet cook. The servers are not well versed in the English language, but a chalkboard listing the day's specialties (including, no doubt, *pierogi*) will help you make the right selection. The dinners are moderately priced, as is the case with most Polish dining rooms. You can eat well for under seven dollars. No live entertainment, but there is background music.

Lutnia, *5532 W. Belmont Ave., Chicago,*
(773) 282-5335. Open for dinner daily.

Old-fashioned, authentic Polish food. Specialties include hunter's stew, *pierogi,* pork cutlets, roast goose, and apple blintzes. The waiters flambé many dishes at your table. Live piano music.

Cardinal Club, *5155 W. Belmont Ave., Chicago, (773) 736-4662. Open nightly.*

Big-name guest stars from Poland and musical bands perform on the weekend at this show lounge and saloon with two bars.

Sawa's Old Warsaw Restaurant and Banquet Facility, *9200 W. Cermak Rd. (at 17th Avenue), Broadview, (708) 343-9040. Open for lunch and dinner daily. Credit cards accepted.*

A chain of four family-owned restaurants is now reduced to one. The 1978 recession hit the Sawa family very hard, according to the owner, who started his business at Clark and Ashland in 1963. Sawa's is still a good bargain for a meal, buffet, or private party. There are three private halls.

Staropolska Restaurant, *5249 W. Belmont Ave., Chicago, (773) 736-5230. Open for lunch and dinner daily. Credit cards accepted.*

Inexpensive buffet smorgasbord, all you can eat. Affiliated with the Jolly Inn (see following entry).

Jolly Inn, *6501 W. Irving Park Rd., Chicago, (773) 736-7606. Closed Sundays. Credit cards accepted.*

Adjacent to the Jolly Club, one of the most popular banquet halls on the Northwest Side. Low-priced buffet served all day.

Przyblo's White Eagle, *6839 N. Milwaukee Ave., Niles, (847) 647-0660. Open for lunch and dinner daily. Credit cards accepted.*

There must be something to this large, airy banquet hall and restaurant if it attracted such luminaries as the pope, the president (Carter) of the United States, Illinois governors, and a host of lesser celebrities. Since 1948, the Przyblos have probably hosted more funeral luncheons than any restaurant in the metropolitan Chicago area. But don't interpret that as an omen; St. Adalbert's Cemetery is across the street. Seven banquet halls. Dinners are served family-style.

Polo Restaurant and Bar, *8801 N. Milwaukee Ave, Niles, (847) 470-8822. Open for lunch and dinner Monday–Saturday. Sunday brunch. Credit cards accepted.*

Primarily a dinner restaurant, so the prices here are somewhat more than you would pay at an all-you-can-eat establishment on the Northwest Side.

Halibut in dill sauce, stuffed cabbage, and real potato pancakes are the recommended entrees.

Zofia's, *310 W. Rand Rd., Arlington Heights,*
(847) 259-5050. Open for lunch and dinner daily.
Credit cards accepted.

Inexpensive but deliciously prepared Polish cuisine in the Northwest suburbs. Opened in 1993 and located half a mile west of Arlington Heights Road. Luncheon specials.

Warsaw Inn, *217 N. Route 31 (one mile south of*
Route 120), McHenry, (815) 344-0330. Open for lunch
and dinner Monday–Friday. Saturday and Sunday
lunch and dinner buffets. Credit cards accepted.

Low-priced Polish restaurant.

European Crystal, *519 W. Algonquin Rd., Arlington*
Heights, (847) 437-5590. Open for lunch and dinner.
Closed Mondays.

Excellent and inexpensive Polish and continental cuisine served both buffet style and off the menu. Specialties include chateaubriand, *pierogi, golambki,* and Polish desserts. Banquet facilities and catering service available. Reservations suggested for the weekends.

Media

Polish-Language Broadcasting (Selected Programming)

WCEV (Chicago's Ethnic Voice), 1450 AM, with offices in Chicago, is a foreign-language station owned by Migala Communications.

Voice of Polonia, *hosted by George Migala, who*
doubles as the station manager and vice president.
Migala virtually invented the concept of ethnic radio
by introducing this format to Chicago in 1979. Migala
and his wife Slawa first aired the Voice of Polonia in
1950 when he was an independent producer at WLEY-
FM, 107.01 in Chicago. It is the longest-running daily
Polish radio program in the city. Mondays through
Thursdays, 4:30 to 6:00 P.M.; Saturdays 4:05 to 6:00
P.M. WCEV-1450 AM.

Poland in Music and Song, *hosted by Adam Grzegorzewski. Mondays and Wednesdays, 6:30 to 7:00 P.M.; Saturdays, 6:05 to 6:45 P.M. WCEV, 1450 AM.*

Moments in Polish History, *Hosted by Dr. Joseph Migala. Tuesdays, 6:45 to 7:00 P.M. WCEV, 1450 AM.*

Roman Catholic Mass and Polish Apostleship of Prayer, *religious. Sundays, 8 to 9 A.M. WCEV, 1450 AM.*

Polonia Today, *hosted by Chet and Delores Schafer, Mondays, 3:30 to 4:30 P.M. WCEV, 1450 AM.*

WSBC, 1240 AM, was founded in 1925 by Joel Silverstein, owner of the World Storage and Battery Company (hence the call letters, WSBC). The station features a variety of ethnic programming serving the Polish, Asian, and Hispanic communities.

Sofia Boris Program, *Bob Lewandowski, a pioneer to Chicago ethnic broadcasting, retired in 1991 after 28 years. Sofia Boris took over the show and continues to interview guests, play some music, and discuss the latest news from Poland. Her radio program airs Monday through Friday, 7:00–8:30 A.M. on WSBC, 1240 AM.*

Father Justin Polish Rosary Catholic Program, *religious. Airs at 9 P.M. on Saturdays. WSBC, 1240 AM.*

WEDC, 1240 AM

Sunshine Hour, (Godzina Sloneczna), *formerly hosted by the late Lidia Pucinski, mother of former 41st Ward Alderman Roman Pucinski. Your current host: Halina Grawza. Airs daily from 8:30 to 9:30 A.M. WEDC, 1240 AM.*

WPNA, 1490 AM

Radio Fama, *hosted by Anna Mikulec and M. Adamczyk, weekdays, 5:00 to 6:00 A.M. WPNA, 1490 AM.*

Dzien Dobry Chicago, *hosted by Marek Kulisiewicz, Thursday, 6:00 to 6:30 A.M.; Monday, Tuesday, Wednesday, Friday, 6 to 7 A.M. WPNA, 1490 AM*

Program Pol Zartem, Pol Serio, *hosted by Andrzej Szopa and Barbara Choroszy, weekdays, 7:00 to 7:30 P.M. WPNA, 1490 AM*

Eddie Blazonczyk Polka Show, *hosted by Eddie Blazonczyk, Saturday, 1:00 to 2:00* P.M.; Sundays noon to 1:00 *P.M. WPNA, 1490 AM*

Polish Panorama, *hosted by Stan Lobodzinski, Sundays, 3:00 to 3:30 P.M. WPNA, 1490 AM*

Polish Video

Polish Record and Video Center of America, *2930 N. Milwaukee Ave., Chicago, (773) 486-6700. Open daily. No credit cards.*

Polish and Eastern European films available for rental or sale, including the historical epic, *Knights of the Black Cross,* and the children's special *Bolek and Lolek on the Western Frontier.* Music cassettes, albums, and CDs.

Bodak Video, *two locations: 3248 N. Pulaski, Chicago, (773) 777-3129, and 4195 S. Archer Ave., Chicago, (773) 927-6991. Open daily.*

A Polish-American video center that stocks the classic black-and-white films made during Poland's golden age in the 1930s. In addition to the latest U.S. films available for rental, the owner also carries contemporary Polish films with English subtitles. Foreign films can be ordered and will arrive in the store within seven days.

Polish-American Video, *5231 W. Belmont Ave., Chicago, (773) 725-1025. Open daily.*

More than 600 Polish and American movies for sale or rental.

Avondale: Chicago's Little Warsaw

A twisting Indian trail that was once home to a handful of farming families who arrived in the 1840s now leads to the most concentrated Polish neighborhood in Chicago. Originally a plank road built to expedite the transfer of produce and dairy products to Chicago's Randolph Street market, Milwaukee Avenue has since the 1880s been the main street of Polish Chicago. Middle-class Avondale is the most refined and suburban of the city's remaining Polish neighborhoods. A square bounded by Addison Street, Diversey, and the Kennedy Expressway, Avondale's fourth side is Pulaski Road, which was called Crawford until several Northwest Side aldermen pushed through a bill in the City Council to rename the thoroughfare in honor of the Polish military hero.

Until large numbers of Germans, Scandinavians, and Poles began settling the area in the 1880s and 1890s, Avondale was a distant farm. A building boom that lasted into the 1930s saw the construction of thousands of sturdy, unassuming brick bungalows and two-flats, most of which have been carefully maintained ever since.

On Saturdays and Sundays, Milwaukee Avenue between Central Park and Pulaski is a hub of commercial activity, as the residents shop in congested delicatessens and retail and grocery stores, dine at the intimate Polish restaurants, and meet and greet each other before the bells of St. Hyacinth signal the call to Mass. Avondale remains a slice of Eastern Europe in Chicago's ethnic pie.

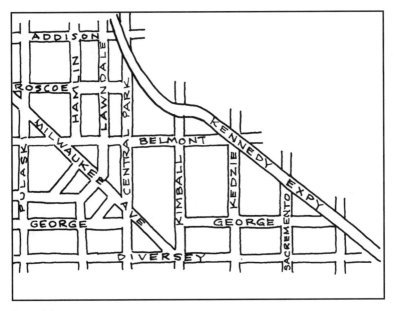

Avondale

Italian Chicago

History and Settlement

The family matters. Ask Chicago Italians and they will tell you so. The sense of family and community spanning the generations is what the Italian-American experience is about, dating back to the 1880s when they began arriving in Chicago in great numbers. Regional identification in Italy was so strong that the newcomers did not consider themselves Italians until the Americans began calling them that. Before 1890, the Italians entering the United States came from the prosperous, economically advanced regions of the north: Venetia, Piedmont, Genoa, and Tuscany. After 1899, the new arrivals were for the most part southern Italians attempting to escape the feudal structure and class stratification of the Old World. Economic opportunity—that great equalizer among peoples—fostered the first wave of emigration. Ironically, though, the first significant population shift from the Kingdom of Italy during the early years of the nineteenth century was toward Latin America, not the United States. Brazil and Argentina were economic magnets until the industrial revolution reached the shores of America and the need for unskilled laborers willing to work for a few pennies a day encouraged a northerly exodus.

The Italians were latecomers. U.S. census figures showed that only 43 of them lived in Illinois in 1850, compared to 27,000 Irish, 38,000 Germans,

18,000 English and 4,000 Scandinavians. By the 1860s there were only 100 Italians in Chicago. But this would change drastically by the turn of the century with the arrival of the *contadini,* or peasant farmers. Very often the Italian immigrants processed through Castle Garden in New York were following the footsteps of their relatives who had settled in Chicago to work as shoemakers, tailors, grocers, meat packers, and carpenters. Many were "sojourners," who stayed only long enough to earn money to purchase farmland in Italy. Others waited months, even years, but then found that peasant life, which seemed so idyllic from their tenement building in the core of the city, had changed. These nomadic "Americani," who were torn between two divergent cultures, often returned to the U.S.

The early arriving northerners who were counted in the 1850 census followed the Germans, Irish, and Swedes into the central city. Frank and August Lagorio were two important figures in the development of the first Italian community in Chicago. The brothers left their native Genoa in 1852 and, following a perilous seventy-day ocean voyage, they passed through Castle Garden in New York and made their way to Chicago.

The Lagorios purchased a home at Kinzie and Kingsbury streets and opened a small neighborhood import business that sustained them for many years. In 1857, Frank Lagorio's wife gave birth to a son whom they named Antonio. Eventually, this son of Genoese immigrants completed his studies at the Rush Medical College, and he later served as president of the Chicago Library Board. The other brother, August Lagorio, was a member of the city's volunteer fire department, which was composed entirely of business and civic leaders. The trail-blazing Lagorios encouraged their friends and relatives to emigrate, and within a few years a thriving Genoese colony was founded near Kinzie Street.

By 1870, there were Italians in all twenty wards except the Irish Seventh. Ominous political events taking shape in the Kingdom of Italy that year contributed directly to the second wave of immigration. As a result of Giuseppe Garibaldi's defeat by a French force at Mentana, many refugees from Naples, Tuscany, Piedmont, Venice, and Sicily poured into the city. Less than a year later, on July 2, 1871, Italian unification was completed when the Roman people overwhelmingly approved a union with the kingdom. The price of peace was economic deprivation and widespread unemployment. Thus, on the brink of starvation, thousands of Italians made their way to the United States and its large urban centers.

An 1884 Board of Education survey determined that the largest concentration of Italian immigrants lived south of the Chicago River near Harrison and 12th Street. Later, just as thousands of immigrants poured into the city from Southern Italy, the poorest of them settled between Van Buren and

12th Street. This was the longtime political domain of Republican Alderman Johnny "de Pow" Powers, saloon keeper, gambler, and sachem of the Nineteenth Ward, who ruled the neighborhood from 1888 until the 1920s. Known as the "Prince of Boodlers" for his rapacious tactics in the city council, Powers greeted the new arrivals with characteristic swagger. "I can buy the Italian vote with a glass of beer and a compliment," he snorted.

The 19th Ward was a classic Chicago melting pot, populated by twenty-six different nationalities. In 1898 there were 48,190 residents living in squalid tenements along Ewing, Forquer, Taylor, and DeKoven (between Halsted and Canal). The 5,784 Italians were viewed with a mixture of suspicion and mistrust by the firmly entrenched Irish and native Anglos. "Here the urbane expression gave way to a censorious one," commented a *Tribune* reporter who tramped down the wood-block streets of the ward on May 13, 1898. And the change was reflected in the countenance of a sympathetic friend. "'Tis a shame," said the friend, "I thought the laws had been passed to keep them out." "They are a noisy, quarreling set," continued the first speaker. "They are not even friendly with one another."

It was a polyglot community. Few of the southern Italians owned property. They crowded together in poorly lit hovels, sometimes housing three families per floor. Economic deprivation and unfamiliarity with the language and the customs created despair and a feeling of powerlessness. Beginning in the 1890s, several key figures within the community joined forces with Jane Addams, the founder of Hull House, to elect candidates more inclined to represent their interests. In 1898, for example, the community rallied behind aldermanic candidate Simeon S. Armstrong, an Irishman who was endorsed by Addams. Responding to the insults heaped upon them by Powers, the newspapers *L'Italia* and *La Tribuna Italiana* launched an ambitious registration drive. The initial results were discouraging. Powers rolled on to victory by a 2 to 1 margin and continued to rule into the Prohibition era. "I am what my people like, and neither Hull House nor all the reformers in town can turn them against me," Powers gloated.

The inevitable revolt against the Irish boss began after 1910 and was led by a man of dubious character—the unfrocked priest Anthony D'Andrea, whose ties to the Black Hand and criminal elements within the neighborhood were well known. D'Andrea was a force in labor union politics and president of the *Unione Siciliana,* the largest and most influential Italian fraternal society in Chicago, which had been founded at the turn of the century. On April 13, 1920, D'Andrea ran unopposed for the office of ward committeeman and was elected. Though the Italians had made important strides working within the system, the results of that election were invalidated by the state supreme court, and Powers regained his former position of committeeman.

Thus by 1921 the Italians were the single largest ethnic group in the ward, yet had no real say-so in policy-making. Powers employed a handful

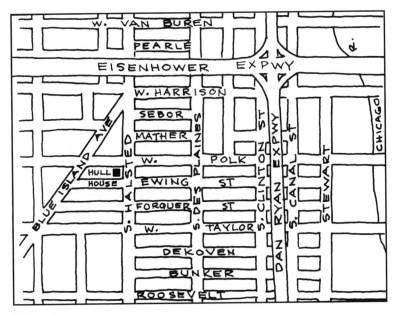

Little Italy

of Italians in his own organization, but they were viewed with suspicion and mistrust by the *paesani* (compatriots).

D'Andrea challenged Powers in the aldermanic election that year in a violent, bloody political campaign characterized by the free use of the bomb and shotgun. The Municipal Voter's League refused to endorse either candidate, though D'Andrea commanded immense popularity among the members of the Chicago Building Trades Council. The vendetta raged through the spring and summer months. In March, Paul Labriola, one of the Powers men who served as bailiff of the Municipal Court, was ambushed and killed. "Labriola was my best friend," Powers sobbed. "I don't know of any enemies he had."

Symbolic of the murderous intent of these two groups was a poplar tree that stood on Loomis Street in the heart of the district. Here the rivals would post the names of their next victims. Nearly thirty men who lost their lives in the Powers-D'Andrea feud saw their names carved on the "Dead Man's Tree" at one time or another. One of the last was D'Andrea himself, who was cut down at the height of his career on May 10, 1921, in front of his doorstep on Ashland Avenue. The Italian-language newspapers decried the violence, but reserved judgment. On election day, several months before his untimely death, D'Andrea had gone down to defeat by a scant thirty-eight votes.

The Nineteenth Ward vendetta presaged the rise of the modern crime syndicate, and illustrated the sense of despair many earnest, hardworking

Italians felt as they attempted to rise above the nightmare of poverty, discrimination, and exclusionary laws they encountered in the United States. In the minds of many native Chicagoans, the new arrivals were either mainland Communists or Sicilian Black Handers who had imported an ancient feudal system to America. The North Side Italian community, bounded by the industrial districts of Goose Island, North Avenue, Wells Street and Chicago Avenue, became known as "Little Hell."

According to Chicago census statistics published in 1920, Little Hell was taken over by the Italians, who comprised 28 percent of the area's population. In the shadow of the opulent Gold Coast, less than a mile to the east, lived thousands of Sicilians who worked on Goose Island, formerly the home of Irish laborers who cluttered the north branch of the Chicago River with their shanties and wild geese (hence the famous nickname). These new arrivals moved into the neighborhood in the 1880s, displacing many Swedes, who moved farther north along Belmont Avenue.

The majority of these Italians came from the island of Sicily. They established autonomy along Gault Court and Milton Avenue between Chicago Avenue and Division Street, and later they pushed across Division to North Avenue. The intersection of Oak and Milton (now Cleveland) gained a fearful notoriety in the first decade of the twentieth century. Here the Black Hand gangsters practiced their extortions, impervious to the police. In this tightly woven ethnic Italian enclave, thirty-eight victims of the Black Hand met death in a fifteen-month killing spree between January 1910 and March 1911. There was little a shopkeeper or private citizen could do if he received the dreaded letter with the hand imprint on it. Pay up or die.

From the pages of *La Tribuna Italiana Transatlantica,* editor Allessandro Mastro-Valerio decried the violence. "Yesterday this one, today that one; tomorrow it may strike even you!" The Chicago police were often blamed by community leaders for their complacency and inertia. The implication, of course, was that the police were "on the take."

The Black Hand flourished in Chicago until the early 1920s, when the modern crime syndicate organized to reap the bountiful harvest of Prohibition. Compared to the fabulous profits from bootlegging, the activities of the old-fashioned "Mustache Petes" were strictly small-time. With the assassination on May 11, 1920, of James Colosimo, a rotund gangster fond of Enrico Caruso and the Chicago Opera Theater, an era of terror ended—only to be replaced by something altogether different.

The rise of Johnny Torrio, Al Capone, and their minions deeply embarrassed the community at large. During the height of the "booze wars" in the 1920s, the Italian periodicals went out of their way to minimize and downplay the significance of the crime problem. The 1929 St. Valentine's Day Massacre, in which eight Irish gangsters were lined up against the wall and shot by the Capone mob, received no attention from the community press.

Instead, *L'Italia* championed Judge Bernard Barasa of the Municipal Court as a role model for the community.

In 1923 Barasa became the first Italian American to announce his intention to run for mayor of Chicago. He entered the Republican primary after Mayor William Hale Thompson dropped out, due to the taint of scandal that surrounded his eight-year reign. Unfortunately, Barasa's name was linked to "Thompsonism," and despite carrying the Nineteenth Ward, the judge was swamped in the primary. The non-Italians proved unresponsive to the Barasa campaign. Since 1923, no Italian has seriously challenged the office of mayor in a city that was until recently dominated by Irish politicians.

Political progress was slow. In the 1920s, four Italians sat on the bench of the Municipal Court: Judge John J. Lupe, Judge Francis Allegretti, Judge Francis Borrelli, and Judge John Sbarbaro (who also owned the city's most famous undertaking parlor). By the 1980s, Chicago's Italian community was well represented in the City Council by Aldermen Vito Marzullo, William Banks, and Michael Nardulli. In Congress, Frank Annunzio of the Eleventh Congressional District was recognized as a leader and an eloquent spokesperson for the National Italian-American Foundation, a lobbying group.

In the scientific realm, one name stands alone—that of Enrico Fermi (1901–1954), the architect of the nuclear age. Born in Rome, Fermi was a brilliant physicist who conceived the idea of inducing artificial radioactivity through a new and ingenious method of reducing the speed of neutrons by passing them through paraffin. In 1938, Fermi was named a Nobel laureate in physics for his work with radioactive elements. The Fascist government granted him permission to attend the award ceremonies in Stockholm, Sweden, but Fermi and his Jewish wife, Laura Capon, fled Italy for a safe haven in the United States. After a brief period in New York, Fermi joined the faculty at the University of Chicago.

As the war clouds gathered over Europe, Enrico Fermi and two of his colleagues alerted President Franklin Roosevelt to the grave dangers posed to the United States if the Nazis should succeed in developing an atomic bomb. Their letter to the president, dated October 11, 1939, convinced Roosevelt of the necessity of developing the bomb before the Nazis. Thus the top-secret Manhattan Project was launched in 1942, with Fermi heading a team of scientists who worked around the clock in a makeshift laboratory constructed on the squash court under the stands of Stagg Field on the University of Chicago campus. On December 2, 1942, Fermi and his associates produced the first self-sustaining chain reaction. Later, the bomb project was moved to Los Alamos, New Mexico. FermiLab in west suburban Batavia is named after the great physicist.

North Side Italians attended Mass at the Assumption of the Blessed Virgin Mary Church. Construction of this magnificent edifice began in 1880, but the city's first Italian parish was not officially dedicated until August 15,

1886. The second Italian congregation was formed six years later, when St. Mary's of Mount Carmel opened its doors at 67th and Page streets on the South Side.

For years church parishes have filled a vital social and religious role in the lives of their Italian members. The *festa* was an expression of devotion to a particular saint and also an important social occasion, much like an old-fashioned country fair. Dating back to the 1890s, the Chicago street fest is patterned after the traditional religious celebrations in Italian villages. The religious festival in Chicago embodied the Old World flavor in a modern urban setting. The "Flight of the Angels" became an annual summer ritual on the Near North Side beginning at the church of St. Philip Benizi. The men of the parish would pull a float in the shape of a sailing vessel with the statue of the patron saint sitting on top.

To be selected one of the two "angels" was the highest honor accorded an Italian family; the two girls chosen not only had to read and write, but they also had to be fluent in the native tongue. The honor carried with it a $20 prize, put up by the sponsoring fraternal society. Dressed in ornamental white gowns, the two "angels" were affixed to a mechanical pulley strung across the rooftops of the convent school and an adjacent building. The girls slowly advanced toward each other suspended in mid-air. This tableau of the angels was traditionally held in late August. At its conclusion celebrants would visit outdoor booths selling tasty Italian dishes, such as *graticola*—fished marinated in vinegar or lemon and then grilled above an open fire.

The Flight of the Angels is but a memory today. However, similar festivals, such as the Our Lady of Mount Carmel celebration in Melrose Park in July and the Santa Maria Lauretana Fest in the Harlem-Cermak neighborhood in September, are a reminder of this rich heritage imported from across the ocean.

The number of Italians living in Chicago has dwindled in recent years. Construction of the University of Illinois campus in the early 1960s displaced thousands of second- and third-generation immigrants residing in the Taylor-Halsted neighborhood on the near West Side. Little Hell is also gone. The Francis Cabrini-Dwight Green housing project, completed in 1962, occupies much of what was once the heart of Little Italy. But the culture—the fests—are preserved on the lower West Side near 24th Street and Blue Island Avenue.

At the turn of the century this neighborhood was settled by Italians from the Tuscany region lured by the promise of good-paying jobs at the McCormick Reaper Works (later International Harvester, now Navistar). In 1903 historic St. Michael's Church in Old Town was built on the foundation of what was formerly a Swedish Methodist-Episcopal church. On the South Side, "La Colonia del Sessantanove Strada" (the Colony of 69th St.) near

Hermitage was developed in 1890 by the *contadini* from Oliveto Citra, a village in the province of Salerno.

Like other immigrant groups before them, the third-generation Italians began to leave the city neighborhoods for improved housing and economic opportunity in the suburbs. It began in the era of rising expectations in the 1920s and continued through the 1960s, when River Forest, Melrose Park, Riverside, and Oak Park took on a decidedly Italian character.

The Italians have been characterized as an ethnic group that remains behind in the "old neighborhood" forever, seemingly unresponsive to the realities of change. *Campanilismo,* or the sense of place, tied the Italians to their communities, be it through the fraternal societies, the ethnic press, or the magnet-like influence of the church parish. Suburbanization accelerated after World War II, but it had its roots in the 1890s, when a small group of Italians moved into Chicago Heights, thirty miles south of the city. The 300 Italians listed in the 1900 census worked at the brickyards or for Gaetano D'Amico, a former railroad section hand, who was the founder of "Mama Mia" spaghetti products.

Italians moved into Melrose Park as early as 1890. Ten years later they accounted for nearly 70 percent of the village population. Smaller but still viable Italian neighborhoods can be found in north suburban Highwood, west suburban Riverside, and in the Chicago neighborhoods of Belmont-Cragin on the Northwest Side, Bridgeport on the South Side, and the storied Tri-Taylor District, which endures in the shadow of the sprawling University of Illinois campus.

The new Little Italy, though, is concentrated on the far western outskirts of the city, along Harlem Avenue between Irving Park Road and North Avenue. The residents call it *Corsa Italia* (the Italian Boulevard), and it bears little resemblance to the congested inner city ghetto that existed on the near West Side at the turn of the century. The Harlem Avenue commercial strip, with its Italian banquet halls, beef stands, and small, independently owned businesses front blocks of single-family bungalows and ranch-style houses that are neatly maintained in a neighborhood that is relatively crime free.

There is no scarcity of Italian culture in Chicago, despite the frequently heard lament of community residents, who hearken back to a time when the Sicilians, Neapolitans, and Calabrians celebrated the festivals of the saints, the birth of their children, and the passing of the elders in the "city of immigrants." "Neighborhoods were missed by folks who had moved to the suburbs," commented Dominic Candeloro, a research associate at Governors State University. "They looked back and saw a time when everybody knew everybody else and helped everybody else." It has been said that in the heart of every man there is one small corner that is Italian. Some of the neighborhoods may be gone now, but the belief in spirituality, love of family, and the inner dignity Chicago's Italians hold will never be destroyed.

====================== **Attractions** ======================

Cultural Institutions

National Italian American Sports Hall of Fame
2625 Clearbrook Dr., Arlington Heights, (847)
437-3077. Open Monday–Friday. Admission is free.

George Randazzo is an Italian-American who satisfied his passion for professional boxing and the pride he felt in the achievements of his people in the athletic arena by founding a Boxing Hall of Fame in 1977. From these modest beginnings, various sports-minded Chicagoans of Italian descent urged Randazzo to expand the Hall of Fame to honor Italians whose noteworthy contributions to all fields of sport captured the imagination of the American public. In 1978 the immortal "Yankee Clipper," Joe DeMaggio, became the first inductee in Randazzo's revamped Hall of Fame, which was originally headquartered at 7906 W. Grand Avenue, in Elmwood Park, Illinois. Present at the ribbon-cutting ceremony were such luminaries as Dodger manager Tom Lasorda; former Yankee catcher Yogi Berra; Mary Ann Marciano, daughter of prize fighter Rocky Marciano; and pool champion Willie Mosconi.

In 1980, the highly successful *Red, White, and Green* was launched, a monthly sports tabloid dedicated to promoting Italians in sports. The publication has a national circulation. On April 4, 1987, thanks to the generous support of Edward J. DeBartolo of Youngstown, Ohio, the NIASHF moved into spacious new quarters located on seven acres of land in Arlington Heights, where the latest in state-of-the-art technology permits visitors to experience a "hands-on" approach to sports history. Thousands of pieces of memorabilia are on display, including the race cars driven by Mario Andretti and his son Michael; Rocky Marciano's heavyweight championship belt; and Olympic gold medal mementos won by Matt Biondi, Mary Lou Retton, and Mike Eruzione.

Throughout the year, the museum hosts a number of special events, including the March Annual Awards Ceremony honoring the athlete of the year (or decade) from the prep, college, and professional ranks. The induction ceremony and sports memorabilia auction is held in July or August, with refreshments served on the grounds. *Recommended.*

Italian Cultural Center *(Under the Aegis of the*
Scalabrini Fathers and Brothers), 1621 N. 39th Ave.,
Stone Park, (708) 345-3842. Open Monday–Friday.
Donations are encouraged. Membership available.

Two blocks east of bustling Mannheim Road (Route 45) and two blocks south of North Avenue (Route 64), the Italian Cultural Center has enhanced the appreciation of the literary, religious, and artistic endeavors of Chicago's large Italian community. The three-story museum was opened in May 1970 when the original seminary of the Scalabrini Fathers and Brothers moved into a newly constructed wing on Division Street, in Stone Park. Tucked away on 22 acres of ground in a quiet residential neighborhood, the Cultural Center features a first-floor library, an important research archive that contains 113 oral history transcripts and 2,500 volumes of Italian history, biography, philosophy, religion, and arts. Second-floor exhibits chronicle the Italian settlement in Chicago, with particular emphasis on neighborhoods, the working experience, and the *festa*. The John Cadel Art Gallery is down the hall, featuring the works of this celebrated painter, who died in 1977. Various oil paintings, bronzes, ceramics, original prints, and Italian crafts are included in the collection. The Savoia Exhibit, a 1:100 scale model of St. Peter's Basilica in Rome and St. Mark's Square in Venice, Italy, occupies much of the available floor space on the third level. Italian-language classes for children and adults are held during the week and on Saturdays. *Recommended.*

Italian Cultural Institute (*Instuto Italiano di Cultura*), *500 N. Michigan Ave., 14th Floor, Chicago, (312) 822-9545. Open Monday–Friday.*

Founded in the mid-1980s, and sponsored by the Italian consulate in Chicago, the Cultural Institute is a not-for-profit center for the arts that regularly hosts gallery exhibitions, lectures, musical concerts, and panel discussions emphasizing the customs, heritage, and creative expression of contemporary Italy. The Institute sponsors Italian-language classes and provides travel services to Europe. Call or drop by to be added to the mailing list.

Galleria Marchetti, *825 W. Erie St., Chicago, (312) 421-4354. Admission fee charged.*

A few years after launching the Como Inn, Giuseppi Marchetti decided to invest a portion of his earnings in a cherished prize: a 1929 Cord automobile. Marchetti and his four sons had a lifelong love affair with the automobile, especially sleek, high-performance racing cars. Ferraris. Joe Jr. began collecting them in 1963. His fixation with the vintage Italian racing machines began that year when he housed his collection in a garage across the street from the Como Inn. The garage at Erie and Halsted was first a showroom and dealership, and then a showcase for art exhibitions and a banquet hall for private parties of up to 250. The Galleria Marchetti is a unique and picturesque spot within the old industrial corridor of West

Town. In October 1989, the Marchettis hosted an extravaganza of Italian design called the *Oggi* (the literal translation means "today") exhibit. It featured a display of contemporary furniture, home accessories, painting, film, and fashion from Milan. *Oggi'*89 was magnificently received, with the proceeds going to the Rinascimento Foundation, which promotes cultural exchanges between Italy and the United States. The *Oggi* exhibit has become another Como tradition.

In 1980, Joe Marchetti founded the Chicago Historic Races at Road America at Elkhart Lake, Wisconsin. Fifty drivers and 500 visitors turned out the first year to preview a fine collection of sports and racing cars built prior to 1973. Since that time the International Challenge for the Chicago Historic Races has attracted as many as 330 cars and drivers, and 10,000 to 15,000 spectators a year. The annual event, held the second weekend in July, features a stunning "Race Car Concours D'Elegance" exhibition at Elkhart Lake, a dinner at Siebken's Resort, qualifying sessions, and an awards ceremony capped off by the Sunday feature races. Each of the events is separately priced, and inquiries should be directed to the Galleria Marchetti. They will be happy to send a registration form and information about entry requirements. The Marchettis abide by a simple philosophy when it comes to vintage racing: "Winning is not the sole purpose, and thoughtless driving will not be allowed."

Annual Events and Celebrations

Columbus Day Parade, *Monday closest to October 12. Call Joint Civic Committee of Italian Americans at (312) 828-0010 for information.*

Each year Chicago's Italians pay tribute to the great navigator whose voyage of discovery led to the permanent settlement of the New World. Whether the Vikings preceded Christopher Columbus or not remains a hotly debated issue. It is a moot point on Columbus Day, of course, as thousands of people line the parade route, which stretches along Dearborn Street between Wacker Drive on the north to Van Buren on the south. Lavishly decorated floats, some 175 marching bands, and a score of politicians and celebrities have turned out each year since 1952 to laud the accomplishments of Columbus. "It's a great day to be Italian!" exclaimed former Lieutenant Governor Neil Hartigan—an Irishman—who was in attendance at the 1990 parade.

The night before the gala downtown parade, the Sons of Italy sponsor a Columbus Day Banquet, traditionally held at a suburban hotel. Call the Order of the Sons of Italy in America, 7222 Cermak Road, Riverside, (847) 447-6304.

Festa Italiana, Arvey Field, the south end of Grant Park at 12th St. and Columbus Dr. Third weekend of August. Tickets are available at local Dominicks and Butera Finer Food stores or at the gate. Call (312) 829-8888 for information.

Three-day folk fair. Since 1976, this popular family event has become a perennial favorite of Chicagoans. That year, the event was a side attraction to the Columbus Day weekend festivities, and was held in relative obscurity at the O'Hare Hyatt Regency in suburban Rosemont. In 1979, under the direction of attorney Anthony J. Fornelli, *Festa Italiana* moved to Navy Pier to become the city's first important ethnic folk fair. Fornelli envisioned more than just an arts and crafts, eat-all-you-want festival. He did not want to lose sight of the cultural and religious aspects of Italian-American life. Sculptors, painters, and artisans from the Chicago area display their work during the weekend in order to educate and inform the public about the achievements of Chicago's Italians. *Festa Italiana* features more than the usual food booths and balloons. There are two main stages showcasing such local and national talents as Frankie Avalon, the singing restaurateur Tony Spavone, and Rick "Elvis" Saucedo. An impressive fireworks display caps off the festivities on Friday and Saturday. *Recommended.*

Annual Italian Heritage Ball and Cotillion, *Grand Ballroom of the Conrad Hilton Hotel, 720 S. Michigan Ave., Chicago. Call the Joint Civic Committee of Italian Americans at (312) 828-0010 for tickets and information.*

The Joint Civic Committee of Italian Americans (JCCIA) is an umbrella organization of leaders representing more than forty fraternal societies who joined forces in 1952 to combat bigotry and prejudice against Americans of Italian descent. The Women's Division, organized in 1966, sponsors an annual Heritage Ball and Cotillion held the second Friday of December. The black-tie event began in 1966, and it marks the debut of the prettiest and most talented Italian-American debutantes between the ages of 15 and 21. The young ladies and their escorts perform a sequence of choreographed dance routines before the assembled guests, which may include the Bishop or Cardinal.

A Touch of Italy, *Near West Side along Taylor St. between Halsted and Morgan St. Call (312) 243-3773. Donations requested.*

Food fest and entertainment. Two stages of continuous entertainment featuring such Italian-American entertainers as Al Martino. An annual event in the old neighborhood since 1989.

St. Joseph's Day Celebrations

According to religious scholars, the custom of offering a "St. Joseph's Table" of food and beverage to the hungry and the homeless began in Sicily, when the people, appalled by the treatment shown the Holy Family, restaged the biblical event in their towns and villages. Others claim that it recalls St. Luke's account of the Nativity, in which Mary and Joseph found only the barest of essentials when they arrived in Bethlehem to give birth to the Christ child. The Sicilians adopted March 19 as the traditional St. Joseph's Day—a time when they opened their doors and their hearts to the street people, offering unlimited food in a symbolic anticipation of the Holy Family's arrival. The custom is recreated at several Chicago-area parishes in March as both a feast and fund-raising event.

Our Lady of Pompeii Church, *1224 Lexington Ave., Chicago, (312) 421-3757.*

Table opens after Mass.

Scalabrini Village, *480 N. Wolf Rd., Northlake, (708) 562-0040. Donations requested.*

Mass at Villa Scalabrini Chapel (procession to Casa San Carlo dining room afterward).

Notre Dame/St. Callistus Parish, *2167 Bowler St., Chicago, (312) 243-7400. Donations accepted.*

A tradition since 1957, held in the school gym. Festivities begin with a procession to the statue followed by Mass.

Our Lady of Ransom Parish, *Paluch Hall, 8300 N. Greenwood, Niles, (708) 823-2550. Donations accepted.*

Outlying Areas

The Annual Feast of Our Lady of Mt. Carmel,
outdoor Mass and procession through the streets of Melrose Park. Sunday closest to July 16. Call (708) 865-9746 for details.

Since 1893, members of Chicago's Neapolitan communities have observed this important religious festival in various surroundings. It began in the inner city neighborhoods north of the river, but with the suburban population shift, the traditions have been imported. After the Sunday noon Mass, the statue of Our Lady of Mount Carmel is carried through the streets of Melrose Park from the grounds of the Civic Center, at 25th and Lake Street. The sacred image, which stands six feet tall, was brought to the United States in 1894, and is held aloft by six strong men. The procession sometimes stretches eight blocks or more.

Italian Day Picnic, *Italian Cultural Center, 1621 N. 39th Ave., Stone Park, (708) 345-3842. First Sunday in August. Admission is free.*

An outdoor feast accompanies the outdoor Mass. Italian food may be purchased on the grounds.

Villa Day Celebration.

Popular Italian food festival is held annually and it features the best in local, live entertainment including Tony Spavone, Dick Contino, and Tony Ocean. The event promotes family unity and it is scheduled for the last weekend in July. Sponsored by the Scalabrini Home For the Aged, 480 N. Wolf Road, Northlake, IL Call: (708) 562-0040 for scheduled times. Admission: $25 for adults, children 6–13, $5.00 includes all you can eat.

St. Francesco di Paola Society, *Italian Cultural Center, 1621 N. 39th Ave., Stone Park, (708) 345-3842. Mid-August on the grounds of the Cultural Center.*

An outdoor feast accompanies the Sunday outdoor Mass. Entertainment. Italian food may be purchased on the grounds.

Feast of Santa Maria Lauretana Society, *22nd and Harlem, Berwyn, (312) 736-3766. Labor Day weekend.*

A four-day festival featuring food, entertainment, fireworks, and the time-honored "Flight of the Angels" procession on Sunday.

Feast of St. Anthony of Padua, *Our Lady of Mount Carmel Church, 1101 N. 23rd Ave., Melrose Park. Second Sunday in June. Call Ann Eboli at (708) 345-0630 for details.*

Solemn High Mass followed by a religious procession. Refreshments served in Carmel Hall following the procession. St. Anthony's bread is also blessed.

Places to See

The Near West Side

Parts of the Near West Side offer a good glimpse of what Chicago was like in the heyday of the great Eastern European immigration, back when Hull House opened in one of the most densely populated regions in the world. The average slum district on the West Side housed 270 persons per acre, crowded together in dimly lit, unsanitary brick slum buildings known as "double-deckers." These buildings were three or four stories high, and typically extended over the entire lot. A 1901 survey found 127 people huddled together in a set of three small rooms.

The West Side neighborhoods remained crowded and often squalid until the process of renovation took hold, beginning in 1943 with the construction of the Robert Brooks Homes at 14th and Loomis. In 1955, the year that Richard J. Daley won his first mayoral election, the Grace Abbott Homes opened on a ten-block site on Roosevelt Road, not far from the Maxwell Street Market.

Then in 1961 came the announcement that the new Chicago campus of the University of Illinois would be built adjacent to the Congress (Eisenhower) Expressway. This occurred at a time when community and business leaders were attempting to reclaim and gentrify sections of the old Italian neighborhood. The fight against the university was waged in part by Florence Giovangelo Scala and the Near West Side Planning Board, who fought to preserve their neighborhood as they knew it. The legal wrangles continued into the mid-1960s, and though much of the old neighborhood was lost, much of what remains retains an Italian flavor and considerable charm.

The university proved to be a boon to the Taylor Street merchants, and stabilized single-dwelling housing. In fact, by 1980, housing prices soared in the Tri-Taylor Historic District, which was buoyed by young homeowners eager to rehab the old buildings to live in a historic yet modern urban setting.

To get a notion of the area's architectural variety, head south on Halsted from Madison Street, passing through Greek Town and over the Eisenhower Expressway to the University of Illinois at Chicago campus. Two blocks south of the expressway is Hull House, a restored red brick house on the right. Go two blocks farther south to Taylor Street and head five blocks west, past all the university buildings.

This is the Italian section of Taylor Street, a lively strip of excellent restaurants, sports bars, Italian delis, and street vendors selling Italian ices. At Loomis Street, turn right again to Arrigo Park. Small apartment buildings line the southern edge of the park; along its northern border on Lexington Street are several elegant blocks of Victorian homes. Once this area was called the Irish Gold Coast; since the 1920s, it's been mainly Italian. Some suburban-like tract homes mix only somewhat uncomfortably with elegant brick homes built before the turn of the century. An extraordinary combination, and only a mile from the Sears Tower.

Tri-Taylor District

Bounded by Oakley Avenue (2300 W.), Taylor Street (1000 S.), and the Penn Central Railroad tracks, the Tri-Taylor Historic District features a charming, wonderfully preserved collection of row houses and two- and three-story flats, typical of the kinds of buildings that existed in this neighborhood in the 1880s and 1890s. Tri-Taylor was added to the National Register of Historic Places in 1983, and it continues to be rehabbed under historic guidelines established by the government. The homeowners are for the most part young Italians, Mexicans, Germans, and Irish who have banded together to preserve the architectural aesthetics of one of the oldest residential communities in Chicago.

Our Lady of Pompeii, *1224 Lexington Ave., Chicago, (312) 421-3757.*

A storied Italian church constructed in 1910, and rebuilt in a Romanesque style thirteen years later.

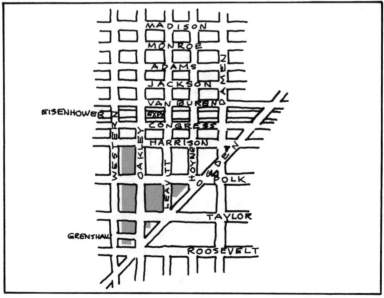

Tri-Taylor Historic District

Jackson Boulevard Historic District, *Jackson Boulevard east of Ashland, in the 1500 block (near Halsted). The Chicago Architecture Foundation conducts a two-hour walking tour of the district on three Sunday afternoons, in June, July, and September. Call (312) 326-1393.*

At a time when the West Side was little more than an inner-city slum with little chance of revival, a group of visionary Chicagoans rescued this block of Victorian mansions from the wrecker's ball, and in the process set the tone for urban renovation in the years to come. Thirty-one Victorian row houses were saved, which stand as a reminder of a simpler, more elegant era. It is doubtful that the poor southern Italians who crowded along Taylor Street could have afforded homes like these, but it is important that we understand the class differences of the era through its architecture.

Outlying Areas

Montefiori: Redefining an Exotic, Lost Age

The air is still, the setting reminiscent of West Egg, and the Long Island estate of F. Scott Fitzgerald's fictional playboy Jay Gatsby, who welcomed the jazz babies and high-living millionaires from the big city to share in the revelry of the times. Montefiori, a sprawling 55-acre retreat located 25 miles southwest of Chicago near the Cal-Sag Channel in Lemont, hearkens back to that opulent era of champagne and roses, especially when Joe Marchetti sponsors the International Concours D'Elegance, featuring vintage car collectors showing off their road machines in Gatsby-era costumes. In 1989, Baron Hans Freiherr von Richthofen, grandson of the Red Baron, was in attendance at Montefiori to lend his name to the festivities.

Montefiori was added to the growing Marchetti empire in 1924, when Giuseppe decided he had to construct a Palladian-style replica of his birthplace in San Ginese. The summer home now belongs to Paul Marchetti, who maintains the estate in style. A camel, twelve llamas, six species of swans, and forty exotic birds ensure that the Montefiori estate lives up to its name, "mountain of flowers." The Marchetti family opened Montefiori to the public ten years ago, and during the summer months the family hosts a series of festivals evolving around collector automobiles, jazz dance, the Lyric Opera, and the beauty of flowers. A schedule of events, beginning in May and continuing through September, includes *Festa Campagnola,* an Italian-style picnic, the Great Gatsby Weekend and International Concours D'Elegance, performances of Shakespeare, and classic Italian opera. In mid-September the Marchettis celebrate "Immagini di Toscana" in the beauty of the countryside. Montefiori is located along Routes 83 and 171.

For additional information about seasonal events at the estate, please call Janet Fisk at (708) 442-8382.

Shops

Scafuri Bakery, *1337 W. Taylor St., Chicago, (312) 733-8881. Closed Sunday and Monday.*

Luigi Scafuri immigrated from Naples and opened this bakery in the 1890s. Today it is owned and operated by his daughter Annette, who was born on nearby Loomis Street and lived above the bakery. She still uses Luigi's traditional recipe for bread. The fresh, unusual flavor comes from the way the bread is prepared: in old-fashioned boxes. According to Annette, Italians come from all over the Midwest to buy the bread, which can be frozen and stored. *Recommended.*

D'Amato's Bakery, *1124 W. Grand Ave., Chicago, (312) 733-5456.*

One of the city's legendary Italian bakeries, located about two miles north of Taylor Street. D'Amato's bakes the best sourdough bread, according to *Chicago Tribune* columnist Bill Grainger, and will sell you uncooked pizza dough if you ask for it.

Conte Di Savoia, *1438 W. Taylor St., Chicago, (312) 666-3471. Open daily.*

Italian grocery store with a small self-service café in the front that caters to the weekday lunch crowd. Vito Cambio started and operated the business at Taylor and Halsted in the 1930s, until the university bulldozed acres of private and commercial buildings in 1960. Mike DiCosola, the current owner, is one of the third-generation Italians who fled to the suburbs but was lured back to the old neighborhood when the Tri-Taylor district underwent gentrification. Imported sausages, pastries, tortellini, cavatelli, fine wines, and standard American groceries are sold here.

Chiarugi's, *1447-1449 W. Taylor St., Chicago, (312) 666-2235. Closed Sundays.*

Where else but on the near West Side can you find a retail emporium that displays toilet seats in the front window? Keep an open mind. Chiarugi's is a charming, old-fashioned hardware store with creaking wooden floors and display cases containing a variety of goods, including wine-making tools, bottles, and corks.

Outlying Areas

Italian Records and Video, *7172 W. Grand Ave.,*
Chicago, (773) 637-5300. Closed Wednesday. Credit
cards accepted.

Charming family-owned store now at its third location near Elmwood Park.
The business began more than sixty-seven years ago on the West Side, but
is now owned by Pompeo Stillo, author of three books about Italian life.
Flags, jackets, greeting cards, and Italian cassettes and records are available
for purchase. Ermida Cassano, one of the employees, is a wealth of information about Chicago's Italian community.

Capodimonte Imports, *5958 W. Addison, Chicago,*
(312) 283-2412. Closed Thursday.

Flowers and assorted gift items attractively presented in this small, independently owned store.

Gino's Italian Imports, Ltd., *3420-3422 N. Harlem,*
Chicago, (773) 745-8310. Open daily. Credit cards
accepted.

Gino Bartucci built his Mediterranean-style shopping plaza in 1981 to house
the specialty imports he offers for sale, including cheeses, sausages and
pasta, kitchen tools, and handmade china.

Minelli Brothers Italian Specialties and Liquors,
7780 N. Milwaukee Ave., Niles, (847) 965-1315. Open
daily. No credit cards.

Homemade roast beef, pizza, and Italian sausages.

l'appetito Imported Italian Foods, *30 E. Huron St.,*
Chicago, (312) 787-9881. Closed Sundays.

Complete line of Italian imported groceries. Deli service, party trays. No
liquor products.

La Bomboniera, *3429 N. Harlem Ave., Chicago,*
(773) 725-9000. Closed Sundays. Credit cards
accepted.

Imported gifts, party favors for all occasions.

Pasta Fresh Co., *3418 N. Harlem Ave., Chicago*
(773) 745-5888. Open daily.

Located next to Gino's in the "Piazza Italia" plaza on Harlem Avenue. Pasta and delicatessen products imported from Italy.

Restaurants

Al's Italian Beef, *1079 W. Taylor St.,* and **Mario's Lemonade Stand.** *(Taylor, between Aberdeen and Carpenter).*

Al's, a four-star chain, started here. During the summer buy your sandwich and stroll the street to sample a frosty Italian snowball and *lupini* at Mario's—where the Gray Line tour buses make an obligatory stop as they make their rounds in Chicago. Mario's opens for the season on May 1.

Trattoria Roma Terza, *1119 W. Taylor St., Chicago, (312) 226-6800. Open for lunch Monday–Friday and dinner daily. All major credit cards accepted.*

Small, unpretentious dining room amid the artful Roman-ruins faux finishes. Appetizer table. Daily specials.

New Rosebud Café, *1500 W. Taylor St., Chicago, (312) 942-1117. Open for lunch Monday–Friday and dinner daily.*

This is without doubt one of the most popular Italian eateries in the city, catering to the patrons of the United Center, who fill the place to overflowing after the Bulls and Blackhawks games. The homemade pastas are served in huge ceramic bowls. Reservations strongly suggested.

Falbo's, *1335 W. Taylor St., Chicago, (312) 421-8915. Closed Sundays.*

Delicatessen and submarine sandwich shop that sells imported Italian sausage, olive oil, and cheeses. Established 1912.

Gennaro's Restaurant, *1352 W. Taylor St., Chicago, (312) 243-1035. Open for dinner. Closed Monday–Wednesday.*

One of the old-line Taylor Street eateries since 1959. Pasta and pizza are the standard fare.

Outlying Areas

The Como Inn, *546 N. Milwaukee Ave., Chicago,*
(773) 421-5222. Open for lunch Sunday–Friday and
dinner daily.

The story begins in 1920, when "Papa" Giuseppe Marchetti left his home in the Tuscan village of San Ginese near Lucca. He arrived in Chicago at the age of 17, ragged, hungry, and filled with ambition. Joe Marchetti became a partner in a small restaurant at Grand and Halsted. In 1924 a nearby grocery store suddenly became available, and young Marchetti, realizing the golden opportunity that comes to each man but once, bought out the business and founded the Como Inn Restaurant. In the early days it was your typical white tablecloth Italian restaurant, but after World War II, the Como Inn evolved into its present neoclassical design. Today the Como Inn is a restaurant complex, with thirteen dining rooms. The Marchettis serve Northern Italian cuisine, and can accommodate large private parties. The Como Inn is tucked away in the sleepy West Town neighborhood bounded by Grand Avenue, the Kennedy Expressway, Division, and Ashland. *Recommended.*

La Gondola, *2425 N. Ashland, Chicago,*
(773) 248-4433. Open for dinner daily. Credit
cards accepted. Parking in rear.

Southern Italian cooking served in a pleasing old-fashioned family atmosphere. The paintings of familiar Venetian scenes grace the walls and provide an interesting European backdrop as you dine on steamed mussels, fresh ravioli, and fried calamari. Nothing fancy here, just down-home style in West Lincoln Park.

Italian Village, *71 W. Monroe St., Chicago,*
(312) 332-7005. Open for lunch and dinner daily.
Major credit cards accepted.

A downtown institution housing three restaurants in one. On the main level you'll find the "Viviere," which is gourmet cooking at its best. Viviere is actually the old Florentine Room. The "Village"—most popular with opera aficionados—is less expensive and is on the second floor. The basement "La Cantina" is a wine cellar grotto and ideal for a quick lunch.

Carlucci's, *2215 N. Halsted St., Chicago,*
(773) 281-1220. Open for dinner daily. Credit
cards accepted.

Elegant decor and sophisticated Italian cooking.

Da Nicola, *3114 N. Lincoln Ave., Chicago, (773) 935-8000. Open for lunch Monday–Saturday and dinner Friday and Saturday. Closed Sundays. Major credit cards accepted.*

Pricey family-style portions served in a pleasing, homey atmosphere. The appetizers are exceptional.

Pizzerias Uno and Due, *29 E. Ohio St. and 619 N. Wabash Ave., Chicago, (312) 321-1000 and (312) 943-2400. Open for lunch and dinner daily.*

Two of the best deep-dish pizza parlors in the city are only a block apart. Both restaurants are usually crowded, so it's best to phone your order ahead. Off-times tend to be the best.

Scoozi!, *410 W. Huron St., Chicago, (312) 943-5900. Open for lunch Monday–Friday and dinner daily.*

This large Italian eatery that seats 320 people is usually crowded during the dinner hour, but roasted meats and smoked pheasant dishes are worth the wait. *Recommended.*

Spiaggia, *980 N. Michigan Ave., Chicago, (312) 280-2750. Open for lunch Monday–Saturday and dinner daily. Credit cards accepted.*

The decor is impressive, the servers are well versed and attentive, but the prices of the pasta are high, as pastas go. Spiaggia on Boul Mich is certainly worth a look, though it is a far cry from the homey little places along Oakley (Marzullo) Avenue. *Recommended.*

Lou Malnati's, *four locations: 441 N. Wells St., Chicago, (312) 828-9800; 6649 Lincoln Ave., Lincolnwood, (847) 673-0800; 1050 E. Higgins Rd., Elk Grove Village, (847) 439-2000; 88 S. Buffalo Grove Rd., Buffalo Grove, (847) 980-1525. Open for lunch and dinner daily.*

Lou Malnati's is a top-drawer, down-home, deep-dish pizzeria that is a favorite of Chicago sports fans. Autographed posters and photographs of Chicago sports greats line the walls of the restaurants. In Buffalo Grove there is a miniature museum on display. But the décor is not the reason to drop by; the pizza's the thing.

Va Pensiero-Margarita Inn, *1566 Oak Ave.,*
Evanston, (847) 475-7779. Open for lunch
Monday–Friday, and dinner Monday–Saturday.
Closed Sundays. Credit cards accepted.

At center stage is the cooking of executive chef Peggy Ryan, whose superb pastas and veal shank are highly recommended. Wonderful desserts and an exceptional wine list. A North Shore delight.

Tony Spavone's Ristorante, *266 W. Lake St.,*
Bloomingdale, (630) 529-3154. Open for dinner daily.
Credit cards accepted.

It's where the owner sings to his customers—but you can only catch Tony Spavone's act on weekends, so it's best to call ahead for reservations. Tony, a fixture at *Festa Italiana,* has been featured on WBBM-TV's "Two On Two" segment. His restaurant is consistently rated among the best in metro-Cook County.

Oakley Avenue & 24th Place in Pilsen:
Northern Italian Restaurant Row

Thousands of northern Italian immigrants, primarily from the Tuscany region, poured into this industrial neighborhood in the 1890s. They were lured by the promise of jobs at the McCormick Reaper Works on nearby Blue Island Avenue, and by affordable housing once occupied by the Germans, Swedes, and Irish. After World War II, a second wave of Italian immigrants—this time from the Piedmont region—poured into this corner of Pilsen which comprises the 25th Ward.

Through the 1950s, 1960s, and 1970s, the first- and second-generation immigrants were represented in the Chicago City Council by Alderman Vito Marzullo, a Sicilian politician who sat at the throne of Mayor Richard J. Daley. Marzullo was chairman of the powerful transportation committee and an important cog in the Daley machine through six terms. It was fitting, therefore, that the council should reward Marzullo's loyalty by renaming Oakley Avenue, from Blue Island to Cermak Road, Vito Marzullo Avenue. After all, Charles Oakley (1792–1849), for whom this street in Chicago was originally named, set an early example for Chicago's ward characters by turning the Illinois-Michigan Canal project into a massive patronage trough, in his capacity as a state-appointed trustee.

Today, the 25th Ward has lost much of its Italian character. Thousands of Hispanics now reside in Pilsen, but for several blocks along Oakley (Marzullo) Avenue it is still possible to experience Northern Italian cuisine served by these restaurateurs.

La Fontanella, *2414 S. Oakley Ave., Chicago,*
(773) 927-5249. Open for lunch and dinner daily.
Checks accepted, but no credit cards.

Family owned and operated. A small, out-of-the-way Italian eatery.

Bacchanalia Ristorante, *2413 S. Oakley Ave.,*
Chicago, (773) 254-6555. Open for lunch
Monday–Friday, dinner Wednesday–Monday. Closed
Tuesdays. Checks accepted, but no credit cards.

The tortellini and chicken Vesuvio are the house specialties.

Alfo's, *2512 S. Oakley Ave., Chicago, (773) 523-6994.*
Open for lunch Tuesday–Friday, and dinner
Tuesday–Sunday. Closed Mondays.

Family style, informal surroundings. Specialties include *vitello* (veal), *fritto misto* (fried veal), and chicken á la Alfo.

Toscano, *2439 S. Oakley Ave., Chicago,*
(773) 376-4841. Open for lunch Tuesday–Friday
and dinner Tuesday–Sunday. Closed Mondays.

Seafood specials.

Bruna's Ristorante, *2424 S. Oakley Ave., Chicago.*
Open for lunch and dinner daily.

Bruna Cane and her husband opened this small neighborhood restaurant in 1934. It's a neighborhood kind of place specializing in veal and fettuccini.

Villa Marconi, *2358-2354 S. Oakley Ave., Chicago.*
Open for lunch and dinner Monday–Friday and
dinner Saturday. Closed Sundays. All major credit
cards accepted.

Traditional northern Italian cuisine.

Fontana Brothers Bakery, *2404 S. Oakley Ave.,*
Chicago, (773) 847-6697. Open daily.

John Toschi, an Italian baker, opened his business more than seventy years ago. Like other ethnic Italian bakers, this family-owned business specializes in bread, be it twists, ryes, or sticks. Cookies, but no fine pastries.

Media

Italian-Language Radio Programming

Pomeriggio Italiana, *sponsored by Italian Records and Video. Airs on WEEF-1430 AM, 2:30–3:00 P.M., Tuesdays and Thursdays.*

Mattinata Italiana, *sponsored by Italian Records and Video. Airs on WEDC-1240 AM, 9:30–10:00 A.M., Saturdays.*

Taylor Street: A Touch of Italy on the Near West Side

The old neighborhood along Taylor Street dwells in the hearts and minds of Chicago's Italian community. Much of this West Side enclave was swallowed up by the University of Illinois campus in the early 1960s, and the Cabrini Housing Project on Taylor Street occupies land where Italian homes and businesses once stood. Though diminished in stature, Taylor Street retains its essential Italian character despite an increasingly wider ethnic diversity.

A collage of elegant southern Italian (Calabrian) restaurants can be found between Halsted on the east and Racine on the west. While most of the 500,000 Italian-Americans live in the outlying neighborhoods and suburbs, many of them come back each year to relive the customs and celebrate Mass at Our Lady of Pompeii Church, especially on Columbus Day. According to Anthony Sorrentino, former executive director of the Joint Civic Committee of Italian Americans, "They begin to recall their rich memories, not only of the hard times, but of their varied social life in the family, church, club, neighborhood and world of work. These and other thoughts came to mind when hundreds attended the Mass for the Columbus Day Parade at Our Lady of Pompeii Church.

"One Italian-American who attends this event every year said: 'I bring my children here every year so that they will have some link with my roots and my heritage.' It is true that you can't turn the clock back, but I believe that this proves that you can go home again—if only to discover who you are and where you should be going."

Greek Chicago

═══════ History and Settlement ═══════

"When Greek meets Greek they start a restaurant!" or so wrote Peter Lambros, community historian and founder and editor of the *Star,* Chicago's oldest established Greek newspaper. Lambros was recalling a time in the 1890s when his compatriots were first making their mark in the city.

The great exodus from the Peloponnesus began in the late nineteenth century, when the price of currants—a staple crop of the peasant farmer—fell to record lows. These Greeks had heard all of the familiar stories about the favorable prospects for Europeans seeking their way in America. Years earlier, during the Greek War of Independence (1821–1828), hundreds of orphaned boys whose parents had been slaughtered by the rampaging Turks had been sent to the United States, where they were given good homes with American families. Many of these youths prospered in their new surroundings as they grew to adulthood, and word of their success had passed back to their homeland.

Prior to 1871, there were only a few Greek immigrants in Chicago. One of the earliest arrivals was Captain Nicholas Pappas, who settled on Kinzie Street in 1857. He lived in Chicago until his death in 1927. The first Greek marriage in Chicago took place shortly after the Civil War, when Nicholas Brown, owner of a Kinzie Street barber shop, married an American-born woman.

The cataclysmic fire of 1871 was the milestone event in the history of the Greek settlement of Chicago. The terrible disaster that scorched miles of prime city real estate encouraged large numbers of strong-bodied Greek men to come to Chicago to take part in the great rebuilding. Word of mouth—that great intangible of the European immigration—was important in luring the Greeks. Christ Chacona, known as the "Columbus of Sparta," was a pied piper in his own right. Realizing that there was money to make here, Chacona returned to his home in Tzintzina, Sparta, to convince his relatives to sell the farm and come back with him to Chicago. Because of Chacona and others like him, the Greek colony near Clark and Kinzie streets on the near North Side became the largest of its kind in the United States, numbering 1,000 residents. The immigrants, for the most part, came from Laconia and Arcadia.

The Greek experience in Chicago in many ways paralleled that of the Chinese. Until 1885, there was not one woman counted by the census takers. This began to change with the arrival of Mr. and Mrs. Peter Pooley (Panagiotis Poulis) from Corfu in 1885. Peter Pooley was a sea captain who was familiar with the city from his earlier excursions up the Mississippi River from New Orleans. Impressed with Chicago and all it had to offer, Pooley returned to Corfu, where he was joined in marriage to Georgia Bitzis. Together, the young couple crossed the ocean and headed straight to Chicago, where in 1885, the spirited, dynamic Georgia organized the Greco-Slavonian Society, the first benevolent association of its kind.

In 1887, the Therapnon Society was formed to promote the religious ideals of the homeland. Its members were instrumental in bringing to the United States the Reverend Peter Phiambolis, the first Greek Orthodox priest to emigrate to America. The church was located in modest surroundings—a rented loft space in a building at Randolph and Union streets. The church was consecrated by Greek Orthodox church leaders on March 25, 1893, during a visit to the World's Columbian Exposition by Bishop Dionysius Lattas of Zante. This oldest Greek Orthodox congregation in the United States later worshiped in a converted Episcopal Church at 1101 S. Peoria from 1897 until 1963. Here in the West Side "Delta" (bounded by Halsted, Harrison, Blue Island, and Polk streets and named for the triangular Greek letter), Chicago's largest, most important Greek settlement, generations of devout worshipers attended services and paid their dues to support the *koinotis* (community).

The role of the Greek Orthodox Church in the *koinotis* was paramount. Every Greek immigrant who resided in the Delta was automatically a member of the *paroikia* (colony). But only those persons who contributed a share of their earnings to support the church and its sponsoring institutions could be said to belong to the *koinotis*. This rigid social structure bound its members to the neighborhood and provided an important identity through the benevolent, fraternal, and social organizations.

Chicago's Greeks were also united in their support for Jane Addams, founder of Hull House and its director from 1885 until her death in 1935. Addams was a friend to the community. She encouraged the Greeks to preserve their rich cultural heritage—so crucial for the survival of the folk traditions. The first Greek play in Chicago was presented at the Hull House Theater in December 1899. It was a classical tragedy titled *The Return of Odysseus,* sponsored in part by the Greek fraternal societies. The play attracted favorable attention from the newspaper critics, which no doubt encouraged a number of the society women, including Bertha Honore Palmer, to purchase tickets. In May 1900, the play was transferred to the spacious Studebaker Theater for the benefit of all Chicagoans.

At Hull House, the Hellenic League for the Molding of Young Men was organized in 1908 to provide paramilitary and athletic training for Greek youth. Instruction was provided by former Greek army officers, who had the unit whipped into shape for the visit of former President Theodore Roosevelt in 1911. Commenting on Roosevelt's visit, the Chicago *Tribune* noted that he had come to Hull House "not to teach, but to learn." When Jane Addams died, she was mourned by the Greek community, which eulogized her as the "Saint of Halsted Street."

The Delta attained significance beginning in the 1890s, when thousands of immigrants poured into the city. Many of them became fruit and vegetable peddlers, or pushcart vendors, dispensing smoking sausages on a bun to lunch patrons in the Loop. Competition was often fierce between the Greeks and the Italians. Sometimes it evolved into fistfights between these two immigrant groups familiar with each other's culture and language. In 1904 the Grocer's Association complained to the City Council that the Greek peddlers were undercutting its business. The pushcart entrepreneurs defended themselves against their upscale competitors by telling the aldermen that they provided an indispensable service to the community, selling produce at reduced prices. In 1909 the city restaurant lobby attempted to ram through the council a bill that would raise the license fee from $25 to $200 a year. The street peddlers only postponed the inevitable, for Mayor Carter Harrison II put his stamp of approval on a City Council measure to ban the sale of food on the streets of Chicago.

The Greek merchants engaged in the fruit, vegetable, confectionery, and ice cream trades re-evaluated the options open to them. All those who could scrape together a few dollars to open a restaurant did so—very often mortgaging their lands back in the old country to pay the first month's rent. Chicago's Greeks were to become in a few years some of the city's most skilled restaurateurs. They began selling food in the streets, then realized the business potential of storefronts. Some were pioneers in their respective industries. The first soda fountain was opened in a Greek-owned ice cream parlor in the Security Building. By 1927, according to Peter Lambros, the

Greeks operated 10,000 stores—500 of them in the Chicago Loop—paying an aggregate monthly rental that exceeded $2,500,000.

Typical of the many success stories in the food service industry was that of John Raklos, whose chain of restaurants numbered forty-five by 1930. During the war years and through the 1950s, Chicago's best-loved Greek restaurateur was "Billy Goat" Sianis, whose lower Michigan Avenue café was the favored watering hole of the city's left bank. Sianis, as the story goes, tried to purchase a seat in the grandstand for his pet goat, who very much wanted to see the Cubs play the Tigers in the 1945 World Series. When owner Phil Wrigley denied the ornery goat his place in the sun, Sianis placed a curse on the ball club that has endured to this very day. Sam Sianis took over after his father passed away, but could do little to assist the hapless Cubbies, who have yet to win another pennant, even after the goat's descendent was invited back to Wrigley Field on the 50-year anniversary of the 1945 pennant. They still lost!

The Greeks were also prominent in banking, real estate, and Chicago's burgeoning financial and investment industry, then located at South Water Street and Randolph. An estimated $250,000,000 was transacted annually with Greek merchants.

Prominent in the entertainment field was a man who would become synonymous with the big band sound. Andrew Karzas, who arrived in Chicago in 1904, erected a monument to the immigrant spirit in 1922—the magnificent Trianon Ballroom—on the same location where he began his career hustling newspapers and candies. The Trianon at 63rd and Cottage Grove Avenue on the South Side is gone but certainly not forgotten by those who patronized it. Later, Karzas gave to the North Side the Aragon Ballroom, where Paul Whiteman, Guy Lombardo, Wayne King, and Glen Gray and his Casa Loma Band played to starry-eyed romantics for so many Saturday nights.

The Delta was synonymous with Greek culture in Chicago until the late 1950s, when the Eisenhower Expressway and the new University of Illinois campus displaced thousands of residents and eventually forced the closing of Holy Trinity. The congregation had dwindled to only a handful of parishioners, but the faithful few re-established the church on the far Northwest Side, where it is now located. The Socrates School followed the congregation, moving from 42 S. Ada Street, where it was replaced by a statue of Christopher Columbus. The children who attended classes at the Socrates School were the offspring of first-generation immigrants. Today all that remains of the dismantled Delta is a string of ethnic Greek restaurants in a two-block stretch along Halsted Street. At the Parthenon Restaurant at 314 S. Halsted, a passerby is often reminded of those former times by the sight of a whole pig or lamb roasting on a spit in the window.

After 1904 a second Greek settlement sprang up along 63rd Street between Wentworth and Cottage Grove avenues. It was founded by a group of malcontents from the Delta, who were instrumental in the formation of Saints Constantine and Helen Church at 61st and Michigan in 1904. The original church stood until 1926, when a fire gutted the interior. It was rebuilt with the help of Andrew Karzas. The church continued to serve the neighborhood until 1948, when the building was sold to the Episcopal congregation of St. Edmunds. The changing racial makeup of Washington Park, hastened by the influx of southern blacks into the city before and after World War I, influenced the decision to abandon the neighborhood for a new location farther south at 74th and Stony Island Avenue. In 1972, the congregation again moved for much the same reason, this time to south suburban Palos Hills.

The Washington Park Greeks are but a memory today. The spirit of those former times is being kept alive by Harry Mark Petrakis. Petrakis has written a string of award-winning novels, including *Pericles on 31st Street, Hour of the Bell,* and *Nick the Greek.* Petrakis lives in Indiana now, but like other Chicago expatriates, the city is never very far from his thoughts.

Today, much of the Lincoln Square neighborhood along Lawrence Avenue on the far North Side also has a distinctive Mediterranean presence, apparent mainly in the mural-decorated restaurants specializing in traditional lamb dishes. Since 1928 St. Demetrius Greek Orthodox Church at Winona and

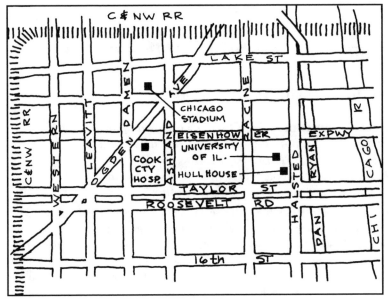

Greektown

Washtenaw has also kept Greek religious traditions alive in Lincoln Square, which is noted for its ethnic diversity. The Greeks, who accounted for 10 percent of the neighborhood's population according to the 1980 census, share living space with the Germans, Asians, Irish, and Hispanics. The St. Demetrius complex contains a community center, a library, and the Solon Afternoon Greek School, fostering pride in classic Greek culture.

Chicago's 250,000 Greeks are now widely dispersed through the Chicagoland area. They are linked together culturally, socially, and politically by the United Hellenic American Congress, an umbrella group founded in 1974 to coordinate the diverse activities of the community. Every May since 1965, the societies have sponsored the annual Greek Independence Day Parade, a festive event featuring ecumenical leaders, the Greek *evzones* (the presidential guard of honor), attired in colorful folk costumes, floats, and, of course, a queen.

Hellenism has survived and indeed prospered in the urban ethnic frontier of Chicago . . . or Chicagonopolis, if you will. Hellenic traditions have been maintained and handed down to a younger generation, thus preserving the duality of two worlds.

Getting There: By cab or on foot, Greektown at Halsted and Van Buren is only minutes from the Loop. If you take the CTA, catch the Madison (#20) bus and ride several blocks west to Halsted Street. That puts you just two blocks north of the restaurant strip.

For additional information, call the CTA at (312) 836-7000.

═══════════ Attractions ═══════════

Cultural Institutions

Hellenic Museum and Cultural Center, *National Bank of Greece Building, 168 N. Michigan Ave., 4th Floor, Chicago, (312) 726-1234. Open Wednesday– Friday. Admission free, but donations encouraged. Special arrangements available for groups.*

Incorporated in 1989, the Hellenic Museum documents and preserves the history of the Greek experience in the United States, with special emphasis on the Midwest. The museum features exhibits, musical and dance performances, seminars, movies, drama, folk art, a research library, and a gift shop selling imported icons, ceramics, and books. The museum was originally headquartered in River North, but moved into its present (interim) location in May 1992. The Board of Directors has explored various sites for a permanent, free-standing building of its own. This is contingent upon the progress of "Greektown Redevelopment," with 45-foot Greek columns depicting the high points of classical Greek history, perched high above the exit ramps of the nearby Kennedy Expressway. The redevelopment of Halsted Street revolves around the museum, the restaurants, and neo-classical Greek architecture recreated on the West Side. The project is already underway, but promoters move forward and talks with the city regarding a permanent location for the museum continue. The Hellenic Museum features at least three new exhibitions and special programs each year with guest lecturers and author readings.

Annual Events and Celebrations

Greek-American Parade, *Michigan Ave., from Lake St. to Van Buren. Second Saturday in May. Sponsored by the United Hellenic American Congress, 400 N. Franklin St., Suite 215, Chicago, (312) 822-9888.*

Everyone loves a parade, especially Chicago's Greek community, which turns out in full force every year to celebrate its independence from Turkey, which actually took place on March 25, 1821. However, the yearly threat of inclement weather in Chicago and the health risks posed to the 10,000 or so children who participate in this event prompted officials to wait until May and the customary end of the school year. The parade is sponsored by the United Hellenic American Congress (UHAC), which was organized to promote ethnic ideals and tradition and to foster support for tiny Cyprus, which was invaded by an ancient foe in the region—Turkey. Beginning with the very first parade in 1965, UHAC has attached a yearly theme to the festivities. In 1981 the parade tied in with the "Search for Alexander" exhibition that was touring the U.S. Three years later promoters again paid homage to the ancient world with A Salute to the Olympics. The 1991 event marked "25 Years of Hellenic Unity!" Thousands of celebrants line the parade route to hear traditional ethnic music, view the visiting *evzones* and to greet the "Queen of Greek Heritage Week," chosen in a contest held every year during the first week of May.

Greek Heritage Night, *held at alternating churches the night before the annual parade in May. Call UHAC at (312) 822-9888 for specific times and location. Admission free.*

Greek Heritage Week begins with a historical pageant recalling the 1821 War of Independence. The parade queen and her court are introduced, followed by a presentation given by the *evzones*, and the Greek dance troupes, including the Opa Dancers of the Hellenic Society, and the Greek Macedonian Society of Chicago. The yearly pageant rotates between the North, West, and South Side Greek Orthodox churches in Chicago, and is sponsored by the Greek Heritage Committee. Two days before the actual parade, the *evzones* will perform a series of Greek dances at the Chicago Civic Center, 50 W. Washington Boulevard, beginning at noon.

Annual UHAC Banquet, *held at the Chicago Hilton and Towers, 720 N. Michigan Ave., Chicago. Second week of November. Call UHAC at (312) 822-9888 for the time, date, and ticket price (usually $125).*

Since 1975, the United Hellenic American Congress has sponsored an annual fund-raising dinner honoring notable Greek personages from Chicago, the United States, and abroad. The proceeds generated from this event are channeled into the UHAC coffers for cultural, religious, philanthropic, and charitable programs. Keynote speaker, music, and entertainment.

St. John Chrysostom Oratorical and Arts Festival, *held in different Chicago and suburban churches. End of April. Sponsored by the Greek Orthodox Diocese. Call the Greek Orthodox Diocese at (312) 337-4130 for times and locations.*

A two-day festival of poetry, iconography, and oratorical expressions of faith. The categories of participants are the Junior Division (7th to 9th grades); Senior Division (10th to 12th grades); and a Young Adult Division (ages 19 to 35). Includes breakfast, awards luncheon, and divine liturgy. The recitations and poetry readings are open to the public.

Greektown Festival on Halsted Street, *between Monroe and Van Buren. Second weekend of August. For information call the festival's administrator, Leo Louchious, (708) 461-1878 (answering machine).*

In 1991, the Greektown Merchants Association (now called the Greektown Chamber of Commerce) launched its first open-air summer festival, with specialty foods prepared by the master chefs of the restaurants, music, and merchandise. The Chamber of Commerce has established its own headquarters in Greektown and can provide additional information about the festival. *Recommended.*

Outlying Areas

St. George Holy Day Dinner Dance, *Golden Flame Restaurant, 6417 W. Higgins, Chicago. Last Sunday in April. Sponsored by St. George Church, 2701 N. Sheffield Ave., Chicago. Admission fee charged (as a donation). For reservations, call (773) 525-1793.*

A social hour begins in the early evening with an open bar, which is open throughout the evening. A complete prime rib dinner is served after the social hour.

Greek Fest, *Annunciation Greek Orthodox Cathedral, LaSalle St. and Oak St., Chicago, (312) 664-5485. Last weekend in July. Admission is free.*

The first Greek Orthodox Church was also called the Annunciation (or *Evangelismos,* meaning happy message), and it was located in a small wooden building at Kinzie and Clark. Philosophical differences and festering internal rivalries between religious factions within the community led to the closing of the first Annunciation Church, but a second one was built in 1910. The lovely yellow-brick Orthodox Church which borrows the earlier name symbolizes the parallel between the Annunciation of the Virgin and the establishment of freedom in the motherland. Many other Greek churches in the United States trade upon the same theme: "Evangelismos-Hellenismos"—salvation and freedom. The last weekend in July is a time to celebrate the enduring ideas that the Greek Orthodox Church in the United States was founded upon. The festival takes place every year on the church grounds, and it features entertainment, Greek bands, singers, food booths, but no carnival rides. A liturgy is celebrated on Sunday.

Flavors of Greece.

Indoor festival features Grecian foods and live entertainment and is sponsored by St. Athanasios Greek Orthodox Church in Aurora. Scheduled for the last weekend in May at the Kane County Fairgrounds, Main Street (Route 64) and Randall Road, in St. Charles. Admission: $2.00 for adults. Call (708) 851-6106 for times.

St. Demetrios Greek Fest, *Winona St. and Washtenaw Ave., Chicago, (312) 561-5992. Weekend following the Assumption (usually the second week in August). Admission fee charged.*

The church sponsors the oldest annual Greek Fest in the city, one that dates back to 1949. Each year hundreds of parishioners, many of whom abandoned the area years ago, come back to rekindle a few good memories, sample traditional Greek food under the tent, and listen to the dance music of Harry Karoubas and his band.

St. George Orthodox Church Greek Fest, *Sheffield Ave. and Schubert Ave., Chicago, (773) 525-1793. Second weekend in June, around Father's Day. Admission fee charged.*

The parish of St. George originally opened at this North Side location as a German Evangelical Lutheran church, but with changing patterns of immigration it became a Greek Orthodox Church. For the last ten years, the church has sponsored an annual Greek Fest in the rear parking lot. No rides, but plenty of good food, live Greek ethnic music, and ice cream.

St. Basil Greek Orthodox Church Greek Fest, *733 S. Ashland Ave. (at Polk), Chicago, (312) 243-3738. Weekend after Labor Day. Admission fee charged.*

Formerly the Anshe Sholom Jewish synagogue, until the Greek community converted it into an Orthodox Church in 1927. The church has played an important role in the Near West Side Greek community and still manages to hold on to its congregation, even though neighborhood displacement has caused many Greeks to leave the area. The traditional Greek festival is the last one on the calendar, and is held in the church hall and adjoining backyard. Music and entertainment. Food booths, merchandise displays, and Greek pastries are sold on the grounds.

St. Andrews Greek Orthodox Church Annual Greek Fest, *5649 N. Sheridan Rd., Chicago, (773) 334-4515. Second Sunday of July. Admission fee charged.*

One of the newer churches to be built in the Chicago area (1956), St. Andrews has hosted a Greek Festival since 1960 on the church grounds at Hollywood and Sheridan near Lake Shore Drive. Food booths, carnival rides, games, Greek food, and dancing.

Saints Constantine and Helen Greek Orthodox Church Greek Fest, *11025 Roberts Rd., Palos Hills, (708) 974-3400. Weekend of or immediately after August 15. Admission fee charged.*

Carnival rides, Greek food, clowns, musical entertainment, and dance troupes. One of the South Side's oldest church festivals.

Father's Day Festival, *St. Nicholas Church, 10301 S. Kolmar Ave., Oak Lawn, (708) 636-5460. Father's Day weekend. Admission fee charged.*

An annual south suburban Greek festival held in the parish parking lot. Food booths, games, music, and dancing.

St. Spyridon Greek Fest, *12307 S. Ridgeland Ave., Palos Heights, (708) 385-2311. Mid-July. Admission fee charged.*

Since 1972, the annual Greek Fest has featured games, food booths, and ethnic dancing.

St. Nectarios Greek Fest, *133 S. Roselle Rd., Palatine, (847) 358-5170. Late July. Admission fee charged.*

The three-day St. Nectarios Greek Fest takes place in the church parking lot. Pony rides, food booths, ethnic dancing, pastries, and an *agora* (marketplace) where imported items are sold.

St. Sophia Orthodox Church Greek Fest, *525 Church Rd., Elgin, (847) 888-2822. Second weekend in July. Admission is free.*

Greek culture celebrated through food, music, games, and a shopping boutique. The St. Sophia dance troupe also performs traditional dances.

St. Haralambros Greek Orthodox Church Foodfest, *7373 Caldwell Ave., Niles, (847) 647-8880. Second or third weekend in July. Admission fee charged.*

A real taste of Greek Chicago, with healthy servings of Athenian chicken, roast lamb, shish kebab, and *pastichio* (Greek lasagna). This annual fundraising event is hosted by Father Dean Botsis. All proceeds benefit the church.

St. Demetrios Greek Orthodox Church, *O'Plaine Rd. on the old Polo Grounds between Highways 137 and 120, Waukegan, (847) 623-0190. June. Admission is free.*

Annual four-day festival has been going strong for nearly thirty years. Greek music, dancing, carnival, gift imports, hay ride, jewelry sales. Scheduled to coincide with the Libertyville Days festival.

Assumption Greek Orthodox Church,
20401 Western Ave., Olympia Fields,
(708) 748-3040. Second Saturday in June.
Admission free.

Greek food in the South Suburbs, special appearance by a selected Greek dance troupe, and a raffle.

Shopping and Dining
in the Halsted Street Greektown

Spurred by the construction of Presidential Towers, a 2,346-unit apartment complex in the West Loop and the redevelopment of Halsted Street with a new pavilion, classical columns, and new attractions, Chicago's Greektown is making a strong comeback following a period of economic decline in the middle-to-late 1960s, when some 30,000 immigrant residents living near Halsted and Harrison were forced to abandon the neighborhood in order to make way for the new University of Illinois campus. With the arrival of many single, upscale professionals who live in the neighboring high-rises, business is better than ever for the Greek restaurateurs and small shopkeepers along Halsted Street between Monroe on the north and Van Buren on the south.

Chicago's Greektown blends the best of the old and the new. The St. Basil Greek Orthodox Church at 733 Ashland Avenue has anchored the community since 1927, when it was purchased by the Greeks for the benefit of those who stood in opposition to the Royalists of the older Holy Trinity Church at 11th and Peoria. The anti-Royalist sentiments after World War I led to a permanent rift in Chicago's Greek community, and it contributed to the founding of St. Basil's in 1921.

In the 1960s, the congregation of St. Basil's dwindled to less than sixty families, but has since grown to more than 250. Many of the parishioners are lured from the distant suburbs by the energetic young priest, Father Chris Kerhules, who assumed his duties in 1989. St. Basil's, originally built as a Jewish temple in 1911, has undergone extensive renovation in recent years. New icons prepared in the traditional Byzantine style have replaced the Renaissance images favored by the founding members of the congregation back in the 1920s. The inside dome has been repainted and given a bright new molding and stenciling.

New immigrants from Greece arrive annually to work in the area's several restaurants and shops, keeping Greektown's ethnic vitality fresh and authentic.

Shops

Panellinion Meat Market, *804 W. Jackson Blvd.,*
Chicago, (312) 726-1081 or 454-9873. Closed
Sundays.

Bustling Greektown butcher shop. Baby back ribs, spring lamb, and goat meat cut to specifications on an ancient wooden chopping block.

Athenian Candle Co., *300 S. Halsted St., Chicago,*
(312) 332-6988. Closed Wednesdays and Sundays.

Off-the-beaten-path religious gift store that sells icons, bibles, exotic spices, mint, and uncut oil by the pound.

Greektown Music and Gift Shop, *330 S. Halsted St.,*
Chicago, (312) 263-6342. Open daily. Checks and
credit cards accepted.

One of the more recent additions to the Greektown scene. It specializes in Greek video movies, CDs, albums, and cassettes. Silver gift items, pins, religious icons, wedding gifts, jewelry, and figurines also stocked.

Athens Grocery, *324 S. Halsted St., Chicago,*
(312) 332-6737. Open daily.

Owned by Jim and Bill Siannis, who opened the business a few doors down in 1962. The shelves are lined with imported Greek foods, olive oil, feta cheese (made from goat's milk and sheep's milk), grape leaves, and several foreign-language newspapers, including Chicago's own *Hellenic Life,* published at 7902 Maple Street, Morton Grove, IL 60053.

Pan Hellenic Pastry Shop, *322 S. Halsted St.,*
Chicago, (312) 454-1886. Open daily. No credit cards.

Owned by Louis Manolakos, an immigrant from Sparta who cooks his own special version of the sweet and gooey desert treat, *baklava. Galactoburiko* is a custard-filled pastry, worth a try; ditto for the *Kadaifi* (shredded wheat with walnuts). You can purchase and eat these delights in the shop.

Outlying Areas

Sparta Grocery, *6058 W. Diversey, Chicago,*
(773) 637-8073. Open daily.

Greek foods, meat, produce, and newspapers.

Hellas Pastry Shop, *2627 W. Lawrence Ave.,*
Chicago, (773) 271-7500. Open daily.

Wedding cakes, birthday cakes, and assorted Greek pastries for all occasions.

New Hellas Imports, *2558 W. Lawrence Ave.,*
Chicago, (773) 271-1125. Open daily. No credit
cards.

Gift shop specializing in party favors for Greek religious observances. Candles, glassware, greeting cards, Greek-language newspapers and magazines.

The Athenian, *4748 N. Western Ave., Chicago,*
(773) 334-5698. Closed Sundays. Credit cards
accepted.

Imported shoes for men and women.

Delphi Food Market, *2655 W. Lawrence Ave.,*
Chicago, (773) 271-0660. Open daily.

Another throwback to the days when the Greeks were both grocers and restaurant owners.

Crystal Palace Imports, *9202 Waukegan Rd.,*
Morton Grove, (847) 965-7844. Open daily. No
credit cards.

Imported gift items, including Greek ceremonial clothing, baptism candles, and crystal from all over the world.

Restaurants

Pegasus Restaurant and Taverna, *130 S. Halsted St.,*
Chicago, (312) 226-4666. Open for lunch and dinner
daily. Valet parking. Credit cards accepted.

Pegasus is a fairly recent addition to the Greektown restaurant row, opened in November 1990. An attractive wall mural painted by Bora Guanovich depicts three of the Greek islands, Mykonos, Paros, and Santorini. The mural provides an appropriate backdrop for the elegant dining. House specialties include *souvlaki,* lamb, *sinagrida* (snapper), octopus, and some delectable appetizers.

Santorini, *800 W. Adams St., Chicago,*
(312) 829-8820. Open for lunch and dinner
daily. Free valet parking. Credit cards
accepted.

Named for one of the islands in the Aegean Sea. Seafood, especially broiled fish, is the order of the day at this charming but rustic eatery in Greektown that was opened in 1988 by Jim Kontos, owner of the Tempo Coffee Shop on Chestnut Street. The lunch menu is the best bargain, but it's advisable to call ahead for reservations since the restaurant critics around town have been falling all over themselves in praise of Kontos.

Greek Islands, *two locations: 200 S. Halsted St.,*
Chicago, (312) 782-9855, and 300 E. 22nd St.,
Lombard, (630) 932-4545. Open for lunch and
dinner daily.

The owners of this restaurant joined in a partnership to open Santorini, which is just down the street. The Greek Islands is one of the busiest locations on the street, and is not recommended for a quiet, late-evening repast. During peak hours, the Greek waiters (no other nationalities will do) can serve up to 1,000 people.

Petro's Dianna, *1633 N. Halsted St., Chicago,*
(312) 332-1225. Open for dinner. Closed Mondays.
All credit cards accepted.

Philoxenia, Greek meaning "love for the stranger," is in abundance at Dianna's, one of Halsted Street's landmark restaurants. In 1961 Petros Kogiones opened the Dianna Grocery and Restaurant in the 300 block of Halsted Street. It was nothing fancy as far as ethnic neighborhood restaurants go. But the personal magnetism of the owner ensured that this former schoolteacher from Nestani, Greece, would be around for a long time. Petros claims to have kissed more women than any man alive. He's danced with them, too, earning the well-deserved sobriquet "King of the Opaa." The Kogiones brothers douse their cheese appetizers with brandy and then set it on fire. "Opaa!"

Petros personally greets each and every one of his female "cousins" at his Halsted Street restaurant, and keeps the festivities moving at a fever pitch. Sometimes the waiters get into the act, and a few dishes are occasionally broken. But it is a small price to pay to experience Petro's Dianna. *Recommended.*

Parthenon, *314 S. Halsted St., Chicago,*
(312) 726-2407. Open for lunch and dinner
daily. All credit cards accepted.

The oldest restaurant on the strip, dating back to 1958 when Chris and Bill
Liakouras bought out a small gyros restaurant that was about to go under.
Complete with music, shouting waiters, dancing, and tasty, flaming
saganaki. (They even say Opaa!)

Costa's Greek Dining and Bar, *340 S. Halsted St.,*
Chicago, (312) 263-0767. Open for lunch and dinner
daily.

Laid-back, understated elegance. Named for the old quarter of Athens, near
the slopes of the Acropolis. Owned by the Liakouras family, who also run
the Parthenon. The piano music of Dimitri Marinos is featured nightly.

Rodity's, *222 S. Halsted St., Chicago, (312) 454-0800.*
Open for lunch and dinner daily. Free parking.

Rodity is Greek for "red wine," which is served here in abundance. Greek
rosé wine is lighter than many, and easier to take in large doses, so be careful. If you're unfamiliar with Greek food, try the Rodity's combination
plate. Homemade bread. Wood-paneled bar.

Outlying Areas

Billy Goat Tavern, *Hubbard St. and (Lower)*
Michigan Ave., Chicago, (312) 222-1525. Open for
breakfast, lunch, and dinner daily. Credit cards?
Forget it!

The "curse of the Billy Goat" has haunted the Chicago Cubs since 1945, the
year that Phil Wrigley decreed his ballpark off-limits to Sonovia, a cantanker-
ous, horned mammal that was the pride and joy of William Sianis, popular
West Side restaurateur and bon vivant. During the '45 World Series, Sianis, an
ardent Cub fan, purchased a ticket for Sonovia so that the beast could bring
good luck to the North Siders. Phil Wrigley, a rather straight-laced, priggish
owner who inherited his daddy's chewing gum empire, decided that his ballpark was no place for shaggy, foul-smelling Sonovia. Ticket or no ticket, the
goat wasn't going to get in. The Cubs went on to lose the series to the Detroit
Tigers, which afforded Sianis the perfect chance to get in a few last digs. He
sent a telegram to Wrigley, demanding to know: "Just who stinks now?" It
certainly wasn't the mountain goat. Billy Sianis prophesied that the Cubs
would never again win the pennant, and the rest, as they say, is history.

Sianis emigrated to Chicago from a rural village in the mountains of Greece in 1909, and within a few years, he opened his first tavern and restaurant at 1855 W. Madison Street, directly across from the Chicago Stadium (now the United Center). A stable of baby goats occupied the rear of the building, but by decree of the owner, no Republicans were allowed to enter the domain. Sports writers and Democrats were always welcome to come in and quaff his Pilsner at thirty cents a glass (or three for a dollar—Billy never was very good at arithmetic), while the neighborhood urchins played with the pet goats. Eventually the old tavern was bulldozed to make way for a parking lot, but this did not deter Sianis from moving to the high-rent district. Billy's East opened on Lower Michigan, and it soon became the poor man's lunch alternative to the glitzy Riccardo's, where the journalistic élite gathered to swap war stories.

The Billy Goat attracted its own literary clientele over the years. Columnists Jack Griffin, Arch Ward, Mike Royko, Studs Terkel, and Dave Condon spent a fair amount of time ingesting greasy "cheezeborgers," chips, and Coke (no Pepsi!) between deadlines. Actor John Belushi and the rest of the Second City cast ate here, too. Years later, Belushi mimicked the short-order cooks who worked for nephew Sam Sianis, in his own comedy sketches for *Saturday Night Live*.

You won't find traditional Greek food here. To sample the finer dishes from the islands, you'll have to backtrack to Halsted Street—but the old-fashioned atmosphere of Billy Goat's makes this Michigan Avenue landmark one of a kind. *Recommended.*

Papagus Greek Taverna, *620 N. State St., Chicago, (312) 642-8450. Open for lunch and dinner daily.*

Adventuresome Greek cuisine in an upscale but comfortable, cozy atmosphere. Specialties include hot and cold *mezedes, saganaki,* grilled shrimp, and chicken *souvlaki.* Full dessert tray, including dried-cherry pistachio baklava.

Grecian Taverna, *4535 N. Lincoln Ave., Chicago, (773) 728-1600. Open for lunch and dinner daily. Credit cards accepted.*

A Greek restaurant the way they used to be. Two chefs cook the gyros over a hot spit in the front, while attending to the delicatessen. In the rear, Greek waiters provide for the luncheon and dinner patrons. Homemade gyros, carry-out foods.

Psistaria, *4711 W. Touhy, Lincolnwood, (847) 676-9400. Open for lunch and dinner daily.*

Large portions of authentic Greek food served in a comfortable taverna atmosphere.

Nikos Restaurant & Lounge, *7600 S. Harlem Ave.,*
Bridgeview, (708) 496-0300. Open for lunch and
dinner Monday–Saturday and for Sunday brunch.

Greek and continental cuisine.

Deni's Den, *2941 N. Clark St., Chicago,*
(773) 348-8888. Open for dinner. Closed
Mondays and Tuesdays. Credit cards accepted.

Features live entertainment nightly, with Greek singers and music every Friday and Saturday night. Advance reservations recommended.

Central Gyros, *3127 N. Central Ave., Chicago,*
(773) 622-5288. Open for lunch and dinner daily.

There are hundreds of gyros stands in Chicago, but we recommend Central Gyros on the Northwest Side, owned by the Apostolou brothers, as our personal favorite. Beer and Greek wine served.

Media

Greek-Language Radio Programming

Athens Radio Hour, *Saturday evenings at 8:00 P.M.,*
hosted by John Diamantis on WSBC, 1240 AM.

Hellenic Heartbeat, *sounds of yesterday and today,*
produced and presented by Vicky Kournetas every
Sunday from 2:00 to 4:00 P.M., on WONX-AM, 1590.

Sunday Hellenic Hour, *hosted by John Nastsos from*
2:00–3:30 P.M. on WSBC, 1240 AM.

The New Greektown at Lincoln Square

An estimated 40,000 Greek Americans reside in a polyglot community directly west of the Lincoln Square shopping mall along Lawrence Avenue, between Talman and Maplewood. The Germans originally settled this neighborhood, but with the breakup of the Delta in the years following World War II, many Greek families relocated to the North Side. A steady flow of immigrants from the old country found the numerous courtyard apartment buildings and two-stories very affordable and within walking distance of the church and the Lawrence Avenue commercial business district. St. Demetrios Greek Orthodox Church at 2727 W. Winona Avenue, a basilica-style structure built in 1928, anchors the North Side Greektown. The 500-student Solon School is the largest afternoon school in the city, and it helps keep the traditions alive for second- and third-generation youngsters who attend classes until the age of sixteen. Their foreign language instruction is fully certified by the Greek government, and credits transfer to Greek schools. The church library serves many of the same cultural functions for the 1,500 families who worship here.

Less touristy than Halsted Street, the new Greektown is fighting to preserve its Hellenic identity amid a growing influx of Korean immigrants, who have opened grocery emporiums, video rental stores, and restaurants on West Lawrence Avenue, very often in storefronts formerly occupied by Greeks and other Eastern European groups. The offspring of the Greek immigrants who settled Lincoln Square after World War II began leaving the community in the 1960s and 1970s in order to purchase single-family dwellings north of Foster Avenue. According to George Stamos, who coordinates the St. Demetrios Festival, the new Greek immigrants are following close behind. Yet the church itself has maintained its congregation and still has a high percentage of "walk-up" traffic from the neighborhood for services.

Lincoln Square is indeed a "Touch of Europe," as it has been promoted by the local Chamber of Commerce in recent years, but increasingly this diverse community has also become a window to East Asia.

African American Chicago

History and Settlement

A sea of windswept prairie grass, a sky of leaden gray, and an expanse of lake, left by an ancient glacier, extending as far as the eye could see—this is how Chicago appeared in 1779 when Jean Baptiste Point du Sable established a trading post in what is now Pioneer Court.

Du Sable was the son of a prominent Quebec merchant and a former slave woman from Santo Domingo. His trading post on the shore of the lake was the hub of commercial activity in the northern Illinois territory in the years before Fort Dearborn was established to guard the waterways from the French and the Indians in 1803. The settlement of Chicago, and the African Americans who were to follow in the intervening decades, rightfully begins with the itinerant fur trapper and "voyageur," du Sable.

Yet, seventy-three years later, the Illinois legislature passed a law forbidding blacks to enter the state. Slavery was expressly forbidden in the state constitution, but the racial issue had simmered in Illinois since the French period. In 1824 a proslavery faction in the legislature ordered a referendum on the calling of a constitutional convention to legalize slavery in the state. Led by Edward Coles, a Virginian who became the second Illinois governor, the antislavery forces triumphed by a margin of 6,640 to 4,972. Coles, who freed his own slaves before leaving for Illinois, spent $4,000 of his own money to see to it that the "peculiar institution" would not infect Illinois politics in years to come.

Despite the noble intentions of Coles and other sympathetic legislators, blacks had no real legal rights in Illinois, and very often freed slaves would be abducted by hired thugs and returned to their former owners in the cotton South. Blacks could not vote, serve on a jury, or join a militia.

With the passage of the second Fugitive Slave Law in 1850, Chicago became an important stop on the Underground Railroad for fugitive slaves making their way north to freedom. Consequently, the black population tripled in the 1850s, and continued to grow steadily until 30,150 African Americans were counted in the 1900 city census. Most of them worked as low-paid household domestics, and though they accounted for only 1.3 percent of the population in 1890, the black community supplied 37.7 percent of the male, and 43.4 percent of the female, servant class.

Blacks were denied the opportunity to join the skilled trade unions, and when better jobs in construction and manufacturing became available, it was usually the result of a bitter labor strike or management lockout that forced frantic employers to meet their production demands by hiring blacks as strikebreakers. This, of course, contributed to the ill will already existing between whites and blacks.

A fledgling black political movement began to take shape during this period, when the patterns of neighborhood segregation in Chicago first became evident. The South Side "Black Belt," an expanding, self-contained community whose borders were defined by Michigan Avenue on the east, Cottage Grove on the west, 31st Street on the north, and 51st Street on the south, was given definition in the 1890s when half of the city's black population resided in three economically depressed wards.

In the immediate post-Civil War period, the most eloquent spokesman for black causes was John Jones, a tailor, the son of a freed slave woman and a German immigrant who brought his family to Chicago in 1845. In 1871 Jones was elected county commissioner on Joseph Medill's "Fire Proof" ticket, which was swept into office as a result of the fire that leveled the city in October. Jones was defeated in his re-election bid four years later, but by virtue of his victory in 1871, he became the first black to hold public office in Chicago. In 1876, grocer John W. E. Thomas was elected to the Illinois legislature, but after the Reconstruction period ended, a political backlash against black candidates negated the advances made by Jones, Thomas, and other blacks nationwide.

A period of black activism began in 1893, the year a college-educated New Yorker named Edward "the iron master" Wright was elected president of the Afro-American League, which promoted blacks for public office.

Wright served several terms on the county board, and finally succeeded in securing the committeeman's post from the 2nd Ward in 1920, following a protracted battle with the white political establishment that ran things in the Black Belt.

Wright was a canny political organizer, and despite his numerous setbacks, he paved the way for other up-and-coming black leaders who profited from his tutelage. Through some rather astute backroom dealing, Ed Wright negotiated the appointment of Ferdinand L. Barnett, who became the first black assistant Cook County State's Attorney. It was a payback for the vote Wright had delivered to candidate Charles Deneen, who was elected state's attorney in 1896.

The black population of Chicago increased from 30,140 in 1900 to 44,103 just ten years later. It was during this time that the nation's most influential black newspaper, the Chicago *Defender,* was founded by a Georgian named Robert S. Abbott. An earlier sheet, the Chicago *Conservator,* was founded by Ferdinand Barnett in 1878 to crusade for the rights of former slaves. In 1895, the year before Barnett was appointed assistant state's attorney, he married Ida B. Wells. She had come to Chicago after a mob of whites had destroyed her Memphis *Free Press* newspaper, which protested the lynching of blacks.

Wells was a gifted and fiery muckraker who drew attention to the appalling mistreatment of Chicago blacks, who were denied entrance to the World's Fair grounds because of their color. By 1915, however, the *Conservator* had folded, leaving Abbott the lone spokesperson for black Chicago. He began his paper with twenty-five cents to his name and a single card table as a desk. Within a decade the *Defender* was a successful, albeit sensational, newspaper that was read by blacks all over the country, distributed in part by Pullman porters who would pass it out from railroad cars throughout the South.

Though Abbott painted a somewhat unrealistic picture of conditions in the industrial North, calling Chicago a mecca of opportunity, his pleading encouraged many blacks to turn their backs on the South and come to Chicago. The *Defender* offered advice on resettlement, the housing market in Chicago, and the job prospects for blacks once they stepped off the train. Abbott struck a responsive chord, as Chicago's black population swelled to 109,458 by 1920.

The outbreak of World War I resulted in a temporary job shortage in the stockyards and steel mills, which Abbott was quick to exploit. On May 17, 1917, scarcely a month after the U.S. entered the war on the side of the Allies, the *Defender* announced its "Great Northern Drive." Abbott encouraged blacks to flee the poverty and oppression in the South, and he was joined in this crusade by Chicago's vocal and flamboyant mayor, William Hale Thompson, whose most powerful ally on the South Side was Second

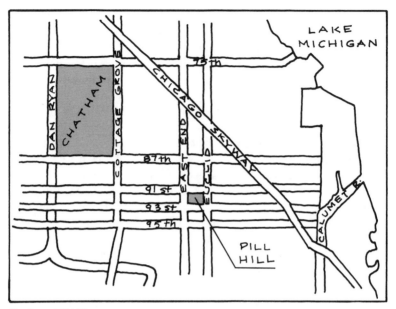

Chatham/Pill Hill

Ward Alderman Oscar DePriest. Thompson solicited the black vote; and, in return for black support, he dropped hundreds of patronage jobs into DePriest's lap to dispense as he saw fit. Encouraged by a sympathetic white mayor, a strong NAACP branch opened in Chicago in 1911; and, lured by the soothing words of Abbott, Southern blacks "went North" by the thousands.

With little in the way of financial reserves, but instilled with unbridled optimism, they boarded trains that took them only as far as their money permitted. African Americans from the southern coastal states of Virginia and Georgia very often ended up in New York or Philadelphia. The Illinois Central "Green Diamond," servicing Mississippi, Arkansas, and Louisiana, conveyed blacks from their rural backwater towns directly to the bustling Illinois Central Station at 12th Street, which commentator Clarence Page has likened to a "Midwest Ellis Island."

Here, Abbott's Chicago stretched out before them. The smokestacks of the factories belched out billowing soot. The stockyard stench was equally foul, especially in the disagreeable July heat. Acres of ramshackle wooden housing in the Black Belt barely kept out the cutting January winds, as two, three, sometimes four families huddled together in the darkness. Overcrowding was a chronic problem. But it was their new home, this Chicago, city of promise.

The reverse of ghetto life were the glitzy jazz honky-tonks up and down State Street, and in the last vestiges of the old South Side levee. After the war, Chicago became the Midwest mecca of jazz music, an emerging art form popularized in New Orleans at the turn of the century. Jazz was something new and daring—a hybrid of West African rhythms, southern banjo music, and the barrelhouse piano styles practiced by midwestern tavern musicians. The fusion of popular ragtime and blues with these earlier musical forms occurred around 1900, when Bunk Johnson, "Jellyroll" Morton, Danny Parker, and Alphone Sicou experimented with the curious new music in the brothels of Storeyville, a legal, thirty-eight-block controlled vice district in New Orleans.

Because black musicians were denied the opportunity to perform in legitimate vaudeville houses, they were forced to find their audiences elsewhere. Often those audiences were made up of chemise-clad strumpets and their well-heeled white customers who patronized the sporting houses dotting the old city's famed Canal Street. Louis Armstrong, Kid Ory, and Joseph "King" Oliver appeared nightly in the bistros, until the reformers had enough and abolished the district for good on November 12, 1917.

Out of work, the young musicians headed north where they assembled their own bands. King Oliver organized his famed Creole Jazz Band, which was recognized as the first black group to record jazz music. In 1922, Louie Armstrong stepped off the train in Chicago. He, too, had read Abbott's *Defender,* and decided to come northward, where he joined up with Oliver's Creole Jazz Band. Armstrong plied his trade in the Black Belt, where the Elite, the Schiller Cafe, the Dreamland, the Royal Gardens, and the Onion routinely booked such top-notch acts as Baby Dodds, Jimmy Noone, and Sidney Bechet.

The Near South Side pulsated with the sounds of Dixieland and Armstrong's Gut Bucket Blues, which he recorded with the Hot Five. A unique Chicago sound—fusing jazz and blues together—had been born. Moralists decried what they called "shameless iniquity" going on within the doors of the "Black and Tan" cabarets—so named because of the free association between white patrons and the African American performers and clientele. The indignation of the white establishment was best summed up by Captain Max Nootbaar of the Chicago Police Department, whose detail closed down several of the Second Ward cabarets in October 1917.

"No place is respectable where young white girls are allowed to drink and dance with Negro men," Nootbaar told the police trial board when he was brought up on charges of racial discrimination by Alderman Louis Anderson and by the old political war-horse, Edward Wright, who was serving as corporation counsel. "I would shoot my wife or daughter if I found them in such places!" Nootbaar roared. The commission found the police captain "justified" in closing down immoral places, but in a rare conciliatory gesture toward the black politicians, Nootbaar was transferred out of the district.

The white jazz impresarios like Bix Beiderbecke, Benny Goodman, Art Hodes, and the Austin High School Gang were unfazed by prevailing narrow-mindedness. They preferred to learn their craft in a dozen gin-soaked, smoke-filled cafés in the Second Ward. The Austin group, formed at a West Side high school and led by Jimmy McPartland, Bud Freeman, Muggsy Spanier, and Mezz Mezzrow, took jazz in a new direction and broadened its popularity with white audiences.

Legendary "Bronzeville"—the Black Belt of yesteryear—encompassed much of Douglas and Grand Boulevard. Its boundaries extended roughly from 26th Street to 47th, and from State Street on the west to the shores of Lake Michigan. It was here, in a string of jumping cabarets, that Duke Ellington, Count Basie and other legendary jazz men performed their music. Sam Cooke and Nat King Cole grew up here under the influence of the new swinging sounds of Chicago jazz.

Jesse Binga founded the first black-owned bank at 35th and State streets, the hub of Bronzeville. The Binga Bank anchored the neighborhood and fueled a prosperous middle-class life-style for many of its residents. By the 1960s, however, Bronzeville was decayed, despairing, with its history all but forgotten except by a handful of community historians and the surviving veterans of the "Great Migration." Now it is on its way back, thanks to an ambitious plan of renovation undertaken by the Mid-South Planning and Development Commission.

The coalition of community organizations comprising Mid-South has identified at least seven sites in Bronzeville for restoration, including the Wabash Avenue YMCA, where historian Carter G. Woodson founded the Association for the Study of Afro-American Life and History in 1915. The Eighth Regiment Armory at 3533 S. Giles Avenue is where Marcus Garvey championed his "Back to Africa" movement in the 1920s, and where the legendary "Fighting Eighth" infantry unit trained before doing battle in France in World War I. Built in 1915, the old Armory has been listed on the National Registry of Historic Places. However, the building was sold to a business consortium for back taxes early in 1996, and its inclusion in the revitalized Bronzeville area is less certain.

Planners intend to develop an entertainment complex, history museums, and a "Muddy Waters Blues District" in this 3.5-mile district bounded by Cermak Road, the Dan Ryan Expressway, and 51st and Cottage Grove Avenue. The Blues District will be patterned along the lines of the successful redevelopment of Beale Street outside downtown Memphis, where this unique African American musical art form first took root.

The Mid-South Commission faces a tough, uphill battle to secure adequate funding. The community is among the poorest African American neighborhoods in the city, and the Illinois General Assembly has been slow to appropriate funds to see the project through to its conclusion. There are hopeful signs, however. The old YMCA building at 3763 S. Wabash Avenue, founded in 1913 but closed since 1981, is slated to re-open in 1998 as a recreational center and apartment complex.

Despite police harassment, the South Side Black Belt was a thriving, self-contained neighborhood throughout the 1920s. Ed Wright was elected to the county board in 1920 and continued his work promoting black politicians. The Binga Bank held $1.5 million in assets, representing one-third of all money deposited in savings institutions by Chicago blacks. In 1928, Oscar DePriest became the first popularly elected black man to win a seat in Congress since the Reconstruction era. (In 1915, DePriest had become the first black elected to the Chicago City Council.) DePriest was a skillful political organizer and businessman. He owned the largest painting and decorating business in any African American community in the industrial North.

The success of Wright, Binga, and DePriest in the political and business arenas belied the growing racial tension with whites, prompted by a shrinking job market, the economic consequences of a rising population, and calls for economic equality. Random acts of violence against the homes of blacks in the summer of 1918 foreshadowed the calamity that was to come a year later.

On July 27, 1919, an outing at the 29th Street Beach on the South Side became a battleground when a 14-year-old boy named Eugene Williams was stoned to death as he crossed the invisible "race line" separating the white and black bathers. When a white policeman named Dan Callahan refused to arrest the perpetrators, angry blacks vented their outrage by hurling stones and bricks at their antagonists.

Before it was over a week later, Chicago had become an armed camp. The Illinois National Guard was deployed along the Black Belt to keep white South Side street gangs like Ragen's Colts from setting fire to the wooden tenements east of Wentworth Avenue. Thirty-eight people died in the rioting, including twenty-three blacks and fifteen whites. A biracial commission impaneled by Governor Frank Lowden examined the cause and effect of the riots and recommended an end to job discrimination, improved educational opportunity for young blacks, and open housing. The noteworthy recommendations of the panel were ignored for the next forty years, until the same vexing issues confronting the races again threatened to overturn the peace.

In the 1920s, blacks continued to penetrate predominantly white neighborhoods. Washington Park on the South Side was a microcosm of social and ethnic displacement, a pattern of mobility that was duplicated in many Chicago neighborhoods for decades to come. In 1920 blacks comprised 15 percent of Washington Park's 38,076 residents. The "white flight" in the

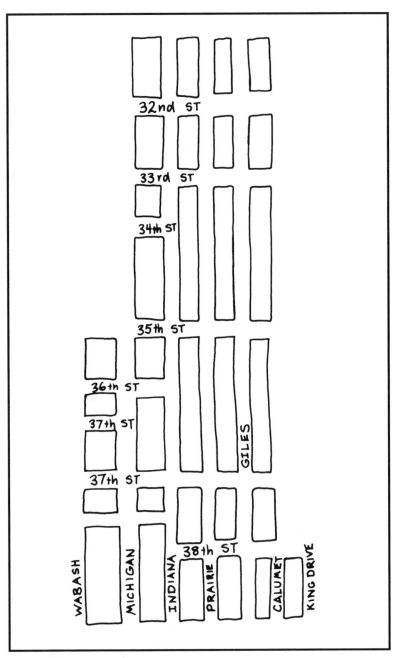

Bronzeville

next ten years was dramatic. By 1930, scarcely 10 percent of the Washington Parkers were white. Much the same scenario was later repeated in East and West Garfield, North Lawndale, and Austin on the West Side.

Political power in the black wards was vested in William Levi Dawson, inheritor of the Wright-DePriest legacy. Dawson was one of two black aldermen to occupy a place in the City Council in the 1920s. Dawson was a Republican at the outset of his career, like so many of his constituents who equated the Democratic Party with the antebellum South and slavery. Dawson was a machine politician who pacified his supporters with jobs and patronage. He served the Thompson forces loyally when the Republicans were the only game in town.

That game changed overnight when Anton Cermak, a Czech Democrat from Lawndale, was elected mayor in 1931. Cermak counted on the black vote, but needed to overcome the community's opposition to the Democratic party. Cermak and his successor Edward Kelly used essentially a carrot-and-stick approach to bring the balky Dawson into the fold. Cermak threatened Dawson with grave political reprisals, and to illustrate this point, the mayor ordered his most capable police officers into the Second Ward strongholds to clean up illegal gambling—an important source of revenue to members of the South Side Dawson machine.

Finally, Kelly offered Dawson a deal: a post as Democratic committeeman in return for black support on election day. Dawson's people worked the five predominantly black wards tirelessly, going door to door trying to convince voters to shift their allegiance to the Democratic party. When the process was complete, Dawson found himself in the enviable position of commanding a vast patronage army. Dawson was the master of all he surveyed, a situation that would not change until the volatile 1960s. The Cook County Democratic Party reciprocated with jobs and relief benefits for thousands of blacks caught in the grind of the Depression.

Under Kelly's stewardship, William Dawson was elected to Congress in 1942 and would serve fourteen continuous terms, until his death in 1970 at the age of 84. Dawson, by his very nature, was an amenable politician that the white aldermen and mayor could "work with." Mayor Richard J. Daley counted on Dawson's South Side clout through his first four terms of office. It was only after Dawson had passed the staff of leadership to a younger, more outspoken generation of black leaders, who were less impressed with his plantation-style politics, that this situation began to change.

During this era of passivity, there were powerful but still muted voices in the black community expressing the collective frustrations of a generation raised in poverty and suffering under the weight of oppression. Richard Nathaniel Wright was born in Mississippi in 1908. He came to Chicago in 1935, where he found work on the Federal Writer's Project. In 1938, Wright published his first book, *Uncle Tom's Children,* a collection of essays dramatizing racial prejudice. His most important work, *Native Son* (1940), explored the horror of ghetto life and its impact on a young Chicago black named Bigger Thomas, who was driven to commit murder. Wright was the spokesman for a generation, and his other notable books, *Black Boy* (1945), *The Outsider* (1953), and *White Man, Listen* (1957), further developed his observations of contemporary black life in the urban centers of America. Richard Wright's quiet outrage against the prevailing conditions was an early yet powerful catalyst of change. Future leaders like Al Raby, Ralph Metcalfe, and Jesse Jackson read his work carefully. It was a marked departure from the era of compliance.

The second great black migration from the rural South occurred after World War II. Between 1940 and 1950, the African American population increased from 277,731 to 492,265. By 1970 the figures surpassed the million mark for the first time, comprising 32 percent of the city's population. As blacks poured into formerly all-white neighborhoods, nervous real estate agents attempted to buck this trend by invoking the restrictive covenant, a legal device inserted into many wills and deeds designed to prevent a residential dwelling from being sold to people of color. The covenants held until the U.S. Supreme Court declared this barrier to open housing unconstitutional.

Alarmed by the specter of economic deprivation in the black community and miles of slum housing on the South Side, the Chicago Housing Authority (CHA) began demolishing the tenements to pave the way for the gleaming high-rise "projects" designed to end poverty and overcrowding. In theory, at least, the urban planners of the 1940s and 1950s believed they held the solution to a festering problem. There was no easy approach to housing conditions on the South Side. Many of the wooden buildings were constructed in the nineteenth century and lacked running water and heat. They could not be repaired, so they had to be bulldozed. That much was true, but what was regarded then as an appropriate solution brought with it a new set of problems.

With the opening of the Ida B. Wells homes at 37th and Vincennes in 1941, and the twenty-three Cabrini buildings north of Chicago Avenue between Larrabee and Hudson in 1942, the twenty-year period of urban renewal in the city began. One by one the black neighborhoods were transformed, almost overnight in some cases. After the Wells homes, building continued with the construction of Stateway Gardens in 1957 at 39th and Princeton, the Raymond Hilliard Homes for senior citizens at 22nd and State streets, and the Robert Taylor Homes, fronting the Dan Ryan Expressway. Their construction, along with that of the integrated middle-class 2,000-unit Lake Meadows complex between 31st and 35th streets, spelled the end of the blighted Federal Street slum. The 16-story Taylor homes were the world's largest public housing facility, but they soon illustrated the advent of new social problems that accompanied the construction of high-rise housing complexes.

Though well-intentioned by 1940s standards, the CHA planners who designed the clean but sterile apartment units ultimately succeeded only in worsening living conditions. Within a few years the Taylor Homes, Cabrini Green, and Stateway Gardens became seedbeds of drugs, crime, and mayhem. The residents were crowded together in insecure, neglected buildings that became safe houses for junkies and pushers. The vision of Mayor Daley, Dwight Green, and others did not extend much past the drawing boards and meeting rooms of City Hall. The positioning of the Taylor Homes on the east side of the Expressway appeared to be little more than de facto segregation on the part of the politicians, who created a manmade barrier to separate the haves and have-nots. Similar plans to build housing projects in all-white neighborhoods were doomed to failure after it was shown that blacks occupied 84 percent of the 45,000 public housing units controlled by the CHA.

By the 1960s, Chicago was forced to come to grips with the Civil Rights movement, which had been in flower since the end of World War II, when thousands of black GIs returned to the United States from their posts overseas. They were in no mind to put up with segregated schools, black-only lunch counters, and the back of the bus. The battle flared in Montgomery, Alabama, in 1955, when Rosa Parks refused to give up her seat on the bus. It reached Chicago a decade later when the Reverend Martin Luther King, Jr. led 10,000 marchers from Buckingham Fountain to City Hall on July 26, 1965, to demand the ouster of Charles Swibel, whom they accused of using federal funds to build segregated public housing.

At the center of the controversy was Chicago's embattled school superintendent, Benjamin C. Willis, who had been under fire since 1963 when he pushed through a plan to build mobile classrooms in overcrowded black districts. The NAACP accused Willis of promoting segregation. Late in 1963, black activists led by Al Raby and Alderman Ralph Metcalfe spearheaded an immensely successful boycott of the public school system. On October 22, 1963, exactly thirty days before John F. Kennedy was gunned down in Dallas, 224,770 of the 469,733 students enrolled in the public school system stayed home.

Congressman Dawson endorsed this first boycott with reservations, but broke ranks with Raby and the NAACP when a second boycott was called in February 1964. Dawson's philosophy was simple and old-fashioned: "We must play the game according to the rules. I always play it that way and I play with my team." The captain of the team, of course, sat on the fifth floor throne of City Hall. The anti-Willis crusade was the humble beginning of black political activism in the 1960s, a turbulent decade that brought profound social change.

In July 1965, comedian Dick Gregory led seventy anti-Willis marchers into Bridgeport, past the Daley residence at 3536 S. Lowe Avenue. "Chicago is the most ghettoized city in the country," complained Martin Luther King, who led an even bigger march into the all-white neighborhoods of Gage Park, Cragin, Chicago Lawn, and South Deering in 1966.

Sporadic rioting broke out on the West Side in 1965 and again a year later. Violence was triggered by the city's misguided decision to turn off the fire hydrants, which ghetto youngsters were likely to play under during the ninety-degree weather. These were the "long, hot summers" of Chicago's recent history.

The West Side went up in flames following the assassination of Dr. Martin Luther King in Memphis, Tennessee, on April 4, 1968. The arson and looting along Madison Street and Roosevelt Road took a heavy toll on the black community. One thousand people were left homeless and acres of one- and two-story buildings were reduced to rubble.

The Kerner Report on the rioting nationwide laid the blame for Chicago's rioting on the city's doorstep. The public school system was inadequate and beset by segregationist policy. The neighborhoods remained hopelessly divided along racial and economic lines, and the threat of renewed rioting hung in the air. By 1967, the Dawson machine was beginning to lose its grip on the voting public. That year two "independents" won seats in the City Council: A. A. "Sammy" Raynor in the Sixth Ward and William Cousins in the Eighth. In each case, machine-backed candidates went down to defeat. After Dawson passed away in 1970, social worker Fred Hubbard bucked the organization and claimed the Second Ward alderman's seat. The old order, for all intents and purposes, was dead.

The 1990 census data showed a slight decrease in the minority population. African Americans accounted for 39.03 percent of the city's ethnic makeup—down from the 39.8 percent registered in 1980. The evidence suggested that the older black communities like Grand Boulevard, Englewood, and West Lawndale, settled between 1920 and 1950, lost significant numbers of residents. A growing black middle class that had refused to linger in the crime-ridden neighborhoods abandoned the core of the city in search of affordable housing in the outlying areas. Black home ownership has steadily increased since 1960. The south and south west suburbs of Markham, Harvey, Phoenix, Dixmoor, and Maywood registered significant increases in their black populations during this time. (African Americans represent 7.5 percent of the suburban population base.)

While much of the original South Side Black Belt lay in ruins, or had been bulldozed years earlier to make way for high-rise housing projects, several black Chicago neighborhoods, notably Park Manor, West Chesterfield, Chatham, and the Jackson Park highlands, were rock-solid bastions of the middle class. Chatham, a quiet, tree-lined "suburb within the city," is bounded by the Dan Ryan Expressway to the immediate west and Cottage Grove Avenue on the east. This bungalow-belt neighborhood was once an ethnic melting pot of Swedes, Irish, and Germans. Now it is almost entirely black and the home of developer and writer Dempsey J. Travis, former Illinois comptroller Roland Burris, and many other leaders from the black professional class. Pill Hill, a smaller residential community to the south and east of Chatham, once home to many white physicians (hence its nickname), also became a middle-class black neighborhood.

The loss of heavy industry and the abandonment of the once-thriving commercial strips in Englewood, Woodlawn, North Lawndale, and Austin created a permanent displaced underclass, becoming communities unsafe for blacks and whites.

However, in 1983 the black community scored its most significant political victory since Oscar DePriest's aldermanic election in 1915. In November of that year, former congressman Harold Washington rode the tide of discontent into the mayor's chair. Washington, a product of the old Third Ward Democratic organization, had broken with the machine in 1977. The Washington revolt attracted thousands of young liberal whites, Hispanics from Pilsen and the near Northwest sides, and a unified black constituency into a "Rainbow Coalition," which relied heavily on religious and ethical symbolism to wrest control away from the white ethnics.

Racial divisiveness underscored the campaign that year. Republican challenger Bernard Epton's campaign literature tapped into the deepest fears of thousands of Poles, Germans, Lithuanians, and Irish on the Southwest and Northwest sides. They feared the "ghettoization" of their communities, and, for their part, precinct workers were quick to exploit this anxiety on both primary and election day. "Epton—Before It's Too Late!" the campaign preached.

Mayor Washington defeated Epton in 1983 and was reelected in 1987. His untimely death shortly after the election left the African American community without a clear political leader. A block of politicians formed the Harold Washington Party after the mayor's death to promote black candidates. The party hasn't yet garnered the support it seeks, but continues to be an active player in Chicago politics.

The Epton campaign's terse, grim appeal to racial antipathy illustrates the caste system under which Chicago continues to operate. Nowhere in America is this fierce sense of community more prevalent than in Chicago. Commenting on this essential character of Chicago life, Connecticut writer Richard Conniff noted in the pages of *National Geographic* that "the neighborhoods are the city's strength and its weakness. . . . There is of course a flip side to the appeal of neighborhood intimacy. Every neighborhood enforces its own brand of conformity, and the old mold doesn't necessarily fit new arrivals."

=============== **Attractions** ===============

Cultural Institutions

Du Sable Museum of African American History,
740 E. 56th Pl., Chicago, (773) 947-0600. Open daily.
Membership available.

Named after Chicago's first permanent settler, the Du Sable Museum in Washington Park explores the history, contributions, and culture of the African nations and people of African American descent. Founded in 1961 by Charles and Margaret Burroughs, the unique collection of sculpture, masks, folk dolls, and jewelry was originally housed at 3806 S. Michigan Avenue, in the former headquarters of the Quincy Club, which served as a meeting place for African American railroad workers. In 1973 the Du Sable Museum purchased a gray-stone building in Washington Park that once served as the South Side lockup for the Chicago Park District Police, an adjunct of the city police department until the two agencies were merged in 1959. The exhibits are shown on the first level, and they include a portrait gallery of prominent local and national African Americans, including Langston Hughes, Booker T. Washington, Robert S. Abbott, and Oscar DePriest. A wooden bas-relief mural carved by Robert Will Ames, completed in 1965 after six years of labor-intensive work, depicts forty episodic scenes and 225 identifiable figures who helped shape the African American experience from the time of the European slave trade up to the twentieth century. A separate room is devoted to the life and times of Harold Washington, including a display of 287 awards received by the late mayor between 1983 and 1987. A research library, auditorium, and gift shop are located on the grounds. During the year, the Du Sable Museum sponsors an Arts and Crafts Promenade, African American history courses, a "Know Your Heritage" bus tour of the city, African mask-making workshops, Family Day, an annual book fair, and a series of summer concerts and festivals. For a calendar of events, call the museum. *Recommended.*

African-American Cultural Center, *Addams Hall,*
830 S. Halsted St., Chicago, (773) 996-9549. Open
Monday–Friday; weekends by appointment.
Admission free.

Cultural center dedicated to the presentation and preservation of African American arts. The Center invites visiting artists to display their work in solo exhibits, providing contemporary artists public exposure. The Center also maintains a permanent collection. The public is welcome to use the

Center's research library, study room, and community meeting rooms. The Center frequently hosts lectures on African American art and culture.

ETA Creative Arts Foundation, *7558 S. Chicago Ave., Chicago, (773) 752-3955. Admission fee charged. Visa and MasterCard accepted.*

A black-owned performing arts center founded in 1971 by Harold Johnson, Abena Joan Brown, Al Johnson, and Archie Weston, Jr., to promote African American drama, dance, and musical events under one roof. Six main stage productions are given on Thursday and Saturday nights throughout the year. Such critically acclaimed dramatic works as *Stoops* and *Good Black* (both staged at ETA) have been nominated for Jeff Awards in the past. In the spring of 1991, the theater sponsored the play *Survival,* a tribute to Winnie and Nelson Mandela and the struggle to end apartheid in South Africa. ETA also sponsors dramatic workshops for children six years and up, and theater classes for adults.

Black Ensemble Theatre, *4520 N. Beacon St., Chicago, (773) 769-4451. Admission fee charged. Visa and MasterCard accepted.*

A center for the performing arts founded by Jackie Taylor in 1976. In recent years audiences have delighted to the stage adaptation of *A Streetcar Named Desire, The Other Cinderella*, and *Muddy Waters: the Hootchy-Kootchie Man.* The theater was originally located on Wells Street in Old Town, and moved to its present location in 1986. Five plays are given each year, and are held Friday and Saturday nights and Sunday afternoons.

Afro-American Genealogical & Historical Society (AAGHS). *Mailing Address: PO Box 377651, Chicago, IL 60637. Membership available.*

Meets the second Sunday of the month at the South Shore Cultural Center, 7059 South Shore Dr., Chicago, (312) 747-2536. The AAGHS has 150 active members in Chicago, and an additional 600 on the mailing list who are tracing their family history through hands-on workshops, field trips to the Allen County Library in Fort Wayne, Indiana (the largest genealogical library in the nation), regular Sunday meetings, and an annual conference held the last Saturday in February at the South Shore Cultural Center. The group was organized in 1979, and has nine standing committees dedicated to archival work, computer research, publications, special events, and publicity. AAGHS publishes a newsletter four times a year, and sponsors a workshop in October, which teaches people family research methodology.

Nicole Gallery, *230 W. Huron, Chicago,*
(312) 787-7716. Open Tuesday–Saturday, Sunday
and Monday by appointment. Credit cards accepted.

Painting and sculpture by African, Haitian, African American, and other American artists.

Isobel Neal Gallery, *200 W. Superior St., Chicago,*
(312) 944-1570. By appointment only. Credit cards
accepted.

Contemporary paintings, sculpture, three-dimensional construction, and prints done by African American artists.

Woodshop Art Gallery, *441 E. 75th St., Chicago,*
(773) 994-6666. Closed Sunday.

Largest retail dealer of African American art in the city.

Annual Events and Celebrations

Bud Billiken Day Parade. *Second Saturday*
in August. For additional information, call
(773) 225-2400.

A lavish, annual back-to-school parade kicking off from Oakwood Boulevard and King Drive, proceeding south on King to 55th Street in Washington Park. The history of this parade dates back to 1929 when Robert Abbott, publisher of the Chicago *Defender,* decided to pay tribute to the newsboys who hawked his paper on the street corners. The employees of the *Defender* would walk with the youngsters from 35th Street to Washington Park, where everyone would participate in a day-long picnic. The afternoon picnic and the selection of the king and queen by the newspaper staff are time-honored customs that are features of every Billiken parade. Abbott named his event after the ancient Chinese billiken doll, which according to legend is supposed to watch over little children. A "Buddy Billiken" doll stood on his desk for many years.

With more than 300 entries and sixty floats participating every year, Chicago's Bud Billiken Parade is the third largest parade in the country, following the Tournament of Roses Parade in California on New Year's Day, and Macy's Thanksgiving Day Parade in Manhattan. The marching bands come all the way from Texas, Missouri, Nebraska, Kansas, and Iowa. For the politicians who regularly turn out for this event, it's only a short ride from City Hall. For the best public transportation routes, call the CTA at (312) 836-7000. *Recommended.*

African Liberation Day. *Third Saturday in May.*
For more information, call (773) 268-7500,
ext. 154.

Parade, speeches, picnic, and entertainment sponsored by the National
Black United Front, Chicago Chapter. The three-mile parade, resplendent
with floats, school bands, marchers and politicians, kicks off from Austin
Avenue and Jackson Street, on the West Side, and proceeds to Garfield Park
for a day-long festival and ceremony marking the African independence
movement that took shape in Ghana during the 1950s. Under the leadership
of Kwame Nkrumah, the people of Ghana threw off the last shackles of
British colonialism in the early 1950s. This helped spark a broader-based
independence movement that took shape in French Guinea and the Belgian
Congo. As a result, the Organization of African Unity was organized in May
1963, when thirty-one African heads of state convened a summit meeting to
proclaim the fourth Saturday in May an international holiday. The first ALD
was staged in the United States nine years later, on May 27, 1972. The event
includes live music and dance performances; sales of African art, clothing,
and jewelry; and speeches.

African Festival of the Arts, *Du Sable Museum,*
740 E. 56th Pl., Chicago. Labor Day weekend.
For additional information, call (773) 955-7742.

Annual three-day street fair featuring food booths, musical entertainment,
story telling, crafts demonstrations, an African puppet show for the children, and video displays. The festival revolves around a different theme
every year. In 1990 the focus was on "Creativity and Survival." "A Window
to Africa" highlighted the 1991 event, which was sponsored in part by the
National Council of Artists, Chicagoland chapter.

Black Harvest International Film and Video
Festival, *Film Center of the Art Institute, Columbus*
and Jackson, Chicago, (312) 443-3733. July.
Admission fee. Membership available. The center is
closed on Mondays and Wednesdays.

Annual film festival presented each year since 1981 by the Film Center of
the Art Institute, and featuring the work of leading contemporary black
directors and producers including Spike Lee, Sijri Bakaba, and local independents, such as Ruby L. Oliver. Conceived and developed by Floyd
Webb, the Blacklight Festival is a series of month-long events and workshops held every July.

African Film Festival, Columbia College, *600 S. Michigan Ave., Chicago, (312) 663-1600, ext. 5170 or 5287. April. Admission free.*

Dr. Alice E. Stephens, an independent filmmaker and professor at Columbia College, coordinated the college's first African Film Festival in 1995. This annual event features screenings of contemporary African, African American, and African Caribbean filmmakers. Since the films are shown at several locations, it is best to call in advance for a schedule. At least one day is devoted to family-oriented films. Columbia College hosts a preview party and benefit reception prior to the festival's start, with music, authentic African or Caribbean cuisine, and a private screening of the festival's films. Call for tickets.

Chicago Gospel Festival, *Grant Park (Jackson Boulevard and Columbus Drive). First or second weekend in June. Admission is free. For a schedule of performers and times, call the Mayor's Office of Special Events at (312) 744-3315.*

Two-day music extravaganza. Unlike the larger, more chaotic city events, such as the Taste of Chicago and the Jazz Festival, which annually lure upwards of 400,000 people, Chicago's Gospel Fest is a celebration of the spirit attended by church-going families. This means very few security problems for the often-overextended Chicago Police Department. The Gospel Fest has been a "religious rite of summer" since 1985. Its roots run much deeper, however. Gospel music is derived from Pentecostal church worship services of the late 19th century and blues singing. The practice of "shouting" is directly related to African circle dances and "speaking in tongues." It became an art form popular with American blacks in the 1920s, and enjoyed a tremendous postwar popularity, due in no small measure to long-time Chicago resident Mahalia Jackson (1911–72), who toured internationally, appeared in films, and was broadcast around the world on TV and radio. The soaring tribute to the big-time gospel composers and singers, including Kenneth Morris, Marvin Yancey, H. W. Brewster, the Edwin Hawkins Singers, the Rev. A. C. Tindley, Sister Rosette Tharpe, New Life, and Mahalia Jackson, is performed on three stages: the Petrillo Bandshell, the Youth Stage, and the Chicago Gospel Stage.

The CTA will add extra buses along the South Side routes. For transit information, call (312) 836-7000.

Chicago Blues Festival, *Grant Park, (Jackson Boulevard and Columbus Drive), in mid-June (usually follows Gospel Fest by a week). Admission free. For a schedule of performers and times, call the Mayor's Office of Special Events at (312) 744-3315.*

A three-day concert showcasing blues artists from Chicago and down south. Though it is no longer exclusively an African American art form, this secular folk music from the black rural South dates back to the post-Civil War period, and is a fusion of work songs, field hollers, minstrel show tunes, and mainstream white compositions. The blues were originally derived from southern black men, who tended the fields under the grueling mid-day sun in Georgia, the Carolinas, Texas, and Mississippi. The first reference to this form of music in a scored composition occurred in 1912 with the publication of W. C. Handy's *Memphis Blues.*

   In the 1920s and 1930s Chicago played the greatest role in the development of the "urban blues" as we know it today, through the recordings of such renowned performers as Big Bill Broonzy, John Lee "Sonny Boy" Williamson, Tampa Red, and Memphis Minnie. After World War II, a young generation of blues musicians came into their own, including Muddy Waters, Elmore James, Otis Spann, Howlin' Wolf (whose records, cassettes, and CDs are sold from a van every Saturday and Sunday at Maxwell and Halsted streets), and Little Walter Jacobs. In the 1950s, the recording studios of Chess Records at 2120 S. Michigan Avenue helped fuse a fledgling music art form known as "rhythm and blues" to mainstream pop. Leonard and Phil Chess opened their studio in 1947, with such blues artists as John Lee Hooker, Jimmy Rodgers, Howlin' Wolf, and Muddy Waters under contract. They added Chuck Berry, Bo Diddley, the Moonglows, Johnnie and Joe, the Tune Weavers, and the Monotones in the mid-1950s when the demand for black R & B music and sentimental "doo-wop" ballads expanded into the white neighborhoods. Allen Freed may have legitimized the new music while working as a disc jockey in Cleveland in 1952–53, but the birth of rock n' roll was foretold several years earlier when the Chicago blues performers stepped into the Michigan Avenue recording studios of Chess Records for the very first time.

   The Grant Park Blues Fest exalts the famous Chicago sound that has become a musical institution. The fest has been going strong since 1984, preserving these earlier traditions on four main stages: the Petrillo Music Shell (Jackson and Columbus Drive), the Front Porch (Jackson Boulevard and Columbus), the Crossroads Stage (Jackson and Lake Shore Drive), and the rotunda at the tip of Navy Pier. *Recommended.*

Chicago Jazz Festival, *Grant Park. Last weekend in August. For Jazz Fest showtimes, call (312) 744-3370. Sponsored by the not-for-profit Jazz Institute of Chicago (JIC) and the Mayor's Office of Special Events.*

There was a time, not so long ago, when Chicago was the jazz mecca of the Midwest; when dimly lit nightclubs, like the Happy Medium, the London House, the Blue Note, and a half-dozen smaller bistros near State and Randolph gave out a rich, vibrant sound. The legendary clubs have faded into memory—casualties of the social transformation wrought by the 1960s. Jazz lovers, take heart. The sprawling Grant Park festival has been growing in stature each year since its inception in 1979, and is broadcast coast-to-coast on National Public Radio (NPR), WBEZ (91.5 FM) in Chicago. An exciting array of local, national, and international acts is featured in the Petrillo Music Shell and the Jazz on Jackson Stage (Jackson and Lake Shore Drive) from noon till 10:00 P.M. throughout the festival. What you get is a mixture of traditional jazz, be-bop, swing, and Dixieland. This is probably the only major jazz festival in the U.S. that pays homage to the growing international flavor of the art form, which is disconcerting to some of the purists. One of the gripes expressed by members of the Association of Creative Musicians (AACM) is the inherent conservatism of Chicagoans when it comes to jazz music. Experimental and avant-garde performers have a hard time making their mark in hard-nosed, blue-collar Chicago. Their most receptive audiences are outside the mainstream, and very often found in Europe, where a newcomer is able to catch a break. Innovation, if it is to be found in Chicago, very often comes from some of the smaller clubs around town, like the Bop-Shop at 1807 W. Division Street, and Jazz Showcase, at 59 W. Grand Avenue.

Neighborhood Resident Blues Festival, *Garfield Park, Chicago. First Friday, Saturday, and Sunday in August. Admission is free. Contact Minnie Dunlap, (773) 265-1902.*

Sponsored by the Fifth City Neighborhood Residents Association in conjunction with Habilitative Systems, Inc., at 417 S. Kimbark. The Garfield Park Blues Fest is a community event that has been held every year since 1971. Local jazz performers are showcased on Saturday night. Pop singers and balladeers share the spotlight on Fridays. Food vendors. Clowns. Plenty of down-home Chicago music.

Jazz Fest, *South Shore Cultural Center, 7059 South Shore Blvd., Chicago, (773) 747-2536. First weekend in August. Admission free.*

Two-day series of concerts and jazz workshops held on the grounds of the Cultural Center. In 1974, Geraldine de Haas decided that in order for Chicago to expand its cultural horizons, it was first necessary to install an appreciation for the kind of music that used to be synonymous with the swinging South Side. The political sachems of the Daley administration were cool to the idea. Pork barrels and patronage were what really mattered in those days—but Geraldine was a patient woman. She bided her time until Mayor Jane Byrne came along and decided to spruce up the image of the city by sponsoring a myriad of festivals, weekend outings, and celebrations. Geraldine helped Jane spawn the immensely successful Grant Park Jazz Fest, which served to whet the public's appetite for more of the same. The South Shore Jazz Fest is sponsored by Jazz Unites, Inc., and other agencies. Since 1981 some of the biggest names in contemporary and traditional jazz—including the Count Basie Orchestra, Ramsey Lewis, and the Ray Brown Trio—have headlined the festival. Budgetary constraints make this one of the least publicized musical events in the city, but through word of mouth and public service announcements, the South Shore Jazz Fest has drawn an average of 15,000 people each of the last few years.

Dance Africa, *Dance Center of Columbia College, 4730 N. Sheridan Rd., Chicago. One week in late September or early October. Admission fee charged. Visa and MasterCard accepted. For scheduled times, call (773) 989-3310.*

A yearly festival of African American choreography held in the college's 250-seat theater. Following on the heels of the critically acclaimed "Present Vision/Past Voice: the African American Tradition in American Modern Dance" in 1990, Columbia College has renewed its commitment to offering diversity within the program by presenting this seasonal pageant of African culture.

Ebony Fashion Show. *May. Call (312) 322-9200 for tickets, dates, and location.*

Sponsored by *Ebony* magazine in conjunction with the Chicago Area Club of the National Association of Negro Business and Professional Women's Clubs, Inc. Proceeds from this charitable event go toward scholarship programs and the African American community. The fashion show is usually held at the Holiday Inn, O'Hare, in Rosemont, but the location and price are subject to change.

Walk-a-thon. *First Saturday in June. Admission fee charged (lower group fee available). To register, call (773) 947-0600.*

An annual walk-a-thon to help support the Du Sable Museum's operating expenses for tours, exhibitions, education, and public programs. The day-long event begins at the Du Sable Museum in Washington Park on Payne Drive. It proceeds through the University of Chicago campus in Hyde Park, east to Lake Shore Drive, then west to 57th and Cornell, before ending at the finish line. The total distance is 16 kilometers. Participants receive a T-shirt, a raffle ticket for prizes, a "goodie bag," and a bagged lunch.

Pre-Kwanzaa Celebration, *at the South Shore Cultural Center, 7059 South Shore Dr., Chicago, (773) 509-4900. First or second weekend in December. Admission is free.*

Kwanzaa is a non-religious holiday conceived in 1966 by Maulana Ron Karenga, a civil rights activist who desired to strengthen the African American family unit through a week-long celebration incorporating elements of the traditional African harvest festivals. Nowadays, Mr. Karenga is a professor at California State University and Chairman of the Black Studies program. *Kwanzaa* is a Swahili word meaning "first fruits of the harvest," celebrating *nguzo saba,* the seven principles of unity, self-determination, cooperative economics, collective work and responsibility, purpose, faith, and creativity. Though Kwanzaa is observed from December 26 through January 1, the South Shore Cultural Center kicks things off early with this event, co-sponsored by the Chicago Park District. African American dance troupes, Afro-centric lectures, cooking classes, arts and crafts, doll-making sessions, and other workshops are included in the program.

Kwanzaa Summer Festival, *95th St. and State St. First Saturday in July. Call (773) 264-1298. Admission is free.*

Sponsored by the Soweto Center of Chicago, 19 W. 103rd St., Chicago. Musical entertainment, food, and children's activities.

Black History Month Events

February is Black History Month, celebrating the heritage, art, music, customs, and achievements of African Americans. Local theaters and museums feature an array of interesting events, including lectures, films, theatrical productions, ethnic dance, and gallery exhibitions, which are geared to a different theme every year.

African Heritage Festival, *Field Museum of Natural History, Roosevelt Rd. and Lake Shore Dr., Chicago, (312) 922-9410. Workshop fee and regular museum admission fee charged (museum free on Thursday). For additional information, contact the museum's education department.*

The museum sponsors a month-long program of crafts demonstrations, music presentations, and children's hands-on workshops, where skilled artisans teach young people the art of basket weaving and drum making. Storytelling sessions and a choral presentation by the greater Holy Temple Gospel Choir are regularly scheduled features in February. The Field Museum devotes one day a week in February to these special events.

Black Creativity, *Museum of Science and Industry, 57th St. and Lake Shore Dr., Chicago, (773) 684-1414, ext. 2436. Admission free with a museum ticket.*

Celebrating its 25th anniversary in 1996. The museum's exhibit revolves around a different cultural theme every year. In 1991, visitors were treated to "Music! Music! Music!: An African American Tradition." A juried art exhibit, featuring the works of African American painters, sculptors, and photographers from around the country is a yearly custom. Lectures. Musical concerts. Dance ensembles.

Art Institute of Chicago Exhibition, *Michigan Ave. at Adams St., Chicago, (312) 443-3680 (Museum Education Department). Admission fee charged.*

In addition to an ongoing exhibit in the Gallery of African Art that features wood carvings, textiles, and jewelry from Africa, the museum sponsors a different program every year during Black History Month. The public is invited to attend free lectures, workshops, and special showings that pertain to black artistic endeavor and cultural history. The 1990 program was titled "Yoruba: Nine Centuries of African Art and Thought." During the year, the education department sponsors various other African American exhibitions in the museum. "The Gold of Africa" and "Senufo Woman" were two smaller showings on display during the spring and summer months of 1991.

Chicago Public Library Cultural Center Exhibition, *78 E. Washington St., Chicago. Admission free. For information about the itinerary, times and*

*locations, call the Department of Cultural Affairs
at (312) 744-6630.*

The Chicago Department of Cultural Affairs presents a yearly ensemble of creative dance, musical performances, art exhibits, films, and lectures given by contemporary artists in the meeting rooms of the old library. Other activities are included in the calendar of events, which is drawn up several months in advance of the February showing.

Newberry Library Events, *60 W. Walton St.,
Chicago, (312) 943-9090, ext. 457. Closed Sundays
and Mondays.*

Free symposiums, lectures, and presentations pertaining to local black history and genealogy. The Newberry received a two-year project grant for its "Afro-American Family History Project," which concluded in 1991. The library assisted local scholars and genealogists who traced black family life in Chicago, through extensive archival, manuscript, and catalog material housed at the library. Each year the Newberry sponsors a program relating to Black History Month; the focus is different each time. A Lyceum series, with classes on black genealogy, is held twice a year and is open to the public. The cost of these classes ranges from $50 to $60 per course, and classes can be booked by calling the library at the above number. The Newberry is a fine resource for local history.

Museum of Broadcast Communications, *Chicago
Cultural Center, Michigan Avenue at Washington,
Chicago, (312) 629-6000. Admission fee charged.*

Seminars, workshops, discussions on black ownership of radio and TV stations, and film documentaries about the history of the civil rights movement are held throughout the month. Guest speakers, such as TV newsman Harry Porterfield, recount their experiences in Chicago broadcast journalism over the years. Contact the education department for a program of events (program varies from year to year).

Peace Museum, *314 W. Institute Place, 1st floor,
Chicago, (312) 440-1860. Closed Sundays and
Mondays. Admission fee charged.*

The Peace Museum presents a different theme every year to mark Black History Month in Chicago. In 1990, the paintings and drawings of illustrator and journalist Franklin McMahon were featured in an exhibition titled "An Artist's Notebook: Civil Rights, Selma to Chicago." In other years, the artwork of children living in the crime-ridden Cabrini-Green housing project has been displayed. The special exhibits will run the entire month of February, and sometimes longer.

Chicago Historical Society, *Clark St. at North Ave., Chicago, (312) 642-4600. Admission fee charged (admission free on Mondays).*

The society contributes much to our understanding of African American and Chicago history through special exhibits, lectures, and bus tours of the city conducted year-round. In 1991, the it hosted two exhibitions of note: "I Dream a World: Portraits of Black Women Who Changed America," a photographic study of 75 African American women who helped fulfill the prophecy of essayist and author Langston Hughes (1902–67), who could only "dream a world where all will know sweet freedom's way," and "African American Passport," featuring discussions and lectures given by visiting scholars, a dinner at the CHS, and related programs. Black History Month at the society is indeed a 365-day event, but in February it is likely that special concerts, films, and lectures will be listed on the program calendar. For more information, contact the education department at the society.

Places to See

Kenwood Walking Tour, *conducted by the Chicago Architectural Foundation, 1800 S. Prairie Ave., Chicago, (773) 326-1393. May, June, September, and October. Admission fee charged.*

Two-hour tour of a landmark South Side neighborhood that is remarkably well preserved. Kenwood, described by many as a "suburb within the city," was founded by Dr. John Kennicott, a dentist of Scottish descent who settled here in 1856. The quiet, tree-lined streets were home to some of Chicago's most notable citizens, including Julius Rosenwald and the Gustavus Swift family. As the South Side underwent a profound racial transformation in the twentieth century, the northern portion of Kenwood became closely identified with the all-black Oakland community, while the southern end of the community forged a social, economic, and cultural link with neighboring Hyde Park and the University of Chicago. Included on the tour are homes built by Frank Lloyd Wright, Alfred S. Altschuler, and Howard Van Doren Shaw. Tour guides provide historical interpretation and will answer questions. The tour begins at 1100 E. Hyde Park Boulevard (5100 S) and Greenwood Avenue (1100 E) at the K.A.M. Isaiah Israel Congregation Temple.

Statue of the Black Doughboy, *35th St. and S. King Dr., Chicago.*

The base of the memorial was erected in 1927, and is dedicated to black soldiers who gave their lives in World War I. The statue, designed by Leonard Crunelle, was sculpted in memory of George Giles, a highly decorated World War I veteran. It was placed atop the pedestal in 1936.

Ida Wells/Ferdinand Lee Barnett home, *3624 S. King Dr., Chicago.*

Ferdinand Barnett, founder of the *Conservator,* the first black newspaper in Chicago, and his wife, social reformer Ida B. Wells, lived in this building from 1919 to 1930. In July 1974, the Department of the Interior designated this site a National Historical Landmark. Nearby, on King Drive, between 37th and 39th streets, stands the Ida B. Wells housing project.

Dr. Martin Luther King, Jr. residence, *1550 S. Hamlin Ave., Chicago.*

In the summer of 1966, Dr. King established a temporary living quarters in this West Side apartment building while he fought for open housing and equal justice. As a result, the Leadership Council of Metropolitan Chicago was organized.

Jesse Binga home, *5922 South King Dr., Chicago.*

Binga's amazing business success at a time when few black men prospered in the white man's North is partly explained by the lavish inheritance he received when his brother-in-law, John "Mushmouth" Johnson, passed away in 1907. Johnson was a swaggering gambler from St. Louis, who ran Chicago's South Side policy rackets for nearly twenty years, beginning in the 1880s. Johnson was the proprietor of the Frontenac Club, which catered to an exclusive white clientele that helped him earn an estimated $250,000 in illegal revenue, though he claimed to be down to his last penny shortly before his death. A year after Johnson passed away, Binga opened his bank at State and 35th streets. He was forced to close down in July 1930, bankrupting many depositors. Many people have blamed utilities czar Samuel Insull for Binga's misfortunes, but the Great Depression was already in full force, and it made no racial distinctions. Binga's modest frame dwelling was bombed ten times by whites during the protracted period of racial troubles in 1918 and 1919.

Offices of the Chicago *Defender,* *2400 S. Michigan* *Ave., Chicago.*

Almost singlehandedly, Robert S. Abbott, the son of a slave butler, inspired the great northern black migration in the pages of his sometimes sensational, but always blunt and to the point, Chicago *Defender.* Under the guidance of Abbott's nephew, John Sengstacke, the *Defender* became one of two black papers to publish daily beginning in 1954. This modest stone building on the Near South Side houses the *Defender* editorial staff, and was designated an important "historical site in journalism" by the prestigious Sigma Delta Chi society on May 5, 1975.

The Chicago *Bee* **Building,** *3649-57 S. State St.,* *Chicago.*

Local preservationists came to the rescue of this historic building slated for the wrecking ball. The editorial offices of the Chicago *Bee,* a black-owned newspaper that thrived in the 1920s, were located here during the heyday of "Bronzeville." Anthony Overton managed the paper, and, incidentally, may have been the inventor of cold cream. Now, fortunately, the structure will be converted into a library, thanks to an infusion of state money drawn from the "Build Illinois" program.

Guide to Local Clubs

Wild Hare and Singing Armadillo Frog Sanctuary, *3530 N. Clark St., Chicago, (773) 327-4273. Open* *nightly.*

Live reggae music at this busy North Side nightclub and bar.

Equator Club, *4715 N. Broadway, Chicago,* *(773) 728-2411. Closed Mondays. Cover charge* *varies.*

Bar and nightclub featuring Afro-pop, Caribbean, disco, and calypso music played by a disc jockey.

New Regal Theatre, *1645 E. 79th St., Chicago.* *Closed Sundays. To charge tickets by phone, call* *Ticketmaster at (312) 559-1212. Visa and MasterCard* *accepted. For a recorded message listing upcoming* *events, call (773) 721-9230. Ticket prices vary*

depending on the event, but can be purchased through
Ticketmaster outlets or at the New Regal box office.

Big-name jazz, blues, and gospel performers booked on a regular basis.
WGCI radio sponsors a talent showcase each year, and a limited number of
stage plays and musicals are also included during the year. This is an experience that hearkens back to the days of old vaudeville. Special dinner theater packages available.

Blues

New Checkerboard Lounge #2 (Blues), *1634*
W. 69th St., Chicago, (773) 471-5300. Open nightly.
Cover charge on the weekend.

Some of the big-time rock performers like Mick Jagger and Eric Clapton,
who are heavily influenced by Chicago-style blues music (perfected to a
high art on 43rd Street, otherwise known as "Muddy Waters Drive" during
the blues "Renaissance," and the Lounge's former location) have been
known to drop by to catch the hottest acts from the South and North sides.

Buddy Guy's Legends (Blues), *754 S. Wabash Ave.,*
Chicago (312) 427-0333. Open nightly.

This South Loop blues spot features the music of Buddy Guy (part owner of
the club), who teams up with the John Watkins Group, appearing nightly.
Such international celebrities as Bill Wyman, the late Stevie Ray Vaughn,
and Ron Wood have also performed here. Rock and R & B are featured
occasionally.

B.L.U.E.S., *2519 N. Halsted St., Chicago,*
(773) 528-1012. Open nightly. Cover charge varies.

Small-sized neighborhood blues club that is very popular with the out-of-
town set, who elbow their way to the front just about every night. Only a
block away from the Biograph Theater, where John Dillinger met his
demise in 1934.

B.L.U.E.S. Etcetera, *1124 W. Belmont Ave., Chicago*
(773) 525-8989. Open nightly. Cover charge.

Spawned by B.L.U.E.S., but the parking is easier and there is greater room
to roam, unlike the Halsted Street location. The club features a number of
out-of-town acts, and special performances are given by musicians from
B.L.U.E.S. The B.L.U.E.S. Etc. club sponsors an annual four-hour "Blues

Cruise" on Lake Michigan, which includes food and music, the third Saturday in July. Tickets are available through all Ticketron outlets. Call (312) 559-1212.

Rosa's Lounge (Blues), *3420 W. Armitage Ave., Chicago, (773) 342-0452. Open nightly. Cover charge varies. Free parking next door.*

Rosa's calls itself the "friendliest blues club" in Chicago, and has done much to promote local blues artists over the years. Located in Logan Square, and maintained by Tony Manguilo and his mother, Rosa, who tends bar. The club features something different every night.

Blue Chicago, *736 N. Clark St., Chicago,* *(312) 642-6261,* and **Blue Chicago on Clark,** *536 N. Clark St., Chicago, (312) 661-0100. Open nightly. Cover charge varies.*

The two locations feature a potpourri of blues styles, but tends to favor such female blueswomen as Gloria Shannon, Dietra Farr, and Katherine Davis. Excellent sound system, very spacious.

Lilly's (Blues), *2513 N. Lincoln Ave., Chicago, (773) 525-2422. Closed Mondays and Tuesdays. Cover charge varies.*

Intimate piano and acoustic blues club in a café atmosphere. The place is a personal favorite of a number of veteran blues performers, including Jimmy Rogers and Big Moose Walker.

Kingston Mines (Blues), *2548 N. Halsted, Chicago, (773) 477-4646. Open nightly.*

One of the oldest established clubs in the city, Kingston Mines promotes itself as Chicago's "Blues Center." Live blues, and two bands, seven days a week.

Koko Taylor's Chicago Blues, *7 W. Division St., Chicago, (312) 337-2583. Open nightly.*

Open blues jam sessions on Sunday. Live blues acts every other night.

Jazz

(Note: For information about what's happening on the local jazz scene in Chicago, call the Jazz Institute Hotline at (312) 666-1881 for a prerecorded message, or stay tuned to WNUA, 95.5 FM, for frequent updates during the day.)

The Bop Shop (Jazz), *1807 W. Division St., Chicago, (773) 235-3232. Open nightly.*

The place for contemporary jazz, Chicago-style. Unpretentious. The look and feel of this Wicker Park club is authentic, so much so that the club sponsors an annual Nelson Algren celebration. (Algren lived and worked nearby.)

The New Jazz Showcase, *59 W. Grand Ave., Chicago, (312) 670-2473. Closed Monday. Cover charge varies.*

Joe Segal's New Jazz Showcase pays homage to all who have gone before: Charlie "the Bird" Parker, Duke Ellington, Dizzy Gillespie. It's a downtown kind of place that has been around since 1947, so expect to pay a hefty cover charge. The Jazz Showcase used to be located in the Blackstone Hotel.

The Green Mill (Jazz), *4802 N. Broadway (at Lawrence), Chicago, (773) 878-5552. Open daily and nightly. Free parking at Lawrence & Magnolia.*

In the days of Prohibition, this was a gangland hangout run by the late Henry van Horne. His son Rudy went on to become a stand-up comic and latter-day vaudevillian. Rudy once sat on Ruth Etting's knee, and performed a nifty tap dance for one of Al Capone's boys way back when. Things are a little more sedate today. The gangsters have been replaced by local jazz impresarios like the Green Mill All-Stars and Ed Peterson, who perform in a 1940s setting. For a change of pace, the Green Mill features poetry readings (the Uptown Poetry Slam) on Sunday evenings, followed by more live jazz.

Pop's for Champagne (Jazz), *2934 N. Sheffield, Chicago, (773) 472-1000. Closed Tuesdays.*

Desire a romantic interlude, at a definitely upscale jazz club in the Clybourn corridor? This is definitely the place for a rendezvous. The wine bar features 100 champagnes, and twelve by the glass. A "jazz brunch" is featured on Sundays. The champagne and all that jazz are pricey, so beware.

Andy's Lounge (Jazz), *11 E. Hubbard St., Chicago, (312) 642-6805. Closed Sundays.*

The informal approach to jazz works best at Andy's, one of the oldest clubs of its kind in Chicago. Andy's features the music of the Chicago Jazz Band, the Rhythmmakers and Swingtet, and the only noontime jazz in the city.

The Bulls (Jazz), *1916 N. Lincoln Park West,*
Chicago, (773) 337-3000. Open nightly. Cover
charge varies.

Basement bar and nightclub featuring local contemporary jazz musicians. The best time to go is during the week, when there are no lines. It has been jumping since way back in 1963, due in no small measure to the fine acoustics.

Oz (Jazz), *2917 N. Sheffield, Chicago,*
(773) 975-8100. Live music Thursday–
Saturday. Cover charge varies.

Contemporary jazz fusion in a cozy storefront surrounding. Very popular with the upscale Lincoln Park crowd.

The Backroom (Jazz), *1007 N. Rush St., Chicago,*
(312) 751-2433. Open nightly. Cover charge.

A former Rush Street hot spot that used to be a horse barn (believe it or not) still reverberates with the sound of jazz, even though the neighborhood isn't quite the adult playground it used to be.

The Other Place (Jazz), *377 E. 75th St., Chicago,*
(773) 874-5476.

Popular South Side spot that disdains the cover charge, but attempts to make up the difference with higher drink prices when the big out-of-town acts perform.

Dick's Last Resort (Jazz), *435 E. Illinois St.,*
Chicago, (312) 836-7870. Open daily and nightly. No
cover charge.

If you enjoy unstructured Dixieland music, Dick's is the place to go. Food and drink are served.

Green Dolphin Street (Jazz), *2200 N. Ashland,*
Chicago, (773) 395-0066. Closed Mondays. Cover
charge varies.

Upscale jazz club serving dinner and more basic bar food. Popular with professionals.

Velvet Lounge (Jazz), *2128½ S. Indiana, Chicago,*
(773) 791-9050. Open nightly.

Live jazz jam sessions on Sunday nights.

Metropole Lounge (Jazz), *Fairmont Hotel,*
Illinois Center, 200 N. Columbus Dr., Chicago,
(312) 565-7444. Closed Sundays.

Live jazz every night but Sunday.

Milt Trenier's Lounge (Jazz), *610 N. Fairbanks Ct.,*
Chicago, (312) 266-6226. Closed Tuesdays.

Live jazz nightly.

The Cotton Club (Jazz & Latin rhythms), *1710 S.*
Michigan Ave., Chicago, (312) 341-9787. Open
nightly.

Maybe one day the owners of the Cotton Club will be able to take credit for the rebirth and development of South Michigan Avenue, which once crawled with jet-setters, society swells, and the ne'er-do-wells of the old levee, eager to partake of the gin spirits of Colosimo's nightclub on Wabash. Colosimo's, and the horn players who carried on there, are ghostly memories now, amid the ruins of decaying warehouses and abandoned courtyard flats. The Cotton Club, with its eclectic variety of Dixieland jazz and down-home blues, is in vogue these days in less-than-elegant surroundings.

Shops

Jazz Record Mart, *444 N. Wabash Ave., Chicago,*
(312) 222-1467. Open daily. Credit cards accepted.

Chicago's largest selection of jazz and blues CDs & Tapes. Located just a few blocks away from where the legendary Clark Street jazz hot spots of the 1920s, '30s, '40s, and '50s once stood—the Hi-Note, the Liberty Inn, The Ship, and the Victory Club—the Jazz Record Mart caters to the serious connoisseur of jazz music, offering the largest inventory of jazz and blues CDs and cassettes in the Midwest. The Mart publishes an annual "Rhythm and News" catalog that is sent to subscribers all around the country, listing current inventory by record label, and news of the local jazz scene. If you happen to be in town for the Chicago Jazz Festival, a side trip to the Record Mart should definitely be included in your itinerary. *Recommended.*

Afrocentric Bookstore, *234 S. Wabash Ave., Chicago,*
(312) 939-1956. Closed Sundays.

One of the few bookstores in the city to specialize in African American books. Stocks over a thousand titles plus audio books, newspapers, magazines, and gifts. Phone and mail orders accepted. Excellent resource for researchers.

Powell's Books, *2850 N. Lincoln Ave., Chicago,*
(773) 248-1444. Open daily.

Large selection of used blues and jazz books.

Harold Washington Library, *State St. and Van Buren*
St., Chicago, (312) 747-4999 (general number). Open
daily.

Compact discs, vinyl records, and books available for check-out and on-site viewing. The library often exhibits photographs and other memorabilia concerning jazz and blues performers.

Window to Africa, *5210 S. Harper Ave., Chicago,*
(773) 955-7742. Open daily. Credit cards accepted.

Traditional and contemporary African paintings, sculptures, beads, jewelry, and textiles for sale.

Boutique Africa, *209 E. 75th St., Chicago,*
(773) 723-1544. Open daily.

Fabric, clothing, jewelry, and prints created by African artists.

Unan Imports, *6971 N. Sheridan Rd., Chicago,*
(773) 274-4022. Open daily.

African creations only, including beads, jewelry, carved statues and masks, baskets, cards, and beautiful tapestries.

Safari Market Place, *1403 W. 111th St., Chicago,*
(773) 233-8307. Open daily.

Wide array of African goods sold, including kente dolls, Zulu beaded dolls, postcards, clothing, and fabric. The store also displays African art in a small gallery. Custom framing.

African Wonderland Imports, *4713 N. Broadway St., Chicago, (773) 334-2293. Open daily.*

Hand-made African art, leather goods, baskets, jewelry, clothing, and ceremonial drums. Owned an operated by Zack Ajayi, a Nigerian immigrant. Located in Uptown.

Restaurants

Soul Food and Southern-Style Restaurants

Army & Lou's, *422 E. 75th St., Chicago, (773) 483-6550. Open for lunch and dinner. Closed Tuesdays. Accepts credit cards.*

Serving up soul food at this location since 1945. Owners Avis and Benjamin Piper have maintained the same high standards in their cuisine, but have tried to incorporate low-fat and low-cholesterol methods into a style of cooking that is no longer consistent with the eating habits of salad-eating, granola-munching joggers. So you forget the diet for a day, that's all.

Jackie's Place, *425 E. 71st St., Chicago, (773) 483-4095. Open 24 hours. No credit cards.*

Specializing in short ribs of beef and other soul foods since 1968.

Nina's Restaurant, *5810 W. Madison St., Chicago, (773) 921-5062. Open for breakfast and lunch daily and dinner Tuesday–Saturday. No credit cards.*

Soul food. Daily luncheon specials.

Barbara's Restaurant, *353 S. 51st St., Chicago, (773) 624-0087. Open for breakfast, lunch, and dinner daily. No credit cards.*

Soul food, including ham hocks, plus roast beef, chicken, and fish.

Richard's Jamaica Club & Restaurant, *303 E. 61st St., Chicago, (773) 363-0471. Open for breakfast, lunch, and dinner daily. No credit cards. Free parking.*

"Blue Monday" every week means chicken.

Alexander's Restaurant, *3010 E. 79th St., Chicago,*
(773) 768-6555. Open for lunch and dinner daily.
Credit cards accepted.

The house specialties include prime rib and roast beef. Live jazz on Thursdays. Music provided by the Jazz Masters in conjunction with Jazz Unites. According to the owners, the Jazz Masters are destined for greatness. Come and see the South Side's best-kept secret. Alexander's has been a South Side institution for more than 50 years.

Soul Queen, *9031 S. Stony Island Ave., Chicago,*
(773) 731-3366. Open for lunch and dinner
daily.

Specialties include short ribs, chitterlings, red beans and rice, sweet potato pie, peach cobbler. All-you-can-eat buffet.

Dixie Kitchen & Bait Shop, *5225 S. Harper Ave.,*
Chicago, (773) 363-4943. Open for lunch and
dinner daily.

The owner describes the menu as "pan-Southern" and "Southern roadside dining," which means you'll find Creole, soul food, Cajun, and other dishes considered quintessentially "Southern." Specialties include hot johnnycakes, fried green tomatoes, crab and corn fritters, gumbos, jambalaya, and blackened catfish.

Brother Jimmy's BBQ, *2909 N. Sheffield, Chicago,*
(773) 528-0888. Open for lunch Saturdays and
Sundays and dinner daily.

Carolina cooking meets Tex-Mex. Featuring basted, spice-rubbed, and smoked barbeque. Sunday brunch. Live blues and soul music on Friday and Saturday nights.

Heaven on Seven (The Garland Café), *Garland*
Building, 111 N. Wabash Ave., 7th Floor, Chicago,
(312) 263-6443. Open for breakfast and lunch
Monday–Saturday. Dinner served the first and third
Friday of every month.

Inexpensive Cajun dishes. The twice-monthly dinner is accompanied by a live jazz band. Considered one of Chicago's best-kept secrets.

Soul Kitchen, *1576 N. Milwaukee Ave., Chicago,*
(773) 342-9742. Open for dinner daily.

The food and music share top billing at the Soul Kitchen. The menu includes traditional southern cuisine, Cajun and Creole from New Orleans, and Caribbean specialties. The "upbeat, funky soul music," while not live, is still an integral part of the experience.

Savannah's, *1156 W. Grand Ave., Chicago,*
(773) 666-9944. Open for dinner daily.

This is the place for Low Country cuisine. This style of cooking comes from the South Carolina coast and is heavily influenced by West African tradition. Crab cakes, oyster sausage, and steak stuffed with smoked oysters and mushrooms are some of the more popular dishes.

Outlying Areas

Hecky's Barbecue, *1902 Green Bay Rd., Evanston,*
(847) 492-1182. Open for lunch and dinner daily.

Chicago Tribune columnist Mike Royko is known to cook up a mean rack of ribs, but our award for spicy Chicago barbecue goes to Hecky's carry out restaurant in Evanston. The smell of cooking ribs permeates the neighborhood, as anyone who lives or works near this part of Evanston will tell you. Smoked duck is the latest addition to the menu, which also includes fried seafood, barbecued chicken, turkey, and links. Catering available. *Recommended.*

African Restaurants

Ethiopian Village, *3462 N. Clark St., Chicago,*
(773) 929-8300. Open for dinner daily. Credit cards
accepted.

Authentic Ethiopian cuisine at modest prices. Live entertainment included on the weekends. Daily vegetarian buffet.

Moulibet, *3521 N. Clark St., Chicago,*
(773) 929-9383. Open for dinner daily. Credit
cards accepted.

Vegetarian and non-vegetarian Ethiopian food served in an amicable storefront location, with live entertainment on the weekends.

Mama Desta's Red Sea Restaurant, *3218 N. Clark St., Chicago, (773) 935-7561. Open for lunch Tuesday–Sunday and dinner daily. Credit cards accepted.*

Fine Ethiopian foods, including chicken, lamb, beef, and vegetarian dishes.

Vee Vee's African Restaurant and Cocktails, *6243 N. Broadway St., (773) 465-2424. Open for lunch and dinner daily. Catering available.*

Predominantly Nigerian cuisine, featuring *ongbonu,* a tropical seed soup, and meat or fish stew with rice.

Addis Abeba, *3521 N. Clark St., Chicago, (773) 929-9383. Open for dinner daily.*

Ethiopian cuisine, including stir-fry chicken and a number of vegetarian dishes. Diners may reserve traditional Ethiopian place settings, which consist of platters of food placed in hand-woven baskets. Occasional live Ethiopian music.

Media

African American Video

African-American Images/Afro-Am Distributing Co., *1909 W. 95th St., Chicago, IL 60643, (773) 445-0322. Ordering number: 1-800-552-1991.*

This Chicago-based mail-order firm sells a full line of documentary videos pertaining to the African American experience in the United States, from the historical and sociological standpoint. A free catalog of titles is available by calling the office phone number during regular business hours.

Chicago Public Library, Dr. Martin Luther King, Jr. Branch, *3636 S. King Dr., Chicago, (773) 225-7543.*

This branch library loans out a number of historically important Hollywood movies that portray blacks in prominent roles or deal with African American themes.

Chinese Chicago

═══════════ **History and Settlement** ═══════════

Eight Chinese laundrymen lived and worked in Chicago the year before the Great Fire of 1871. Their names are lost to history, swept away in the conflagration that reduced the city to ashes and sorely tested the "I Will" spirit of Chicago. Historian Paul Siu identified "Opium Dong," one of the eight, who sold his grocery store to T. C. Moy, who arrived from San Francisco in 1878. Because so little information is available about Opium Dong, T. C. Moy enjoys the distinction of being the first known permanent Chinese settler in Chicago. He lived in a wooden shanty on the teeming West Side, but moved to Clark Street, north of the Chicago River, a few months later.

Life was good in Chicago, Moy reported in glowing terms to his relatives in Hong Kong. There were no discriminatory head taxes or contract labor, and the virulent racism of local whites who competed for scarce jobs during the building of the Transcontinental Railroad was greatly diminished in Chicago. By 1878 Moy had convinced sixty friends and relatives to embark on the perilous journey to Chicago. "They never said to me that the Chinese have got the perfection of crimes of 4,000 years," Moy recalled years later. "They never asked me whether or not I ate rats and snakes. The Chicagoans found us a peculiar people, to be sure, but they liked to mix with us. I was destined not to return to my fatherland, I thought." Even today, the Moy family continues to influence the social and cultural life of Chinatown.

They came slowly, at first. The Exclusion Act signed into law by President Chester A. Arthur in May 1882 stemmed the tide of Chinese immigration for the next twenty years or so. In 1890, 500 Chinese huddled together in dingy hovels along South Clark Street—the squalid vice district know as the Custom House Place Levee. Dr. Wu Ting-Fang, a community organizer and a man of profound insights, realized that if his people were to escape the lowest rung of the social order and prosper in Chicago, it was necessary for the immigrants to disperse across the city. Ting-Fang devised an ingenious strategy. His people would bridge the cultural differences by opening Chinese restaurants that catered to the American public. The first "chop suey" house, King Joy Lo, was located at Dearborn and Randolph. Curious Chicagoans flocked to the restaurant to sample traditional Cantonese dishes. It was a first for the city.

Typical Chinese restaurants of this period featured orchestras and public dancing. But the immigrants arriving from the Port of Canton (the only one open to foreign powers after 1840) were peasant farmers. Few of them were able to make good use of their skills in the large urban centers of the U.S. Instead, most became laundrymen, especially after 1869, when the transcontinental railroad was completed and thousands of contract workers found themselves unemployed. The laundries and restaurants were a peculiarity of the Chinese immigration, since there was a scarcity of laundries and even fewer restaurants in the homeland during this period. By 1900 there were 1,179 Chinese living in Chicago. Most came from the Sai-Ya district near Canton. According to the Lakeside Annual Directory for 1900, 239 of the 255 Chinese who were surveyed were employed as laundrymen. No doubt it was dirty, unpleasant work and a reflection of fierce anti-Chinese biases that denied these people a legitimate share of the American dream.

Ethnic prejudice was a factor in the 1905 uprooting of the immigrants from their homes in "Old Chinatown," in the Custom House Levee, to the modern-day location at 22nd and Wentworth on the South Side. The vice lords who ruled the South Loop from the time of the Chicago Fire until 1905 were a source of continuing embarrassment to the downtown businesspeople. The tippling rooms, panel houses, and wine rooms existed in the shadow of the majestic loop office buildings for years. In 1905 the state's attorney, backed by various civic agencies, drove them south to 22nd and Wabash. At the same time, no provisions were made for the Chinese, who were made to feel equally unwelcome. The anti-Chinese hysteria that had spread eastward in the three decades following the completion of the transcontinental railroad infected the Custom House Place landlords, who raised their rents to exorbitant levels. With no other recourse, the Chinese followed the criminal gangs and vice lords southward to 22nd and Wentworth—the fringe of Chicago's notorious levee district.

The Chinese in Chicago, 1870–1960

Year	Population
1870	1
1880	250
1890	567
1900	1,179
1910	1,778
1920	2,353
1930	2,757
1940	2,013
1950	3,334
1960	5,082

The evil specter of racial prejudice made assimilation into the American culture exceedingly difficult, despite the Chinese capacity for hard work and perseverance. The 22nd Street district on the near South Side was a "badlands." Rents were generally cheap, but police protection was minimal. Open lawlessness and vice in its lowest forms tested the spirits of these hearty immigrants, banished as they were by the city fathers.

It was not so surprising that this unsavory environment fostered criminality within the community. The early 1900s gave rise to the secret societies or "Tongs," which numbered twelve by 1912. Some of these Tong gangs did much good during the early years, providing the community with mutual assistance programs, cultural identity, and a small but certainly viable political lobby. In 1910 Dr. Sun Yat Sen visited Chicago, where he was greeted by a delegation of several hundred Chinese. He imparted to them the idea of organizing a "revolutionary" society in the city. A year later a branch of the Chinese Nationalistic League was formed. The Chicago chapter, a branch of a nationwide movement, was aimed at bringing down the Manchu Dynasty. But as the years passed, members of this secret society concerned themselves more with the advancement of economic issues and working conditions.

Similar to the aims of the Nationalistic League was the Mon Sang Association, organized in 1918 to fight inadequate wages and excessive working hours. In the first decade of the twentieth century Chinese restaurant workers toiled an average of fourteen hours a day. Poor wages denied many of the immigrant men the opportunity to send for their wives and family members stranded in China. The Mon Sangs addressed this grievance, providing members a forum for public debate, music clubs, reading rooms, classes for instruction in Chinese and English, and health insurance programs. The Mon Sangs looked past religious, social, and family issues to become the largest, most influential organization in the community.

The most serious problems facing Chinatown's leaders were the criminal activities of two Tong gangs: the Hip-Sings and the On-Leongs, existing for the purpose of protecting the lucrative gambling rackets and opium trade within the neighborhood. Gambling was a popular diversion for the immigrants, notably lotteries (called *tze-fa*), *fan-tan*, and *tinkou*. Two types of gambling houses had sprung up within the community. One was the establishment given over entirely to games of chance, the other was a commercial business, with back rooms reserved for wagering. Gambling reached the height of its popularity in New Chinatown before the Depression. By 1938 there were only eight gambling dens left in the neighborhood. Declining economic conditions forced many to close their doors. For many years, though, the Hip-Sings and On-Leongs fought a series of protracted gang wars to resolve territorial issues and spheres of influence. The Hip-Sings were composed of members from "Old Chinatown," at Harrison and Clark. The much larger On-Leong gang had its roots near 22nd and Wentworth. Differences were finally resolved through the careful mediation of Chin Kung Fong. Today the On-Leong Merchant's Association and the Hip-Sing engage in much more peaceful endeavors, as they work toward the betterment of the community.

The absence of family life, due to the exclusion laws, no doubt contributed to the crime problem. In 1910 there were 1,713 Chinese men living in Chicago, but only 65 women. This situation began to change after 1943, when the Exclusion Act was repealed by Congress. Non-quota status was given to wives of the Chinese citizens in 1946, which permitted them to stream into the United States without government interference. Through the 1940s, Chinatown continued to serve as the focal point of community life in Chicago. This too began to change, especially after the 1949 Revolution in China, which brought to Chicago a new class of immigrants—the urban professionals. These new arrivals were for the most part Mandarin, and they had little in common with the Cantonese who first settled Chicago. Separated by language differences and cultural links to the homeland, the Mandarin Chinese dispersed across the city and into the Western suburbs. The presence of hospitals and universities on the North Side, in particular, led to a "clustering" of Chinese along Clark Street, Broadway, and other major thoroughfares near the lakefront.

The "New" Chinatown community, extending between Sheridan Road and Broadway along Argyle Street on the city's North Side, is symbolic of the changing realities of postwar immigration. When the Federal Detention Center was erected in the South Loop in 1970, the displaced Hip-Sing Association was forced to seek new headquarters. Under the guidance of noted restaurateur Jimmy Wong, the North Side Chinatown was founded. But to a majority of Chicagoans, the traditional Chinatown will always be the Wentworth Avenue corridor.

In many ways the Wentworth Avenue Chinatown is a hermetically sealed environment. There are residents there who do not speak a word of English. Many of them have lived in the community for fifty years but rarely venture past the street signs marked with Chinese characters. These first-generation Chinese from Taiwan, Hong Kong, and the People's Republic remain relatively unassimilated. It is estimated that 9,000 people live within a narrow ten-block radius. The expanding Chinatown has had its problems in recent years acquiring the land necessary to relieve the residential clog. The Santa Fe Company rejected the community's bid for the abandoned property north of Cermak Road, much of it comprised the old levee before it was turned into rail yards. At one point, city planners envisioned a multi-purpose sports stadium on the site, but that, too, was canceled.

Chicago's Chinatown is a major tourist attraction that has come a long way from its humble beginnings in the early 1900s. Covering eight square blocks of land that was once hemmed in by railroad yards and now by expressways, the future of the community seems assured, due to the steady influx of new immigrants each year from Taiwan and mainland China, and to the new Chinatown Square retail and commercial mall at Archer Avenue and Wentworth. Between 1970 and 1980, the population grew from 14,077 to 29,000, spurred by the U.S. government's decision to relax immigration

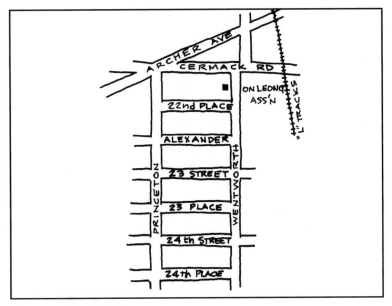

Chinatown (South Side)

requirements following the normalization of relations with the People's Republic of China.

Though many of the older residents are buying homes in nearby Bridgeport, Chinatown is still a residential as well as commercial area. New neighborhoods are taking shape in the abandoned rail yards to the immediate north. "It is the dream of all people in Chinatown to see the community expand," explained Ping Tom, an enthusiastic civic booster and past president of the Chicago Chinatown Chamber of Commerce, who was born in the heart of the neighborhood in 1935. Ping Tom formed a corporation in 1984 to negotiate the purchase of thirty-two acres of the blighted Santa Fe property.

Chinatown Square, fulfilling the vision of Mr. Tom and the Chinese-American Development Corporation, opened in 1992, and added twenty-one new residential units tailored to traditional Chinese custom. The town homes were equipped with small efficiency rooms for parents and relatives. Retailers were excited by the prospects of a 100,000-square-foot Asian trade center. An Oriental garden and a colorful festival square designed by Harry Weese & Associates promised to be an aesthetic delight amid the frantic hustle of Asian commerce.

The new town homes proved to be in great demand, but the occupancy rate of the retail shops fell well below expectations by the time Chinatown Square was officially open for business. "After all, how many more Chinese restaurants can we open?" complained one Wentworth Avenue business owner.

The new concourse featuring a performance facility known as the Pan Asian Cultural Center, was criticized as being sterile and too far removed from the bustling community life south of 22nd Street. However, the demand for affordable housing has not lessened. In the coming years the Chinese-American Development Corporation foresees additional expansion west to Canal. Perhaps there will be as many as 600 new town homes and apartments that will stretch the boundaries of Chinatown well past Ashland Avenue. But it will all depend on the patterns of post-1997 emigration out of Hong Kong.

Visitors to Chinatown encounter a fascinating collage of ethnic sights, sounds, and smells. Whole cooked chickens and ducks hang in the windows of the groceries and delicatessens. At 22nd Place and Wentworth on a busy Saturday afternoon, Italian produce wholesalers unload their goods on the street, while Chinese shoppers sift through the wooden packing crates searching for only the freshest vegetables and fruit to take home for the evening meal.

The grocery stores and gift shops are stacked to the ceilings with exotic foreign spices, herbs, wind chimes, books, Oriental teakwood furniture, artwork, cooking utensils, porcelain tea sets, Chinese fabrics, and, of course, the usual tourist kitsch from Hong Kong and Japan. The overcrowded stores bursting to the seams with merchandise arranged haphazardly and seemingly without purpose are the most successful, by neighborhood standards.

The temple-like Pui Tak Center (formerly the On-Leong Building), 2216 S. Wentworth Avenue, anchors the commercial district of Chinatown. Its reception hall represents the one and only indigenous Chinese shrine in the Midwest. In years past, Chinatown was almost exclusively a bachelor community, and many of the single men who came to the United States to earn their livelihood rented apartment quarters on the second floor of this historic building. Built in 1928 by Michaelsen & Rognstad, the On-Leong Building fell into disrepair in later decades, acquiring an unsavory reputation as a notorious gambling den controlled by organized crime associates and patronized by community residents who played games of *Pai Gow, Fan Tan,* and *Mah-Jongg.* Agents of the FBI battered down the doors of the historic building on April 20, 1988, busting up an operation that netted its proprietors thousands of dollars a day. Chinatown has historically been fertile ground for Chicago's organized crime group known colloquially as the "outfit."

On-Leong remained shuttered and abandoned until 1993, when the Chinese Christian Church purchased the property for $1.4 million. Another $1 million was invested in general repairs.

Given a second chance in life, the building was reopened as the Pui Tak Center in 1995, offering English-language classes and outreach programs designed to help Chinese immigrants assimilate into the American culture. *Pui Tak* means "developing moral character and virtue," and in this sense the On-Leong Merchants Association has been restored to its original purpose. The literal translation of *On-Leong* means "prosperity and peaceful conduct."

The Chinatown branch of the Chicago Public Library in the new Galleria on the south end of Wentworth is another fascinating place to visit. Chinese-language books and cassettes account for nearly half of its total circulation. The Chinatown branch is the largest circulating branch library in the city. Albany Park, which serves a predominantly Korean and Jewish clientele on the far North Side, ranks second in the total number of circulating books. The people you see in the reading room are not simply reading newspapers for pleasure. They are digesting the stories and vicariously experiencing the outside world through the printed word.

The high premium attached to education in the Asian cultures is nowhere more evident than at the St. Therese Elementary School and Catholic Mission at 247 W. 23rd Street, which is built in the Chinese architectural style. The facility operates on an austere budget, but consistently produces one of the highest levels of education in the city. The elaborate sanctuary of the St. Therese Catholic Mission at 218 W. Alexander (about 100 feet off Wentworth) was originally an Italian parish when it was constructed in 1904. The adjacent Chinese garden manse and "Moongate" reflect the predominantly Asian culture of the neighborhood since that time. According to Chinese folklore, the Moongate wards off evil spirits.

It is the restaurants, however, representing the four regional styles of Chinese cooking, that draw the largest share of tourists to the neighborhood. The Eastern Region, especially in the provinces of Kiangsu and Chekiang, is best known for its redcooking method, which uses dark soy sauce simmered by low heat. Seafood and meat dishes sprinkled with a generous amount of vegetables and fresh bamboo shoots are characteristic of this region. The Northern Region dishes, coming from the Hopei, Honan, and Shantung Provinces, are lighter and milder. Scallions, leeks, and garlic are the preferred seasonings. In the Southern Region, stir-frying and blanching are the most popular cooking methods. Dishes braised in dark soy sauce and roasted for hot or cold plates are the standard fare in Canton and the surrounding areas. And finally, the Western Region, dominated by the Szechwan and Hunan provinces, offers up the hottest, most spicy dishes. Oil, mixed with hot spices, garlic, and scallions, seals in the taste of the ingredients.

The Wentworth Avenue Chinatown also remains the city's only real source for Dim Sum—the traditional Chinese tea brunch—which can be appreciated by the casual gourmet only with an empty stomach and an adventurous spirit.

Today Chinatown remains very much as it was fifty to sixty years ago: a slice of the Old World in the shadows of urban Chicago. You know you are there when you cross under the imposing Chinatown Gate at the corner of South Wentworth Avenue and Cermak. The tile-ornamented structure is the brainchild of George Cheung, a restaurateur and civic promoter who conceived the idea in 1971. Cheung led the campaign to raise $70,000 in city and private funds to build an arch that embodied ancient Chinese customs. Cheung envisioned a more contemporary motif, but architect Peter Fung decided to go with a more traditional approach. A number of the decorative tiles were shipped from Taiwan in 1973, but not nearly as many as originally planned, which led to some last-minute difficulties, since native craftspeople were not available to complete the project. Work continued right up to the moment of dedication in November 1975. The decorative panels on the pagoda contain messages of peace, harmony, and the spirit of cooperation between people—echoed in the words of Dr. Sun Yat-sen, who proclaimed that "the world is for all," and Chiang Kai-shek's admonition that mankind should respect "Propriety, Justice, Integrity, and Conscientiousness."

Getting There: Take the Lake-Dan Ryan elevated train in the Loop southbound from the Lake Street or Wabash stations. By bus southbound from the Loop, board the Wentworth (#24) bus, starting at

Clark and Wacker; the Archer (#62) bus, starting at State and Kinzie (get off at the Archer/Cermak stop and walk one block east); the Wallace-Racine (#44) bus, starting at State and Kinzie; or from the west, take the Cermak (#21) bus, starting at 54th and Cermak. By car from the south, exit the Dan Ryan Expressway (I-94) at the 22nd Street-Canalport turnoff. From the north, exit the Dan Ryan Expressway at 18th Street. From the Loop, drive south on Michigan Avenue to 22nd Street (Cermak Road), and turn right. Proceed west on Cermak for five blocks. There is a public parking lot at Wentworth and Cermak, on the right-hand side of the street.

For additional information, call the CTA at (312) 836-7000.

Attractions

Cultural Institutions

Cathay Gallery, *980 N. Michigan Ave., Chicago,*
(312) 951-1048. Open by appointment only.

A fine collection of Chinese museum-quality antiques, dating from the Neolithic period up to 1900 is included in the collection. Porcelain, ivory, jade, carvings, and snuff bottles round out the collection.

Annual Events and Celebrations

Chinatown New Year Parade and Lion Dance
January or February. For information, call
(773) 326-5320.

If you happen to be dining in one of the many fine Cantonese restaurants in Chinatown during the day of the big New Year Parade (which is always held the Sunday after Chinese New Year's Day in February), do not be too surprised if a ferocious looking man-lion, decked out in black and red sweatpants and a papier-mâché head seasoned with herbs and the blood of a rooster, comes bursting through the front door. It is customary for the lion (costumed members of the Chicago Lion Dancers, who perform at the Chinese Community Center, 250 W. 22nd Place), to accept gifts of food and money from the house as a way of fending off evil spirits in the coming year. This is but one of many traditions that are carefully maintained in Chinatown, which remains a tightly woven, highly insulated community, despite the presence of so many out-of-town tourists and local sightseers who crowd into the restaurants and shops near 22nd and Wentworth. During the New Year celebration, the local restaurants begin serving special seasonal banquets to patrons, many of whom are second- and third-generation Chinese who have left the neighborhood, but are lured back for sentimental reasons. The annual parade begins at the corner of 24th Place and Wentworth Avenue, and ends at Cermak Road and Princeton Avenue. Because the date of the Chinese New Year changes every year, it is necessary to check with the local Chamber of Commerce before February. *Recommended.*

Chinatown Summer Fair, *held on Wentworth Avenue. Last Sunday in July or first Sunday in August. Call the Chinese Community Center at (773) 225-6198 for dates and times. Admission is free.*

Showcase of Asian food, art, and dance. The main stage between 24th Street and 24th Place features Chinese, Japanese, Korean, and Philippine dance troupes. Chinese artists display their paintings and etchings, while vendors hawk traditional items such as lanterns, Indian silk scarves, and assorted Asian foods. A farmer's market begins mid-morning. Children's activities include a carnival in the main parking lot with puppeteers, clowns, and animals from the Lincoln Park Mobile Petting Zoo. This event lures upwards of 70,000 people, so it is advisable to take public transportation, if possible. The Summer Fair was originally conceived and developed by local restaurateur and noted long-distance runner George J. Cheung. It is now jointly sponsored by the Chinatown Chamber of Commerce, the Merchant's Association, and the American Legion Post.

Double-Ten Parade, *Sunday closest to October 10. Call the Chinese Community Center at (773) 225-6198 for information.*

Marks the overthrow of the Manchu dynasty by Sun Yat-Sen's Kuomintang (Nationalistic Party) in 1911. Lion dancers, marching groups, and music. The parade travels down Wentworth Avenue from 24th Place to Cermak and Princeton. The Double-Ten Parade observed its twenty-second anniversary in 1995.

Chinatown Moon Festival, *community parking lot at Cermak and Wentworth Ave. Held in September. Call (773) 326-5320 for information.*

One-day event held in the refurbished Chinatown parking lot. The proceeds benefit the Chinese Dragon Athletic Association, a youth sports league.

Olga Huncke Scholarship Dinner, *alternating*
restaurants in Chinatown. One Saturday night in June.
Call Eunice Wong at (773) 842-2820 for tickets, date,
and location.

At a time when there was considerable discrimination directed against the
Chinese immigrant population, the deeds of Olga Huncke, an American
educator assigned to the Chinatown community, were especially praisewor-
thy. For the generations of Chinese Americans who passed through the
Chicago Public School System, Olga Huncke was their first encounter with
Western-style education. For many years, Huncke taught kindergarten at the
John C. Haines Elementary School at 247 W. 23rd Place. Her spirit and dedication are remembered today in the form of scholarships awarded to
deserving students who best exemplify her virtues. The year 1992 marked
the twentieth anniversary dinner, which includes a scholarship presentation
to the recipients (typically fifteen to twenty students each year), dinner, and
musical entertainment. The dinner is always open to the public.

Chinese Lantern Festival, *Wentworth Ave.*
and Cermak Rd. Last two weeks in May. Call
(773) 326-5320 for information.

The Chinatown Chamber of Commerce inaugurated the Lantern Festival in
May 1996 to coincide with Asian-American Heritage Month. Highlights
include lantern-making demonstrations, a children's lantern parade, workshops, Chinese calligraphy demonstrations, cultural activities, and ancestral
tributes inside the Pui Tak Center (formerly the On-Leong Building).

New Chinatown (North Side)

Chinese New Year on Argyle, *January or February.*
Call Charlie Soo, (773) 728-1030, for information.

The Chinese New Year begins with the second new moon of winter, which
means that the date of the festive celebration varies from year to year. The
new year generally falls between the second and third weeks in February,
with lavish parades on both the North and South sides. The New Chinatown
parade, with a traditional lion dance and fireworks display, begins at Broadway, proceeds down Argyle, and ends at Sheridan Road. In 1991, there was
a special reason to celebrate. The new $100,000 pagoda, which drapes the
Argyle Street CTA elevated stop, was officially dedicated. The pagoda
symbolizes peace, unity, and prosperity for the area. The Asian-American
Small Businessmen's Association is confident that it will help establish
Argyle Street as the leading purveyor of Oriental food in the Midwest.

Depending on the schedule of events within the Chinese-American community each year, the North Side parade will usually follow the South Side festivities.

Outlying Areas

Hong Kong Film Festival, *School of the Art*
Institute, Columbus Dr. and Jackson Blvd.,
Chicago, (312) 443-3737 for a recorded message,
or (312) 443-3733 for general information.
Every spring.

Until Bruce Lee arrived, the Southeast Asian film industry was an unknown commodity in the West. But in the 1970s, Lee and dozens of imitators popularized the martial arts genre. The low budget "chop and slash" action films gave way to a new, more sophisticated style of movie-making. The School of the Art Institute sponsors the annual Hong Kong Film Festival as a part of its ongoing commitment to bringing the world a little closer to Chicago's doorstep through cinema. Students of the visual arts are afforded a chance to preview the films of some of the Orient's biggest stars, including Jackie Chan, Michael Hui, and Chow Yun-fatt.

Shops

Happy Garden Bakery, *two locations: 2140 S.*
Wentworth Ave., Chicago, (773) 225-2730,
and 227 W. Cermak, Chicago, (773) 842-7556.
Open daily (Cermak location closed on
Thursdays).

Fresh Chinese and French pastries, some gooey and sweet, can be eaten at a leisurely pace inside the store or carried out.

Keefer Bakery, Inc., *249 W. Cermak Rd., Chicago,*
(773) 326-2289. Open daily.

Try the Red Bean Lotus Cake or the Red Bean Puff for something delicious and totally out of the ordinary. Keefer has been at this location for over fifteen years. *Recommended.*

Dong Kee Company, *2252 S. Wentworth Ave.,*
Chicago, (773) 225-6340. Open daily.

Large, prosperous gift shop that sells a variety of Oriental foods, cooking utensils, wind chimes, tea, almond cookies, and dishware.

Woks 'n' Things, *2234 S. Wentworth Ave., Chicago,*
(773) 842-0701. Open daily.

One of the leading suppliers of Oriental cookware in the Midwest. Choose from a large selection of woks and the cookbooks that explain how to use them. Electronic appliances, hardware, and other related items are also found in the store.

Pacific Furniture, *2200 S. Wentworth Ave., Chicago,*
(773) 808-0456. Open daily. Credit cards accepted.

Elegant teakwood furniture, hand-crafted porcelain figurines, tea sets, masks, and some imported items from Japan. Wholesale and retail.

Mandar-Inn Gifts, *2319 S. Wentworth Ave., Chicago,*
(773) 326-5082. Open daily.

Porcelain floor vases, wall hangings, teakwood furniture, and tapestries. Popular with the tourists, and no longer owned by the Mandar-Inn Restaurant.

Dor Fook, *2410 S. Wentworth Ave., Chicago,*
(773) 326-1941. Open daily.

Jeweler and goldsmith who caters more to the neighborhood people than the tourist trade. Birthday, anniversary, and wedding plaques embossed on red velvet. Red is the traditional color of happiness in China.

Oriental Boutique, *2262 S. Wentworth Ave., Chicago,*
(773) 842-3798. Open daily.

China, jade, and Oriental gifts from Taiwan. Kung-fu supplies, slippers, and pajamas. Porcelain figurines.

Ten Ren Tea & Ginseng Co. of Chicago, Ltd., *2247*
S. Wentworth Ave., Chicago, (773) 842-1171. Open
daily.

The Ten Ren Co. of Taipei, Taiwan, owns and operates thirty-six chain stores and five factories worldwide that manufacture and sell ginseng—the "king of herbs." For generations, ginseng has long been regarded as a restorative elixir with a high concentration of effective nutrients. Ten Ren grows cultivated ginseng in a 120-acre plantation in Wisconsin, which is considered the ideal geographic location for ginseng-growing in North America today. Wisconsin Ginseng Co., Inc., a subsidiary of the parent company, harvests 500,000 pounds each year, much of it winding up in domestic markets such as this one. People come from all over the Midwest and the Great Plains states to purchase from among fifteen high-grade teas and ginseng at this branch location. There are always one or two samples available to taste.

Sun Sun Tong: Chinese Herb, Ginseng, Gifts, & Food Co., *2260 S. Wentworth Ave., Chicago, (773) 842-6398. Open daily. Credit cards accepted.*

Chinese herbs, ginseng, and nutritional health foods. Wholesale, retail, and mail order. Tea sets, vases, and figurines round out the gift line. Margaret Lau, the resident herbalist, is available on Sunday to answer your questions about the healing powers of ginseng.

That Porcelain Place, *2239 S. Wentworth Ave., Chicago, (773) 225-3888. The best oriental porcelain in the city. Open daily. Free U.P.S. service. Credit cards accepted.*

Bark Lee Tong: Ginseng, Tea & Herbs Company, *229 W. Cermak Rd., Chicago, (773) 225-1988. Open daily. No credit cards.*

A thousand different herbs, teas, and Chinese pharmaceuticals sold by Andy Hoi-Csiu Chan, owner of this family-run business that has been a fixture in the Chinatown community for thirty-five years. Andy is also an artist in residence. He serves as president of the Chinese Artist's Association of North America, and is an art adviser to the People's Republic of China. In the basement underneath his herb store, Andy Chan teaches painting, conducts photography workshops, and hosts poetry readings for the Chinese-American community. Chinese art supplies, including rice paper, water colors, and brushes are available for purchase. For information about the workshops, poetry readings, and other ongoing creative activities within the Chinatown neighborhood, ask for Andy Chan. *Recommended.*

Tai Wah Grocery, *2226 S. Wentworth Ave., Chicago,*
(773) 326-4120. Open daily.

Barbecued hogs and ducks hang seductively in the window. Inside you'll
find some exotic Asian foods that you may want to try if you're in an adventurous frame of mind. Dried octopus, barracuda, and anchovy are sold in
clear plastic bags. That way, you can see just what it is you're getting yourself into. To wash this down, you may wish to sample imported sugar cane
juice, sold in pop-top cans.

Wing Chan Bar-B-Q, *2157 S. China Pl., Chicago,*
(773) 791-9389. Open daily.

The best spot in Chinatown for barbecued pork, chicken, and duck "to go."

World Journal & Bookstore, *2116 S. Archer,*
Chicago, (773) 842-8080. Open daily. Credit cards
accepted.

Chinese-language books, magazines, greeting cards, audio tapes, newspapers, and gift items.

New Chinatown (North Side)

Kim San Jewelry Sale and Gift Shop, *1008 W.*
Argyle St., Chicago, (773) 878-5666. Open daily.
No credit cards.

Toys, jewelry, Chinese shell art, and ceiling fans.

Double Happiness Bakery and Restaurant, *1061 W.*
Argyle St., Chicago, (773) 334-3735. Closed
Tuesdays.

Chinese bakery located in the front, with snack tables in the rear in case you
desire to indulge your sweet tooth on the spot.

Trung Viet Co., Inc., *4940-4942 N. Sheridan Rd.,*
Chicago, (773) 561-0042. Closed Tuesdays. No credit
cards.

Ethnic Chinese grocery that services the local restaurant trade. Frozen foods, Chinese herbs, bulk rice, meats, and fish.

Tan Thanh Books & Gift Co., *1135 W. Argyle St.,*
Chicago, (773) 275-8687. Open daily. Credit cards
accepted.

Specializing in a wide assortment of jade, figurines, wind chimes, audio cassettes, and Chinese magazines and newspapers.

Outlying Areas

Scholars Bookstore, *1379 E. 53rd St., Chicago,*
(773) 288-6565. Open daily.

Chinese-Japanese bookstore and full-line computer supplier. The store also sells Chinese audio tapes.

Restaurants

Emperor's Choice, *2238 S. Wentworth Ave., Chicago,*
(773) 225-8800. Open for lunch and dinner daily.
Credit cards accepted.

Seafood and poultry, especially Peking Duck (which you should order a day in advance) are the preferred menu choices at this modestly styled eatery housed in a former antiques store. You'll dine amid the emperors . . . whose likenesses are reproduced in paintings on the wall.

Chee King, *216 W. 22nd Pl., Chicago,*
(773) 842-7777. Open for lunch and dinner
daily. Credit cards accepted.

This modest storefront restaurant specializes in seafood but also offers the full gamut of Chinese cooking ranging from hot Szechwan and Hunan to the milder dishes of Canton. Peking duck is usually available at a moment's notice. Complete carryout service.

Hong Min, *221 W. Cermak Rd., Chicago,*
(773) 842-5026. Open for dim sum, lunch,
and dinner daily. Credit cards accepted.

An unassuming storefront restaurant specializing in Cantonese and Mandarin foods, especially seafood, and beef dishes. Most of the items on the menu are exceptional.

Sixty-Five, *2414 S. Wentworth Ave., Chicago,*
(773) 842-6500. Open for lunch and dinner
daily. Credit cards accepted.

Reasonably priced seafood restaurant that is always crowded. The reason is the outstanding food, which is always served in generous portions. Whether you have it steamed or stir-fried, you won't be disappointed. Family-style dinners are included on the menu.

Three Happiness, *2130 S. Wentworth Ave., Chicago,*
(773) 791-1228. Open for dim sum, lunch, and dinner
daily. Credit cards accepted.

A large, spacious eatery that quickly fills to capacity when the dim sum carts roll out of the kitchen during the mid-day. You'll want to sample the steamed dumplings, a rich assortment of cold meats, and some very fine Chinese pastries. Dim sum is excellent. The regular menu items are only fair, by comparison.

Mandar-Inn Restaurant, *2249 S. Wentworth Ave.,*
Chicago, (773) 842-4014. Open for lunch and dinner.
Closed Mondays.

A neighborhood institution that serves the four main styles of Chinese cooking: Mandarin, Cantonese, Hunan, and Szechwan.

Royal Pacific Restaurant, *2217 S. Wentworth Ave.,*
Chicago, (773) 842-4444. Open for lunch and dinner
daily. Credit cards accepted.

Specializing in tropical drinks and Cantonese dishes. A large, spacious restaurant on two stories. The second-floor window seating offers a fine view of Wentworth Avenue and the imposing On-Leong Merchant's Building. No dim sum. *Recommended.*

Cantonesia, *204 W. Cermak Rd., Chicago, (773) 225-0100. Open for lunch and dinner daily. Credit cards accepted. Free parking in the rear of the building.*

Cantonese and Szechwan food. Full bar service, business luncheons, and banquet rooms available for up to 100 people.

Moon Palace Mandarin Restaurant, *216 W. Cermak Rd., Chicago, (773) 225-4081. Open for lunch and dinner daily. Credit cards accepted.*

Hot and spicy food and poultry and pork dishes are the specialties here. Full cocktail service, banquet rooms, and carry-out, but no dim sum.

Wing Wah Restaurant, *208 W. Cermak Rd., Chicago, (773) 225-4611, or (773) 225-2817. Open for dim sum, lunch, and dinner daily.*

This restaurant is the old Lung Fung, but under a new name and at a new location. Wing Wah specializes in Cantonese and Mandarin food, and is always crowded.

Junk Restaurant and Lounge, *2143 S. Archer Ave., Chicago, (773) 326-3311. Open for dinner daily. Credit cards accepted.*

Located in the "suburbs of Chinatown," an appropriate description supplied by owner George Cheung. It was Cheung who spearheaded the drive to construct the colorful Chinatown Gateway arch, which opened in 1975 and spans Wentworth Avenue at Cermak Road. The civic-minded Cheung was born and raised in Chicago, and is the cofounder of the Junk Running Club, headquartered in his popular restaurant and bar across the street from the Chinatown Square shopping mall and commercial center. The Cheungs have been in business for over twenty years, serving the usual Chinese standbys with such exotic names as "Shanghai Sally," "Captain's Delight," and the "Coolie Caper." The atmosphere is pleasing, and a trip to the "suburbs" is highly recommended the next time you visit Chinatown. Full cocktail service.

King Wah Restaurant, *2225 S. Wentworth Ave., Chicago, (773) 842-1404. Open for lunch and dinner daily. Credit cards accepted.*

Since 1962, the Lee family has made frequent trips to Hong Kong and Taiwan to keep up-to-date with the latest techniques in ethnic Chinese cooking. The result: some excellent Cantonese and Mandarin menu items, including the chef's special—spicy chicken and shrimp. The Marco Polo steak and tea-smoked duck are also recommended. One of the more upscale restaurants on the street.

Evergreen, *2411 S. Wentworth Ave., Chicago,*
(773) 225-8898. Open for lunch and dinner daily.
Credit cards accepted.

Szechwan, Hunan, and Cantonese cooking. This is one of the newer China-town restaurants, located near the Galleria on the south end of Wentworth Avenue.

New Chinatown (North Side)

Sun Wa Bar B-Q, *1134 W. Argyle St., Chicago,*
(773) 769-1254. Open for lunch and dinner daily.
Credit cards accepted.

Located in what used to be a Japanese restaurant. This modest establishment moved here from New York several years ago. Standard Chinese food served, with a mixture of barbecue dishes, including pig, duck, and chicken. Carry-out service available in the front.

Furama Restaurant, Inc., *4936 N. Broadway St.,*
Chicago, (773) 271-1161. Open for lunch
Monday–Friday, breakfast and dinner daily.
Credit cards accepted.

Spacious two-story Chinese restaurant that was an automotive repair garage in its former life. With a little imagination, you might be able to visualize lube jobs and ball joint repairs as you dine on your dim sum (served for breakfast and lunch daily).

Mei Shung, *5511 N. Broadway St., Chicago,*
(773) 728-5778. Open for lunch and dinner.
Closed Mondays.

Serving both Mandarin and Taiwanese cuisine. Specialties include julienne pork in piquant satay sauce, coriander-topped tofu in oyster sauce, and braised-beef noodle soup.

Song Song, *1138 W. Argyle St., Chicago,*
(773) 271-6552. Open for lunch and dinner,
lunch only on Tuesdays. Credit cards accepted.

Chinese cuisine.

Media

Bang Bang Video & Audio, *2337 S. Wentworth Ave.,*
Chicago, (773) 326-9888. Open daily. Credit cards accepted.

Chinese movies from Hong Kong available for sale or rental. Magazines, newspapers, and audio cassettes are also stocked.

Asian Chicago

═ Multiethnic History and Settlement ═

Although they account for less than 4 percent of the Chicago metropolitan population, the combined Asian communities are the fastest-growing ethnic group in the Chicago area. The Asian population increased 70 percent between 1980 and 1988. The 1990 census found that Filipinos accounted for 0.87 percent of the total Chicago metropolitan area population; Asian Indians, 0.78 percent; Chinese, 0.59 percent; Koreans, 0.5 percent; Japaneses, 0.26 percent; and Vietnamese, 0.1 percent. There is a growing Thai community as well. There are Asian pockets in Cook, Du Page, and Will counties, but the greater number of Asian Americans reside in nine wards on the north and northwest sides.

With the loosening of immigration restrictions, and continuing political strife in Southeast Asia, thousands of Koreans, Filipinos, Thais, Vietnamese, and Cambodians swelled this previously small part of the metropolitan area's population. The 1980 census placed their collective number at 166,000. This upward trend is consistent with recent patterns of immigration across the United States. Though language barriers, cultural differences, climatic changes, and housing and employment discrimination are obstacles to progress, Asian immigrants quickly broke these barriers down. Hard work, self-reliance, and a penchant for resourcefulness turned one economically depressed crime-ridden Chicago neighborhood into a major wholesale center of Southeast Asian commerce.

Before 1980, the neighborhood around Argyle and Broadway was a neglected corner of Uptown, a faded, blowsy area overrun by street people, substance abusers, and an economically displaced underclass victimized by various social forces. Since then, Uptown has been on the rebound. It's been given new life by Vietnamese businesspeople who opened grocery stores and restaurants alongside Chinese merchants, who sought to expand the boundaries of the South Side Chinatown.

Argyle and Broadway, known variously as Little Saigon, Little Hanoi, or New Chinatown, is an ethnic success story that draws on values the Asian cultures hold in high esteem: honor, a sense of obligation to the family and society at large, and a profound respect for education. Much attention has been focused on the achievements of Asian children in the U.S. school systems, and their parents in the white-collar sectors of the economy. According to the most recent census data, Asian Americans are more likely than white, Hispanic, or African Americans to hold down professional jobs.

Asians have often been stereotyped as "model minorities." Their high-profile academic and business achievements have brought mixed blessings. On the one hand, American educators marvel at this work ethic. (A 1986 survey commissioned by the U.S. Department of Education found that half of all Asian American high school sophomores spend five hours per week on homework assignments. Contrast this with whites, who spend a third of that time on homework, and African Americans, who spends a quarter of the time. Yet community leaders are quick to point out that these success stories often ignore the economic hardships that many refugees encounter when they make the transition from rural to urban life. Foreign-born Asian Americans are also more likely to hold down the lowest-paying jobs on the bottom rungs of the employment ladder: domestic, manual labor, or table busing.)

One should not, however, generalize when speaking about Chicago's multinational Asian population. Each is group unique, and each would bristle at the thought of being pigeon-holed into one category. Philippine history, for example, is marked by both Hispanic and other Western influences. Within China alone there are more than a hundred nationalities. There are four regional dialects in Thailand, where Buddhism is the prevailing religion. The Vietnamese are also predominantly Buddhist, but there is an overlay of Western influence that lingers from the French colonial period.

These Asian peoples have not yet had much influence on the political process in Chicago. A failure to close ranks in order to achieve a common purpose has retarded progress in the public sector. In 1983 an Asian American Coalition was founded. It is an umbrella group formed to close the cultural and political gulf separating the Asian nationalities. The late Mayor

Harold Washington helped open the door to Asians, who have forced Illinois politicians to re-evaluate their policy toward ethnic groups.

Ken Moy, a Chinese American attorney, is the highest-ranking politician to occupy an office in the tricounty area. He has been a member of the Du Page County Board since 1984. In 1990, an Indian American attorney named Ahmed Patel was slated to run for a Cook County judgeship on the Democratic ticket; another first. Even though Mr. Patel was overwhelmed in the general election by former state's attorney Bernard Carey, and the Asian American population is still not considered large enough to be a crucial swing vote in statewide elections, nearly every major officeholder now has an Asian liaison officer on staff.

Politicians no longer take for granted the Asians' quiet presence and past silence concerning issues of importance. Beginning in the late 1980s, North Side community leaders would set up voting registration booths along the 1200 block of Argyle Street with hopes of registering the 10,000-strong Asian vote. Cook County pols turn out in full force for the annual Lunar New Year Banquet, a cross-cultural social function for the dozen or so Asian ethnic groups scattered across the city. It is testimony to the growing political awareness and voting strength of a segment of the population that will become the trend-setters of the twenty-first century and beyond.

Cultural Institutions

Lizzardo Museum of Lapidary Art, *220 Cottage Hill, Elmhurst, (630) 833-1616. Closed Mondays. Admission fee charged every day except Friday.*

This is one of the largest private collections of Asian jade and ivory in the country. The permanent collection contains more than 150 exhibits, including gemstones, fossils, cameos, and carvings.

Decoro, *224 E. Ontario St., Chicago, (312) 943-4847. Closed Sundays and Mondays.*

The collection includes an interesting variety of antique Japanese kimonos and *mingei* art, Korean *bandaji* chests, and traditional Chinese rugs, chairs, and cabinets.

Saito Oriental Antiques, *645 N. Michigan Ave., Chicago, (312) 642-4366. Closed Sundays. No credit cards.*

Fourth floor at Michigan Avenue and Erie Street. Museum-quality antiques, bronzes, porcelain, and lacquerware from the Shang and Ching Dynasties.

Korean art and Japanese screens, *ukiyo-e* prints, and ivory carvings. Two years at this location.

Asian House of Chicago, *159 W. Kinzie St., Chicago, (312) 527-4848. Closed Sundays.*

Wholesale and retail works of art and antiques from the Orient. Included in the collection are finely crafted porcelain vases, Byobu screens, ornate rosewood furniture, Thai bronzes and tapestries, fishbowls, hand-carved jade, and lamps. Located east of the Merchandise Mart.

Tobai International, *320 N. Dearborn St., Chicago, (312) 661-0394. Closed Sundays and Mondays. Credit cards accepted.*

Original Japanese watercolors, antique paintings and decorative chests from Korea, hand-painted porcelains, selected pieces of artwork from China, Japanese Tansu, and lighting fixtures.

Annual Events and Celebrations

Asian American Coalition of Chicago Annual Lunar New Year Celebration. *January or February. Call Irene Cuatoping at (773) 630-6882 for tickets, date, and location.*

Organized for the purpose of fostering greater political, social, and economic cooperation between the diverse cultures, the coalition is comprised of fourteen different ethnic groups representing Chicago's South and Southeast Asian communities. A banquet has been held in February each year since 1984, revolving around a different theme each time. In 1991, the coalition's slogan was "Together We Can." The location varies from year to year, depending on the preferences of the particular committee responsible for planning the event. During the last three years, the Lunar New Year Celebration has been held at the Hyatt Regency O'Hare, New Grand Ballroom, 9300 W. Bryn Mawr Avenue, Rosemont. Between 1,000 and 1,700 people have attended each year for the past eight years. Since the banquet rotates among the fourteen representative groups in the coalition, it is likely that the location may change in the future. Dinner, guest speakers, and musical entertainment are included in the ticket price. The coalition does not have a central office, so interested parties are encouraged to call Irene Cuatoping.

Argyle Fest, *between Broadway and Sheridan Road. Last weekend in August. Free admission. Call (773) 728-1030.*

One-day Asian-American street festival. Argyle Fest is a coordinated venture of the Chinese Mutual Aid Association, the Vietnamese Association of Illinois, the new Chinatown Chinese Council, and the Asian-American Small Businessmen's Association. This ethnic fair, featuring food vendors from local restaurants, clowns, arts and crafts, Asian and American music, dancers, and children's events, has been held annually since 1985, and lures 15,000 people to the neighborhood. *Recommended.*

Asian Small Business Conference, *Furama Restaurant, 4936 N. Broadway, Chicago. Saturday closest to October 24. Call Charlie Soo, (773) 728-1030, for information. Admission is free (subject to change).*

October 24 is United Nations Day, which sets this conference in its intended context. Charlie Soo chose this date to demonstrate the purpose of his conference: to encourage unity among Asian business owners in the city, especially on Argyle Street. Local politicians, civic and community leaders, and business people deliver a series of presentations while the other participants and members of the audience enjoy Furama's acclaimed dim sum.

Shops

Tiem Vang A Chau (Asian Jewelers), *1019 W. Argyle St., Chicago, (773) 878-0083. Closed Mondays.*

Exclusive jade and gold jewelry imported from Hong Kong by owner Julie Hoa, whose family runs the Nhu Hoa Restaurant across the street. The store will buy scrap gold. Watch and jewelry repair on the premises.

Pailin Gifts, *1114 W. Argyle St., Chicago, (773) 275-7754. Open daily. No credit cards.*

A Cambodian-owned business specializing in porcelain figurines, audio cassettes, watches, jewelry, and other gift items

Kim Huot, Inc., *1107A W. Argyle St., Chicago, (773) 769-6190. Open daily. Credit cards accepted.*

Gold items, gifts, children's dolls, fine silks, shoes, perfumes, and bedspreads. Chaotic, but interesting.

New Chinatown Bakery and Coffee Shop, *1019 ½*
W. Argyle St., Chicago, (773) 784-1700. Open daily.
No credit cards.

Opened in November 1990. Chinese and Vietnamese bakery items, with an adjacent dining area.

New Hong Kong Bakery, *1050-52 W. Argyle St.,*
Chicago, (773) 878-3226. Open daily.

Oven-fresh bakery products, and all kinds of Chinese and American pastries. Everything is baked on the premises.

Mien Hoa Market, Inc., *1108-1110 W. Argyle St.,*
Chicago, (773) 334-8393. Open daily.

Grocery, delicatessen items, and candies.

Mya Market, *1100 W. Argyle St., Chicago,*
(773) 878-7126. Open daily.

Formerly a drug store. Now it's a full-line Asian grocery store. Things change fast on Argyle Street.

Restaurants

Thai Binh Restaurant, *1113 W. Argyle St., Chicago,*
(773) 728-0283. Open for lunch and dinner daily.
Credit cards accepted.

Catonese, Szechwan, Vietnamese, and Thai cuisine. Two separate dining rooms that don't seem to be too busy on Saturdays. This restaurant recently underwent an expansion.

══ Japanese History and Attractions ══

Immigrants from the rural farming districts of Japan arrived in the United States in the late 19th century, but few made it as far as Chicago. Kameno-suke Nishi, who lived in San Francisco prior to the 1893 World's Fair, was among the first Japanese residents here. He made a fortune for himself operating a gift shop at the corner of Cottage Grove Avenue and 27th Street.

Not until the middle years of World War II did the Japanese community in Chicago begin taking shape. Beginning in 1942, a steady stream of former internment camp inmates established temporary residence in Chicago's Little Tokyo, near Clark and Division. The proliferation of Japanese Americans, who had become refugees in their own country, were lured to the city by the abundance of light manufacturing, clerical, and wartime jobs. The city provided steady employment until the cessation of hostilities and the lifting of wartime restrictions that barred the Japanese from returning to their West Coast homes.

In 1945, a number of Chicago's *Nisei* (second-generation Japanese), who were concerned about the well-being of the former internees, organized the Japanese American Service Committee for the purpose of locating affordable housing and jobs in the private sector. The JASC was assisted in this endeavor by the United Way, the Community Trust, the Catholic Church, and the American Friends. The JASC marked its 50th year of service to the community in 1995.

Before Pearl Harbor, there were only 390 people of Japanese ancestry living in the city. Most were students living in Hyde Park-Kenwood dormitories and attending classes at the University of Chicago. Then, after the war, Japanese arrived in greater numbers until 1950, when the population stabilized at 10,829. These numbers increased only slightly in the next three decades, due in no small measure to improving economic conditions in postwar Japan.

The history of the Japanese settlement in Chicago is characterized by rapid assimilation and social mobility. The anti-Japanese phobia of the West Coast was never a factor in Chicago. Jobs were plentiful and the prejudicial attitudes of employers and landlords were minimized.

Buddhism, Japan's principal religion, teaches interdependence. Western cultures teach rugged individualism and the virtues of self-reliance. The success of the Japanese in the face of historic racial discrimination reflects the tenets of Buddhism: respect for the family and the educator, hard work, and pride in achievement. There is a high premium placed on success and, conversely, shame awaits those who do not produce.

The Japanese community that had once settled in Old Town was dispersed by commercial and residential development in the 1960s and 1970s. Sandburg Village, along Clark Street between Division and North, occupies a site formerly inhabited by many ethnic Japanese. All that remains of "Little Tokyo" is the Midwest Buddhist Temple, designed by Hideaki Arao and opened at Menomonee and Hudson avenues in 1972. Life continues to revolve around this North Side house of worship, even as more and more Japanese make their way into the suburbs.

As presently constituted, the Japanese are still one of the smallest ethnic groups in the suburban sprawl, but they have moved from the inner-city neighborhoods for much the same reasons as the Europeans: to ensure that their children will profit from better schools and drug-free environments.

What this ultimately means is a shift away from the activities revolving around such institutions as the temple, though the Futabakai Japanese Day School in Niles continues to instill Asian culture in the third and fourth generations.

Cultural Institutions

Japanese Cultural Center, *1016 W. Belmont Ave., Chicago, (773) 525-3141. Open daily.*

Year-round activities include classes and lectures in Zen meditation, traditional martial arts, Japanese language, and Japanese cultural ceremonies (including the tea ceremony).

Annual Events and Celebrations

Japanese Summer Festival (Natsu Matsuri), *1151 W. Leland Ave., Chicago. Saturday and Sunday before the Fourth of July weekend. Admission fee charged. For additional information, contact the Midwest Buddhist Temple at 435 W. Menomonee, Chicago, (773) 334-4661.*

A two-day fund-raising event sponsored by the Midwest Buddhist Temple. The Summer Festival has been going strong since 1945, featuring judo, aikido, kendo, and karate demonstrations; Japanese classical and folk dancing; flower arrangements, ceramics, and bonsai miniature plants. Plenty of Japanese food available on the grounds, including sushi, barbecued chicken teriyaki, and *yakisoba.* During the year, the temple conducts religious services, which are open to the public every Sunday morning following the meditation classes. The Midwest Buddhist Temple also sponsors Japanese language classes for adults at 1151 W. Leland, Chicago. Summer classes last seven weeks. Call the temple for information.

Obon Odori Festival, *Midwest Buddhist Temple, 435 W. Menomonee, Chicago, (773) 943-7801. Second Saturday evening in July. Admission is free.*

Also known as the Festival of Lanterns, because the *cho-ching* (paper lanterns) decorate the parking lot of the temple where the traditional folk dancing and Japanese music are enjoyed by the spectators. *Obon* means "a bowl or tray with which one serves guests," expressing hospitality and sincere welcome. It is in this spirit that the Obon Odori Festival is sponsored each year. The customary Obon religious service (*Hatsu-bon*), which honors the loved ones who have passed away during the previous year, is held the following morning.

Annual Ginza Holiday, *Midwest Buddhist Temple, 435 W. Menomonee, Chicago, (773) 943-7801. Third weekend in August. Donation requested.*

Three-day festival of Japanese culture, martial arts, demonstrations by the *Waza* master craftspeople from Japan, classical and folk dancing, Buddhist *Taiko* (drum) group, prize drawing, and ethnic cuisine held for the past thirty-six years. The event is named after the Ginza, a busy and colorful shopping center and street in the heart of Tokyo. Three hundred years ago, that area was a marshy swamp, inhabited by wild ducks. In 1873, housing construction began on the site. The Ginza became the first street in Japan with brick houses and pavement.

Shops

Japan Books and Records, *3450 W. Peterson Ave., Chicago, (773) 463-7755. Open daily.*

Located in the same building with Seoul Books and Records. Specializing in Japanese paperback books, magazines, and audio.

Scholars Bookstore, *1379 E. 53rd St., Chicago, (773) 288-6565. Open daily.*

Chinese-Japanese bookstore and full-line computer supplier. The store also sells Chinese audio tapes.

Kiyo's Oriental Gift Store, *2831 N. Clark St., Chicago, (773) 935-0619. Open daily. Credit cards accepted.*

Japanese gift items ranging from inexpensive kitsch up to fine porcelains, jewelry, and shoji screens. Try on the kimonos for size. Kiyo's has been at this location for over twenty years.

J. Toguri Mercantile Co., *851 W. Belmont Ave. (near Clark), Chicago, (773) 929-3500. Closed Sundays. Credit cards accepted.*

Japanese imports, including magazines, books, records, tapes, and household items such as tableware, lacquerware, and china (some of it actually coming from China).

Aiko's Art Material Import Co., *3347 N. Clark St.,*
Chicago, (773) 404-5600. Closed Sundays and
Mondays. No credit cards.

Chicago's leading supplier of Japanese art materials and handmade papers used for printmaking, bookbinding, screens, and book restoration. Japanese greeting cards, artwork, ceramics, and artist's tools are available for purchase.

Star Market, *3349 N. Clark St., Chicago,*
(773) 472-0599. Open daily. No credit cards.

One of the original ethnic Japanese groceries to open in Chicago. In business now for nearly forty years. Fresh fish, produce, and other perishables. Canned and frozen foods.

Outlying Areas

Asahiye Bookstores, U.S.A., Inc., *100 E. Chicago*
Ave., Mt. Prospect, (847) 228-9851. Closed Mondays.
Credit cards accepted.

This is a full-line Japanese magazine and bookstore, with a limited number of English-Japanese language-instruction manuals. No audio or video equipment.

Restaurants

Midori, *3310 W. Bryn Mawr Ave., Chicago,*
(773) 267-9733. Open for lunch Monday–Saturday
and dinner daily. Credit cards accepted.

Japanese restaurants tend to be among the most expensive of Asian cuisines. Midori is the exception, with the lunch and dinner menu very reasonably priced.

Restaurant Suntory, *11 E. Huron St., Chicago,*
(312) 664-3344. Open for lunch Monday–Friday
and dinner daily. Credit cards accepted.

Much like the Italian Village, Restaurant Suntory combines three elegantly appointed dining areas under one roof. The sushi bar is one of the most extensive in the city in terms of variety.

Tokyo Marina, *5058 N. Clark St., Chicago,*
(773) 878-2900. Open for lunch and dinner
daily. Credit cards accepted.

Seafood, soups, and casseroles are the preferred menu items, and the sushi is generally fresh. A selection of Chinese entrées is also included on the menu.

Sai Café, *2010 N. Sheffield Ave., Chicago, (773) 472-8080.*
Open for dinner daily. Credit cards accepted.

The place to go for sushi. The chefs can do wonders with a cutting knife and are a delight to behold as they carve up raw but tender pieces of fish before your eyes.

Kyoto, *2534 N. Lincoln Ave., Chicago, (773) 477-2788.*
Open for lunch Monday–Friday and dinner daily.

Traditional Japanese cuisine and more inventive dishes share the menu. The sushi is excellent, and so are the rice rolls with scallops and spicy mayonnaise.

Shiroi Hana Japanese Restaurant, *3242 N. Clark*
St., Chicago, (773) 477-1652. Open for lunch
Monday–Saturday and dinner daily.

Inexpensive, fresh sushi and sushi rolls. Close to Wrigley Field.

Kamehachi of Tokyo, *1400 N. Wells St., Chicago,*
(312) 664-3663. Open for lunch and dinner. Closed
Mondays. Lunch only during the winter.

Popular for its sushi, both cooked and traditional; *nigri* (sushi pressed on rice); and *maki-mano* (rolled sushi wrapped in seaweed).

Outlying Areas

Kuni's, *511 Main St., Evanston, (847) 328-2004.*
Open for lunch Monday and Wednesday–Saturday.

Open for dinner Wednesday–Sunday. Closed Tuesday.
Credit cards accepted.

This world-famous sushi bar presided over by master chef Yuji Kunii has pleased area residents for over twenty-four years. House specialties include beef, chicken, teriyaki, tempura, and softshell crab.

Media

Tokyo Video of Chicago, *7353 N. Clark St., Chicago,*
(773) 528-3592. Open daily.

Hundreds of Japanese-language films and television documentaries for children and adults are available for rental or sale.

⚊⚊ Korean History and Attractions ⚊⚊

A handful of Koreans arrived on U.S. shores as early as 1903, but local exclusionary laws prevented a mass immigration until 1965, when the door to the West opened ever so slowly. The next year, 2,000 Koreans, who preceded the exodus of boat people from Laos, Cambodia, and Thailand, pooled their savings and came to America. Nearly two-thirds of these people were college-educated professionals, seeking acceptance and economic gain within the American capitalist system. By 1973, the number of foreign-born Koreans had increased substantially to more than ten times the 1966 figure.

For the Koreans who arrived in the late 1960s, the adjustment to American life was arduous. There were language and serious cultural barriers to overcome, and compromises to be made with the traditional Korean values. Since 1962, the Korean American Association of Chicago has served as a community outreach agency, bridging the cultural gap between East and West.

Unofficially at least, the president of the KAAOC is the "mayor" of the Korean community; some holders of this office have even had a strong voice at City Hall through the Mayor's Advisory Council on Asian-American Affairs. Despite knowing that they'll be working out of a cramped, windowless office at 5941 N. Lincoln Avenue, the ambitious have competed fiercely for this unsalaried position as the leader of the Korean community (which, according to 1990 census figures, numbers 150,000 people in the six-county area).

The Koreans have demonstrated strong entrepreneurial skills. They are a resourceful people, unafraid of putting in long hours and painful sacrifice.

The borders of Chicago's Koreatown were first defined in the early 1970s, when the immigrants began buying commercial property in Albany Park, from Foster and Pulaski on the north and west; Montrose on the south, and the north branch of the Chicago River.

The Koreans inherited a community experiencing the first signs of urban decay. Empty storefronts, escalating crime, and a blaze of neon signs on Lawrence Avenue beckoned lonely men to spend their money in a score of corner adult bookstores and peep shows. In the late 1970s, the Koreans opened dry cleaning stores, groceries, martial arts emporiums, and gift shops, all of which restored stability along the commercial strip between Kedzie and Elston.

The Korean Businessman's Association has worked very hard to promote the Asian ethnic flair of Albany Park while local churches and the Korean Services Agency began sponsoring family counseling programs, language translation, and day-care centers for the children of working parents. One such program is the Employment Service for Indo-Chinese refugees, which places not only Koreans but Vietnamese, Cambodians, Laotians, Hmong, and Chinese into good-paying jobs in service industries and the white-collar sector.

A high point in the revitalization of Albany Park was reached several years ago with the opening of the Moo-Goong Terrace, a seventy-five unit

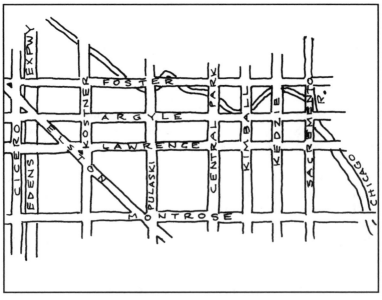

Albany Park ("Seoul of Chicago")

senior citizen complex at Kedzie and Lawrence. It was built in partnership with the federal Housing and Urban Development agency.

In April 1993, the city of Chicago recognized the growing strength of the Korean-American community by designating as "Seoul Drive" a 14-block stretch of Lawrence Avenue, beginning at the north branch of the Chicago River and extending to Central Park Avenue. Ceremonial brown street signs were tacked to lampposts, but not all of the residents of Albany Park were pleased with them. A furious protest from many non-Korean homeowners, many of whom came to Albany Park in the 1970s, prompted city officials to order the work crews to take down the offending signs the next day.

The protestors marshalled their forces, and the newly formed "Citizens For a Democratic and Diverse Albany Park" pointed out to City Council members that the 1990 census revealed that Korean-Americans comprised only 7 percent of the residential population of this polyglot neighborhood. Conversely, the storefront businesses along Lawrence Avenue were 60–90 percent Korean-owned. Needless to say, this presented a delicate problem for 39th Ward Alderman Anthony Laurino, who recalled a time in recent memory when Lawrence Avenue was virtually a ghost town.

After the Jewish-owned businesses abandoned the area in the 1960s, Koreans bought up the empty storefronts and helped provide economic stability to a neighborhood in imminent danger of being invaded by gangs and drug pushers.

The honorary signs recognizing Seoul Drive and extending all the way west to Pulaski Road would remain . . . for the time being. In return, Korean merchants agreed to install English-language signs on many of the storefronts to encourage shoppers of all ethnic and racial backgrounds to patronize their establishments. In other quarters of the city, the Koreans encountered a different kind of acrimony which was not as easily resolved.

There is a flipside to the American dream that immigrant groups since the time of the Irish potato famine know all too well—the decay overtaking the inner city, which is the only place offering hope of advancement for new arrivals. The Koreans, like others who have gone before, are often steered to these high-crime areas by well-meaning business contacts who understand that the lowest rents can be found here. Opportunity sometimes exacts a terrible price, however. In recent years Asian and Arabic shopkeepers have been victimized by thieves and ghetto gunmen. In addition, Asian business-people have encountered a backlash from the African-American community over alleged double standards.

The problem crystallized in the Far South Side community of Roseland on Michigan Avenue. Blacks have complained that the Korean American merchants there are insensitive to consumer needs and that they suspiciously view each customer as a potential threat. Picket lines were set up outside Korean business locations and a widespread consumer boycott was threatened by frustrated residents in the summer of 1990.

Blacks advised Ninth Ward Alderman Robert Shaw that the Koreans were absentee landlords who took their money out of the neighborhood and failed to provide employment to local residents. Store owners replied that Roseland was a dangerous place in which to run a business. Shoplifting, burglary, and vandalism were chronic problems and contributed to escalating insurance rates. The impassioned Shaw read from a prepared statement titled "Let's Take Control of Our Community!" and was accused of fanning the flames of discontent. Meetings were set up between the Commission on Human Relations and the two feuding factions. Both sides indicated a willingness to resolve the difficulties. It will take time, but a spirit of cooperation will emerge from this painful period of social adjustment. Rivalries between ethnic and racial groups in Chicago are as old and historic as the city itself.

Annual Events and Celebrations

Korean Fest (*Kyng-Ro-Jan Chi:* The Day to Respect and Honor Elders), *Bryn Mawr between Kedzie and Kimball, Chicago. Second or third Saturday in September. Admission free. For additional information, contact the Korean-American Association of Chicago, (773) 878-1900.*

Korean-style entertainment, with food booths, merchandise sales, contests, and music. Shortly after the festival begins, there's a parade down Lawrence to the festival.

Korea Day (*Chu Shunk*). *Second or third Sunday in September in alternating even-numbered years. Admission free. For the date, place, and time, call (773) 878-1900.*

Food booths, folk dancing, and music, sponsored by the Korean Association of Chicago, 5941 N. Lincoln Avenue, Chicago.

Places to See

Bultasa Buddhist Temple of Chicago, *4358 W. Montrose, Chicago, (773) 286-1551. Open daily.*

One of five Korean Buddhist temples in the Chicagoland area. This one is unique, however, because it features the lovely "1000 Buddha Temple Altar," believed to be the only one of its kind in the Midwest. The monks in residence are happy to lead visitors on a guided tour of this facility, which until four years ago still housed residential apartments upstairs. To arrange a tour, or for information about the Zen meditation group that meets regularly, please call Ron Kidd at (773) 327-1695.

Shops

Seoul Books and Records, *3450 W. Peterson, Chicago, (773) 463-7756. Open daily.*

Korean magazines, books, newspapers, cassettes, and records. A limited selection of cookbooks in English.

Hundai Video, *3513 W. Lawrence Ave., Chicago, (773) 588-8737. Open daily. No credit cards.*

Hundreds of imported Chinese and Korean movies available for rental or purchase.

Hokyong Market, *3519 W. Lawrence Ave., Chicago, (773) 267-2746. Open daily. Credit cards accepted.*

Southeast Asian herbs and ginseng root sold for medicinal purposes. Groceries. Korean newspapers.

First Gift Store, *3550 W. Lawrence Ave., Chicago, (773) 463-3533. Open daily. Credit cards accepted.*

Gift items, clothing, and imports from Korea and the Orient. Video rental of Korean-language films at the back of the store.

Arirang Super Market, *4017 W. Lawrence Ave., Chicago, (773) 777-2400. Open daily. No credit cards.*

A grocery store that sells Korean foods only.

Word of Life Books, *3523-A W. Lawrence Ave., Chicago, (800) 654–5124. Closed Sundays. Credit cards accepted.*

A neat and well-organized store that stocks Korean religious books and gift items. Drinking mugs, children's books (some in English), and audio cassettes.

Modern Gift, *3432 W. Lawrence Ave., Chicago, (773) 588-6055. Closed Sundays.*

Pharmacy, cosmetics, and general merchandise distributor.

Asiana Jewelry & Handicraft, *3773 W. Lawrence Ave., Chicago, (773) 539-2886. Closed Sundays.*

Imports from Korea and Japan. Figurines, wind chimes, religious items, telephones, plates, and toys. More of a tourist trap than anything else.

Master Cookware Corp., *3212 ½ W. Lawrence Ave., Chicago, (773) 588-3232. Closed Sundays. Credit cards accepted.*

A large selection of woks and Asian cooking utensils. Tea sets, teak wood chests, and electric appliances.

Restaurants

Bando Korean Restaurant, *2200 W. Lawrence Ave., Chicago, (773) 728-7400. Open for lunch and dinner daily. Credit cards accepted.*

An indoor waterfall enhances the pleasing decor at Bando, regarded by many as the best Korean restaurant in town. Entrées are reasonably priced, and they include seven to eight side dishes per person. There is a barbecue grill at every table. Chicken, pork, beef, and short ribs are the house specialties. *Recommended.*

Shilla, *5930 N. Lincoln Ave., Chicago, (773) 275-5930. Open for lunch and dinner daily. Credit cards accepted.*

Any one of the eight private banquet rooms captures the essence of the Orient, if you care to reserve a private party in elegantly appointed surroundings. Japanese and Korean dishes, including barbecued short ribs, sashimi, and shrimp tempura are the house specialties.

Chun Soo Chang, *3534 W. Lawrence Ave., Chicago, (773) 539-2444. Open for lunch and dinner daily. Credit cards accepted.*

Four of the tables in the restaurant are equipped with gas grills, so you can cook your own pot of seafood, or pork or beef dish, depending on your tastes. No poultry dishes, but there is plenty to choose from on the menu. Like many of the Korean stores and restaurants up and down Lawrence Avenue, the servers and counter help speak faltering English.

Korean Restaurant, *2659 W. Lawrence Ave.,*
Chicago, (773) 878-2095. Open daily 24 hours.

Open around the clock, in case you desire a late-night *kim chee* feast. The decor is not fancy, but an extensive menu, including an array of noodle dishes, marinated and grilled beef, and spare ribs make up for lost ambience.

Gin Go Gae, *5433 N. Lincoln Ave., Chicago,*
(773) 334-3895. Open for lunch and dinner daily.
Credit cards accepted.

An established North Side Korean restaurant with an impressive assortment of side dishes. You may want to try the octopus in hot red sauce for something out of the ordinary.

Filipino History and Attractions

Since the 19th century, the designation of "Filipino" has been applied to the Christian Malays who populate the islands constituting the Philippine archipelago. During the the Spanish conquest, the term Filipino was loosely applied to persons of Spanish descent born in the Philippines. The Spanish presence officially ended on June 12, 1898, when General Emilio Aguinaldo proclaimed the first Philippine Republic and unfurled the state flag for the first time. However, the Treaty of Paris, signed on December 10, 1898, which ended the Spanish-American War, also ceded the entire island nation to the United States in return for a payment of $20 million.

Philippine insurgents fiercely resisted American military and civilian rule for the next forty years. The struggle to establish home rule was resolved by the passage of the Tydings-McDuffie Bill in 1934, which guaranteed Philippine independence by 1946. The Republic was formally established that year, coinciding with the anniversary of the American Declaration of Independence on July 4.

The first Filipino settlers arrived in North America in 1765, via the Spanish galleons. They settled in what is now New Orleans. Filipino immigration into Chicago picked up after World War I. St. Mary's, located in downtown Chicago and one of the oldest Catholic parishes in the city, was the first to welcome the new Asian arrivals. A Christmas tradition of the homeland is kept alive there in the *Simbanggabi* (Night Mass), part of a nine-day celebration that makes the Philippine Yuletide season the longest in the world. Simbanggabi dates back more than 300 years, when the Spanish introduced Catholicism to the Philippines. Up until the mid-18th century, the Philippine Christmas was a two-day festival, including the December 24 "Vespera."

According to Philippine history, a parish priest was overwhelmed by the piety of a certain group of farmers in a Bulacan town, people who prayed on their knees around a *siga*—or bonfire—for nine straight days. The priest asked for official sanctions from Rome to adopt this *psalamat* as a part of the Christmas observance. The papal grant was awarded and the Simbang-gabi Mass followed.

The nine-day holiday (commencing on December 16), has served as a powerful unifying force in the Philippines, which is known as a bastion of Christianity in the Far East, but is divided by political and cultural ideology. The Simbanggabi in Chicago is tailored to the specific requirements of American life, but is a nostalgic reminder of family and homeland.

The Filipino community in Chicago began taking on some formal shape in 1937, when the resident commissioner of the Philippines in the United States sent his assistant, Francisco Varona, to Chicago to organize a central committee to represent Filipino immigrants in all matters of social and political concern. Varona convinced the numerous social clubs scattered across the city to form the Council of Clubs, which evolved into the National Filipino American Council of Chicago (NFACC). In 1953, this umbrella group, representing thirty-four regional provisional groups, was incorporated as a nonprofit organization.

Later, the Dr. Jose Rizal Memorial Fund was created to acquire a community center. That dream became a reality on May 7, 1966, when the first NFACC building was dedicated at 1139 W. Webster Street on the North Side by Estela Sulit, consul general of the Philippines in Chicago. Four years later the Filipino American Political Association was organized as the political arm of the NFACC, with Roberto D. Roque, an attorney and prominent community leader, elected charter president. Under the direction of Roque, the first Philippine Week celebration, with a lavish downtown parade and special exhibits at the Museum of Science and Industry, was held during the week of June 12–19, 1970. It is now a yearly tradition, in which thousands of Filipino Americans pause to reaffirm their appreciation and affection for the national heritage.

A steady tide of Filipinos began arriving in Chicago in the 1960s, when changes in immigration laws encouraged many professional people with medical and technical skills to emigrate. They found employment in the city's abundant hospitals, medical clinics, and extended health care facilities.

Filipinos' economic status and familiarity with the English language made the process of acculturation relatively easy. Though they are a close-knit community, the Filipinos are widely dispersed across the North and Northwest sides. Many can be found in Edgewater and Uptown, which is close to the Howard-Englewood-Jackson elevated line—the best mode of transportation to the hospitals and medical clinics that dot the lakefront.

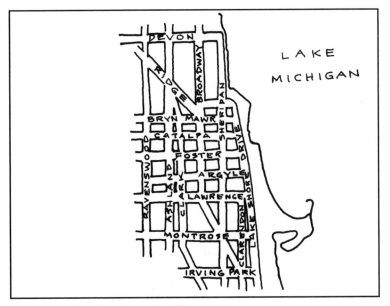

Argyle-Broadway-Sheridan (New Chinatown)

In recent years Chicago's Filipino-American colony has spread into the affluent western suburbs of DuPage County. Forty-eight-year-old Juventino "Ben" Fajardo broke ground in April 1995 with a stunning electoral victory in Glendale Heights, a suburb of 27,973 residents. Seven percent of the residents there are Filipino Americans.

Mr. Fajardo, who fled the Philippines in 1972 after President Ferdinand Marcos declared martial law, made history by becoming the first Asian-American to be elected mayor of an Illinois municipality. The reserved Fajardo is one of three Filipinos to be elected trustees in diverse Glendale Heights since 1989. He is conciliatory, not confrontational, which is a virtue in the tumultuous world of Illinois politics.

Community life continues to revolve around the representative organizations of the NFACC, now headquartered at the Jose Rizal Memorial Center, at 1332 W. Irving Park Road on the North Side. The yellow and blue brick building was originally constructed for the Orphei Singing Club, a Swedish choral and fraternal society. But with the changing patterns of immigration, the few remaining Orphei members disbanded the club and sold the property to the Filipino community in 1974. Such are the ethnic realities of Chicago. Neighborhoods are nothing more than temporary harbors in a sprawling urban center, the only defining quality of which is change.

Annual Events and Celebrations

Philippine Week Events

Philippine Independence Parade and Picnic at
Labagh Woods, *Cicero and Foster, Chicago. Saturday closest to June 12. For additional information please call Roberto D. Roque, (312) 744-0833.*

The Commonwealth of the Philippines was established in 1935 in an attempt to pave the way for political and economic independence from the United States, which had been autonomous in the region since 1898. The Japanese occupation and World War II delayed this process until July 4, 1946, when the Republic of the Philippines was established, with Manuel Roxas installed as the first president. However, the lavish Chicago parade featuring twenty floats and three to four marching bands commemorates the political separation from Spain, which occurred on June 12, 1898. Chicago's first Philippine Independence Day parade was staged on June 12, 1970, but the parade did not become a yearly event until 1980. Festivities begin along the Dearborn Street parade route between Wacker Drive and Van Buren. The parade is co-sponsored by the local fraternal organizations within the Philippine Week Committee. A ceremony marking Philippine independence is held in the Daley Civic Center during the noon hour on the day before the actual parade, as a part of the city's "Under the Picasso" ongoing program of entertainment. Short speeches by local dignitaries are featured.

Open House at the Rizal Memorial Center, *1332 W. Irving Park Rd., Chicago, (773) 281-1210. Second week of June. Admission is free.*

In 1974, the Filipino American Council of Chicago (FACC) purchased the former home of the Swedish Orphei Singers, and converted the facility into a social club, dinner theater, and cultural center. The center features Filipino entertainment and food that is available to the public on Friday evenings. During Philippine Week, the Rizal Center often sponsors a one-day open house, featuring exhibits and mementos from the Filipino Historical Society. Nominal charge for food and beverages.

Independence Day Picnic at Labagh Woods Forest
Preserve, *Cicero and Foster, Chicago. Sunday closest to June 12. Admission is free. Call (773) 965-2874 for details.*

Food, music, and games held the Sunday following the big downtown parade.

Community Ball, *Hyatt Regency O'Hare Hotel, 9300 Bryn Mawr Ave., Rosemont. Saturday evening closest to June 12. Admission fee charged. Call (773) 965-2874 for tickets and time.*

Cocktails, dinner, musical entertainment, and speeches marking Philippine independence.

Shops

Philhouse Market, *5845 N. Clark St., Chicago, (773) 784-1176. Open daily. Credit cards accepted.*

Tucked into a steadily growing colony of Asians who inhabit the Swedish Andersonville and Edgewater communities, the spacious Philhouse Market is a full-line grocery store and fresh produce exchange that also sells roast pork on the weekends. Wall posters, books, records, and tapes are available for purchase.

Philippine Grocery and Gift Shop, *5750 N. California Ave., Chicago, (773) 334-4628. Open daily. Checks, but no credit cards.*

Imported foods from the Philippines, newspapers, and a limited selection of gift items. Filipino movies on tape available for rental.

Villamar Food Mart and Gifts, *5949 W. Fullerton Ave., Chicago, (773) 637-1686. Open daily. No credit cards.*

Imported foods from the Philippines and a line of gift items.

3R's Food Market, *two locations: 5200 W. Grand Ave., Chicago, (773) 745-1701, and 2712 W. Montrose, Chicago, (773) 539-4714. Open daily. Credit cards accepted.*

Stocking plenty of Filipino food items at both locations.

DeLeon's Oriental Store, *3143 W. Irving Park Rd., Chicago, (773) 539-2178. Closed Sundays. No credit cards.*

Filipino movies (many current titles with subtitles) are carried in stock, and are available for purchase or rental.

Restaurants

Feliz Cakes and Restaurant, *3056 N. Lincoln Ave.,*
Chicago, (773) 549-4188. Open for lunch and dinner.
Closed Sundays and Mondays. No credit cards.

Bakery and café, specializing in Filipino barbecue foods, pastries, and meat cakes. Various American and European foods also served.

Little Quiapo Restaurant, *4423 N. Clark St.,*
Chicago, (773) 271-5441. Open for lunch and
dinner. Closed Mondays. Credit cards accepted.

Small, homey restaurant located on the North Side.

═ Vietnamese History and Attractions ═

Bewildered, alone, and afraid, thousands of Vietnamese, Cambodians, and Laotians who had been forced into refugee camps along the Thai border, or cast adrift in the raging current of the South China Sea, found a new home in America in the weeks and months following the U.S. pullout from Saigon in 1975. The Vietnamese who were fortunate enough to escape their homeland following the war faced additional perils on the open sea from marauding Thai "river pirates" in search of precious gold *taels*—finely-crafted wafers accepted as payment for a safe passage to Malaysia. Those who were able to smuggle their families out of Vietnam with a few of the valuable ingots in their possession sewed the wafers into the linings of their coats for safekeeping. The Thai pirates knew about the manufacture of gold wafers, which weighed about 1.2 troy ounces, and systematically attacked refugee boats on the high seas. The passengers would be forced to strip before the boat was plundered and burned. Very often the refugees would be shot to death, or simply tossed overboard.

Still, over 130,000 Vietnamese managed to escape their war-torn land, but they often found themselves impoverished by the time they arrived in the United States, where immigration officials herded them into resettlement camps. Life in the camps was an ordeal, but a small price to pay for freedom. The last refugee camp, Fort Chaffee, Arkansas, closed in December 1975. For those who were left, the time had come to adjust to the rigors of American life. Chicago took in 2,000 Vietnamese in those first few months. That number soon tripled and this population has continued to grow. There are now approximately 74,000 Vietnamese living in the Chicago metropolitan area.

Finding a job in a recession-wracked economy proved to be the toughest challenge. Many highly-skilled clerical workers who had served the pro-

Western South Vietnamese government were forced to accept menial jobs in the service economy. The Vietnamese are the newest immigrants to seek their fortunes in Chicago. Now twenty years past the great upheaval, the close-knit community has made tremendous strides. The Argyle-Broadway-Sheridan Road neighborhood is a busy, thriving retail corridor, where hard work and self-reliance carry great weight. It is an old story with a new twist when sixty-five-year-old refugees eagerly sign up for English classes at nearby Truman College. You have to start over somewhere.

Annual Events and Celebrations

Vietnamese Catholic Community Fair and Dance,
St. Thomas of Canterbury Church, 4827 N. Kenmore Ave., Chicago, (773) 784-1932. Saturday following the Lunar New Year in February. Tickets required for the dance, but admission free to the fair.

Ethnic fundraising folk fair includes food, games, and entertainment in the parish hall. The dance is held the night before.

New Year Celebration, *Vietnamese Buddhist Temple, 4429 N. Damen Ave., Chicago, (773) 275-6859. First Saturday of New Year in February.*

Day-long activities planned. Regular services are held in early morning, Monday through Saturday, and at noon on Sunday. To arrange a guided tour of the temple, call the temple.

Shops

Hoang Kim, Inc., *1025 W. Argyle St., Chicago, (773) 271-3132. Closed Wednesdays.*

Fine Vietnamese jewelry, custom design. A specialist in diamonds and gemstones. Wax carving and casting; faceting and polishing of jade. Jewelry appraisals.

Le Dung Cosmetics and Gifts, *1028 W. Argyle, Chicago, (773) 989-7850. Open daily.*

Southeast Asian imported items including furniture, jewelry, Laotian flutes, decorations, cosmetics, jade, and porcelain figurines. Most of the decorative artwork is done by Vietnamese artists living in the United States.

Hoa Nam Grocery, Inc., *1101-3 W. Argyle St.,*
Chicago, (773) 275-9157. Open daily.

You'll discover that many of the Asian shopkeepers in the New Chinatown do little in the way of display advertising. Merchandise is stacked high to the ceilings, and often arranged in a haphazard manner. Because stores like Hoa Nam cater to a regular neighborhood clientele that buys its groceries here every week, it is not necessary to lure new business off the street with special sales, come-ons, or gimmicks. The goods are moderately priced, and the store is always congested.

Viet Hoa Plaza, Inc., *1051 W. Argyle St., Chicago,*
(773) 334-1028. Open daily. Free parking.

The owners of the Viet Hoa Plaza, on the other hand, just completed a $30,000 renovation of their building. With or without the new exterior, this Cambodian-Vietnamese marketplace will no doubt continue to lure Asian shoppers from all over the Midwest. Offering a wide variety of Southeast Asian foods that appeal to every taste, including canned goods, seasonings, live crabs, and bakery items, Viet Hoa is one of the busiest stores on the street.

Restaurants

Ba Le European and Oriental Gourmet and
Sandwich Shop, *5108-20 N. Broadway, Chicago,*
(773) 561-4424. Open for lunch and dinner daily.
No credit cards.

Elegant French pastries and croissants are sold in the bakery. Gourmet sandwiches and soups can be eaten on the premises or carried out. The menu items are inexpensive and very tasty, reflecting the fusion of two divergent cultures that clashed during a pivotal moment in the world history—French and Vietnamese.

Le Bistro Restaurant and Cocktail Lounge, *5025 N.*
Clark St., Chicago, (773) 784-6000. Open for dinner.
Closed Mondays. Credit cards accepted.

Oriental and French cuisine priced moderately. Stylish, understated elegance. The house specialties include sautéed crab (*Cua Rang Muoi*), Vietnamese pancakes (*Banh Xeo*) and marinated sliced beef with lemon grass and sesame oil (*Thit Nuong Banh Hoi*). A selection of finely cut steaks are also available for the less adventurous diner.

Nha Trang, *1007 W. Argyle St., Chicago,*
(773) 989-0712. Open for lunch and dinner
daily. Credit cards accepted.

Vietnamese and Chinese cooking. Chicken, seafood, and Vietnamese steamed rice noodle dishes are the house specialties. You may want to try some of the more unusual menu items, including *Ca Chien Cary* (spicy catfish, with curry and coconut sauce) or the *Muc Xao Ot Xa* (cuttle fish stir-fried with lemon grass and chili) if you enjoy sea food with an exotic flavoring.

MeKong Restaurant, *4953 N. Broadway Ave.,*
Chicago, (773) 271-0206. Open for lunch and
dinner daily. Credit cards accepted.

Vietnamese food served by the new owners who bought this restaurant in 1988. Formerly located on State Street. Buffet all-you-can-eat luncheon served Monday through Friday. Carry-out service.

Pho Xe Lua (The Train), *1021 W. Argyle St.,*
Chicago, (773) 275-7512. Open for breakfast,
lunch, and dinner daily. No credit cards.

Vietnamese and Chinese cuisine. By the looks of things, this restaurant is appropriately named. The Train is just as busy and congested as Argyle Street on a Saturday morning, when the residents come out to do their shopping. The house specialties include a variety of beef and chicken dishes, and rice noodle soup.

Nhu Hoa Cafe, *1020 W. Argyle St., Chicago,*
(773) 878-0618. Open for lunch and dinner.
Closed Mondays. Credit cards accepted.

Dine on Vietnamese and Laotian food in an elegant surrounding, and watch big-screen color television at the same time. The restaurant is owned by the same family that also runs the Tiem Vang A Chau jewelry store across the street at 1019 Argyle.

Haugiang Restaurant, *1104 W. Argyle St., Chicago,*
(773) 275-8691. Open for breakfast, lunch, and dinner
daily. No credit cards.

Fine Vietnamese cuisine and cocktails. Dine in or carry out.

Pho Hung Restaurant, *1129 W. Argyle St., Chicago,*
(773) 275-1112. Open for breakfast, lunch, and
dinner. Credit cards accepted.

"Thumbs up" for this Vietnamese restaurant, according to the local restaurant critics. Reasonable prices, a cheap luncheon special (typically $3.59), and good service are the reasons. This is also the place to go for chicken livers in pig's tripe.

Hoang Yen Cafe, *1010 W. Argyle St., Chicago,*
(773) 275-6411. Open for lunch and dinner daily.
No credit cards accepted.

Vietnamese and Chinese menu items.

══════════ Thai Attractions ══════════

Annual Events and Celebrations

Thai Food and Cultural Festival, *Siam Square*
Restaurant, 622 Davis St., Evanston, (847) 475-0860.
June and July. Free parking at the Sherman/Grove
garage.

A two-month festival featuring Thai gourmet foods prepared in the courtyard, and served by waitresses dressed in traditional ethnic clothing. Original mural artistry is on display, and Thai classical dance is performed at designated times. Reservations recommended.

Places to See

Thai Buddhist Temple (*Wat Dhummram*),
7059 W. 75th St., Bridgeview, (708) 594-8100.

For more than fifty years, the Thai Buddhist Temple has served the religious needs of Chicago's Asian community. Guided tours of the building are held on Thursdays and Sundays or by special arrangement. To schedule a special tour, call the temple.

Shops

Thai Grocery, *5014 N. Broadway Ave., Chicago,*
(773) 561-5345. Open daily. No credit cards.

A Thai delicatessen and grocery that stocks sausages, fresh meats and poultry, prepared foods, fish, and exotic Asian ice cream.

Thailand Plaza, *4821 N. Broadway Ave., Chicago,*
(773) 561-5345. Closed Sundays.

Full-service grocery and newsstand selling videos, newspapers, cassettes, cookbooks, and Asian food.

Restaurants

Arun's Restaurant, *4156 N. Kedzie Ave., Chicago,*
(773) 539-1909. Closed Mondays. Credit cards
accepted.

Small but delightful surroundings enhance the food, which ranges from mild to highly spiced. The pork satay, chicken curry, and *tom yum goong* are recommended.

Wild Ginger, *2203 N. Clybourn Ave., Chicago,*
(773) 883-0434. Open for lunch Monday–Friday
and dinner daily. Credit cards accepted.

Located in the trendy and oh-so-upscale "Clybourn Corridor," which until the arrival of the Yuppie rehabbers was just another inner-city neighborhood on the slide. You wouldn't expect to find a Thai restaurant here, but then again, maybe you would, given the eclectic tastes of the local residents. The food is only mildly seasoned, so you won't be shedding any unnecessary tears. Ginger beef, Singha shrimp, and the crab and shrimp sausage are all worth a try.

P. S. Bangkok, *3345 N. Clark St., Chicago,*
(773) 871-7777. Open for lunch and dinner.
Closed Mondays. Credit cards accepted.

The food is heavily seasoned with curry and red peppers, as you might expect; but the extensive menu allows the patron to experiment with a variety of Thai dishes. The oil paintings on the wall depict traditional Thai scenes. Sunday brunch.

Siam Cafe, *4712 N. Sheridan Rd., Chicago,*
(773) 769-6602. Open for lunch and dinner daily.
Credit cards accepted.

An inexpensive Thai restaurant located in Uptown. Be sure to order the fried greens with oyster sauce, considered to be the best in the city. Other specialties include pork satay (barbecued ribs), chili chicken, and cuttlefish.

Thai Town, *3201 N. Clark St., Chicago,*
(773) 528-2755. Open for lunch and dinner.
Closed Tuesdays. Credit cards accepted.

Clark Street is home to more than the usual share of Asian restaurants. Thai Town, with its varied and extensive menu selections, pleasing decor, and prompt personal services is among the best on the Near North. Not to be missed from among the more unusual dinner selections is the *beef dad deu* (strips of honey-glazed beef). Thai Town offers an inexpensive buffet every day but Wednesday.

Thai Touch, *3200 W. Lawrence Ave., Chicago,*
(773) 539-5700. Open for lunch and dinner.
Closed Monday. Credit cards accepted.

An "outstanding" Thai restaurant; it's been voted one of the best by several critics.

Outlying Areas

Bangkok Village, *22 E. Chicago, #122, Naperville,*
(630) 369-4510. Open for lunch and dinner daily.
Credit cards accepted.

A moderately priced but elegantly appointed Thai restaurant. Choose from a selection of highly seasoned curry dishes including *panang,* Thai royal chicken, and tasty duck. Rice dishes, poultry, and meat entrées round out the menu. Carry-out service.

Siam Square, *622 Davis St., Evanston,*
(847) 475-0860. Open for lunch Monday–Saturday
and dinner daily. Credit cards accepted.

This annual Thai Festival in June and July is definitely worth a trip to Evanston. (See annual events.) The seafood menu items are served in pleasant surroundings in the lush garden patio. Musical entertainment on the weekends.

Media

Thai Radio Hour, *hosted by Sara Lin, WSBC, 1240 AM, Thursday evenings, 8:00 to 10:00 P.M.*

Argyle Street: Getting Things Done

A Chinese proverb teaches that "a journey of a thousand miles begins with one step." Charlie Soo, the "unofficial mayor" of Argyle Street and the director of the Asian American Small Businessmen's Association of Chicago (AASBA), is a great believer in the wisdom of the ancients. His enthusiasm and buoyant optimism in the face of considerable adversity have gone a long way toward reversing the downward slide of this Edgewater/Uptown neighborhood.

Soo, one of the city's best-known and beloved civic entrepreneurs, was born in Hawaii to Chinese parents but moved to Chicago in the 1950s to attend classes at Roosevelt University. He started a modest import-export business that thrust him into the political realm, where he made the acquaintance of many local politicians, including State Senator Cecil Partee, who kindled his early interest in community re-development.

"The city has money to spend to help the North Side," Partee told Soo, who formulated an ambitious plan of action. He set up a storefront on Argyle Street and began casting about for the grant money Partee spoke of.

In 1978, when Soo and other members of the AASBA began considering the ways and means of revitalizing the commercial strip, they encountered the usual resistance and apathy from local shopkeepers, city bureaucrats, and weary residents who had abandoned hope for their community. Since 1972, when the last remnants of the old Chinatown at Clark and Van Buren were bulldozed to make way for the new state detention center, Jimmy Wong and leaders of the Hip-Sing organization envisioned the formation of a "New Chinatown" on the far North Side. Wong purchased several buildings near Sheridan and Argyle, and things appeared to be on proper course. But within a few years optimism gave way to despair. Storefronts stood empty. Street gangs accosted pedestrians. Sidewalks were littered with broken glass and debris, and within a two-block stretch along Argyle the police counted thirty-six bars and liquor stores. According to Charlie Soo, the area was "a mess."

In other words, the situation was grim, but not hopeless. To lure new business and retail traffic to the area, it was necessary to ensure the public's safety. Soo convinced the Chicago Transit Authority to clean up the dank, filthy Argyle Street elevated stop, which was covered with graffiti and garbage and smelled of urine. The CTA responded by installing a new platform, two heated windbreaker shelters, and a $250,000 lighting system. An Oriental ticket booth inside the station was a part of their "Adopt-a-Station" program (which was supported in part by a $10,000 donation from the neighboring AON Corporation). The inside of the station was painted a bright green and red. (Chicago artist Kathleen Eaton, whose work focuses on architectural spaces in Chicago and on the unexpected solitude and human activities that often accompany such urban spaces, completed an oil painting of the Argyle Station for the Hollister Corporation, which in turn produced 18,000 posters for worldwide distribution.) The colorful Oriental pagoda-style roof, constructed at a cost of $100,000, is the first of its kind in the world, according to Soo. "People will know what is here now," he promises.

A free parking lot was opened at Broadway and Winnemac for the convenience of weekend shoppers and tourists. During the mayoral administrations of Jane Byrne and Harold Washington, new curbs and sidewalks were added. Street crime, which was a chronic problem for many years, was greatly reduced when Commander William Antonick, of the 20th Police District, assigned foot patrolmen to cover the area.

The past decade has witnessed remarkable growth, as the vacancy rate along Argyle Street fell to zero. A steady influx of ethnic Chinese and Vietnamese refugees in the middle-to-late 1970s spurred the remarkable growth of the community. The economic initiative undertaken in the late 1970s has generated over $30 million in private investments in buildings, stores, and other commercial establishments. While much of Uptown remains squalid, business has never been better on Argyle Street. The ethnically rich Argyle Street strip teems with visitors from all over the Midwest, especially on weekends, when shoppers venture into Uptown to purchase freshly-cut sides of pork, goat, chicken, and beef, and produce trucked in from farms throughout Illinois and Indiana. The Argyle Street merchants rack up more than $77 million in annual sales.

The cultural richness of Uptown is reflected in its steadily increasing neighborhood diversity. The Chinese, Vietnamese, Cambodians, and Hmong from Southeast Asia have been joined by an influx of Russians, Nigerians, and Mexicans in recent years. Argyle Street and its thriving business community has helped fuel Uptown's slow but measurable recovery.

Today there are numerous ethnic restaurants, Asian grocery stores, and gift and variety emporiums along Argyle. In 1996, growth continued with the opening of Sun Plaza shopping center on Broadway two blocks south of Argyle, home to a collection of new Asian businesses. Old and new shops alike in the New Chinatown cater to local residents, out-of-town shoppers, and an increasing number of tourists who are eager to experience a fresh slice of Southeast Asia.

Latino Chicago

═ Multiethnic History and Settlement ═

The future of Chicago and the direction it will be taking by the year 2000 and beyond will be heavily influenced by the burgeoning Latino population now occupying the neighborhoods on the West Side and Northwest Side— parts of the city formerly occupied by immigrants from Eastern Europe. By the year 2000 it is expected that one in every four Chicagoans will be of Latino descent: Mexican, Puerto Rican, Cuban, and other Latin and South American nationalities.

Today there are seven predominantly Latino wards in Chicago: the 22nd and 25th, representing the Southwest Side Mexican "barrio" communities of Pilsen and the Little Village, and the 26th, 35th and 31st Wards, encompassing West Town and the Humboldt Park neighborhoods. The number of Latino wards in Chicago increased from four to seven as a result of a controversial 1992 realignment creating new zones of political empowerment for the nine largest Hispanic groups who account for nearly one-fifth of the city's 2.78 million population according to 1994 census data.

On the Northwest Side, where the majority of Puerto Ricans reside, the boundary lines of the 1st, the 26th, and the 35th Wards were redrawn, and Billy Ocasio, a Puerto Rican who served as director of the Center for Community Leadership and Development was elected alderman of the 26th Ward in 1995. Vilma Colom, a bilingual education teacher at Yates Elementary School is the only female Hispanic in the City Council, representing the 35th Ward. She defeated three other candidates in a hotly contested election including Marja Stoll, the first Indonesian-American to vie for a seat in the Council.

Until very recently these wards were controlled by "old guard" white ethnic aldermen like Vito Marzullo, Thomas Keane, and the "regulars" who formed the axle of the seemingly invincible Daley Machine of the 1950s and 1960s. Little attention was paid to the Latino voting constituency, which then was perceived to be indifferent to city politics and at odds with itself.

Though all the divergent Latino groups share the Spanish language, cultural, political, and socioeconomic differences among them have created a wide gulf, which translates into political inertia at City Hall and the State House in Springfield. So while there is a Latino community in Chicago, its members have often failed to unite to achieve political parity. In this regard there is little sense of community among the Latino groups.

Many of the Mexicans, for example, who have been a factor in Chicago life for generations, consider themselves culturally distinct from other Latino groups; their traditions and customs more closely parallel the experiences of the white ethnics who once populated their neighborhoods. The Mexicans, for the most part, comprise the blue-collar, laboring classes, while at the other end of the economic spectrum the Cubans generally are white-collar professionals who came to Chicago as political refugees following the Castro revolution of 1959. The Cubans identify more closely with the political right and are more likely to vote for those conservative candidates who would support military intervention to topple Cuba's Communist regime. A University of Florida poll conducted in 1991 indicated that 57 percent of Cuban-Americans would favor some form of overt military action against Fidel Castro.

Puerto Ricans, who are second in number to the Mexicans in Chicago, are U.S. citizens by birth, but rank low on the economic scale. They are less concerned with immigration and repatriation issues than the Mexicans or Cubans, and are more likely to be assimilated into the mainstream Anglo culture. The Latino population in Chicago stands at 545,852, according to 1990 census figures. There were 352,560 Mexicans, 119,866 Puerto Ricans, 10,044 Cubans, and a scattering of Guatemalans, Colombians, Ecuadorians, Peruvians, Spanish, Hondurans, Chileans, El Salvadorans, and fewer Panamanians, Dominicans, and Argentineans.

Despite a cumulative population of 422,063 Latinos in the Metro-Suburban area in 1980, the community was represented by only two public officials: a Democratic Cook County Commissioner (Irene Hernandez) and a University of Illinois trustee (Arturo Velazquez, Jr.). Velazquez was emblematic of a new breed of Latino politician who was no longer content to play by the old guard's rules—in this case, crusty old Vito Marzullo, alderman of the 25th Ward since 1953. Marzullo, who was a product of the Italian quarter, never missed a chance to speak his peace. Concerning well-meaning reformers and liberals like Velazquez, Vito had this to say: "You give them ten dollars and they couldn't get your dog out of the pound!" Marzullo's campaign rhetoric must have counted for something with his Mexican constituency. Velazquez garnered only 41 percent of the vote in 1983.

In 1980, the magazine *Illinois Issues* published an article titled "Mañana Will Be Better: Spanish American Politics in Chicago." The authors predicted great strides within the Latino community in the coming decade. It might have come to pass in 1981 when 29-year-old Rudy Lozano organized community support to battle the machine regulars. Lozano, a labor organizer, failed in his aldermanic runoff by the narrowest of margins: seventeen votes. The popular and charismatic leader accused his opponents of purging Latino names from the poll sheets before the election. Lozano enjoyed the support of Mayor Harold Washington in his bid to unseat incumbent Alderman Frank Stemberk. It never came to pass. Lozano was murdered on June 8, 1983, allegedly by a youthful gang member named Gregory Escobar. The tragedy underscored the larger inability of the community to coalesce to achieve mutually advantageous goals.

Even though Latinos received key political appointments during Mayor Richard M. Daley's first term—Matt Rodriguez was named General Superintendent of Police, Miriam Santos earned high marks as the independent-minded City Treasurer—Latinos lagged far behind other ethnic groups in receiving their fair share of the pie. Juan Solis, Luis Guittieriez, Regner Suarez, and Jesus Garcia took their place in the City Council in the 1980s. Ambrosio Medrano, Riccardo Munoz, Vilma Colom, and Billy Ocasio followed in their footsteps in the 1990s, but the larger goals of political empowerment remain unfulfilled, indicating that *mañana* has not yet come.

Cultural Institutions

Phyllis Kind Gallery, *313 W. Superior St., Chicago, (312) 642-6302. Closed Sundays and Mondays.*

Special exhibitions during the year of Latino (and European) painters. Represents artists Martin Ramirez and Luis Jiminez.

Latino Chicago Theatre Company at the Firehouse Theatre, *1625 N. Damen Ave., Chicago, (773) 486-5120. Call for tickets. No credit cards.*

Latino Chicago showcases the work of American playwrights of Latino descent. The company stages three productions a year (most are in English, but from time to time a few may be presented in Spanish) at the Firehouse, a tiny North Side theater that seats 90. In 1990, a television documentary focusing on the "Puffin Project," a collaboration between Mexico and the Latino Chicago Theatre Company during the International Theatre Festival of Chicago, was aired on PBS. Plays, musical performances, poetry readings, and dance are presented year-round. Tickets can be purchased at the box office up to fifteen minutes before curtain.

Annual Events and Celebrations

Hispanic Festival, *Museum of Science and Industry, 57th and Lake Shore Dr., Chicago. Late September through mid-October. Standard museum admission fee charged.*

A 17-day ethnic folk fair highlighting the cultural heritage of the Latino peoples in music, classical and folk dance, theater, and a juried art exhibition presented in the museum's West Pavilion. The special programs are held in conjunction with National Hispanic Month activities in Chicago, held each year from September 15 through October 16. The museum brings in musical performers and guest speakers from Spanish-speaking countries, including Bolivia, Cuba, Guatemala, Mexico, Panama, and Spain. In 1991 a special traveling exhibition, "Spain/U.S.A. Hall of Fame," focusing on the individuals from the Latino community who have made the greatest impact on communications, aviation, and technology, made its national debut at the Museum of Science and Industry. There is no additional charge for admission to the exhibitions and performances after the standard entrance fee has been paid.

Hispanic Heritage Month: *"Celebracion,"* *Field Museum, Roosevelt Rd. and Lake Shore Dr., Chicago, (312) 922-9410, ext. 658. October. Admission is free.*

Four days of activities and exhibits at the museum, including music, art, and performances by local Latin American talent. The exhibits deal with themes relating to the ancient cultures of Latin America. The demonstrations, workshops, lectures, and performances are for the most part aimed at school groups, but the public is invited to view the special exhibits.

Pan-American Festival, *Soldier Field, Chicago. Mid-August. Admission fee charged. Call (312) 944-7272 for additional information, or Ticketmaster at (312) 559-1212.*

Two days of music, food and fun from south of the border. Musical headliners from Central America, the Dominican Republic, Mexico, and Puerto

Rico, make this one of Chicago's liveliest, best-attended ethnic festivals. The 1991 lineup included Alejandra Guzman, Banda Blanca, Tito Nieves, Tropical Panama, and Gilberto Santa Rosa. Sponsored by Cardenas and Fernandez Associates. *Recommended.*

Festival of Latin Music, *The Vic, 3145 N. Sheffield, or the Park West, 322 W. Armitage. Two Saturdays in September or October. Tickets can be purchased at the Old Town School of Folk Music, 909 W. Armitage, Chicago, or by calling (773) 525-7793.*

Sponsored by the Old Town School of Folk Music. Featured musical performers from all over Latin America, Mexico, Puerto Rico, and South America have made this one of Chicago's premier musical festivals. The renowned Old Town School of Folk Music has sponsored numerous concerts and special performances presented by artists from all over the world. But the Latin Music Festival is by far one of the most successful and popular events that the school has sponsored. Overflow crowds come to see such acclaimed performers as Flaco Jiminez, Guayaneca, and Los Kjarkas—described by executive director Jim Hirsch as the "greatest Andean group in the world."

Chicago Latino Film Festival, *several locations around Chicago. Mid-to-late April. For tickets, dates, and show times, call the event coordinator, Pepe Vargas, Executive Director, Chicago Latino Cinema, c/o Columbia College, 600 S. Michigan, Chicago, IL 60605, (312) 431-1330.*

A series of award-winning feature-length films from Latin America and Europe that are shown on ten different nights in April. The movies are shown at several locations around the city. It is advisable to purchase opening-night tickets in advance, but there is generally no problem securing walk-up seating on any night afterward.

Viva Chicago!, *Grant Park, Chicago. Weekend following Labor Day. Call (312) 744-3315 for additional details.*

A two-day Latin Music festival sponsored by the Mayor's Office of Special Events. Latin music is more popular than ever, evidenced by the throngs of people who have flocked to the Petrillo Bandshell and the "Day Stage" at Jackson Boulevard and Lake Shore Drive each year since 1989 to catch the hottest acts, be it pop singer Gloria Estefan, Los Angeles rockers Los Lobos, percussionist Mongo Santamaria, salsa stars Ruben Blades and Eddie Santiago, or balladeer Beatrize Adriana. There's something here to suit everyone's musical tastes, ranging from mambo to meringue. Virtually every Latin musical style is represented at Viva Chicago! which seems destined to rival the Grant Park Jazz Fest as the premier event of summer. Hours: Saturday and Sunday, noon until 10 P.M. Free admission. Vendors sell Mexican, Puerto Rican, Caribbean, and South American food and beverages in the park.

Hispanic Festival, *at Brookfield Zoo, 1st Avenue and 31st Street, Brookfield, (708) 485-0263. Last week in September. Zoo admission price charged.*

Celebrating the cultures of Central and South America with food, games, music, and story-telling.

═══ Mexican History and Attractions ═══

There are more Mexicans in Chicago than any other Latino group—352,560 according to the 1990 census data. In the span of ten years (1970–80), the Mexican population nearly tripled. As escalating poverty, joblessness, and a sinking peso shattered the Mexican economy, thousands of Mexicans from the interior and the border regions made their way to Chicago in the 1950s and 1960s. The American dream was a powerful motivator for many of these people to abandon their families and friends for the promise of better-paying jobs in the industrial north. The tide of immigration actually began much earlier, when 206 railroad workers were recruited for duty by Chicago firms at the turn of the century. The social and economic chaos following the 1910 Mexican revolution led by Francisco Madero spurred immigration—a process accelerated by the passage of the 1921 Quota Act, which established limits on European immigration into the United States. The Mexicans, meanwhile, provided an affordable, nearby labor force for Yankee industrialists, particularly during times of labor strife. The steelyard strike of 1919 and the meat packing strike two years later provided immediate employment opportunities.

By 1920, some 1,200 Mexican workers, most of them railroad section hands, lived in close proximity to the industrial basin near the Chicago River; South Chicago; Back of the Yards; and farther south, near the steel yards. In 1927 the Catholic Archdiocese, under the direction of George Cardinal Mundelein, designated the first Spanish-speaking parish, St. Francis of Assisi, at 12th Street and Newberry Avenue. By this time the Mexican population of Chicago had grown to nearly 26,000.

The coming of World War II marked the next major influx of Mexicans into Chicago. The international *bracero* contract labor agreements, signed in 1942 and 1943, allowed for the temporary entry of migrant farm laborers to fulfill manpower shortages in the Southwest brought on by the war. In the Midwest the labor drain was particularly acute, as the factories and industrial plants geared up to meet wartime quotas. The large railroad consortiums, including the Chicago, Burlington and Quincy; the Chicago, Minneapolis, St. Paul and Pacific; and the Chicago, Rock Island, and Pacific lines took advantage of the *bracero* (worker) laws to hire 15,344 Mexicans between 1943 and 1945. Mexican braceros poured into New City, Back of the Yards, and the Lower West Side communities of Pilsen and South Lawndale (now called *Pueblo Pequeño* or Little Village), and the adjacent "Heart of Chicago" neighborhood. It is bordered by 17th Street on the north, the city limits on the west, and the South Branch of the Chicago River on the south and east.

Mexicans forced out of their Near West Side neighborhood by construction of the new University of Illinois campus in the early 1960s moved southwest and displaced the Bohemians of Pilsen. South Lawndale, once called "Cesca California" by the Czechs who lived there, was dubbed the "Little Village" by Mexicans, who have given this immigrant neighborhood a decided south-of-the-border flavor. Every year on September 16, the residents of the Little Village celebrate Mexican Independence Day with a large, colorful parade that winds its way down 26th Street from Kedzie to Cicero.

Pilsen and the Little Village continue to serve as the most important port of entry in Chicago for newly enfranchised Mexicans. Grocery stores, restaurants, and newsstands along the commercial strips of 18th and 26th streets cater more to the Spanish-speaking residents than to the small tourist trade that may visit this community in the course of a year. The numbers tell the real story. Between 1960 and 1980, the Mexican population exploded from just 6,972 to 83,385. A decade later, the census taker noted that the Mexican presence in Du Page had doubled from 17,302 to 34,567. It is estimated that a full 90 percent of the Hispanics in DuPage County are Mexican. The new immigrants from south of the border are bypassing the large metro areas in favor of the manufacturing and service jobs that have followed the great inner-city exodus into the suburbs. Half of all Latinos now residing in the western suburbs are here illegally. They are the *indocumentados,* who become the unwitting tool of factory owners who exploit the system for economic gain.

In the 1950s, amid the postwar prosperity of the Eisenhower years, the Mexican-American community in the United States experienced the first major backlash against undocumented workers. It resulted in the "Operation Wetback" roundup of thousands of Mexicans, who were returned to their native land. With stricter immigration laws enacted by the government, fewer Mexicans came to Chicago.

Meanwhile in Chicago, Mexican community leaders banded together in an effort to advance their social and political status in the face of the crackdown. The Catholic church took up the cause of the *indocumentados* in the summer of 1982, when federal immigration officials detained over 2,000 Mexicans in a military hangar at O'Hare Airport. Father Fred Brandstrader of the Providence of God Roman Catholic church, (7171 W. 18th Street), organized his fellow priests from the six parishes serving the Pilsen community to protest the actions of the government. Father Brandstrader presided over one of the largest Mexican parishes in the city; one that had shed its Lithuanian character by the 1960s, when many of the older residents had either moved out of the neighborhood or had died. The march he organized in 1982 was symbolic of the strong ties forged between the church and the community.

As a result of Father Brandstrader's crusading efforts on behalf of the *indocumentados* and his overriding sense of fair play, the City of Chicago has discontinued the practice of confining undocumented aliens in large, dehumanizing holding "pens" at O'Hare Airport. "The purpose of our march was to draw attention to the mistreatment of the Mexican community," the priest explains. "And in this instance I think we were successful."

Father Brandstrader, a gutsy champion of social justice, has worked in Chicago's Mexican *barrio* since 1968—even as that community expanded its horizons into suburbia. Presently he is attached to St. Joseph the Worker parish in Wheeling, where a sizable Mexican-American population goes to worship.

Over the years, other agencies have assisted the community. A $100,000 grant from the Office of Inter-American Affairs resulted in the formation of the Mexican Civic Committee in 1943, then later in 1950, the Mexican American Council. A Mexican Social Center opened in 1945, and was dedicated to the memory of Manuel Perez, who had won the Congressional Medal of Honor during World War II. These coordinated efforts showed that cooperation was not only desirable, but fruitful.

Years later, in 1977, this community spirit was again felt among members of the Pilsen Neighbors Community. They won a major victory over city bureaucrats who had attempted to bus Mexican-American children out of the district against the wishes of the parents. The Board of Education desired to bolster sagging enrollments across the city, but the plan was opposed by Teresa Fraga and others within the Pilsen neighborhood, who called for the construction of their own school. The community fought hard over this issue for nearly four years, until the city decided to build them a new facility at 2150 S. Laflin Street. The discordant voices of 1,000 community residents were heard outside the offices of the Board of Education the day of the vote, until the members caved in to the tremendous political pressure and agreed to build the spacious Benito Juarez High School, which

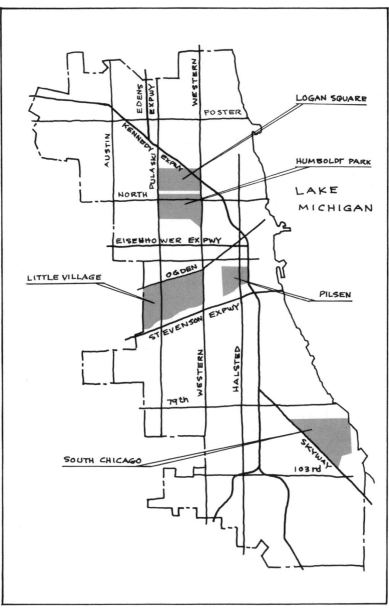

Latino Neighborhoods

was designed by a Mexican architect named Ramirez Vazquez. Juarez, which offers bilingual instruction, is the crown jewel of Pilsen, which has the highest-density Latino community in Chicago.

Because Pilsen and the Little Village were overcrowded, and much of the housing old and dilapidated, many Mexican-Americans who had accumulated savings left the neighborhood and moved to the suburbs. Cicero, Aurora, Joliet, Waukegan, Melrose Park, Wheeling, and West Chicago absorbed much of the city overflow in the 1970s and 1980s. In Aurora alone, there are at least 30,000 Latinos, comprising 3.8% of the residential population. This trend is likely to continue into the next decade, as Mexican-Americans continue to make economic strides. Those who remain behind have valiantly banded together to fight the scourge of drugs, gangs, and crime. The Latin American Job Center, begun in 1972, was formed to train workers for higher-paying, skilled union jobs, and to assist small contractors desiring to do business in the community. On September 10, 1984, solidarity became evident in Pilsen, when 1,200 residents marched in support of the church's efforts to establish the Pilsen Catholic Youth Center, aimed at taking youngsters off the streets to give them religious instruction and provide them with a wholesome place in which to meet socially.

For Chicago's Mexican community, it has been a hard climb. But now at last, the time of *prosperidad* seems to be at hand. The number of independently owned businesses continues to grow—there were about 5,000 of them, according to 1987 census figures. That number has steadily risen. Thanks to minority set-aside programs and a 1994, $200 million federal grant to help impoverished inner-city neighborhoods that provide assistance to Latinos seeking to break into the markets, immigrants who would have otherwise ended up in factories can now share in the entrepreneurial spirit that has been the lifeblood of the city. Of course most of these businesses are of the storefront variety and are confined to the Latino neighborhoods, but if history teaches us anything, it is that small deals and big dreams sometimes point the way toward a brighter future.

Pilsen: The Color of a Great Historic Neighborhood

Chicago, for all of its individual might and "I Will" entrepreneurial spirit, is no more than the sum total of its parts, a delicate weave of interlocking communities separated by culture, ideology, and the tide of history. Neighborhoods become half-way houses, receiving the poor, the hungry, and the uprooted masses in search of a better way. The neighborhood of Pilsen is often referred to as the "Port of Entry," and with good reason.

Irish and German immigrants arrived first, and soon provided a steady and dependable work force for the brickyards and small manufacturing concerns that sprang up along the south branch of the Chicago River. After the 1871 fire, displaced Bohemians from other parts of the city and from Europe began pouring into the neighborhood, which had miraculously escaped the conflagration. The Bohemians were joined by Lithuanians, Poles, Slovenians, and Italians within a few years.

Bohemians shaped the direction of the community for seventy years. Their historic presence can still be felt on 18th Street, if only in the architecture. Like dinosaur bones unearthed from a long-forgotten age, these wonderful old stone buildings are a last testament to Chicago's "age of empire." With a little imagination, it is possible to visualize the Czech craftspeople applying the final touches to the elaborate cornices and mansard roofs of the remarkably well-preserved nineteenth-century storefronts and two-flats that loom over 18th Street west of Halsted.

Pilsen has endured the profound changes that altered the character of the South Side since the 1920s. Massive construction of public housing units, the corresponding deterioration of neighborhoods, and the exodus of industry exacted a heavy toll on much of the surrounding neighborhoods, until all that remains, really, are Pilsen and sections of Bridgeport to stand as testaments to the currents of history. The churches of Pilsen are cathedrals of hope for the individual who is trapped in the industrial corridor of a tough city. St. Procopius, at 18th and Allport, was designed in 1883 by Paul Huber for the Czechs. St. Adalbert's at 17th and Paulina is done in an enduring beaux arts style with clock towers and pink Corinthian columns. St. Adalbert's, which has withstood the test of time, once served the Polish community of Pilsen. The Providence of God Church at 18th and Union was Lithuanian. Today it is almost entirely Mexican.

Pilsen continues to be a "stopping-off point," a temporary way station before the rich harvest. With ingenuity, thriftiness, gritty determination, and a little luck, many of the Mexican residents who arrived here from the central highlands in the 1950s have already moved farther south to the slightly more upscale "Little Village," or to western and northern suburbs such as Waukegan. Those who remain behind channel their efforts toward community improvement. Amid the specter of abandoned factories and vacated manufacturing plants that once provided an important source of continuing employment for the European immigrants, there are hopeful signs of economic turnaround. (The old Schoenhofen Brewery at 18th and Canalport is a good example. The relic of pre-Prohibition Chicago was boarded up and rat-infested for many years until it was placed on the National Historic Register and privately rehabbed. It is a curious twist of fate that the old German brewery is today the Schoenhofen Artesian Water Company.)

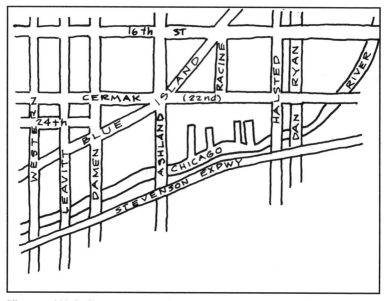

Pilsen and Little Tuscany

A flourishing artists' colony centered near 18th and Halsted provides an important, emerging outlet for creative expression on the Southwest Side. It was founded by John Podmajersky in the 1960s, after he failed in his efforts to sell a renovated tavern. Instead, the second-generation Pilsen native converted the building into a studio loft and within a few short years he was joined by other working artists, writers, and photographers who established residence between 18th and 19th streets. Each year in October the "Pilsen East Artists" sponsor an open house in the 700 block of West 18th Street and the 800 block of West 19th Street, in which the public is invited to attend a special showing of the artists' work.

The Pilsen Neighbors Community Council combines the resources of numerous neighborhood organizations. It seeks to promote the collective good through voter registration drives, the construction of a new field house and gymnastic center at Harrison Park, and the "New Homes for Chicago" program. (The housing program was launched by Mayor Richard M. Daley to provide affordable housing for community residents.) Founded in the 1950s, when the neighborhood was still essentially Eastern European in its character, Pilsen Neighbors is the only community-based organization in the city to be funded under the terms of the "New Homes for Chicago" program. The Pilsen Neighbors Community Council is a powerful voice of hope within the inner city.

On September 7, 1989, the Rudy Lozano branch of the Chicago Public Library was officially dedicated at 1805 S. Loomis Street after years of bureaucratic foot-dragging. The results were certainly worth the wait. The graceful lines of the new library feature a pre-Columbian terra cotta design inside and out, and a twenty-five-foot-high glass dome skylight arching over a Royal Fan palm tree. Named in honor of the 22nd Ward community activist who was gunned down by a reputed gang member in June, 1983, the building houses the largest Spanish-language collection in the city's library system. Among its holdings are books, newspapers, magazines, and video cassettes.

As you stroll along 18th Street, the blare of Latin music can be heard from inside the Victorian buildings. From the second-floor windows, young children and old men gaze at the passing street traffic. In the hot days of summer, few people can afford air conditioning. As you walk past the family-owned *taquerias* (grocery stores), department stores, and corner taverns advertising *cerveza fria* (cold beer) on a warm afternoon, your appetite is whetted for another helping of Mexican food. Street vendors are there to oblige, selling floury Mexican pastries from pushcarts. The walk-up windows dispense tacos and hot corn on the cob, spiced with lemon and hot pepper. You linger for only a moment, and then continue on to preview raw, creative expressionism at its finest. Twenty hand-painted wall murals depicting historical, cultural, religious, and political themes are scattered throughout Pilsen. They include the murals at 1305 W. 18th Street; the 16th Street viaduct (near Blue Island); Casa Aztlan at 18th and Racine, where portraits of Mexican and Latin leaders adorn the exterior wall; Miller and 18th; and, finally, another artistic motif at 18th and Blue Island. The murals came into being during the 1960s and 1970s and were executed by such artists as Ray Patian and Aurelio Diaz.

A Marxist-Leninist book store near Ashland Avenue and 18th Street is a gentle reminder of the political discontent that has simmered beneath the surface of this community for several years. In this regard, the Mexican community of Pilsen carries on the historic traditions of dissent that began with the Bohemian socialists in July 1877. During the tense days of the nationwide railroad strike, they had rioted for better wages and a shortened work week at the 16th and Halsted viaducts.

Getting There: The Douglas elevated line stops at 18th Street in Pilsen. By car, exit the southbound lanes of the Dan Ryan Expressway at 18th Street and proceed west.

For additional information, call the CTA at (312) 836-7000.

Bienvenidos a Little Village:
The "Suburbs" of Pilsen

At first glance, the old South Lawndale neighborhood seems like an unlikely place to resurrect the American dream of home ownership, two chickens in every pot, and a shiny new Ford in the garage. Because as you will observe in your walking tour, the ominous looking Metropolitan Corrections Center at 26th and California stands opposite the festive gateway arch that leads into the *Pueblo Pequeño* (Little Village). The solemnity of the jail, its barbed wire walls, and imposing guard towers offer an unsettling yet conspicuous contrast to the inner vitality of 26th Street—the *Calle Mexico*—the shopping, restaurant, and nightclub area between the Little Village Mall at Albany and the Chicago Central Industrial Park farther west at Kostner Avenue.

Mexicans first arrived in the Little Village in the 1950s. Most had migrated from nearby Pilsen, and in all likelihood would have continued to move farther westward into Cicero and Berwyn if not for the prevailing social attitudes toward minorities in those two suburbs. Making the best of a tough situation, the Mexican community has prospered in its Southwest Side surroundings. Property values continue to rise, and the storefronts along 26th Street are nearly at full occupancy. Old-fashioned inner-city retailers like Goldblatt's and Three Sisters continue to serve a predominantly Latino clientele. In other neighborhoods, these kinds of stores are boarded up, burned-out, deserted shells—grim reminders that the economic well-being of some neighborhoods has been sapped by the influx of gangs, crime, and poverty. But in the Little Village, Goldblatt's, a respected name in Chicago retailing for generations, seems to be making a go of it.

The merchants, supported by an enthusiastic Chamber of Commerce and Community Council, promote the stability and togetherness of the Little Village, reflected in the colorful wall murals—far less political than the outdoor artwork of Pilsen. Murals are located at the Bank of Chicago, 26th and Homan; 25th and St. Louis; 25th and Pulaski at the Second Federal Savings; and in back of the Los Camales Restaurant at 26th and Kedzie, opposite McDonald's. The "Broken Wall Mural," as it is called, was painted by the Marshall Savage Boys and Girls Club. The message of faith is poignant in its simplicity: "Beyond the walls of doubt there is a great reward that can only be reached through faith in God."

The most visible landmark in the community is the welcome arch next to the Little Village Mall at Albany and 26th. The pink-colored gateway, which in some ways is reminiscent of the Chinatown arch, was financed by local subscription and private donation. The formal dedication ceremony took place on April 30, 1990. Then on April 11, 1991, the former Mexican president, Carlos Salinas de Gortari (now living in self-imposed exile in Ireland), inaugurated the clock during a state visit. Some 2,000 well-wishers and city officials, including Mayor Richard M. Daley, witnessed. As a symbol of good will between the two respective nations, this stretch of 26th Street was rechristened the "Calle Mexico."

The storefronts are well-maintained family businesses, due in part to a city and federal Façade Rebate Program, which provides financial and technical assistance to the owners and tenants of buildings that have street-level commercial space. The improvements listed under the rebate program are intended to promote and revitalize Chicago's neighborhood commercial retail areas, which have suffered a slow decline since the advent of the large suburban shopping malls. The independent merchants of 26th Street sell clothing, books and records, and imported grocery items from Mexico. The owners of these establishments often find themselves in friendly competition with street-corner hustlers hawking sharply discounted music cassettes from Mexico, fresh fruit, and tee-shirts. Copies of *El Mañana* and *La Raza*—the largest-circulating Latino newspaper in the city—can be purchased in the stores or in the corner boxes. *La Raza* and the seven Spanish-language community papers provide some of the few links to the distant culture of Mexico, preserved here in the Little Village.

In many respects the neighborhood mirrors Chinatown in its expansive economic growth, but it is much less touristy. You will not find the proliferation of gift shops selling inexpensive souvenir paraphernalia and gadgets. However, restaurants and Mexican nightclubs may abound. In fact, you'll find two, three, maybe even four restaurants, ranging from fast food to quasi-elegant, on every block. The difference lies in the clientele. Since the Little Village is an undiscovered treasure, the owners cater, for the most part, to the neighborhood residents.

In 1990 plans were unveiled for Plaza de Mexico, a $30-million shopping mall. The idea for a 351,000-square-foot plaza was put forward by the Matanky Realty Company on Halsted Street. The developers encountered a storm of protest from the 600 local business owners, who feared that the long-term consequences of such a mall would destroy their livelihood and the viability of the community. Young boys selling wholesale cassettes on the street is one thing. A well-publicized real estate development costing millions of dollars is something else again.

A sagging real estate market in the early 1990s, environmental protection issues, and economic uncertainty discouraged Matanky Realty from moving forward with their plans. Only a small portion of the industrial plot was redeveloped—the City of Chicago constructed a new public school on the disputed parcel of land.

"It is very difficult to open up an ethnic area such as Pilsen," explained Jim Schmidt of Matanky, who points to the need for cultural sensitivity and addressing community concerns on the part of the large firms seeking to commit their resources to the inner city.

Without the addition of the first "Mexican Theme Mall" in the Midwest, the future of Little Village seems assured for the time being. Even though the number of votes cast during a typical city election is the smallest here, by percent, that phenomenon is partly explainable by the large population of young children and adolescents who now reside in the 22nd Ward. Once they come of age, they alone will determine the destiny of this blue-collar Chicago neighborhood once known as "Ceska California" in the days when Anton Cermak greeted his Bohemian neighbors on the street. Will the next generation of Mexicans choose to remain behind and preserve the indigenous Latino culture, or will this Little Village be absorbed into the whole, its boundaries virtually indistinguishable from its tragically blighted neighbor, North Lawndale? Only time, and the unpredictable patterns of neighborhood settlement, can provide a clue.

Cultural Institutions

Mexican Fine Arts Center Museum, *1852 W. 19th St., Chicago, (773) 738-1503. Closed on Mondays. Admission is free.*

In recognition of the historic settlement of the Pilsen community by thousands of Mexican immigrants, the Chicago Park District in January 1986, signed an agreement to convert the Harrison Park Boat Craft Shop into a permanent home for the Mexican Fine Arts Center Museum, which was founded in September 1982. The renovation phase began in August 1986, with the festive grand opening taking place on March 27, 1987. A newly remodeled west wing was unveiled on June 8, 1990. It is the first Mexican museum of its kind in the Midwest, and since its founding, it has achieved most if not all of its stated objectives. Those are: (1) to sponsor special events and exhibits that reflect the rich cultural diversity of the Mexican visual and performing arts; (2) to develop a significant permanent collection of Mexican art; (3) to encourage local Mexican artists to achieve excellence; and (4) to offer regularly scheduled educational programs. The Mexican Fine Arts Center Museum has held nearly 40 exhibits in the main gallery since 1987, and has welcomed over 600 groups and 75,000 visitors during that time. The museum houses a permanent collection of prints, photographs, folk art pieces, and selected works of noted artists such as David Alfaro Siqueiros and Jose Clemente Orozco (both famous for their wall-sized public murals depicting pivotal events from Mexican history and culture), Alfredo Zalce, Jose Guadalupe Posada, and Rufino Tamayo. A gift shop, small auditorium, main gallery, and courtyard gallery are located in the building. *Recommended.*

Annual Events and Celebrations

Mexican Independence Day Parade (Downtown).
*Saturday closest to September 15. Call
(312) 744-3315 for additional information.*

Marks Mexico's political separation from Spain, an event that occurred in
1820 when Guerrero and Agustin de Iturbide negotiated a status quo independence with the colonial government following a protracted and violent
struggle that first took shape in 1810. An insurrection led by Miguel Hidalgo
y Costilla was brutally suppressed. Jose Maria Morelos y Pavon's military
campaign against the Spanish in 1814 met with similar failure. But in 1823,
Mexico was declared a republic, and a federal constitution patterned after
the United States Constitution was adopted a year later. Each year, over 130
floats, bands, marching groups, and even the Chicago Police Department's
much-heralded Emerald Society Band takes part in this extravaganza. The
parade route (south on Dearborn Street from Wacker Drive to Van Buren) is
annually witnessed by 250,000 spectators proudly waving Mexican flags.
Many of them sport huge sombreros and brightly colored folk costumes.
The parade is organized by the Mexican Civic Society.

Mexican Independence Day Parade (Little Village).
*Sunday afternoon following the downtown parade, or
September 16. For dates and time, call (773) 521-5387.*

Festive neighborhood celebration that winds its way down 26th Street
between Kedzie Avenue and Cicero in the heart of Chicago's Little Village.
It is a rollicking good time, with floats, marching bands, costumed mata-
dors, dancers, men on horseback, and of course, the "Miss Little Village"
parade queen. The Grand Marshal of the 1991 parade was Illinois governor
Jim Edgar, who was eager to cultivate the good will of Chicago's sizable
Mexican community during his first year in office. The event is sponsored
by the Little Village Chamber of Commerce.

El Grito Parade, *47th Street, from Damen Avenue to
Ashland. Second weekend in September. For
information, call (773) 247-5100.*

Annual Mexican Independence Day celebration sponsored by the Back of
the Yards Council. Mexican bands, floats, and entertainment.

Fiesta en la Villita (Little Village Festival), *26th St.
and Albany, in the Little Village Mall, Chicago.
Thursday before the Mexican Independence Day*

Parade in September. Admission is free. For
information, call the Little Village Chamber of
Commerce, (773) 521-5387.

Four days of music, carnival rides, and live performances of Mexican folk
and contemporary music.

Fiesta del Sol, *Blue Island Ave. between 18th Street*
(on the north) and Cermak Rd. (on the south),
Chicago. July or August. Free admission. On-street
parking available near the festival. For additional
information, contact the Pilsen Neighbors at 2007 S.
Blue Island Ave., Chicago, or call (773) 666-2663.

Four-day street fair. The festival, one of the largest in the city and sponsored
by the Pilsen Neighbors Association, began as a block party in 1973 to celebrate the Board of Education's decision to build Benito Juarez High
School. Since that time, Fiesta del Sol has become one of the most important
social events in the Mexican community. The proceeds of the event benefit
the Pilsen YMCA, the various neighborhood parishes, and El Hogar del
Niños (a daycare center). There are carnival rides; an arts and crafts promenade; free medical exams for children; local jazz and rock artists and well-
known performers like Elsa Garcia, a Texas-based singer, Suzy Gonzalez,
and Antonio de Jesus, who are flown in especially for the occasion. The
savory Mexican food, including tostadas, gorditas, and the famous enchiladas prepared by Jovita Andrade and other past and present Pilsenites, are
a mainstay of the festival.

Viva Mexico!, *Soldier Field, Chicago. Mid-July.*
Admission fee charged. Call (773) 944-7272 for
information.

Two-day street fair and folk festival that has attracted upwards of 100,000
people each year since its inception in 1986. The reason: Festival promoters
book some of the top musical acts from Mexico each year, who are well
known to the Latino residents of the Pilsen and Little Village communities.
Food vendors dispense Mexican burritos, enchiladas, chimichangas, and hot
salsa. There is a carnival midway and games for youngsters. Sponsored by
Cardenas and Fernandez Associates and participating advertisers.

Viva Aztlan Street Festival, Casa Aztlan, *1831 S.*
Racine St., Chicago, (773) 666-5508. July.

One-day outdoor street festival at Casa Aztlan, a multi-service community
and cultural center. Casa Aztlan was founded as the Howell Neighborhood

House eighty years ago, when Pilsen was a port of entry for thousands of Eastern Europeans. Through its various youth, family services, and education divisions, Casa Aztlan promotes self-determination within the Mexican community it now serves.

Del Corazon Festival of Mexican Performing Arts,
Mexican Fine Arts Museum, 1852 W. 19th, Chicago,
(773) 738-1503. Spring festival from March to June,
fall festival from September to November.

Traditional Mexican music and dance performed at the museum and other spots around the city, including the Skyline Theater at Navy Pier.

The Way of the Cross *(Via Crucis), Providence of*
God Church, 717 W. 18th St., Chicago, (773) 226-2929.
Good Friday.

Religion is a powerful, unifying force in Latino life; deeply rooted in mysticism, spirituality, and centuries-old traditions that succeeding waves of immigrants have carried with them into the northern cities of the United States. On Good Friday, hundreds of worshipers from the eight Catholic parishes that serve the Pilsen community participate in the stirring dramatization of the Passion Play in the basement of the Providence of God Church, and a reenactment of the walk to "Calvary" (in this case, Harrison Park). The members of the cast are dressed in costume, and a mounted Roman centurion clears 18th Street so that the actors portraying Christ, the Virgin Mary, and the twelve Apostles may proceed past hundreds of onlookers to Harrison Park. The Way of the Cross is a powerful affirmation of faith and a custom that dates back to antiquity. It was brought to Mexico by the conquering Spanish armies hundreds of years ago, and is recreated each year in the small ranches and rural villages high in the mountains. *Via Crucis* starts at Providence of God Church (where, by the way, Pope John Paul conducted an open-air mass in 1979) and ends at St. Adalbert's Church, 1650 W. 17th St., Chicago. *Recommended.*

Cinco de Mayo Celebration.

Commemorates the historic 1862 Battle of Pueblo in which the Mexican Army under the leadership of President Benito Juarez rallied their troops to defeat the forces of French Emperor Napolean III. Until a few years ago few people outside the Mexican community were unaware of the broader significance of the day. But now all of Chicago celebrates the pride of Mexico with a festive parade that travels west-bound along Cermak Road (22nd Street) from Damen Avenue to Kedzie, starting at noon on the first Sunday in May. The parade features strolling mariachi musicians, horseback riders and floats.

The activities also include an open-air carnival at Douglas Park, 1401 S. Sacramento Avenue on Chicago's West Side, with plenty of carnival rides, food booths, games, and merchandise sales. The entire event is simulcast over WTAQ-Radio, AM-1300. Call (312) 747-7670 for scheduled times.

Day of Our Lady of Guadalupe, *Providence of God Church, 717 W. 18th St., Chicago, (773) 226-2929. December. Call the church for the date and time.*

About 450 years ago, the Blessed Virgin appeared before a poor Mexican peasant named Juan Diego. She ordered the man to go before the bishop of Mexico City and to tell him to build a church in her honor. When the bishop twice refused, the Virgin again appeared, and caused roses to grow out of the rocks in the hills. The disbelieving bishop refused a third time. The image of the Virgin then appeared on Juan Diego's apron. Legend or miracle, call it what you will, but it remains the most important religious feast day in Mexico, and for that matter, in Chicago's Pilsen community as well. At the Providence of God Church, where so many Lithuanian parishioners once worshiped, the Pilsen community attends an evening mass conducted in Spanish by a visiting priest from Mexico. A mariachi band with three guitars, two violins, and a trumpet accompany the choir in the *magnanitas,* a hymn that speaks of faith, devotion, and hope. When the service has ended, Mexican pastries are served in the church basement.

Shops

Panaderia Bakery, *3117 W. 26th St., Chicago, (773) 254-0006. Open daily.*

An unusual self-service bakery located in the Little Village Mall. Select from an assortment of Mexican pastries, bismarcks, and donuts, which are arranged along the walls. The metal serving trays are available at the counter.

El Nopal Mexican Bakery, *two locations: 3648 W. 26th St., Chicago, (773) 762-9204, and 1844 S. Blue Island, Chicago, (773) 226-9861. Open daily.*

Fancy puff-dough pastries, wedding cakes, and sweet rolls. Two locations— in the Little Village and Pilsen.

Coral Bakery, *two locations: 3807 W. 26th St.,*
Chicago, (773) 762-4132, and 3424 W. 26th, Chicago,
(773) 522-8121. Open daily.

Cookies, pound cakes, sliced and buttered bread, and tarts for every occasion.

Supermercados "La Justicia," *two locations:*
3644 W. 26th St., Chicago, (773) 277-6148, and
3435 W. 26th, Chicago, (773) 521-1593. Open
daily.

Two friendly neighborhood grocery stores owned by Ruby, Julio and Sergio Martinez. Imported food items from Mexico, fresh produce, canned goods, and Spanish-language magazines and newspapers.

Armando's Finer Foods, *2627 S. Kedzie Ave.,*
Chicago, (773) 927-6688. Open daily.

Mexican supermarket with a full line of imported foods, bakery items, meats, produce, and magazines.

Libreria Giron, *3527 W. 26th St., Chicago,*
(773) 521-5651. Open daily.

Spanish-language books and magazines, CDs, cassettes, greeting cards, and newspapers.

Restaurants

Su Casa, *49 E. Ontario St., Chicago, (312) 943-4041.*
Open for lunch and dinner daily. Credit cards
accepted.

A long-time Chicago favorite that seems to improve with age. The food is still a bargain, despite its location in one of the priciest neighborhoods in town. The standard Mexican dishes: shrimp chimichanga, enchiladas, and chicken fajita are recommended.

Frontera Grill, *445 N. Clark St., Chicago,*
(312) 661-1434. Open for lunch and dinner. Closed
Sundays and Mondays. Credit cards accepted.

For people who really know their Mexican food. This North Side eatery is owned by Rick and Deann Groen Bayless, authors of a cookbook listing recipes for dozens of regional dishes from the "Heart of Mexico." Saturday brunch. *Recommended.*

Lindo Mexico, *2642 N. Lincoln Ave., Chicago, (773) 871-4832. Open for lunch and dinner daily. Credit cards accepted.*

Festive atmosphere, new menu items, and reasonable prices complement the existing charm of this restaurant. Recommended dishes include garlic-sautéed shrimp or boneless chicken served with toasted ancho chilis, lime, and cilantro.

Las Palmas, *1773 W. Howard St., Chicago, (773) 262-7446. Open for lunch and dinner daily. Credit cards accepted.*

Fine Mexican cuisine at reasonable prices.

Topolobampo, *445 N. Clark St., Chicago, (312) 661-1434. Open for dinner. Closed Saturday–Monday. Credit cards accepted.*

Adjacent to the Frontera Grill, and named for a Pacific Coast town, Rick Bayless's latest creation comes highly recommended. The Mexican dishes as prepared by Rick and Deann are original and savory.

Concordia Restaurant and Nightclub, *3801 W. 26th St., Chicago, (773) 521-4095. Open for breakfast Saturdays and Sundays and for lunch and dinner daily.*

Mexican cuisine with a special emphasis on seafood and *parrillada.* The small dance floor can get very crowded on the weekends, when the live entertainment appears. For a quiet Mexican lunch at very reasonable prices, it's best to stop by on a Saturday afternoon, when the waiters have little else to do but to gaze out at the street traffic.

Hat Dance, *325 W. Huron St., Chicago, (312) 649-0066. Open for lunch Monday–Saturday and dinner daily.*

The striking white-on-white decor and excellent blend of traditional and experimental Mexican cuisine have made Hat Dance very popular. Reservations are strongly recommended.

Las Cazuelas, *4821 N. Elston Ave., Chicago,*
(773) 777-5304. Open for lunch Tuesday–
Friday and dinner Tuesday–Sunday. Closed
Mondays.

Chef and owner Ricardo Caballero opened a new, larger space in 1996 offering both inside and outside dining. The regular menu items are usually excellent, but patrons strongly recommend trying the daily specials. Try the lobster flautas, grilled salmon, and delicious margaritas.

Decima Musa, *1901 S. Loomis St., Chicago,*
(773) 243-1556. Open for lunch and dinner.
Closed Mondays. Credit cards accepted.

A cozy Pilsen restaurant with occasional entertainment on the weekends. There are definite language barriers to be overcome if you are not fluent in Spanish.

Outlying Areas

El Cortez Restaurant, *three locations: 13414 S.*
Western Ave., Blue Island, (708) 371-9566; 18250 S.
Cicero, Country Club Hills, (708) 798-4223; and
10296 S. 78th Ave., Palos Hills, (708) 599-5080.
Open for lunch and dinner daily.

Traditional Mexican food in a casual, fun setting.

Media

Rolo's Video, *3800 W. 26th St., Chicago,*
(773) 277-2362. Open daily.

Rolando G. De La Vega rents Spanish-language and standard English titles.

Video Mexico, *4204 W. North Ave., Chicago,*
(773) 384-7758. Open daily.

This Northwest Side location stocks thousands of Spanish-language films from Mexico that are available for rental only. There are some American films dubbed in Spanish.

═ Puerto Rican History and Attractions ═

Puerto Ricans are a young immigrant group, though one can hardly call the Puerto Ricans immigrants, since the three islands were ceded to the United States on December 10, 1898 by terms of the Treaty of Paris ending the Spanish-American War. Puerto Rico was granted commonwealth status on July 25, 1952.

In 1980, the average age in the Puerto Rican community was only 21. A full 59% of the population was under the age of 25. These numbers suggest—and the reality of their urban existence bears out—the point that they are among the poorest of Chicago's ethnics, suffering from chronic unemployment, low per capita income, and a high drop-out rate as reflected in the 1982 graduating class at Roberto Clemente High School. Of the 855 eligible seniors, 55.7% of the Latino students dropped out before commencement.

Assimilation into the Anglo culture has been difficult ever since the first great exodus from the island began after World War II. Like the Mexican farm workers who crossed into Texas and the American Southwest in the early years of the century, the Puerto Rican immigrants were also agrarian farmers who harvested coffee, sugar cane, bananas, pineapples, and rice on small, uncompromising plots of land. By the 1950s, the Puerto Ricans began supplanting the Italians, Poles, and Ukrainians in the ethnically diverse West Town community on the lower part of Milwaukee Avenue. This process of displacing older European groups was hastened by the construction of the Kennedy Expressway in the later 1950s.

In 1960 there were 32,371 Puerto Ricans counted in the census, but a full 10,000 of them lived in Spanish-speaking West Town. In the next twenty years, the growth of the community was explosive. While West Town continued to serve as a port of entry for new arrivals, other Puerto Ricans who had lived in Chicago for a few years pushed farther north into the historic Humboldt Park, which until its incorporation into Chicago in 1869, was far removed from the bustle of downtown Chicago, and was inhabited for the most part by ethnic Germans and Norwegians.

The Puerto Ricans who tried to carve out a better life along the spacious Logan and Humboldt boulevards typically worked on factory assembly lines, in fancy Loop hotels and restaurants, and in various manufacturing concerns. Relief from the drudgery of menial labor could be found through social and fraternal societies like Los Caballeros de San Juan (Knights of San Juan), organized in 1954 to foster a sense of well-being within the Spanish community. Los Caballeros also filled a larger need by helping their members find decent housing outside of the ramshackle tenements of West Town and locate better-paying jobs. The organization began in the Woodlawn community, but quickly re-formed into twelve *concilios* (councils) throughout Chicago. Beginning in 1956 and continuing through 1965, the fraternal society sponsored an annual *El Dia de San Juan* (St. John's Day) celebration, which included a banquet and a dance. After 1965 this event became known as *La Parada Puertorriqueña* (The Puerto Rican Parade), which took into account all of the Puerto Rican societies and promoted a sense of sorely needed community pride.

This occurred at a time when jobs were increasingly harder to find, and when conditions in the "barrio" were nearly intolerable. Job discrimination and an unresponsive city administration contributed to a feeling of growing despair that culminated in the first Puerto Rican riot in United States history—on June 12, 1966, when 21-year-old Arcelis Cruz was shot and killed on Division Street by police officers during the annual parade. For the next two days and nights the West Town streets became an armed battleground that saw sixteen people injured and fifty buildings damaged. And then, after another eleven years had passed, violence flared anew when two more Puerto Ricans were shot down by police.

Out of this turmoil came the realization by city officials of the special needs of the Puerto Rican community. The Spanish-speaking Coalition for Jobs drew attention to discriminatory practices against Latinos and sought to address the broader problems that cut across the dominant Latino cultures. In 1975 the Latino Institute, bringing the different Latino organizations together under one roof, was founded with a two-year grant of $70,000 from the Community Fund of Chicago. Sensitive to the divided loyalties of the community leaders, the Institute was headquartered downtown at 105 S. LaSalle Street. To build a facility in West Town or in Pilsen would seem to favor one group at the expense of the other.

In 1981 Mayor Jane Byrne, recognizing the growing political influence of Chicago's Puerto Ricans, appointed Jose Martinez interim alderman of the 31st Ward, which extends from West Town into Humboldt Park.

Martinez wasn't the first Puerto Rican to hold a council seat. During World War I, Alderman William Emilio Rodriguez served two terms in the City Council representing the 15th Ward. Rodriguez was born in Naperville in 1879, and had actually visited Puerto Rico during military service in the Spanish-American War. However, Alderman Rodriguez downplayed his ethnicity, completing his term with little or no fanfare. Political empowerment for Chicago's Puerto Rican community would have to wait for many more decades.

After Martinez's appointment, Edward Nedza, the only white Democratic ward committeeman to slate Latinos before 1986, selected Joseph Berrios as the party's standard-bearer for the 9th District seat in 1982. Berrios was reelected in 1984. Interestingly, Nedza was ousted as a state senator in the 1986 Democratic primary by another Latino, Miguel del Valle. Del Valle was named chairman of the Mayor's Advisory Commission on Latino Affairs in 1983.

The Puerto Rican community of Chicago looks forward to a brighter day when it might consolidate these modest political achievements to formulate a new social order, which will hopefully close the economic chasm preventing them from harvesting the fruits of prosperity.

Cultural Institutions

Pedro Albizu Campos Museum of Puerto Rican History and Culture, *1457 N. California Ave., Chicago, (773) 342-4880. Open Thursday–Sunday. Admission is free.*

Dr. Pedro Albizu Campos spent much of his adult life behind bars in Puerto Rico because of his nationalistic leanings. Dr. Campos championed a free and independent Puerto Rico and was jailed for seditious conspiracy in 1937—the first of many prison terms for this political dissident. The Puerto Rican Museum, named in his honor and opened in September 1993, sponsors folkloric dancing, poetry readings, lectures, and art exhibits. Paintings, drawings, and mixed media work by Puerto Rican artists. Group tours, cultural workshops available by appointment.

Juan Antonio Corretjer Puerto Rican Cultural Center, *1671 N. Claremont, Ave., Chicago, (773) 342-8023. Open Monday–Friday.*

Located in the Wicker Park-West Town neighborhood. The Center features wall murals of Puerto Rican political dissidents. Cultural events are held inside the coffeehouse at various times during the year. A legal clinic, day care center, and high school classes are offered to community residents.

Annual Events and Celebrations

Puerto Rican Day Parade, *Michigan Ave., from Wacker Dr. to Van Buren. Second Saturday in June. For information and dates, call the Puerto Rican Parade Committee at (773) 292-1414.*

There is no special significance attached to the date of the Puerto Rican community's gala event. It just happened to fit into the City of Chicago's prearranged schedule of cultural events, and has remained a yearly tradition since 1966. It's all about being Puerto Rican, and the heartfelt pride that goes with it. There is no political message or solemn anniversary to be commemorated, just a lively Caribbean salsa beat, an army of baton twirlers, the Roberto Clemente High School Marching Band, beauty queens, 150 floats, and a score of dignitaries, which in 1991 included Chicago's treasurer Miriam Santos, who appeared with the grand marshal, Mayor Richard M. Daley. The parade and the accompanying festival held in Humboldt Park are sponsored each year by the Puerto Rican Parade Committee, which was losing money every year until Daniel Ramos took over in 1985 and reversed this pattern. A second Puerto Rican parade, more political in nature than this one, proceeds down North Avenue on the same day before winding up at Humboldt Park for the special festivities (see entry below).

Fiestas Patronales Puertorriqueñas, *Humboldt Park, 1400 N. California Ave., Chicago. June. Free admission. Sponsored by the Puerto Rican Parade Committee, 1237 N. California, Chicago, (773) 292-1414.*

A six-day outdoor festival marking Puerto Rican Week activities in Chicago, which coincides with the two major city parades. Over sixty food vendors dispense such Puerto Rican delicacies as codfish fritters, stew of pig's ears, and boiled green bananas. A midway carnival entertains the children, while older people relax under the shade playing bingo with their friends. Caribbean music performed by noted salsa musicians fills the air. Vendors from seventy-eight Puerto Rican cities exhibit their crafts, ranging from sculptured glass and pottery to leather work. Regardless of the weather, which usually tops out at a sultry ninety degrees, there's something here for everyone, evidenced by the 50,000 to 100,000 people who show up each year.

Puerto Rican Parade Committee, Beauty Queen Pageant. *Last Saturday in May. Sponsored by the Puerto Rican Parade Committee, (773) 292-1414. Admission fee charged. Call for tickets and information.*

It is quite an honor to be crowned "Queen for a Day," and the competition among the sixteen finalists hoping to represent Chicago's 120,000-strong Puerto Rican community on parade day is quite intense. Many of the contestants who vie for the coveted "satin sash" (which guarantees them a $2,000 scholarship, a white sable coat, and round-trip tickets to Puerto Rico), are Americans unfamiliar with their own Latino heritage. Very often the grueling competition is a "baptism by fire." The girls are required to spend long hours studying their history, language, native dance, and folk traditions, while developing the necessary poise and charm to win the hearts of the judges. In addition to the coronation of the queen, big-name performers like Danny Rivera and Lourdes Robles—major celebrities in Puerto Rico—are flown in to entertain the audience.

Restaurants

La Village Cafe, *510 N. Western, Chicago, (773) 455-9253. Open for lunch and dinner daily.*

The tropical decor fits the menu, which includes seafood-stuffed plantain and pork chops served with bananas and rice with peasant peas. Live music and dancing on Friday and Saturday nights.

===== Cuban History and Settlement =====

Before 1960, the Cuban community in Chicago was virtually nonexistent. On March 17, 1958, one of the epochs of political history in the Western Hemisphere began when Fidel Castro, a former lawyer, engaged in guerrilla activities and announced his intentions to lead a general revolt against the entrenched regime of Fulgencio Batista. In 1955, after several years of military rule, Batista had restored constitutional rule and granted amnesty to political prisoners. Castro and his supporters stormed into Havana on January 1, 1959, and drove Batista into permanent exile. With him went thousands of political refugees, many of them skilled workers from the professional classes who were lucky to escape with only the shirts on their backs. Some 20,000 Cuban exiles poured into Chicago. They were provided relocation assistance by the Catholic Charities of Chicago, and were generally warmly received, not only because they were fervent anticommunists during the height of the Cold War, but also because the Cubans brought with them skills that would benefit American society.

Their assimilation into American culture was far easier than that of the Mexicans and Puerto Ricans for these same reasons. Published statistics in 1979 showed that 45% of Cuban Americans in Cook County owned their homes, compared with only 35.8% of other Latino groups. An employment survey, conducted by the U.S. Immigration and Naturalization Service in the late 1970s, still showed that 10% of Cubans in the work force were professional or technical, while 7.7% were employed in the white-collar sector as clerical and office personnel. This survey was commissioned at a time when a number of working-class Cubans, unable to speak English and less prepared for the challenges of the marketplace, began appearing in the United States. This "second wave" of immigrants left Cuba for purely economic reasons and, unlike the 1960 refugees, were far less likely to resettle on the island even if the hated Castro government were to be toppled. The economic outlook hasn't changed much for the Cubans, Ecuadoreans, Colombians, and Peruvians in the 1990s. These four groups account for only 25,000, or less than 5% of the city's total Latino population but are at the top tier in terms of income, education, and housing.

Unlike the Puerto Ricans and Mexicans who are concentrated in their "barrio" neighborhoods, the Cubans are widely dispersed across the North and Northwest Sides of Chicago. The refugee immigrants, determined to locate in inexpensive housing near the Spanish-speaking neighborhoods (but not caught up in the barrio itself), tended to settle between the north branch of the Chicago River and Lake Michigan. In 1980 the largest concentration of Cubans was in the Logan Square neighborhood (1,590), and the Far North Side Edgewater community (1,441). Their desire to live among the white ethnics no doubt contributed to some rancorous feelings and heightened mistrust that have characterized the relationship between Cubans and the rest of the Latino community. According to sociologist Ruth Horowitz, in her 1983 study of Chicago's Mexican population, it is the community culture, *chicanismo,* that allows other Latinos to proclaim that "those people are like us and those others are not."

But there is no denying that the Cubans have overcome tremendous adversity and have prospered in the Anglo culture. Thirty-five percent of the Cubans residing in the Chicago metropolitan area have migrated to the suburbs, far and away the highest percentage of any Latino group.

However, the economic success of the 1960 arrivals belies the problems encountered by the 1980 Mariel boat lift refugees, exported to U.S. shores by Fidel Castro, who relaxed immigration policies to permit only malcontents and criminals to leave the island. Until 1984, these people were not eligible for immigrant status under U.S. laws. Following the Mariel boat lift, the Castro government held fast to its long-standing policy of permitting only men over 45 and women 40 or over to visit relatives in the United States.

In 1995, 40,000 Cuban boat people seeking political asylum in the U.S. crowded into a squalid tent city at the Guantanamo military base on the island. The immigration debate flared up anew—following a significant shift in foreign policy stemming from the Clinton White House.

The President reversed a 35-year precedent of granting all Cuban refugees immediate political asylum by ordering all Cuban exiles arriving on American shores returned to the island. The Cuban-American community in Chicago continues to monitor these ominous developments, but as each day passes the prayer for a free and democratic Cuba seems less of a certainty. Hope is an eternal kind of thing, however, and when that day finally comes, it will be cause for celebration.

The Cuban community today reflects a peculiar dichotomy in that it is both settled and transient. To build a sense of unity with other Latinos remains an unfulfilled goal.

Restaurants

Ambassador Cafe, *3605 N. Ashland Ave., Chicago, (773) 404-8770. Open for lunch and dinner. Closed Sundays.*

At first glance, you wouldn't think that a restaurant with the unlikely name of Ambassador Cafe is a preferred choice for gourmet Cuban cuisine. Actually, the name was inherited from the previous owners, but Omelio Rodriguez decided to retain the moniker when he took over in 1990. The restaurant is small, but the menu items are very savory. Cuban sandwiches, a variety of seafood items, and meat entrées are included on the menu. You should also sample a "mamey" milkshake, made from South American fruits.

Cafe Bolero, *2252 N. Western Ave., Chicago, (773) 227-9000. Open for lunch and dinner daily.*

Cuban cuisine with an extensive tapas selection. The menu includes an interesting Cuban dish with Yugoslavian influences called *cevapcici* (sausage with roasted peppers and feta cheese). The roast pork with *congri* (white rice with black beans) is also popular.

━━━━━ Spanish Attractions ━━━━━

Annual Events and Celebrations

American-Spanish Dance Festival,
Northeastern Illinois University, 5500 N. St. Louis Ave., Chicago, (773) 583-4050, ext. 3015. Two weeks in July.

Presented by Ensemble Español, the premier Spanish dance company in the United States to have "in residence" status at a university, in this case Northeastern Illinois University. The ensemble has presented thousands of performances throughout the United States. Founded in 1976 by "Dama" Libby Komaiko (a Chicagoan of Russian-Lithuanian descent who performed in Jose Greco's company), the Ensemble promotes cultural pluralism at the community, state, national, and international levels, and collectively through the two-week American-Spanish Dance Festival. Seminars, college credit classes, films, and workshops highlighting all aspects of flamenco, classic, and folkloric dance are presented each day and night. You can register for the daytime non-credit program or single classes. Performances are generally given Wednesday and Thursday evenings. Spanish films are shown throughout the festival.

Songs of Spain and Latin America, *at the North Lakeside Cultural Center, 6219 N. Sheridan Road, Chicago, IL (773) 743-4477.*

Designed by architect Myron Henry Church in 1910 for S. H. Gunder, president of the Pazzinni Pharmacal Corporation, the historic Prairie style mansion fell into disrepair and was seemingly destined for a rendezvous with the wrecking ball by the time the North Lakeside Coalition took control of the property from the Chicago Park District and converted it into a visual and performing arts center in 1988. The not-for-profit association sponsors an artist in residence program, author readings, Sunday afternoon musical concerts, and theatrical presentations throughout the year. The Songs of Spain and Latin America Festival debuted in 1996, and it features the compositions of noted musicians from Spain, Latin America, Mexico and Argentina. Scheduled for mid-May. Admission: $5.00 for adults. Street parking. Call for dates and performance times. NLCC hours: Tuesday–Friday, 9:00 A.M.–5:00 P.M.; Sunday: 1:00–5:00 P.M.

Restaurants

Cafe Ba-Ba-Reeba, *2024 N. Halsted St., Chicago, (773) 935-5000. Open for lunch Tuesday–Saturday and dinner daily. Credit cards accepted.*

The pleasant decor and ambiance of this restaurant make it a real favorite of Chicagoans who wait in line each night for seating. This is more than just a *tapas* (Spanish for "little dishes," or appetizers that should be shared) bar. The menu is substantial, including regional specialties of Spain such as grilled squid, paella, baked goat cheese, tuna cannelloni, and dessert delicacies like bananas with caramel sauce and flan.

La Paella, *2920 N. Clark St., Chicago, (773) 528-0757.*
Open for dinner. Closed Mondays. Credit cards
accepted.

If you're planning a quiet, romantic dinner in a quaint Spanish setting, La Paella, which incidentally is also the "dish of Spain," is a good choice.

Tania's, *2659 N. Milwaukee Ave., Chicago,*
(773) 235-7120. Open for lunch and dinner daily.
Credit cards accepted.

Spanish and Cuban cuisine, with seafood as the house specialty. Be sure to try some of the gourmet Cuban food, like *ropa vieja* (shredded beef in tomato sauce) and *lechon asado* (roast pork). Latin dancing and music till early morning. Lambada, meringue.

Chef Tony's Taste of Spain, *86 W. Dundee St.,*
Buffalo Grove, (847) 520-8222. Open for lunch
Sunday–Friday and dinner daily.

Gourmet Spanish tapas, seafood, steaks, and imported Spanish wine. Stylish setting, knowledgeable waiters.

Viva Madrid, *3923 N. Lincoln Ave., Chicago,*
(773) 325-0066. Open for dinner. Closed Mondays
and Tuesdays.

Tapas and seafood in a casual atmosphere. Specialties include mahi-mahi, *queso de cabra al horno,* steamed mussels, and *pollo en salsa picante.*

Cafe Iberico, *739 N. LaSalle St., Chicago, (312) 573-1510.*
Open for lunch and dinner daily.

Tapas in a busy, well-decorated bar/restaurant. Popular with young Loop professionals.

Tapas Barcelona, *two locations: 111 W. Hubbard*
St., Chicago, (312) 467-1091; and 1615 Chicago,
Evanston, (847) 866-9900. Open for lunch and
dinner daily.

Specializing in Spanish tapas and Catalan cuisine.

Outlying Areas

Emilio's Meson Sabika, *1025 Aurora Ave.,*
Naperville, (630) 983-3000. Open for lunch
Monday–Friday and dinner daily. Credit cards
accepted.

Located in a quaint, old-fashioned mansion in Naperville that was built in 1847. In Spanish the name means "house on the hill." And indeed, the three chandeliered dining rooms are as pretty as a postcard. Emilio Gervilla opened at this location in 1990. The menu is nearly identical to his place in Hillside, which is the sister restaurant.

Emilio's Tapas Bar Restaurant, *4100 W. Roosevelt*
Rd., Hillside, (708) 547-7177. Open for lunch
Monday–Friday and dinner daily. Credit cards
accepted.

A pleasing taste of old Spain brought to you by Emilio Gervilla, who earned critical acclaim when he was a chef at Cafe Ba-Ba-Reeba. The menu lists eighteen different tapas dishes with a complement of daily specials. Begin with the cold appetizers before moving on to the main entrées. Intimate, cozy, and highly recommended.

Caribbean, Central, and South American Attractions

Cultural Institutions

Gallerie Thomas R. Monahan, *1038 N. LaSalle St.,*
Chicago, (312) 266-7530. Open by appointment only.
Credit cards accepted.

Contemporary European art, with special emphasis on a Latin American artist's colony in Paris that in recent years has produced some of the finest paintings in the surrealistic genre. This group of influential artists includes Carlos Aresti and Mario Murua of Chile, Eduardo Zamora and Heriberto Cogollo of Colombia, and Roberto Matta, an avant-garde painter considered by many to be the founder of surrealism. The Monahan gallery has a collection of the artist's work dating back to the 1930s.

Annual Events and Celebrations

Central American Independence Day Parade. *First Saturday in September following Labor Day. For additional information call (312) 744-3315.*

In 1989, when this colorful pageant first began, the theme revolved around Guatemalan independence. Now it is a cross-cultural event honoring all of the Central American nations. The parade travels along Dearborn Street from Wacker Drive to Van Buren.

Restaurants

Caribbean Delight, *(773) 743-2900.*

Jamaican food, including spice steak, curried goat, and jerk chicken. The owners also serve as food consultants. They closed their restaurant at 7303 N. Damen, Chicago, in 1996, and began evaluating new locations. Call for their new address.

Chez Delphonse, *2201 N. Clybourn Ave., Chicago, (773) 472-9920. Open for lunch and dinner daily.*

Jamaican and French-Caribbean cuisine, including seafood gumbo and steak with tomato and cilantro sauce.

El Nandu, *2731 W. Fullerton Ave., Chicago, (773) 278-0900. Open for lunch Monday–Saturday and dinner daily.*

One of the only Argentinean restaurants in the area. Specialties include tomato salad with oregano, *empanadas, churrasco encebollado,* and *dulce de batata.* Live music Thursday, Friday, and Saturday nights.

Rinconcito Sudamericano, *1954 W. Armitage St., Chicago, (773) 489-3126. Open for lunch and dinner daily. Credit cards accepted.*

Peruvian cuisine. A storefront location that serves hearty portions of seafood and shellfish to beef, veal, and lamb. If you order a dinner for two, you'll be able to experience the full spectrum of Peruvian cooking.

El Tinajon, *two locations: 4638 N. Western Ave.,
Chicago, (773) 878-5862, and 2054 W. Roscoe St.,
Chicago, (773) 525-8455. Open for lunch and dinner
daily. Credit cards accepted.*

Serving Guatemalan dishes in two storefront locations. The prices are low, and the variety of menu items are bound to please.

Outlying Areas

Julio's Latin Cafe, *95 S. Rand Rd., Lake Zurich,
(847) 438-3484. Open for lunch Tuesday–Friday and
dinner daily.*

Popular for its interesting blend of Caribbean, Mexican, and South American cuisine. Live music on Fridays and Saturdays.

chapter seventeen

Indian and Pakistani Chicago

History and Settlement

There was a time during the 1960s when Chicago's growing population from the Indian subcontinent considered the city to be only a temporary residence while they acquired their education at American universities or advanced their careers with American firms and gained a perspective on Western culture.

Like the earlier European groups, the Indian people soon discovered that there was no going back. In every respect they had assimilated into the cultural mainstream and had planted roots in Chicago that were not easily severed. India, the world's largest democracy, is home to 850 million people. It has sent more of its sons and daughters to New York and Chicago than to any other American cities. Only in recent years, however, has there emerged a readily identifiable Indo-Pakistani community. It is located along the congested Devon Avenue commercial strip between Western and California avenues in West Ridge—formerly an all-Jewish neighborhood.

The genesis of this bustling retail district dates back only about twenty-five years, to 1971, when a Hong Kong-based Indian firm named the Sun Palace decided to sell some items from its product line in the Harrison Hotel. The overwhelming response encouraged these entrepreneurs to eventually open a branch outlet on Devon Avenue, adjacent to an existing Indian import store, the India Sari Palace.

The India Sari Palace at 2534 W. Devon opened for business in 1973 and was the first Indian-owned business on the street. By the mid-1980s, Devon Avenue featured the second-largest cluster of Indian grocery stores, wholesale electronics outlets, and clothing shops in the United States, ranking behind the community of Jackson Heights, New York.

The steady influx of Indian merchants was alarming to the Jewish merchants who witnessed with growing concern the sudden erosion of their community life. Controversy flared in early 1983 when a block of storefronts on Devon Avenue between Rockwell and Maplewood were bought up by Indian businessowners and rented to East Asian concerns.

The former store owners who vacated their buildings, with more than the usual reluctance, claimed that their rents had been doubled from $600 to $1,200 a month by landlords eager to drive them out of the neighborhood.

The process of assimilation was not an easy one for the emerging Indian community along Devon Avenue, despite their familiarity with the English language resulting from years of British rule in the Indian sub-continent. Storefront windows were shattered in random acts of vandalism by street thugs who mistook the Indians for Iranian nationals in the wake of the 1980 hostage crisis in the Middle East. Ignorance of Indian culture contributed to this unfortunate act of bigotry.

Since that time, an exotic collection of vegetarian and nonvegetarian restaurants, sari shops, Indo-Pakistani video rental stores, and import groceries catering to the tastes of Chicago's 70,000-strong Indian community has slowly squeezed out the string of Jewish businesses that were fixtures in this community for years. In the last few years, a tiny but steadily growing Assyrian and Arabic presence on Devon Avenue between Oakley and Western shows signs of significantly altering the ethnic composition of West Ridge once again. Devon Avenue, designated the "Gandhi Marg" by the City Council, remains one of Chicago's most frequently overlooked ethnic treasures.

This apolitical group is scattered across Cook County, but in South Suburban Lemont, the Hindu Temple of Greater Chicago has become the most important religious shrine for adherents of that faith. The large white temple, covering nearly twenty acres of land, was sanctified in October, 1987, and is dedicated to Rama, a Hindu deity representing the human body. According to Hindu legend, Rama was the heir to the kingdom of Ayodhya. He is the central figure of the Sanskrit epic poem the *Ramayana,* which tells of a plot hatched by his enemies to banish him from his rightful place on the throne. In this tale, Rama spent the next fourteen years living in exile with his wife, Sita, his half-brother Laksmana, and the monkey general Hanuman, who helped the deity rescue Sita from Ravana, the demon-king of

Lanka (now Sri Lanka). Rama is worshiped as the seventh incarnation of Vishnu, the major god of Hinduism popularly regarded as the preserver of the universe. Images of him and his attending figures are located in the *mahamandapum,* or main prayer hall, in the Lemont shrine. Images of other Hindu deities, including Sri Venkataeshwaram, Bhoo Devi, Krishna, Radha, and Sri Ganesh, are located in two side halls. Construction of this impressive building began in 1984 and cost $4 million, of which $1.4 million came in the form of bank loans.

Chicago's Sikh population, though comparatively small at 3,000, has its own religious society of *gurdwara* in Palatine, and the World Sikh Organization is located in Schaumburg.

The Pakistani community is less than one-third the size of the Indian population in Chicago. According to 1990 census data, only 9,035 Pakistanis reside in Illinois compared to 64,200 Indians. However, they have closely followed the Indian patterns of immigration and neighborhood settlement, coming into the United States during the late 1960s and early 1970s and dispersing along the lakefront in Uptown and West Rogers Park. The predominantly Islamic Pakistani community is separated by a widening religious

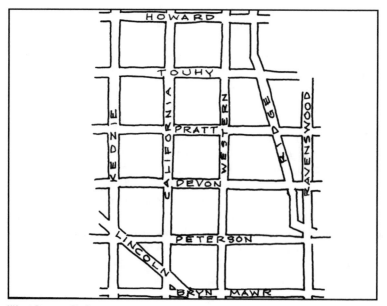

West Rogers Park

and cultural gap from the Indian community, who, for the most part, follow the Hindu faith. Political tensions in India and Pakistan, monitored closely by both ethnic groups, only serve to exacerbate the problem.

The Pakistanis observe their Independence Day with an annual parade along Devon Avenue in August, marking the end of British rule of the Indian sub-continent in 1947. The Indian parade is held a day earlier.

"At this point the community has seemed to successfully maintain its cultural and religious identity while still taking part in mainstream local activities," comments Dr. M. Arshad Mirza of the Indus Society of America. Others are not so sure.

The Indian and Pakistani communities, highly insulated within a myriad of their own civic and private fraternal organizations, have largely been ignored by the Chicago press corps, and this has impeded progress. "The media should use these people as the source of their stories, publish their pictures, cover their cultural functions," recommends Moin H. Kahn of the *India Tribune*.

Attractions

Annual Events and Celebrations

India Independence Day Parade. *First Saturday in August. For dates and times, call the Mayor's Office of Special Events at (312) 744-3370, or 744-3315.*

Marks the formal political separation of India from the British Empire, achieved on August 15, 1947, after years of nonviolent struggle led by Mohandas K. Gandhi and supporters of the India National Congress. The Chicago parade is held on Michigan Avenue between Wacker Drive and Van Buren. The Federation of India Association, an umbrella group representing twenty different fraternal organizations in the city, sponsors the annual pageant, which includes a noontime rally featuring dance troupes, speakers, and musical bands in the Daley Center Plaza the day of the parade. The decorated floats depict the regional customs of India, revolving around a different theme each year. In alternating years, there may be a second Independence Day Parade held on Michigan Avenue the Sunday afternoon preceding the holiday. At other times, the sponsors of this much smaller parade may join forces with the Federation of India Association for one large extravaganza.

Pakistani Independence Day Parade. *First Sunday in August. For dates and times, call the Mayor's Office of Special Events at (312) 744-3370, or 744-3315.*

Pakistan achieved independence from Britain on August 14, 1947. The independence movement, however, began twenty years earlier. In the early 1930s, Muslim residents of British India began calling for a separate Muslim state in the northern regions of the colony. The movement was led in the 1940s by Muhammad Ali Jinnah, head of the Muslim League. Pakistanis celebrate independence by marching along Devon Avenue from Damen to Western Avenue.

Federation Banquet, *held at alternating sites in metro Chicago or in the suburbs. Second week in May. Admission fee charged. Call Mr. Anil Pillai at (847) 674-7694 for information.*

Dinner and drinks. Testimonial speeches by the Indian Consul General or elected officials from Cook County. Musical entertainment. An annual event for the Indian community for over a decade.

Taste of Devon Festival, *Devon at Rockwell Ave., Chicago, (773) 743-6022. First weekend in August.*

Showcasing the multi-national flavor of East Devon Avenue, but with special emphasis on the Indian-Pakistani community. The two-day event is scheduled to coincide with the Indian-Pakistani parades in early August. Sample the delights of the East Asian restaurants in an outdoor food court while listening to Indian rock bands and folk music. No merchandise vendors. Sponsored by the Devon Northtown Business Association since 1995.

Diwali—The Indian Festival of Lights *Begins Nov. 10—extends for approximately five days.*

The biggest holiday for Hindus is celebrated on Devon Avenue with sparkling lights and special sales and events. This is a family holiday that celebrates the triumph of good over evil, commemorating the return of a banished prince, Lord Rama, to his home in central India. Festivities include raffles, entertainment and special dishes and sweets served in the food establishments. Sponsored by the Devon North Town Business Association. For further information call (773) 743-6022.

Outlying Areas

Taste of India Festival, *Chino Park, Illinois Blvd.*
and Evanston St., Hoffman Estates. First Sunday in
September. Admission is free. Call Mr. Anil Pillai at
(847) 674-7694 for information.

A one-day arts and crafts bazaar with food supplied by some of the more notable Indian restaurants around town. Cultural entertainment. Music. Games for children. This event was launched in 1991 by the Federation of India Association.

Places to See

Hindu Temple of Greater Chicago, *12 S. 701*
Lemont Rd., Lemont, (630) 972-0300. Open daily.
Admission is free, but donations accepted.

Located high atop a hill on a wooded thirty-acre lot in Du Page County, the majestic Hindu Temple is open for guided tours. Sunday afternoon is the preferred time to explore the religious customs and traditions of Southern Asia. On the last Saturday in July, the temple hosts an annual Great Lakes Hindu Youth Conference, featuring lectures, a cultural program, outdoor activities, and group discussions. Call ahead for times and date.

Shops

Kamdar Plaza, *2646 W. Devon Ave., Chicago,*
(773) 338-8100. Closed Tuesdays. Credit cards
accepted.

Grocery and retail store all in one. In the food section, select from a variety of Indian spices, sweets, and canned and bulk foods. The other side of the store features saris and other imported clothing items.

Silver Arts Jewelers, *2721 W. Devon (773) 465-2466.*

This is the only jewelry store on Devon that carries nothing but 100% silver items. Owners Himanshu and Neela Parekh sell giftware and silverware from India along with jewelry from Italy and Thailand. They do engraving and watch repairs as well. Credit cards as well as personal checks are accepted. Hours are 11:00 A.M.–8:00 P.M. Closed Tuesdays.

India Books and Journals, *2551 W. Devon*
(773) 764-6567. Hours: 11:30 A.M.–8:30 P.M.
closed Tuesdays. Credit cards accepted.

Owner Mahesh Sharma operates the only newsstand in Chicago devoted exclusively to Indian and Pakistani publications. The bookstore features a wide variety of fiction and non-fiction titles, cassette tapes, and gift items.

Patel Brothers, *2610 W. Devon Ave., Chicago,*
(773) 262-7777. Open daily.

A pioneer retailer in Indian and Pakistani groceries. The store also sells cookware, *thalis* (dinnerware), appliances, fresh produce, mango pulp, ground flour for making Indian bread, rice, Ceylon tea, and vegetarian and nonvegetarian foods. The aromatic fragrance of Indian spice hangs in the air.

Zabiha Meat Market, *2907 W. Devon Ave., Chicago,*
(773) 274-6700. Open daily.

Middle Eastern. Among the many Indian businesses on Devon Avenue, this one serves the needs of West Ridge's growing Assyrian and Iranian population. Exotic spices, frozen goat meat, rice, and some Indian and Pakistani foods are sold.

Jainson International Corporation, *2514 W. Devon*
Ave., Chicago, (773) 262-8787. Closed Tuesdays. No
credit cards.

Importer of Indian spices, bagged rice from Pakistan, flour for making Indian *chappati* bread, canned foods, and audio cassettes.

I.S.P. (India Sari Palace), *2534 W. Devon Ave.,*
Chicago, (773) 338-2127. Closed Tuesdays.

The sari material is sold by the yard and is available in an incredible array of colors and patterns. I.S.P., Devon Avenue's original sari shop, also sells imported gift items, luggage, handbags, CDs, and Indian video movies.

Sari Sapne, *2623 W. Devon Ave., Chicago, (773) 338-*
SARI. Closed Tuesdays. Credit cards accepted.

Their phone number tells it all. For exclusive Indian and Japanese Saris, this is the place to go.

Jai Hind, *2658 W. Devon Ave., Chicago, (773) 973-3400. Open daily. Credit cards accepted.*

In Jai Hind, you'll find cookware, fresh produce, and groceries. Don't forget to sample the tasty dessert *kulfi,* which is similar to ice cream in its consistency.

Zaveri Jewelers, Inc., *2603 W. Devon Ave., Chicago, (773) 764-8185. Closed Tuesdays.*

Imported gold items from London and India.

Video Palace, *2315 W. Devon Ave., Chicago, (773) 262-3990. Closed Tuesdays.*

Indian and Pakistani movies available for sale or rental. Same-day conversion and film transfer. The store also sells a line of electronic appliances.

VIP Video Vision, *2524 W. Devon Ave., Chicago, (773) 465-3344. Closed Tuesdays.*

The latest American, Indian, and Pakistani movies available for rental or sale. VCR repair service. CDs and records.

Restaurants

Bukara, *2 E. Ontario St., Chicago, (312) 943-0188. Open for lunch and dinner daily. Credit cards accepted. Reduced-rate parking across the street.*

Bukara features cooking from India's Northwest Frontier, and may not be quite what you expect from this part of the world. Cloth bibs are provided by the waiters, since all foods are eaten with the fingers. The house specialties include *shimla mirch,* Khyber *tikka,* and *sikandari raan.* Buffet-style lunch.

Klay Oven, *414 N. Orleans St., Chicago, (312) 527-3999. Open for lunch and dinner daily. Credit cards accepted.*

Plush surroundings, an extensive menu, and attentive wait staff ready to explain Indian cuisine make the Klay Oven one of the top-notch Indian restaurants in the city. Owner Prem Khosla stocks a large wine cellar and has made great strides toward having this become one of the top ethnic restaurants in the city. Buffet lunch. *Recommended.*

Raj Darbar Indian Restaurant, *2350 N. Clark St.,*
Chicago, (773) 348-1010. Open for lunch and dinner.
Closed Sunday. Reduced parking available. Credit
cards accepted.

One of Chicago's newest Indian restaurants. Northern Indian cuisine and a lunch buffet on the weekends.

Standard India, *917 W. Belmont Ave., Chicago,*
(773) 929-1123. Open for lunch and dinner. Closed
Tuesdays. Credit cards accepted.

A vegetarian/non-vegetarian restaurant. Buffet lunch on the weekends. Vegetarian buffet dinner served on Tuesdays and Thursdays.

Viceroy of India Restaurant, *2516 W. Devon Ave.,*
Chicago (773) 743-4100. Open for lunch and dinner
daily. Credit cards accepted.

An institution for many years, owned by Shashi and Surinder Jain, who decided to move back to Devon Avenue after operating in Villa Park for a while. The food is reliable, and any one of the three chef's specials are recommended for the culinary novice unfamiliar with Indian cooking. Vegetarian/non-vegetarian. A daily lunch buffet includes tandoori chicken, goat meat, and *masala dosa* (an Indian crepe).

Natraj Restaurant, *2240 W. Devon Ave., Chicago,*
(773) 274-1300. Open for dinner daily.

Southern Indian cuisine, and the meeting place for the Krishna Yoga Foundation on Sundays. Buffet dinner.

Gandhi India Restaurant, *2601 W. Devon,*
(773) 761-8714.

One of the oldest restaurants on Devon Avenue, owners Deven Parikh and Nand Kishore serve both southern and northern Indian cuisine in this charming restaurant. Both vegetarian and non-vegetarian dishes are available and they have a lunch buffet which changes daily. Lunch hours are 11:30 A.M.–3:30 P.M. Dinner is served nightly from 5 P.M.–10 P.M. week-days and 5 P.M.–11 P.M. on week-ends making it one of the later establishments on the street. Full bar available; credit cards accepted.

Tiffin—The Indian Kitchen, *2536 W. Devon,*
(773) 338-2143.

This new addition to Devon Avenue serves a variety of vegetarian and non-vegetarian dishes in an elegant upscale setting. Here you'll find the same delectable dishes that the tiffenwallahs carried through Bombay's busy streets. There are regional specialties from different parts of India and the wine list has domestic offerings as well as French and Italian. Lunch features a buffet and is served 11:30 A.M.–3:30 P.M. Dinner is from 5:00 P.M.–9:30 P.M. Monday through Thursday, 5 P.M.–10 P.M. Friday and Saturday and 5:00 P.M.–10:30 P.M. on Sunday. Credit cards accepted.

Woodland of Madras, *2340 W. Devon, (773) 338-8550.*

This is a unique restaurant specializing in South Indian vegetarian cuisine. The chef uses only fresh, all natural ingredients and emphasizes the spices of coriander, turmeric and chili powder. Their specialty is paper thin crepes called *dosai* with a variety of fillings. Other dishes include Indian pizza, curries and lentil donuts. Lunch buffet from 11:30 A.M.–3:30 P.M. Open 11:30 A.M. to 9:30 P.M. on weekdays and until 10:00 P.M. on weekends. Free parking available at Devon Bank parking lot, 6445 N. Western Ave.

Moti Mahal Restaurant, *2525 W. Devon (773) 262-2080. Hours are 12:00 P.M.–9:30 P.M. Monday–Thursday, and Sunday and 12:00 P.M.–11:30 P.M. on Friday and Saturday. Credit cards accepted.*

Owner Surjit Sikand operates not only an Indian restaurant but a banquet hall and a carry-out food and grocery shop at this one location. The restaurant emphasizes North Indian cuisine and serves a popular lunch buffet from 12:00 P.M.–3:30 P.M.

Gaylord India Restaurant, *678 N. Clark St., Chicago, (312) 664-1700. Open for lunch and dinner daily.*

Gaylord has been serving excellent northern Indian food for over thirty years. Specialties include tandoor-roasted bread, curried lamb, and *kulfi,* an Indian ice cream. Buffet lunch available.

India House, *two locations: 2548 W. Devon Ave., Chicago, (773) 338-2929 and 855 E. Schaumburg Rd., Schaumburg, (847) 529-3007. Both locations open for lunch and dinner daily.*

The chefs use the traditional *tawa* (an iron plate) and *kadhai* (an iron wok over hot coals) to cook most of the menu items.

Kanval Palace, *2501 W. Devon Ave., Chicago, (773) 761-7270. Open for lunch and dinner daily.*

Traditional northern Indian food, including lamb *tikka masala,* red-curried shrimp, and a number of vegetarian dishes. Lunch buffet daily.

Outlying Areas

New Delhi, *30 S. Meacham, Schaumburg, (847) 894-6900. Open for lunch and dinner daily.*

Northern Indian cuisine served in a casual setting. The menu features a variety of chicken, lamb, vegetarian, and seafood dishes.

Gateway of India, *417 E. Ogden Ave., Naperville, (630) 717-7600. Open for lunch and for dinner daily. American Express accepted.*

Chef Kanwarjit Chhatwai serves it up spicy or mild in the Western suburbs with a modestly priced menu that will appeal to all budgets

Peacock Indian Restaurant, *701 N. Milwaukee Ave., Vernon Hills (847) 816-3100. Open for lunch and dinner daily. Major credit cards accepted.*

Chicken and lamb dishes are the specialties. Fish or giant blue crabs from India skewered and prepared with Indian barbecue sauce is also a recommended dish. Carry-out service available.

Media

Hindu-Pakistani *programming on WSBC, 1240-AM, Wednesday evenings, 8:00–9:00 P.M. Hosted by Nasees Rahim.*

Middle Eastern Chicago

History and Settlement

Assyrians

A thousand years ago the empire of the Assyrians stretched from Northern Iraq into Northern Iran. A proud but ancient desert empire was forged in the shifting sands of the Middle East by warlike conquerors whose people were closely knit in language, culture, and religion. They were among the world's first astronomers, mathematicians, and lawmakers.

It appeared that the seemingly invincible Assyrians were destined to rule the Middle East for centuries to come, but internal strife, political intrigue, and palace revolts doomed the empire to a slow and painful disintegration—a process all but complete by 609 B.C.

Assyria no longer exists as a modern nation—its borders dissolved by conquest and war—but its descendants cling to their rich social and religious customs and proudly point to the indisputable fact that they were among the first practicing Christians in the world.

Religious services are still conducted in Aramaic—the ancient language believed to have been spoken by Christ. According to Assyrian custom, a piece of the original bread consecrated at the Last Supper was preserved, placed in flour and guarded by the faithful. Each time a batch of dough is prepared, a portion is retained for Leaven which must then be consecrated by the patriarch, bishop, or priest. The majority of Assyrian-Americans belong to the Apostolic Catholic Assyrian Church of the East.

Religious persecution in the Arab world scattered many Assyrians to the four corners of the world, a process that greatly accelerated after Saddam Hussein seized control of the Iraqi government in 1979 and forced Assyrian men into the military, and kept them in the service against their will for many years.

A small pocket of émigrés were counted in the Chicago city census as early as 1901, but it wasn't until 1917 that St. Michael's Assyrian Church on the Near North Side, their first parish, was built. One hundred families, coming from not only Iraq and Iran, but Jordan, Turkey, Lebanon, and Syria as well, formed a colony around the mother parish. The modern nation of Syria, as any proud Assyrian will quickly point out, should not be confused with the vanished empire from antiquity.

Ethnic displacement, the result of large numbers of Italians pouring into the neighborhood, pushed the original Assyrian enclave, anchored in the vicinity of Division and Wells after World War I, farther north—to Belmont and Halsted, then populated by a large concentration of Swedes.

A hard-working, industrious people who gravitated toward the law, mercantile pursuits, and investments, Chicago's Assyrian community grew slowly but steadily in the coming decades. During the Lebanese Civil War of 1975, thousands more emigrated to the United States—choosing Detroit and Chicago as their preferred destination points. Nearly 3,000 war refugees were air-lifted out of Beirut with the help of the Assyrian-American community.

By the mid-1970s there were at least six Assyrian churches conducting the liturgy in Aramaic. In September of 1995, Patriarch Mar Dinkah IV of the Assyrian Church of the East, one of the world's oldest Christian denominations, moved the Church's headquarters to Chicago. Dinkah himself came to the United States from Tehran in 1979, shortly after becoming patriarch. Dinkah recently negotiated a settlement with Pope John Paul II that healed a 1,500-year-old schism between the church leaderships. In addition to being patriarch, Dinkah serves as pastor at St. George's Patriarchal Cathedral at Touhy and Ashland in Chicago.

It is estimated that there are 70,000 Assyrians scattered along the lakefront in Uptown, Edgewater, Rogers Park, and the suburbs. Chicago is home to the largest Assyrian population in the United States, second in the world only to Iraq.

In the early 1970s the Assyrians and other Middle-Eastern nationalities were integrated into the Scandinavian community of Andersonville at Clark and Foster. Swedish bakeries and delicatessens co-exist with Middle Eastern and Filipino restaurants and shops offering us a blueprint in ethnic harmony.

At Lawrence and Kedzie, adjacent to the bustling Korean-American neighborhood of Albany Park and due west of the original North Side German and Greek settlements, the Assyrians opened coffee shops, markets, and groceries. They had become a viable community presence within a cultural melting pot.

Despite the recent immigration from the Middle East, Assyrian elders, like other immigrant cultures that have assimilated into the United States after many years, lament the "Americanization" of their heritage. Their concerns may be unfounded. Most Assyrians are trilingual and are fluent in Assyrian, English, and Arabic or Farsi.

"You can take the boy out of Assyria but you can't take Assyria out of the boy," quips Paul Newey, a noted attorney of Assyrian-American descent whose father, the Reverend Paul S. Newey, Sr., published a newspaper for his fellow immigrants from 1915–1921 out of a small print shop located at Superior and Chicago avenues on the Gold Coast.

Reverend Newey, who was greatly admired and respected by movers and shakers of his generation, including Chicago Mayor William Hale Thompson and U.S. Senator Paul Douglas, was born at the foot of Mount Ararat. He settled in the United States in 1906, and served as pastor of the Assyrian Congregational Church from 1919 until the time of his death in 1960. His son Paul, licensed to practice law in Illinois for the past fifty years, speaks of his father and Chicago's Assyrian community with understandable pride.

He has not allowed the historical tradition and sense of achievement to fall by the wayside, nor has anyone else in the Assyrian community. The tradition and respect for the ancient culture is preserved and maintained to this day by the Assyrian-American Civic Club of Chicago and the Assyrian-American Council of Illinois.

Iranians

Chicago's Iranian community is much smaller in number than the entrenched Assyrians. Its members are still striving to stake their rightful claim within the urban tapestry.

Until 1935, Iran was still known by its traditional name from antiquity—Persia—the conventional European designation in use in the West. The kingdom of Persia was overrun by Muslim Arabs during the reign of Yazdegerd III (632–641 A.D.). Islam replaced Zoroastriansim as the state religion, and the lands were incorporated into the caliphate and ruled from Damascus and Baghdad. Gradually the old religious customs vanished and henceforth the nation of Iran was a Muslim country, but it was vulnerable to outside attack and would be subjected to a succession of foreign invasions beginning with the Seljuk Turks, then the Mongol hordes led by Genghis Kahn, and finally the European colonialists who gained hegemony in the oil-rich lands beginning in the 18th Century.

The Muslim presence in Chicago was negligible at the turn of the century; only a dozen followers of the Islamic faith were identified within the boundaries of Chicago.

The stirrings of immigration from this sector of the Middle Eastern world occurred shortly after World War I—a result of continuing political persecution in Asia Minor against the indigenous peoples by British and Russian occupiers. The newcomers to Chicago lived in the vicinity of what is now the luxurious Gold Coast—Oak Street south to Chicago Avenue and Huron, and between LaSalle and Rush Street. However, the growth of the Iranian (or Persian) community was severely restricted by quotas placed on immigration which in 1921 limited them to only 78 per year.

Because of the U.S. backlash most of the Iranian immigrants were single men—unskilled laborers—who settled in lodging houses north of the Chicago River. The Iranian situation was analogous to the plight of the ethnic Chinese who lived in Chicago for years without the companionship of women and children. Later, when the restrictive quotas were eased, women and children were permitted to cross the ocean and families were once again reunited.

The abbreviated Iranian migration curtailed in the 1920s and would remain dormant for the next 45 years. The 1980 census listed only 3,500 Iranians residing in the Windy City, a figure disputed by community leaders who pegged the figure to be closer to 6,000. More than half of them had come over between 1975 and 1979, when the nation was still a constitutional monarchy under the leadership of Shah Muhammad Reza Pahlavi, who was brutally deposed by Muslim fundamentalists in January 1979.

By the mid-1980s, when the bitter memories of the hostage crisis involving 66 American diplomats at last began to fade away, Chicago's Iranians finally were able to close the book on the troubled past but harbored lingering concerns for the future.

The Iranian émigrés who never expected to become permanent American citizens were faced with a painful readjustment. Could they return to their native land now guided by the Islamic fundamentalists who had turned their back on Western culture and technology? Those who chose to stay opened restaurants, worked as cab drivers, or in the entrepreneurial spirit of former times, saved their money and opened small retail shops and restaurants in densely populated inner-city neighborhoods—beginning in the early 1970s in Andersonville, north of Lakeview.

The history of the Iranian-American experience in Chicago is of brief duration, but in the decades to come, as the ethnic and racial transformation of Chicago accelerates, it is likely that this small but growing community will leave its unique imprimatur on the cultural milieu of the city.

Syrians

Among the earliest settlers from the Middle East to seek refuge in Chicago were a small detachment of Syrian merchants who came here in 1893 to sell fine embroidered laces, Persian rugs, olive wood novelties, and other imported items to the visitors of the World's Fair along the ornate Midway Pleasance.

At the time of the Chicago World's Fair, Ottoman Turks ruled Syria, which had functioned as an important overland trade route to the Far East since the days of the Roman conquest. Syria, an Islamic Republic which threw off the last vestiges of British and French colonialism in 1946 to forge a strong, independent military presence in the Mideast, has sent fewer of its sons and daughters to the United States in the modern era than any of its neighboring states.

Following the 1893 World's Fair, an event of historic proportions that established Chicago as an *international* city, a Syrian colony sprang up at the foot of 18th Street near State on the South Side. St. John the Baptist on the West Side served the religious devotions of the community.

However, immigration stalled in the 20th century. Those who settled in Chicago did so because of religious persecution back home at the hands of the Maronite clergy of Lebanon—the Christian community of Arabs supported by the French colonial government centered there, but also existing in Cyprus, Syria, and Palestine. By 1938, there were only 30 Syrian families assembled in Chicago—most lived in relative isolation just north of downtown or in a small pocket on the West Side.

Many Syrian-Arabs fled the West Bank after the Six-Day War in 1967, matriculating into densely populated city neighborhoods like Albany Park where the Koreans had already established hegemony along the congested east-west thoroughfares of Lawrence, Foster, and Montrose avenues. However, Chicago's Syrian population is less than half the size of the Palestinians who came here as political refugees. The Syrians who chose to leave the Middle East for reasons unrelated to politics are, for the most part, physicians or nurses or are engaged in other white-collar professions.

A mixed Syrian, Palestinian, and Iraqi business community has taken root in recent years near the Ravenswood Elevated line along Kedzie Avenue between Lawrence and Montrose avenues. A strip of Middle Eastern travel agencies, grocery stores, and retail emporiums provide added diversity to one of the most colorful, chaotic, noisy, and fascinating neighborhoods in the city.

Palestinian Arabs

The Gulf War of 1991, preceded by a decade of turmoil, hostage-taking, and assorted random acts of terrorism, bombings, and hijackings in the Middle East, contributed to an unfortunate climate of mistrust and ethnic stereotyping that has left many Arabs in this country questioning the fundamental values of democracy and fair play.

It has been a long, painful journey from the Middle East to the Midwestern heartland. In Detroit, Michigan, and its surrounding suburbs, 100,000 Arabs with roots in 19 different Middle Eastern and North African nations comprise the largest Arabic community in the United States. The Arabic language and Islamic religion provide the common cultural thread linking the ethnic peoples together.

According to unofficial estimates, Chicago ranks second in population, with 80,000 Arab-American residents, of whom 60% are of Palestinian descent. They may well be the least visible immigrant groups in the city—preferring to conduct their lives in quiet, unassuming ways, free of outside influences. By the same token, Arab-American leaders decry long-standing misconceptions. "We don't want to be viewed as terrorists or camel drivers, or tent dwellers," explained Taysar Yunis, a Palestinian affiliated with the Arab Information Center in downtown Chicago. "We want to be viewed as human beings like anyone else."

The war to establish the modern state of Israel in May 1948 vanquished five Arab armies and produced 780,000 Palestinian refugees. Many thousands fled the Middle East out of desperation and panic but proudly clung to their ethnic identity, though the U.N. Charter all but erased the national boundaries of Palestine.

The Six-Day War in June 1967 accelerated the exodus and fueled the stirrings of immigration to the United States. It was at that time that large numbers of West Bank refugees, including a mix of Syrians, Lebanese, and Iranians, first poured into Chicago.

Although many Palestinians scattered across the city, most gravitated to the South Side, where a residential pocket formed on 63rd Street between California and Western Avenues. Arab entrepreneurs purchased small grocery stores, servicing fellow immigrants in harmony with their new surroundings.

Orthodox Muslims have opened forty-eight mosques in the greater Chicagoland area. The largest mosque in the city is located at 92nd Street and Harlem Avenue.

In the African-American neighborhoods lining 63rd Street, dozens of Arab-owned grocery stores sprouted in the 1970s, much to the chagrin of politicians who hoped to create enterprise zones for black businesspeople. Relations were strained between the new arrivals who replaced fleeing white European merchants, and the African-American residents, who complained of rude treatment and callous remarks from the shopkeepers while patronizing their stores.

In an effort to iron out differences between the two divergent groups, the Reverend Jesse Jackson, whose wife visited the Mideast in 1978, organized a series of face-to-face meetings between community leaders in what he termed a "mission of peace." Inner-city Arab business leaders pledged financial support to Reverend Jackson's Operation PUSH organization, and agreed to invest in the redevelopment of depressed South Side communities like Woodlawn.

While the cultural gap existing between American-born blacks and Arab immigrants has never been fully reconciled, there are fewer bruised egos and heated confrontations these days. A rising concern to the leaders of the Palestinian community is the portrayal of Islam by the media.

Echoing the opinions of Taysar Yunis regarding ethnic stereotyping, Nazir Hasan, a building contractor who immigrated to Chicago from the Middle East in 1951, believes that the press has intentionally fueled the fires of ethnic discord. "This is the problem—the media goes after Islam," he said. "If a Muslim commits a crime, they say a Muslim did that—not a John Doe. Islam is the fastest-growing religion in America, and it teaches a complete commitment through Almighty God, and to respect government and to serve it."

Hasan served the United States military with distinction during the Korean conflict. He expresses remorse over the imperialistic adventuring of Iraqi dictator Saddam Hussein and others in the Middle East who have contributed to the prevailing ill will around the world. But by the same token: "Not all Muslims can be blamed for the unfortunate actions of one. We must come to know one another. We are all the children of Adam and Eve."

Hasan, who hosted an Islamic cable television program at one point in his career, charts the movement of the Palestinians away from the South Side. Today, he points out, the community is widely dispersed across Cook County. Many of the original Palestinian-owned businesses that sprouted near 63rd Street and Western in the mid-to-late 1970s have already left the area because of mounting concerns over encroaching street gangs, drug peddling, and prostitution.

A number of the restaurant and grocery store owners, who are there to serve the dietary needs of the Islamic population, abandoned their former locations and have moved farther west on 63rd Street, settling between Pulaski and Sacramento Avenues, where, it is reported, business thrives and there is renewed hope for the future. This westward migration along the busy thoroughfare of 63rd Street gained strength in the early 1990s.

In recent years, there has been an influx of Jordanian Arabs into the South Side due to political instability and a depressed economy back home. Their presence ensures that the Middle Eastern population will continue to expand in the years ahead.

Many Arab families abandoned inner-city life altogether in favor of affordable housing in outlying areas like Elk Grove Village, Orland Park, Justice, Burbank, Oak Lawn, and Bridgeview, where the Bridgeview Mosque Foundation was opened. The building provides an important social and cultural outlet as well as an Arabic language school.

The Muslim Community Center, at 4380 N. Elston Avenue on the city's Northwest Side was opened by the Pakistanis, but the MCC serves the entire Islamic community and provides free speakers to churches and schools, lectures by renowned Middle Eastern scholars, five-times-daily Muslim prayer rituals, and free classes every Wednesday night.

While many Arab-Americans no longer observe the prayer ritual, Ramadan, the 30-day fasting marking the time in history when the revelations of the Qur'an (Koran) were first revealed to the prophet Muhammad, is universally celebrated within the Islamic community.

According to the Koran, the fast of Ramadan, occurring in the ninth month of the Islamic year, provides believers with the opportunity to "cultivate piety." The fast begins each day at dawn, when, according to custom, "the white thread becomes distinct from the black thread." At dusk the fasting period concludes. Before bedtime the faithful recite special congregational passages in which long passages from the Koran are recited. The *imam* (prayer leader) sings poetic passages from the book, often from memory.

The day after the end of Ramadan is called the Fast-Breaking, and it is celebrated with special prayers and festivities. Chicago's Muslims, eager to strip away the veil of ignorance, mistrust, and wrongful misperception of their faith on the part of the outside world, invited hundreds of local officials to attend closing services of Ramadan in 1996. However, few availed themselves of the opportunity, indicating that, at least for now, there is still a long way to go toward mutual understanding.

Attractions

Cultural Institutions

Oriental Institute Museum, *University of Chicago, 1155 E. 58th St., Chicago, (773) 702-9521. Closed Mondays. Admission is free.*

This wonderful museum has long been overlooked by both tourists and Chicagoland residents. In 1996, the Institute undertook a major renovation and expansion project to present more of its treasures from the Near East.

The museum focuses on the cultures, history, and archaeology of ancient Egypt, Mesopotamia, Anatolia, Iran, and Syria. Exhibits covering nearly 8,000 years of history include a Babylonian archway, Egyptian mummies, statuary, and ancient documents. Gift shop. The museum sponsors a variety of public programs, both on the grounds and in the community, including adult education classes, family events, workshops, and films. The museum has been undergoing a three-year renovation and has been closed to the public. Call (773) 702-9521 for progress updates.

Annual Events and Celebrations

Assyrian New Year Parade (Khab-Ne-Ason),
Western Ave. between Peterson and Touhy on or about April 1. Call the City of Chicago at (312) 744-3315 for date and time.

The festive parade marking the start of the New Year began some years ago in downtown Chicago, but has since moved to the North Side to be near the emerging Assyrian settlement on Devon Avenue. In fact, this stretch of Western Avenue (from Peterson to Devon) has been given the honorary designation "King Sargon Drive" in honor of Sargon II, a ruler who forged a mighty empire during his 17-year reign, from 722–705 B.C. An Assyrian restaurant owner, Hanni Baba, led the movement to rename the street, and the city rededicated it on June 14, 1992.

Shops

Al Anwar Grocery, *3058 W. 63rd St., Chicago. Closed Sundays.*

This family-owned Palestinian grocery store has been in the neighborhood since 1980. Imported Middle Eastern foods, Arabic-language films for rent, and newspapers.

Fadi Foods, *3536 W. 63rd St., Chicago, (773) 476-4964. Open daily.*

Exotic imported Middle Eastern foods, grains, spices, and household items complement an assortment of musical cassettes, rental videos, Arabic-language newspapers, and books. At this location since 1990.

Noor Middle Eastern Pastries, *3530 W. 63rd St.,*
Chicago, (773) 776-4366. Open daily.

One of the largest Palestinian bakeries in the United States. Does a land office business shipping packages of exotic Middle Eastern confections and pastries like *Mammoul, Herrisch, Ghaibeh,* and *Kunafelt* across the country. Owned by the Bahbur family, the "sweet shop" (as Palestinians refer to their bakeries) is named in honor of Mrs. Bahbur's daughter, who was named for Queen Noor. Bakery items selected from the display cases in the front can be taken to the seating area at the rear of the store and eaten.

Restaurants

The Helmand, *3201 N. Halsted St., Chicago,*
(773) 935-2447. Open for dinner daily.

Afghani cuisine in an exotic setting. Specialties include *kabuli* (roast lamb with carrot, raisin, and brown rice with cinnamon) and Afghan ravioli (pastry filled with leeks, with mint garlic sauce under the ravioli and a beef sauce on top). Vegetarian dishes also available.

Uncle Tannous, *2626 N. Halsted St., Chicago,*
(773) 929-1333. Open for lunch and dinner
Tuesday–Sunday and dinner on Mondays.

Lebanese cuisine. According to the owners, Uncle Tannous introduced tapas to Chicago diners. A standard tapas meal here features 20 to 30 different dishes. The lamb chops, kebabs, snapper, and other seafood items are also popular. Live Lebanese music on Saturday with belly dancers.

Cafe Istanbul, *2732 N. Clark St., Chicago,*
(773) 525-3091. Restaurant open for lunch
and dinner daily; club open Thursday–Sunday
nights.

This Turkish restaurant turns into a dance club on the weekends. The menu features traditional Turkish items, including *baba ghannouj, hummus,* grape leaves, eggplant salad, kebabs, and cabbage *sarmi.* The club features Turkish and Albanian music and dancing. Amid the splendor and mystery of Turkish culture, the owners have discovered that "Israeli Nights" also bring out larger-than-expected crowds, mostly Russian-born Jews. Belly dancing on Tuesday, Friday, and Saturday nights. No cover and no minimum.

Ali Baba Restaurant & Lounge, *2241 W. Devon (773) 338-9999. Hours: Open seven days from 10:00 A.M. to 2:00 A.M. Credit cards accepted.*

Owner Najwa Pria operates an elegant restaurant serving everything from gyros to quail and shish kabob. There is ethnic entertainment on week-ends and the waitresses dress as genies and even perform on stage. There is limousine service available for $50 for those customers who don't want to deal with driving or parking.

HaShalom, *2905 W. Devon Ave., Chicago, (773) 465-5675. Open for lunch and dinner.*

Storefront featuring inexpensive Israeli and Moroccan cuisine in a casual atmosphere. Specialties include *hummus, baba ghannouj, bourekas,* kebabs, tahini, and strong Israeli coffee.

Cedars of Lebanon, *1618 E. 53rd St., Chicago, (773) 324-8959. Open for lunch and dinner daily.*

Lebanese cuisine. Some of the more popular items are the lamb kebabs, a variety of vegetarian dishes, falafel, and *hummus.*

Jerusalem Restaurant, *3534 W. 63rd St., Chicago, (773) 776-6133. Open for lunch and dinner daily.*

Middle Eastern food served in intimate surroundings adjacent to the Noor Middle Eastern Pastry Shop.

Ali Baba Restaurant, *3508 W. 63rd St., Chicago, (773) 778-7017. Open for lunch and dinner daily.*

Palestinian menu includes *Shauarma* (a roasted beef and lamb dinner), *fatah, kibbeh,* and an assortment of kebabs prepared by chef Khalid. Cozy, store-front ambiance, six tables, and friendly service.

Al Khayam, *2326 W. Foster Ave., Chicago, (773) 334-0000. Open Friday–Sunday nights.*

The seven-piece Al Khayam orchestra provides background music for an up-tempo format featuring some of the top international recording artists from the Middle East, including Adil Fadel, an Egyptian-born violinist. The owner of the Lakeview cafe, Albert Baba, delights his audience with songs sung in Hindu, Arabic Assyrian, and Kurdish. The action gets going around midnight and continues into the wee hours. Dancing. Drinks. Lots of music. No cover charge, but a two-drink minimum.

Reza's, *two locations: 5255 N. Clark St.,*
Chicago, (312) 561-1898; and 432 W. Ontario,
Chicago, (312) 664-4500. Open for lunch and
dinner daily.

Very popular and critically acclaimed Persian cuisine. Specialties include lamb shank, shrimp and filet shish kebabs, stuffed green peppers, and quail. Live piano music every night. Banquet rooms, delivery, and catering available.

Izmir Restaurant Clark, *5625 N. Clark St., Chicago,*
(312) 728-6699. Open for lunch and dinner. Closed
Mondays.

Traditional Middle Eastern cuisine, including *iskembe*. Late hours.

Pars Cove, *435 W. Diversey Ave., Chicago,*
(312) 549-1515. Open for dinner daily.

Persian cuisine in a romantic, exotic dining room. The chef specializes in Persian seafood. Live piano jazz.

Geja's Cafe, *340 W. Armitage St., Chicago,*
(312) 281-9101. Open for dinner daily.

Moroccan fondue. This has long been considered one of Chicago's most romantic restaurants. The fondue, intimate lighting, and nightly live guitar music combine to make this a memorable dining experience. The annual November wine festival features a different variety of wine each year.

Old Jerusalem, *1411 N. Wells St., Chicago,*
(312) 944-0459. Open for lunch and dinner
daily.

Lebanese and Middle Eastern cuisine. Excellent, inexpensive, and fresh food. The restaurant does not serve alcohol, so the owners invite patrons to bring their own beer, wine, or liquor.

Tuttaposto, *646 N. Franklin St., Chicago,*
(312) 943-6262. Open for lunch Monday–Friday
and dinner daily.

Mediterranean cuisine. The menu changes every few weeks, but usually features the popular wood-roasted rare tuna steak and a variety of vegetarian items.

Uncle Tutunji, *615 N. Wells St., Chicago,*
(312) 587-0721. Open for lunch and dinner daily.

Middle Eastern and Mediterranean cuisine, including the popular Uncle Tutunji platter (rice; grilled filet mignon; grilled pepper, onion, tomato, beef, and lamb; and grilled chicken breast) and well-prepared standards such as falafel, *dolmeh, hummus,* and *baba ghannouj.*

Tribal Café, *1365 W. Erie St., Chicago,*
(312) 829-4514. Open for lunch and dinner daily.

Tribal Café's impressive menu includes traditional dishes from Turkey, Morocco, Iran, and India.

Outlying Areas

Sayat Nova, *20 W. Golf Rd., Des Plaines,*
(847) 296-1776. Open for lunch Tuesday–Friday
and dinner Tuesday–Sunday. Closed Mondays.

Armenian cuisine in a cozy dining room. *Hummus,* lentil soup, *boereg* (cheese and spinach wrapped in phyllo), and grilled kebabs are among the most popular dishes.

La Perla del Mediterráneo, *2135 S. Wolf St.,*
Hillside, (708) 449-1070. Open for lunch and
dinner daily.

Mediterranean cuisine, including Spanish tapas and Moroccan lamb sausage pizza, in an exotic, colorful setting. Live jazz or Latin music on Friday and Saturday, with flamenco and tango dancing. The management suggests calling ahead for the entertainment schedule.

Multiethnic Festivals

Chicago Ethnic Fair, *5100 block of Western Ave.,*
Chicago. First weekend in August. Admission is free.
Call (773) 585-6085 for information.

Three-day street fair, carnival, and crafts show. Neither rain nor the staggering humidity of August have deterred the promoters of this wide-ranging event celebrating Polish, Lithuanian, African American, Croatian, and Irish culture from holding the fair as scheduled. The fair emphasizes the public services available to all Chicagoans, but it also features ethnic dance troupes, specialty foods, and boutiques selling handmade arts and crafts from the representative ethnic groups in attendance. For the children there is a petting zoo, carnival rides, and a magic show. Senior citizens may wish to play a game of bingo or take advantage of free medical testing and immunization shots available to all ages. The Veteran's Administration is also on hand, to provide free health care to vets. The event is sponsored by the Chicago Ethnic Fair, Inc., a not-for-profit agency, in cooperation with the City of Chicago.

Suburban Ethnic Fair, *Square D Company, Roselle*
Road and Euclid, Palatine. First Saturday in August.
Times and location subject to change. Call
(847) 382-6922 for information.

Sponsored by the Northwest Cultural Council. The family event provides a unique cultural and ethnic program for northwest suburbanites who do not make the long drive into the city to attend the Chicago Ethnic Fair. The festival promotes ethnic music and dance, including Japanese Fujima and Spanish Flamenco. Also included in the afternoon's events are storytelling, gourmet ethnic foods, photography exhibits, and a raffle.

International Banquets at Kendall College.

The nationally acclaimed culinary school at Kendall College in north suburban Evanston was established in 1984. Their dining room is a classroom for service and food preparation and the public is invited to feast on sumptuous servings of ethnic delicacies from around the world in a series of international banquets served on selected Monday evenings from July through September. Proceeds benefit the Kendall College scholarship program. Dine in style with the Consul Generals, business leaders from the representative ethnic communities in Chicago, and award-winning chef Kenn Andersen, who supervised the S.A.S. flight kitchen at London's Gatwick Airport before coming to Kendall College to impart his considerable skills to aspiring gourmet chefs. The four-course banquets feature exotic foods from Europe, the Americas, Southeast Asia, Africa, and the Near East. It's important to plan early. Write to Kendall College at 2408 Orrington Avenue, Evanston, IL 60201 or call (847) 866-1399. Major credit cards accepted.

Evanston Ethnic Arts Festival.

More than sixty-five representative cultures spotlighting 120 artists. The annual lakefront festival has been going strong for over a decade, and it includes two sound stages showcasing various forms of ethnic-cultural entertainment, 20 food vendors, workshops and demonstrations. Dawes Park, Church Street and Sheridan Road in Evanston. Scheduled for the third weekend in July. Free admission and free parking on the Northwestern University grounds with shuttle bus transportation to and from the lot. Call Theresa Pacione at the Evanston Arts Council (847) 328-2100 ext. 2470, for scheduled times and additional information.

Festival of Nations, *International House on the University of Chicago campus, 1414 E. 59th St., Chicago (773) 753-2274.*

A week-long panorama of music, films, international cuisine, displays, souvenir stands, and folkloric dance of 25–30 representative ethnic groups staged by the University of Chicago students for the community. Founded by John D. Rockefeller in 1932, the International House is a program and residential facility for both American and international graduate students studying in Chicago. Over the years almost every nation on earth has been represented. The annual Festival of Nations pageant has been held the first or second Sunday in May every year since at least the 1930s. At various times during the year International House hosts language tables, consular dinners, dance performances, weekend excursions, and sporting events. Hours for the main event: 12:00 P.M.–5:00 P.M. Admission: $5.00 per person, $12.00 per family.

Chicago International Film Festival. *Two weeks in mid-October. Admission fee charged for each screening (usually $6–$10). Call (312) 644-FILM for a schedule.*

The International Film Festival features over 100 different titles from around the world, shown at various theaters in the city. During the year, the Film Festival sponsors various special screenings at the city's art houses. Local newspapers usually carry the screening schedule shortly before the festival begins. *Recommended.*

European-American Festival, *Wicker Park, 1500 N. Damen, Chicago. Saturday closest to September 1. Admission is free. For information call the European-American Association, 2827 W. Division Street, Chicago, (773) 342-5868.*

The European-American Association was organized early in 1991 to provide special assistance to newly arrived immigrants in the form of language instruction, educational support, and job placement. The association sponsored its first day-long ethnic festival in 1991, featuring food and musical entertainment representing the German, Italian, Polish, Lithuanian, Ukrainian, Yugoslav, Czech, and Romanian cultures. In addition to the many gourmet international foods available for purchase, visitors may also feast on standard American and Mexican dishes from the various vendors in attendance. The European-American festival is supported by the City of Chicago, the Mayor's Office of Special Events, and local advertisers. The gala event promises to become one of Chicago's premier ethnic festivals in years to come.

Illinois Humanities Festival, *various locations throughout the city, including the Art Institute, Chicago Public Library Cultural Center, Field Museum, and Orchestra Hall. Second weekend in November. Times and individual admission fees vary. Call (312) 422-5580 for information.*

One-day exploration through words, music, and art of the "alternative" cultures in Chicago. Readings by internationally known authors, lectures, and musical concerts. Presented by the Illinois Humanities Council.

Useful Phone Numbers and Addresses

Activities and Events

City of Chicago, Office of Tourism	(312) 744-2400
Visitor Information Center, Water Tower, 163 E. Pearson St.	1-800-ITS CHGO
Convention and Tourism Bureau	(312) 567-8500
Illinois Information Center, 310 S. Michigan Ave.	1-800-223-0121
*Mayor's Office of Special Events (General Information)	(312) 744-3315
	(312) 744-3370
Film and Entertainment	(312) 744-6415
Chicago Fine Arts Hotline	(312) 346-3278
Chicago Art Dealers Association	(312) 649-0065
Chicago Music Alliance (classical concerts and opera)	(312) 987-9296
Concert Line (popular music concerts)	(312) 666-6667

*Note: During the summer months in Chicago, there are musical concerts, art shows, folk festivals, and street fairs held every weekend. The Special Events Hotline will keep you informed about what is going on around town.

Jazz Hotline	(312) 427-3300
Dance Hotline	(312) 419-8383
Chicago Architecture Foundation (Architectural Tours)	(312) 922-3432
Chicago Park District (Information)	(312) 747-2200

Tour Chicago

Grayline Sightseeing Tours, *17 E. Monroe St., (312) 251-3107.*

Comfortable air-conditioned buses depart from 55 E. Monroe Street every day in the morning and the afternoon, with scheduled pickup at the major downtown hotels. Check with your concierge or doorman to find out the exact times. The standard three-hour tour includes visits to the lakefront, the Gold Coast, and the South Side. Multilingual tours are available with a day's notice for groups of ten or more.

American Sightseeing/Chicago, *(312) 427-3100.*

Two- or four-hour bus tours of the city with a knowledgeable guide on board to explain the many cultural attractions. The bus stops at several locations, including Michigan Avenue and the Museum of Science and Industry. Tours depart daily in the morning and the afternoon from 55 E. Monroe St.

Wendella Sightseeing Boats, *(312) 337-1446.*

Ninety-minute tour of the Lake Michigan shoreline and the Chicago River; embarks from the foot of the Wrigley Building at the northwest corner of the Michigan Avenue Bridge and the Chicago River several times every day.

Spirit of Chicago Lakefront Cruises, *(312) 836-7888.*

Tour the majestic Chicago lakefront and be entertained by a musical revue featuring the renowned *Spirit of Chicago* waiters and waitresses. Expert narration. Freshly prepared buffet lunch and brunch for the afternoon cruises, full dinner for the evening cruises. The boat departs every day and night from the south side of Navy Pier, Grand Avenue and the lake.

Black Heritage Tour, *(708) 799-8032.*

A three-and-a-half-hour tour of the historic African American neighborhoods and historic sites. Stops at homes of noted celebrities and community leaders, many of whom shaped the history of Bronzeville. The city bus tour departs from the Art Institute of Chicago, Michigan and Adams, on Saturday afternoons in the spring and summer.

Chicago Jewish Historical Society Bus Tours,
(847) 432-7003.

Throughout the summer months, the Chicago Jewish Historical Society sponsors a series of day-long bus tours on Sundays to significant locations in the city that pertain to the early Jewish settlement of the community. The "Chicago Jewish Roots" guided tour explores the history of Maxwell Street, Lawndale, Humboldt Park, Logan Square, Albany Park, and Rogers Park. A "Summer Safari" to Northwest Indiana winds its way through Hammond, Michigan City, and Gary, and makes periodic stops at some of the local synagogues. An excursion through the "Southern Suburbs" takes you through Homewood, Olympia Fields, and Flossmoor. The history of the Jewish movement in Chicago and its surrounding suburbs is discussed by local experts. Advance reservations required. *Recommended.*

The Consulates

Austria, 400 N. Michigan Ave.	(312) 222-1515
Belgium, 333 N. Michigan Ave.	(312) 357-0992
Great Britain, 33 N. Dearborn St.	(312) 346-1810
Canada, 180 N. Stetson Ave.	(312) 616-1860
Denmark, 875 N. Michigan Ave.	(312) 787-8780
Dominican Republic, 3228 W. North Ave.	(312) 772-6363
France, 737 N. Michigan Ave.	(312) 787-5359
Germany, 676 N. Michigan Ave.	(312) 580-1199
Greece, 168 N. Michigan Ave.	(312) 750-1014
India, 150 N. Michigan Ave.	(312) 781-6280
Ireland, 400 N. Michigan Ave.	(312) 337-1868
Israel, 111 E. Wacker Dr.	(312) 565-3300
Italy, 500 N. Michigan Ave.	(312) 467-1550
Japan, 737 N. Michigan Ave.	(312) 280-0400
Korea, 455 City Front Dr.	(312) 822-9485
Luxembourg, 180 N. LaSalle St.	(312) 726-0354

Mexico, 300 N. Michigan Ave.	(312) 855-1380
Netherlands, 303 E. Wacker Dr.	(312) 856-0110
People's Republic of China, 100 W. Erie St.	(312) 573-3070
Peru, 180 N. Michigan Ave.	(312) 782-1599
Philippines, 30 N. Michigan Ave.	(312) 332-6458
Poland, 1530 N. Lake Shore Dr.	(312) 337-8166
Commonwealth of Puerto Rico, 8770 W. Bryn Mawr Ave.	(312) 693-6810
Spain, 180 N. Michigan Ave.	(312) 782-4588
Sweden, 150 N. Michigan Ave.	(312) 781-6262
Switzerland, 737 N. Michigan Ave.	(312) 915-0061
Thailand, 35 E. Wacker Dr.	(312) 236-2447

appendix C

Suggested Reading

The following books, essays, and unpublished research papers deal with important aspects of Chicago's neighborhood settlements, and are recommended reading for anyone interested in researching the ethnic history of the city. All of the books are available in the Chicago Public Library's Social Science and History collection.

Beijbom, Ulf. *Swedes in Chicago: A Demographic & Social Study of the 1846–1880 Immigration.* Stockholm: Laromedelsforlagen, 1971.

Bicha, Karel B. "The Survival of the Village in Urban America: A Note On Czech Immigrants in Chicago to 1914." *International Migration Reports,* vol. 1, Spring 1974 (pp. 72–74).

Fremon, David K. *Chicago Politics Ward by Ward.* Bloomington & Indianapolis: Indiana University Press, 1988.

Heimovics, Rachel Baron. *Chicago Jewish Sourcebook.* Chicago: Follett Publishing Co., 1981.

Hellenism in Chicago. Chicago: United Hellenic American Congress, 1982.

Hispanics in Chicago. The Chicago Reporter and the Center for Community Research and Assistance of the Community Renewal Society, 1985.

Holli, Melvin, and Peter Jones. *Ethnic Chicago.* Grand Rapids: William B. Eerdmans Publishers, 1977.

Hofmeister, Rudolf A. *The Germans of Chicago.* Chicago: University of Illinois Press, 1976.

Horowitz, Ruth. *Honor & The American Dream: Culture and Identity in a Chicano Community.* New Brunswick, NJ: Rutgers University Press, 1983.

Lane, Kerstin B. "Andersonville: A Swedish American Neighborhood Landmark." Unpublished paper.

McCaffrey, Lawrence J., and Charles Fanning, Michael Funchion, and Ellen Skerrett. *The Irish in Chicago.* Urbana & Chicago: University of Illinois Press, 1987.

Mayer, Harold, and Richard Wade. *Chicago: Growth of a Metropolis.* Chicago: University of Chicago Press, 1969.

Nelli, Humbert. *Italians in Chicago: 1880–1930.* New York: Oxford University Press, 1970.

Olson, Anita. "North Park: A Study In Community." Covenant Archives & Historical Society, North Park College. Unpublished paper.

Pacyga, Dominic A., and Ellen Skerrett. *Chicago: A City of Neighborhoods.* Chicago: Loyola University Press, 1986.

Padilla, Felix. *Puerto Rican.* Notre Dame: University of Notre Dame Press, 1987.

Poles of Chicago, 1837–1937. Chicago: Polish Pageant, 1937.

Rethford, Wayne and June Skinner Sawyers. *The Scots of Chicago: The Illinois St. Andrew Society and its Legacy.* Kendall-Hunt Publishers, 1996.

Ropka, Gerald. *The Evolving Residential Patterns of the Mexican, Puerto Rican, & Cuban Population of Chicago.* New York: Arno Press, 1980.

Scamon, Robert A. *Back of the Yards: The Making of a Local Democracy.* Chicago: University of Chicago Press, 1986.

Spear, Allan H. *Black Chicago: The Making of a Negro Ghetto, 1890–1920.* Chicago: University of Chicago Press, 1967.

Strauss, Terry, ed. *Indians of the Chicago Area.* Chicago: NAES College Press, 1990.

Wilson, Margaret Gibbons. "Concentration and Dispersal of the Chinese Population of Chicago, 1870–Present." Master's thesis, University of Chicago, 1969.

Other Books by Richard Lindberg

Stuck on the Sox (1978)

Who's On Third? The Chicago White Sox Story (1983)

The Macmillan White Sox Encyclopedia (1984)

Chicago Ragtime: Another Look at Chicago, 1880–1920 (1985)

To Serve and Collect: Chicago Politics and Police Corruption from the Lager Beer Riot to the Summerdale Scandal (1991)

Stealing First in a Two Team Town (1994)

Chicago by Gaslight: A History of the Chicago Netherworld (1996)

Quotable Chicago (1996)

Contributing Writer

A Kid's Guide to Chicago (1980)

The Encyclopedia of Major League Team Histories (1989)

The Encyclopedia of World Crime (1990)

The Baseball Biographical Encyclopedia (1990)

American National Biography (1997 Revision Series)

A Message To Our Readers

Passport's Guide to Ethnic Chicago welcomes your comments and suggestions. If we have failed to include your favorite community event, festival, or ethnic restaurant in Chicago and its surrounding suburbs, please send us some information and we will be happy to provide a listing in future editions of this best-selling guidebook. Or if you wish to share some insights into the neighborhood history discussed in these pages, we would enjoy hearing from you. Please direct all correspondence to:

Richard C. Lindberg,
c/o *Passport's Guide to Ethnic Chicago*
NTC Publishing Group
4255 W. Touhy Ave.
Lincolnwood, IL 60646

TRAVEL AND CULTURE BOOKS

PASSPORT BOOKS
a division of *NTC Publishing Group.*
Lincolnwood Illinois U.S.A.